A PRIMER OF MODERN STANDARD HINDI

A Primer of Modern Standard Hindi

MICHAEL C. SHAPIRO

MOTILAL BANARSIDASS PUBLISHERS
PRIVATE LIMITED • DELHI

First Edition: Delhi, 1989
Reprint: Delhi, 1990, 1994, 2000, 2003

ISBN: 81-208-0475-9 (Cloth)
ISBN: 81-208-0508-9 (Paper)

Also available at:
MOTILAL BANARSIDASS
41 U.A. Bungalow Road, Jawahar Nagar, Delhi 110 007
8 Mahalaxmi Chamber, 22 Bhulabhai Desai Road, Mumbai 400 026
236, 9th Main III Block, Jayanagar, Bangalore 560 011
120 Royapettah High Road, Mylapore, Chennai 600 004
Sanas Plaza, 1302 Baji Rao Road, Pune 411 002
8 Camac Street, Kolkata 700 017
Ashok Rajpath, Patna 800 004
Chowk, Varanasi 221 001

Printed in India
BY JAINENDRA PRAKASH JAIN AT SHRI JAINENDRA PRESS,
A-45 NARAINA, PHASE-I, NEW DELHI 110 028
AND PUBLISHED BY NARENDRA PRAKASH JAIN FOR
MOTILAL BANARSIDASS PUBLISHERS PRIVATE LIMITED,
BUNGALOW ROAD, DELHI 110 007

PREFACE

This book arises from a sense of dissatisfaction with the teaching materials that are available for the Hindi language. Those materials written during the past three decades, particularly those published in the United States, have concentrated almost exclusively on the inculcation of oral skills in Hindi. Inadequate attention has been given to formal grammar, reading, and writing. It has been my experience that as a result of this emphasis, many students of Hindi in the United States have been seriously deficient in basic literacy skills. Other Hindi instructors with whom I am acquainted likewise have decried the lack of emphasis on written skills in available language courses, grammars, and the like. There has been a growing sentiment among Hindi teachers that instruction in the language should effect a more even balance among reading, writing, and speaking skills than it currently does.

The title I have selected for this book, *A Primer of Modern Standard Hindi*, has a decidedly old-fashioned ring to it. This is by intention. The book is a primer, that is, a systematic introduction to its topic. Subjects have been included and arranged on the basis of pedagogical efficacy. The work presupposes no prior knowledge of Hindi or its writing system. Moreover, this is a primer of standard, as opposed to colloquial, Hindi. It tries to impart knowledge of that style of Hindi that is taught in Indian schools and that is used in the various Indian media. The book is not a manual of colloquial Hindi. For that, other materials are readily available. This is not to say that much of what is said in this book about formal Hindi is not applicable to the structure of the conversational language. On the contrary, there is a considerable degree of overlap between the two styles or registers of the language and many of the peculiarities and idiosyncrasies of the colloquial language cannot be explained except in reference to the structures of standard written Hindi. But in the end the imparting of literacy skills and the developing of speaking skills in Hindi are enterprises sufficiently different from one another to warrant that they be accomplished by different techniques and in conjunction with different materials.

In writing a book such as this it is difficult to know what to include and what to leave out. My overriding concern has been to include all of the "nuts and bolts" of Hindi grammar that I believe a student needs to master during the first two years of a college level instructional program. The specific points of grammar that have been treated in this work are, for the most part, those recommended in a recent three-year curriculum for the Hindi language.[1] In addition, I have included a core vocabulary,

1. Michael C. Shapiro, Manindra K. Verma, and Bruce R. Pray. *A Three-Year Curriculum in Modern Standard Hindi*. Final report for the U.S. Department of Education Grant # G008002118, University of Washington, Seattle, Washington, 1980.

distributed across the various chapters, of approximately fifteen hundred items. These items have been chosen after examining several published core vocabularies for Hindi.[2] The sequencing of grammatical information in this book is in accordance with my own preferences and teaching practices. I have not aimed for an exhaustive treatment of Hindi grammar in this work—such would be appropriate in a comprehensive reference grammar—, but rather for a systematic and logical exposition of those aspects of the language whose mastery is essential for the development of basic literacy skills.

A Primer of Modern Standard Hindi consists of 31 chapters divided into six parts. Part I (Chapters 1-4) provides some general information about the Hindi language and describes the language's sounds and writing system. The core of the book, Parts II-VI (Chapters 5-31) comprises a step-by-step introduction to the basic grammatical categories and inflections of the language. Each chapter contains discussions of several facets of the language, a vocabulary section containing approximately 50 entries, and a set of written exercises[3]. Hindi forms are given both in the Hindi (or Devanāgarī) writing system and in Roman transliteration through Part III. The Roman transliteration is eliminated beginning with Part IV. In order to provide the student with samples of Hindi of greater than sentence length, a set of supplementary reading passages has been included at the end of each of Parts II through VI. These are graded in order of difficulty and include both prose and poetry texts. The passages have been taken from diverse sources. Many are from children's readings in use in India. Others are from newspapers, books of riddles, anthologies of children's literature, and All India Secondary Board examination papers in Hindi. Special vocabulary sections have been appended to these reading passages. Following the 31 chapters are two supplements that should be of assistance to the students. These are a Guide To Further Study of Hindi and a Hindi-English Glossary.

---

2. Central Hindi Institute, हिंदी की आधारभूत शब्दावली, Agra, 1967; India (Republic) Central Hindi Directorate, *Basic Hindi Vocabulary—2000 Words*, Agra, 1967; Karine Schomer and Geoffrey G. Reinhard, *Basic Vocabulary for Hindi and Urdu*, Center for South and Southeast Asia Studies, University of California, Berkeley, 1978.

3. No exercises are given, however, in Chapters 29-31.

ACKNOWLEDGEMENTS

In writing this primer I must acknowledge a debt of gratitude owed both to previous writers on the topic of Hindi grammar and to friends, colleagues, and students. It would not have been possible to write this book had there not been a substantial corpus of grammars, readers, lexicons, etc. of Hindi already extant. I have read widely in this literature and been influenced by it. My analyses of specific points of grammar have often been influenced by the insights of other grammarians and language teachers. On a few occasions I have used or modified particularly apt sample sentences appearing in standard reference works. It would be impractical to list here each of the many publications that I have consulted at one time or another while mulling over particular points of grammar or phonology. I have, however, provided a short bibliography of useful reference works on Hindi in the section "Guide To Further Study" that follows immediately after Part VI.

There are many people to whom special thanks are due. For the past few years students in elementary Hindi at the University of Washington have been using drafts of this primer as a classroom text. On the basis of the comments of many of these students, I have corrected errors, clarified points, and, hopefully, improved the overall readability of the book. Several individuals, Professor George Cardona, Ms. Saroj Gupta, Dr. Edeltraud Harzer, Professor John S. Hawley, Ms. Naseem Karmali Hines, Dr. Robert A. Hueckstedt, Professor Roy Andrew Miller, Professor Richard Salomon, and Professor Harold F. Schiffman, read through all or portions of the manuscript and made detailed comments and suggestions. Most of the work of preparing the Hindi-English glossary was carried out by Ms. Maureen Haley-Terada. I extend my sincerest thanks to each of these individuals.

A special word of thanks must be given here to Dr. Dhanesh K. Jain and Ms. Kusum Jain, who have helped in countless ways in the preparation of this book. Both of them went over the work with me in Delhi between September, 1982 and May, 1983. Numerous improvements in the work are the result of their keen insights and helpful criticism. I am eternally grateful to them for all of their efforts. Lastly, I wish to thank the firm of Motilal Banarsidass, and particularly Mr. N.P. Jain and Mr. J.P. Jain, for undertaking to publish this volume and make it available to a wide readership.

CONTENTS

PART IV

PART V

ABBREVIATIONS

The following abbreviations have been employed in this primer:

adj.	adjective
adv.	adverb
alt.	alternate
blut.	best left untranslated in this context
conj.	conjunction
f.	feminine
fam.	familiar
hab.	habitual
i.	intransitive
imper.	imperative
indecl.	indeclinable
int.	intimate
inter.	interrogative
interj.	interjection
m.	masculine
n.	noun
neg.	negative
non-prox.	non-proximate
num.	number
obl.	oblique
p.	present
part.	participle
partl.	particle
pass.	passive
perf.	perfective
pl.	plural
pol.	polite
poss.	possessive
post.	postposition
pron.	pronoun
prop.	proper noun
prox.	proximate
psmt.	presumptive
refl.	reflexive
rel.	relative
s.	singular
si.	simple
Skt.	Sanskrit
t.	transitive
v.	verb
1	1st person
2	2nd person
3	3rd person
I	Class I
II	Class II
*	hypothetical form
~	alternates with

The following abbreviations have been used in citing the sources of supplementary reading passages and in referring to Hindi reference materials:

APS — आओ पढ़ें और सीखें : मेरी चौथी पुस्तक. राष्ट्रीय शैक्षिक अनुसंधान और प्रशिक्षण परिषद्. New Delhi. 1968.

BGMH — *A Basic Grammar of Modern Hindi*. 3rd edition. Central Hindi Directorate, Ministry of Education and Social Welfare, Government of India. New Delhi. 1975.

BKSK — बच्चों की सौ कविताएँ. Harikrṣṇa Devasare (ed.). Śakun Prakāśan. New Delhi, 1972.

DBSSE Delhi Board Secondary School Examination (Hindi Paper I, 1977). Published by Shiv Das and Sons, Delhi, 1983.

HKPP हिन्दी की पहली पुस्तक. Satyanārāyaṇ and Avadhanandan. दक्षिण भारत हिन्दी प्रचार सभा. Madras. 1959.

PKK पंजाब और कुल्लू की कहानियाँ. Surjīt. Publications Division, Information and Broadcasting Ministry, Government of India. New Delhi. 1964.

SHP (I) सरल हिन्दी पाठमाला (पहली पुस्तक). Jagdīścandra Jain. Orient Longmans. Calcutta. 1950.

SHP (II) सरल हिन्दी पाठमाला (दूसरी पुस्तक). Jagdīścandra Jain. Orient Longmans. Calcutta. 1952.

SHP (P) सरल हिन्दी पाठमाला (प्रवेशिका). Jagdīścandra Jain. Orient Longmans. Calcutta. 1950.

PART
I

CHAPTER 1: INTRODUCTION

1.1. The Hindi Language

Hindi is one of the most widely spoken languages of the world, possessing speakers of the same order of magnitude as those of English and Russian. In India it has been accorded the status of 'Official Language' and, along with English, is recognized by the central government for use for most administrative purposes. It is spoken natively by at least 150 million persons in the Indian states of Uttar Pradesh, Madhya Pradesh, and Bihar and as a second language by a like number in other states of North India. It is also an official language of Uttar Pradesh, Madhya Pradesh, Bihar, Haryana, Rajasthan, and Himachal Pradesh, as well as of the Delhi union territory. Urdu, a language so closely related to Hindi to allow some to consider the two to be variants of a single tongue, is spoken by tens of millions, either as a first or second language, both in Pakistan and India. Members of emigrant Indian communities the world over use Hindi as a lingua franca. Hindi enjoys some order of official status in countries as diverse as Fiji, Mauritius, and Guyana.

1.2. The Linguistic Status of Hindi

Hindi belongs to the Indo-Aryan family of languages, a subgroup of the Indo-European family. It is thus related to such European languages as English, French, German, Russian, etc. The modern Indo-Aryan languages, including such standardized literary languages as Bengali, Marathi, Konkani, Panjabi, Assamese, Oriya, Nepali, Sinhala (=Sinhalese), Sindhi, Kashmiri, Urdu, and Hindi, are historically derived from Sanskrit, the most important vehicle of communication of classical Indian civilization. These modern Indo-Aryan languages stand in approximately the same relation to Sanskrit as do the modern Romance Languages (i.e., French, Spanish, Italian, Portuguese, Rumanian, etc.) to Latin. With the exception of Sinhala, spoken in Sri Lanka, the Indo-Aryan languages are spread over approximately the northern two-thirds of the Indian subcontinent. Languages of the Dravidian family, genetically unrelated to those of the Indo-Aryan family, are the primary standardized vernaculars of the remaining third of the subcontinent. The most important of these languages are Tamil, Telugu, Kannada, and Malayalam.

1.3. Dialects of Hindi

In its spoken forms Hindi encompasses a wide range of dialects. Roughly speaking, these varieties can be divided into "western" and "eastern" groups, with the former including Braj (western Uttar Pradesh and adjacent districts of Haryana, Rajasthan, and Madhya Pradesh), Bundeli (north-central Madhya Pradesh and south-western Uttar Pradesh), Kanauji (west-central Uttar Pradesh), Bangru (Haryana),

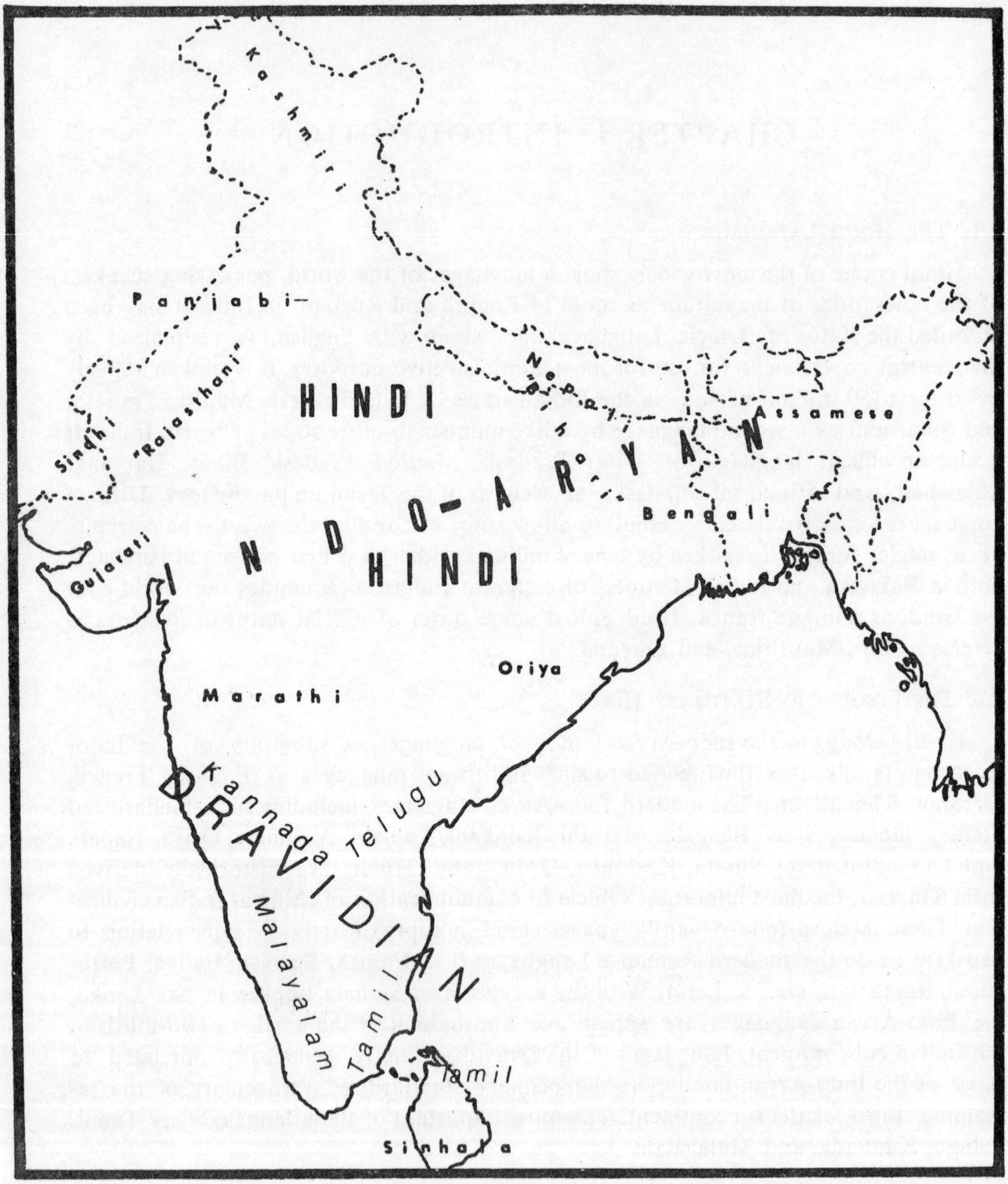

· Figure 1. Major Vernacular Language of South Asia.

and Hindustani (Delhi and its environs), and the latter including Avadhi (north-central and central Uttar Pradesh), Bagheli (north-central Madhya Pradesh and south-central Uttar Pradesh), and Chattisgarhi (east-central Madhya Pradesh). In addition to these western and eastern Hindi dialects, there are several other speech forms that, although counted by some as varieties of Hindi, are properly considered distinct languages. These include a number of Rajasthani languages (of which Marwari is the most widely spoken) and the so-called "Bihari" languages, Maithili, Magahi, and Bhojpuri, of eastern Uttar Pradesh, western and central Bihar, and the Nepal Terai.

The standardized form of Hindi, commonly referred to as *khaRī bolī* (literally 'standing language'), has a somewhat complex history. Before the end of the nineteenth century "Hindi" literary works were for the most part written in normalized forms of regional vernaculars. Tulsīdās and Sūrdās, two of Hindi's greatest medieval devotional poets, wrote in old forms of Avadhi and Braj respectively. The modern standard language (as opposed to regional vernacular or literary dialects) arose through the infusion of considerable external (i.e., non-Hindi) vocabulary into a grammatical skeleton based on the vernacular dialect spoken in the Delhi area. Such non-Hindi vocabulary has included forms from such diverse languages as Sanskrit, Arabic, Persian, Turkish, Portuguese, and English. Beginning in the nineteenth century a heavily Sanskritized form of Hindi, often referred to as *śuddh* (or 'pure') Hindi, began to come into existence. It is this form of Hindi, written in the *devanāgarī* writing system (v. chaps. 2-4), that has been promulgated by the Government of India and that is taught in formal courses of study in India.

1.4. Hindi, Urdu and Hindustani

The terms "Urdu" and "Hindustani" are, unfortunately, often used interchangeably with 'Hindi,' leading to considerable confusion. Urdu, like Hindi, is based on the grammar of the vernacular dialect of the Delhi area. Its vocabulary, however, has been enriched by borrowings from Persian and Arabic. In contrast to Hindi, it is written in a modified form of Arabic script. Whereas *devanāgarī* is written from left to right, Urdu is written from right to left. Literary Urdu can differ quite markedly from literary Hindi. In its most formal varieties the former employs a highly Islamicized vocabulary and may also use a limited set of Persian or Arabic grammatical constructions. Formal Hindi, by contrast, can be extremely Sanskritized, drawing from the rich technical vocabulary of Sanskrit and employing Sanskrit word building devices such as prefixes, suffixes, and other grammatical markers.

The term Hindustani, easily confusable with Hindi, is used in many different, and often contradictory, senses. The most generally accepted of these is a vernacular speech form that is neither excessively Sanskritized nor Islamicized. Hindustani's vocabulary consists of a core of "native" lexical items, as well as a number of forms drawn from either the Sanskritic or the Perso-Arabic lexica. It is this Hindustani that is employed by the vast majority of either Hindi or Urdu speakers for conversational purposes. Hindustani is readily understandable both by individuals who use *śuddh* Hindi for formal written communication and by those who use literary Urdu. Colloquial Hindustani can be easily written in either *devanāgarī* or in Urdu script. Since the partition of India in 1947, it has been increasingly common for citizens of India to write in *devanāgarī* and for those of Pakistan to write in Urdu script. Even in India, however, many individuals, particularly those who received their education before the 1950's or who identify their mother tongues as Urdu, continue to write Hindustani in

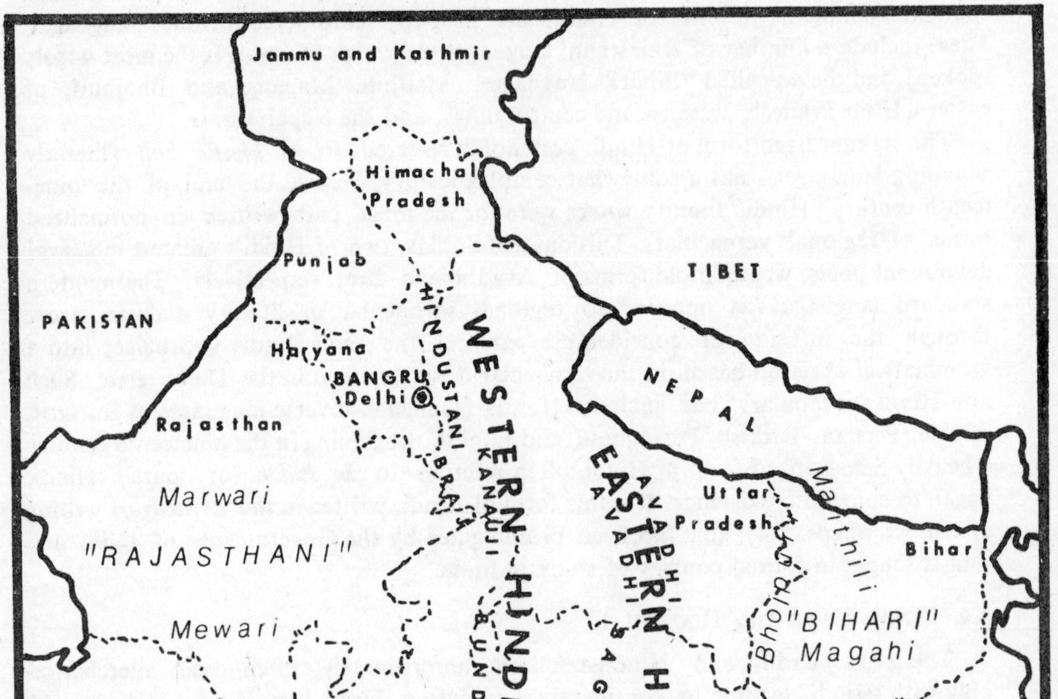

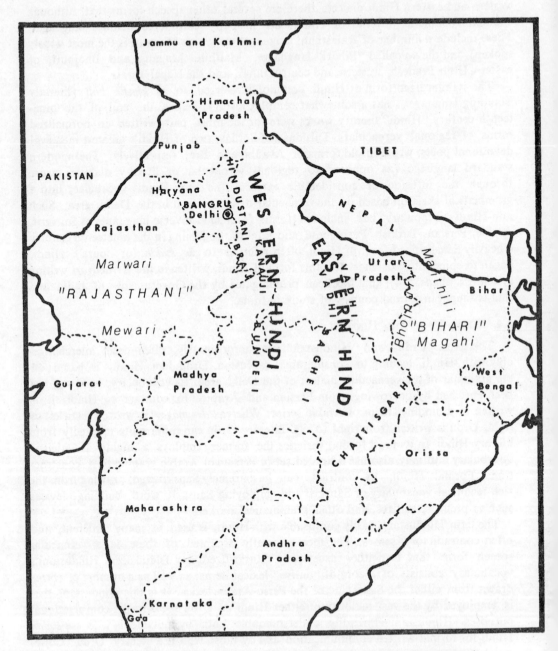

Figure 2. The Major Dialects of Hindi (also "Rajasthani" and "Bihari" languages).

the Urdu script. In Pakistan, Urdu or Hindustani is written almost exclusively in the Urdu script.

In recent years Hindi has come to enjoy a position of preeminence among South

Asian vernacular languages. It has become widely studied throughout India as a result of official efforts in its behalf. Except for English, it is the most commonly employed lingua franca in the subcontinent. Hindi films, manufactured in great number in Bombay, are widely shown in India and to overseas Indian communities. Hindi film songs are enjoyed by hundreds of millions of Indians, and even by the speakers of non-Indian languages, throughout the world. Hindi is an important medium for publication of all kinds, from popular novels to literary works and textbooks. In recent years foreign literature has been extensively translated into Hindi.

I have chosen to call the language discussed in this primer Modern Standard Hindi. It is essentially that form of Sanskritized Hindi taught in Hindi language classes in the Republic of India. I have stressed Sanskritic vocabulary over the Perso-Arabic, although I have included many of those common Perso-Arabic vocabulary items that have entered all styles of the language. The writing system here employed is *devanāgarī* (as opposed to Urdu script). It is my belief that literary Hindi and literary Urdu ought best to be considered two distinct languages, even though the colloquial versions of these two languages overlap to a considerable degree. Readers whose primary interest is in literary Urdu are advised to seek out any of a number of language courses carried out through the medium of Urdu script. Muhammad Abd-al-Rahman Barker's *A Course in Urdu*, 3 vols. (Ithaca : Spoken Language Services, 1975), is particularly recommended.

1.5. Strata of Hindi Vocabulary

The vocabulary of Modern Standard Hindi is both rich and diverse. It draws from the vast lexical resources of Sanskrit, Arabic, Persian, Turkish, Portuguese, English, and other languages with which Hindi has come into contact. Indian grammarians have found it useful to classify some of the different types of vocabulary items that coexist in the language. Those words that are borrowed directly from Sanskrit with little or no phonetic alteration are classified as *tatsama*: e.g., *pakṣī* 'bird', *jal*, 'water', *kārya* 'work, deed', *agni* 'fire'. Items that are ultimately of Sanskritic origin but that have undergone continual phonetic change in the course of their historical evolution are designated as *tadbhava*, e.g., *āg* 'fire', *sab* 'all' (Skt. *sarva*) *ũcā* 'high, tall' (Skt. *ucca*). The Indian grammarians also recognize a class of vocabulary items intermediate between *tatsama* and *tadbhava* forms. These words, categorized as *arddha-tatsama* (or "half-*tatsama*"), are direct borrowings from Sanskrit (as are *tatsama* forms), but show some degree of phonetic modification (like *tadbhava* vocabulary), e.g., *agin* 'fire' (Skt. *agni*), *śanīcar* 'Saturday' (Skt. *śanaiścara*). The *tatsama, arddha-tatsama*, and *tadbhava* vocabularies of Hindi are historically Indo-Aryan, owing their origins to Sanskrit in one way or another. In this sense they contrast with borrowings from such non-Indo-Aryan languages as English, Portuguese, Persian, Turkish, and Arabic.

It is not uncommon to find in Hindi sets of synonyms or near synonyms used for expressing a given concept. For instance, the notion 'to wait' can be translated into Hindi as *pratīkṣā karnā* (literally 'to do waiting') with the *tatsama* form *pratīkṣā* 'waiting', *intazar karna* (with the Arabic-derived noun *intazar* 'waiting'), or as the *tadbhava* verb *ṭhaharnā*. The English noun *water* is rendered into Hindi by the *tadbhava* form *pānī*, by the *tatsama* word *jal*, by the Arabic *āb*, as well as by other words of more limited occurrence.

CHAPTER 2: THE *Devanāgarī* WRITING SYSTEM AND HINDI PRONUNCIATION

2.1. Introduction

Modern Standard Hindi is most commonly written in the *devanāgarī* (or sometimes simply *nāgarī*) writing system. This orthography is also employed for the writing of Sanskrit, Marathi, and Nepali. It is historically related to a number of other writing systems—e.g., those of Bengali, Oriya, Panjabi, Gujarati, Tamil, Telugu, Malayalam, Kannada, Sinhala—current in different regions of South Asia. Several writing systems of Inner and Southeast Asia (e.g., Tibetan, Mongolian, Manchu, Cambodian, Thai) are distantly related to *devanāgarī*, by way of common origin from the ancient Indian Brāhmī syllabary.

2.2. Basic Principles of Devanāgarī

The *devanāgarī* writing system is best considered to be a modified syllabary. Its syllabic nature results from the fact that words written in this system can be analyzed into sequences of block-like figures each of which represents an independent syllable. The syllabary is said to be a modified one because many of these figures can themselves be analyzed into smaller components standing for the individual sounds of which the syllables are composed. Characters of the *devanāgarī* system are written from left to right and are hung from a horizontal cross bar (or *rekhā*).[1] The entire *devanāgarī* system is not very complex in structure and can be learned in a short period of time. The relationship between characters of the writing system and sounds of the spoken language is quite direct. Mastery of Hindi spelling poses few problems once knowledge has been acquired of the forms of *devanāgarī* and the pronunciation of Hindi sounds.

There are thirty-three simple consonantal signs used in *devanāgarī*. To this number must be added a much larger number of conjunct consonant characters representing sequences (or clusters) of consonants. These conjunct consonant characters can, for the most part, be formed by the combination of simple consonants through regular principles. In addition to consonantal forms, *devanāgarī* possesses characters for eleven vowels. Each of these vowels can be represented in two different ways. When the vowel stands by itself for an entire syllable (i.e., when it is not preceded by a consonant or cluster of consonants), it is indicated by an independent character. When the vowel is preceded by a consonant, it is notated by the placement of a mark of some

1. In rapid writing, as well as in artistic varieties of handwriting and printing, the *rekhā* is often omitted.

kind (called a *mātrā*) on or about the sign for the previous consonant or consonant cluster.

In addition, *devanāgarī* possesses several other kinds of orthographic devices. It contains a set of numerals (3.3.), punctuation devices of various sorts (4.4.), and diacritics indicating vowel nasalization (2.3.) or other features of pronunciation. It should be observed that *devanāgarī* employs slightly different inventories of characters when used to represent languages other than Hindi. The reader will be relieved to learn that, unlike Roman, Greek, or Cyrillic alphabets, *devanāgarī* neither makes a distinction between upper and lower case letters nor between cursive and non-cursive varieties.[2]

2.3. Pronunciation of Hindi Vowels

The eleven vowels of Standard Hindi can, for purposes of exposition, be divided into six "simple" vowels (*a, ā, i, ī, u, ū*), an "r-like" vowel (*ṛ*), and four "complex" vowels (*e, ai, o, au*). The four "simple" vowels (*a, ā, i, u*) should pose few problems for English speakers, corresponding closely to the vowels in American English *bun, fond, hit,* and *foot* respectively. The sounds *ī* and *ū* approximate the vowels of English *feet* and *boot*, but without the noticeable diphthongal quality of the pronunciation of these English vowels. Hindi *ī* and *ū* thus correspond more closely to what has often been imprecisely characterized as the "pure" *ī* and *ū* vowels of many European languages than they do to any English sounds.

The pronunciation of the "r-colored" vowel *ṛ* varies considerably in Hindi speakping regions. In one very common version, a consonantal *r*, formed by quickly "tapping" the tip (or apex) of the tongue against the front part of the roof of the mouth, is immediately followed by a brief *i*. In the pronunciation of many Hindi speakers, particularly in regions adjacent to Rajasthan and Gujarat, the consonantal *r* is followed by a short *u* sound instead of an *i*. Other speakers vocalize the Hindi *ṛ* as a sequence of *a* and a following consonantal *r*.

The "complex" vowels *e* and *o* approximate the sounds of the English words *gate* and *boat*. Once again it should be noted that these sounds are pronounced in the European fashion, without any strong diphthongal quality. Considerable variation can be observed in the pronunciation of the remaining vowels *ai* and *au*. In normative varieties of Western Hindi, the first of these has approximately the quality of the vowel in English *cat*. In Eastern Hindi, however, this vowel may be noticeably diphthongal, sounding like a rapid sequence of an *a* or *ā* and an *i*-like sound. The pronunciation of the vowel *au* may cause difficulty for some speakers of English, as many English dialects lack any sound closely corresponding to it. In many Western Hindi dialects the sound has a pronunciation about halfway between that of *ā* and *o*, retaining the lip rounding of the latter. This is the sound that can be heard in many East Coast dialects of American English in such words as *caught, taught, bought,* etc., but without the slight "uh"-like element that can be heard at the end of the vowel in these words. In Eastern Hindi, *au* tends to be dipththongal, sounding like a rapid sequence of *a* or *ā* and a following *u* element. The diphthongal pronunciations of *ai* and

2. In rapid writing, however, many *devanāgarī* characters are frequently abbreviated or modified.

au, although ubiquitous in Eastern Hindi, are viewed as somewhat rustic by speakers of standard Hindi (based, as it is, on a dialect of Western Hindi). The monophthongal pronunciations, by contrast, do not have low status anywhere in the Hindi-speaking regions. A summary of the pronunciation of Hindi vowels is shown in Figure 3 below. The approximate places of articulations of these sounds are indicated on the vowel chart in Figure 4.

With the exception of *ṛ*, each of the Hindi vowels described above may appear in either nasalized or non-nasalized form.[3] The nasal pronunciation of Hindi vowels results from the exiting of the air flow from the body simultaneously via the oral and nasal cavities. The formation of nasal vowels in Hindi is fully analagous to the production of a similar set of sounds in French (e.g., *fin, bon, brun*). Nasal vowels occur in a wide variety of positions in Hindi (i.e., at the beginning, middle, or end of words). When they are not followed by a consonant, care should be taken so as not to make a consonantal closure after the vowel. Thus a word such as *mā̃* "mother" should not be pronounced with an *n* like final consonant, but with a clearly nasalized final vowel.

Vowel	*Phonetic Value (IPA)*[4]	*Pronunciation*
a	[ə]	vowel in American English *but, cup, buck*; initial vowel in *ago, again*.
ā	[a]	vowel in American English *pot, mop*; initial vowel in *father, copper*.
i	[I]	vowel in English *hit, bit, sit,* etc.
ī	[i]	somewhat like vowel in English *feet, meet, weed,* etc., but without noticeable glide. Closer to monophthongal first vowel in French *dire*, German *sieben*, and Italian *riso*.
u	[U]	vowel in American English *put, foot, should, wood.*
ū	[u]	somewhat like vowel in English *moon, June, tooth,* but without noticeable glide. Closer to monophthongal vowels in French *tout*, German *Buhne*, and Italian *muro*.
ṛ	[rɪ]	in Standard Hindi, a sequence of a consonantal "tapped" *r* and a following short *i*.

3. Hindi nasalized vowels are here indicated in transliteration by the placement of a tilde over the sign for vowel (e.g., *ā̃, ī̃, hā̃s, dū̃*).

4. The phonetic transcription of Hindi vowels is done according to the conventions of the International Phonetic Association (*The Principles of the International Phonetic Association* [London: Department of Phonetics, University College, 1949]).

e	[e]	somewhat like vowel in English *gate, rain,* etc, but without noticeable glide. Closer to monophthongal vowel in second syllable of French *epée* or in first syllable of German *geben* and *wesen.*
ai	[æ]	in Western Hindi, similar to vowel in English *cat, mad, fat,* etc. In Eastern Hindi, the pronunciation may be similar to the diphthong in English *bike, like, fine,* etc.
o	[o]	somewhat like vowel in English *boat, mode, cold,* but without noticeable glide. Closer to monophthongal vowel of the vowels in Spanish *todo,* German *Sohn,* and French *côte.*
au	[ɔ]	in Western Hindi, rounded vowel (i.e., uttered with lips pursed, formed halfway between position of *ā* and *o*. Corresponds to the vowel of New York City English pronunciation of vowel in *bought, taught, sought,* etc.

Figure 3. Pronunciation Guide to Hindi Vowels.

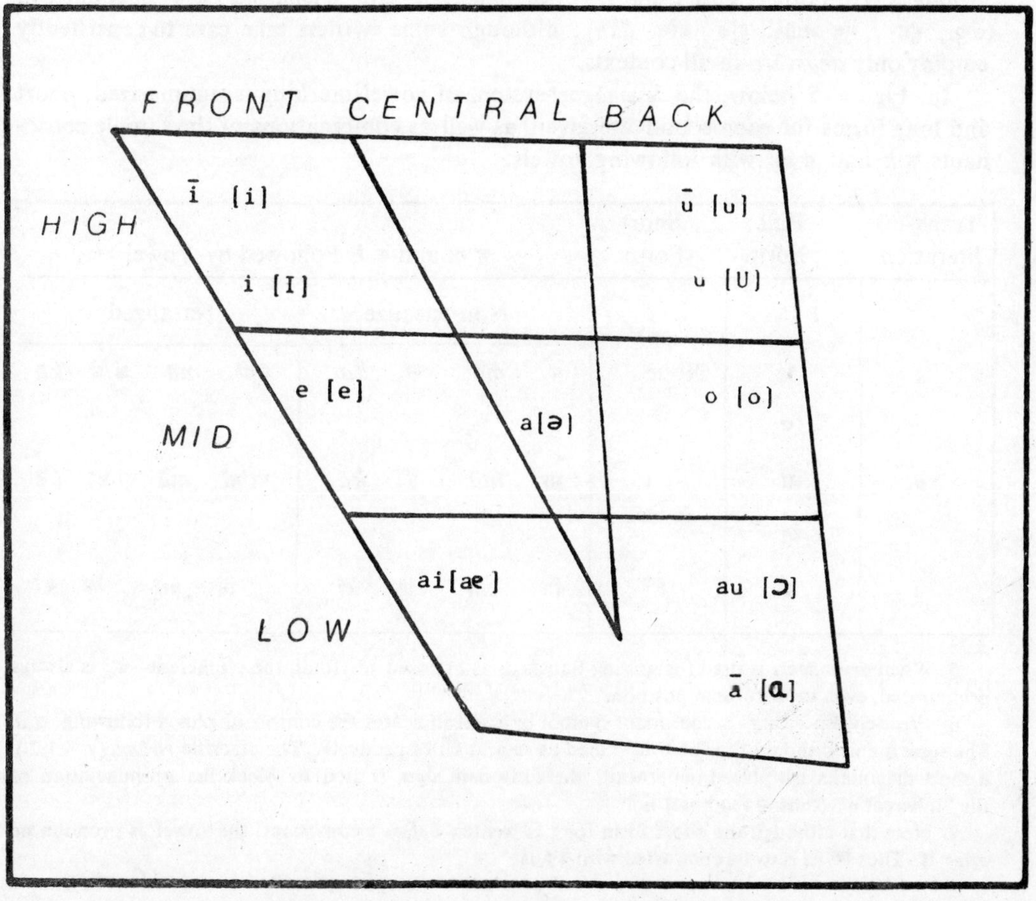

Figure 4. Articulation of Hindi Vowels (Excluding ṛ)

2.4. Devanāgarī Vowel Signs

The *devanāgarī* writing system possesses two different forms for each of the vowels of Hindi. A full form is employed for a vowel that does not immediately follow a consonant or consonant cluster, i.e., in word-initial position or when the second of a sequence of vowels. A short form (or *mātrā*) is used when the vowel immediately follows a consonant or consonant cluster. These short forms consist of lines, hooks, or combinations of both placed above, below, or to the side of consonantal characters. One vowel, *a*, has no special short form. The absence of a *mātrā* adjacent to a consonant suffices to indicate the presence of this vowel. For this reason *a* is often referred to as the "inherent a." At the end of a word, the inherent *a* is not normally vocalized. Thus कक is rendered in Hindi as *kak* instead of *kaka.*[5]

Nasalized vowels are notated by the use of one of two superscript diacritics (*anusvāra*) (ं) and *anunāsika* (ँ) (also called *candrabindu*). Indian grammarians have formulated elaborate rules describing when each of these is used. In practice, the distinction between the two notations is often not observed. Some generalizations, however, can be pointed out. The first of these, *anusvāra*, is always used when the vowel marking (whether short or long form) protrudes above the *rekhā* (e.g., ईं *ī̃*, ऐं *ãĩ*, कों *kõ*, मौं *mãũ*). With other vowel signs, both *anusvāra* and *anunāsika* are encountered (e.g., मुंह / मुँह *mũh*, आंख / आँख *ãkh*), although some writers take care to consistently employ only *anusvāra* in all contexts.

In Figure 5 below, the *devanāgarī* system of vowel marking is summarized. Short and long forms for each sound are given, as well as combinations of the sample consonants क *k* and म *m*[6] with following vowels.

Transliteration	Full Form	Short Form	म *m* and क *k* Followed by Vowel							
			Non-nasalize				Nasalized			
a	अ अ	None	म	*ma*	क	*ka*	मं/मँ	*mã*	कं/कँ	*kã*
ā	आ आ	ा	मा	*mā*	का	*kā*	मां/माँ	*mã̄*	कां/काँ	*kã̄*
i	इ	ि[7]	मि	*mi*	कि	*ki*	मिं	*mĩ*	किं	*kĩ*

5. When *devanāgarī* is used for writing Sanskrit, as opposed to Hindi, the "inherent—a" is always pronounced, even in word-final position.

6. Precisely speaking, a consonant symbol by itself indicates the consonant plus a following अ *a*. The signs म and क should thus be transcribed as *ra* and *ka* respectively. The diacritic *virāma* (v. 4.1.2.), a short diagonal slash placed underneath the consonant sign, is used to block the pronunciation of the "inherent *a*" (thus म *ma* but म् *m*).

7. Note that although the short form for इ is written *before* a consonant, the vowel is pronounced *after* it. Thus कि *ki* is to be contrasted with इक *ik*.

ī	ई	ी	मी	*mī*	की	*kī*	मीं	*mī̃*	कीं	*kī̃*
u	उ	ु	मु	*mu*	कु	*ku*	मं/मुँ	*mũ*	कं/कुँ	*kũ*
ū	ऊ	ू	मू	*mū*	कू	*kū*	मूं/मूँ	*mū̃*	कूं/कूँ	*kū̃*
ṛ	ऋ	ृ	मृ	*mṛ*	कृ	*kṛ*	Do not occur			
e	ए	े	मे	*me*	के	*ke*	में	*mẽ*	कें	*kẽ*
ai[8]	ऐ	ै	मै	*mai*	कै	*kai*	मैं	*mãĩ*	कैं	*kãĩ*
o	ओ ओ	ो	मो	*mo*	को	*ko*	मों	*mõ*	कों	*kõ*
au	औ औ	ौ	मौ	*mau*	कौ	*kau*	मौं	*mãũ*	कौं	*kãũ*

Figure 5. Representation of Hindi vowels in *devanāgarī*.

Several peculiarities can be observed in *devanāgarī* vowel notation. Some vowel characters have alternate full forms. Under the provisions of an orthographic reform of 1953, the letters अ *a*, आ *ā*, ओ *o*, and औ *au* were officially sanctioned in place of अ, आ, ओ, and औ[9]. Both alternates of each of these letters continue, however, to be widely used. Several combinations of consonant and following vowel are anomalous. An र *r* plus a following उ *u* or ऊ *ū* show the irregular forms रु *ru* and रू *rū* respectively. The sequence of ह *h* and ऋ *ṛ* has the special shape हृ *hṛ*.

2.5. EXERCISES

2.5.1. Read aloud each of the following forms and transcribe into Roman using the transliteration introduced in secs. 2.2 and 2.3 :

1. कु, मृ, कों, मू, मिं, के, माँ 2. इक, उक, आँक, ओम, ऋम, ऊक 3. इका, उके, ओंकी, मेकी, मोकू, काकी, आको 4. एकमू, इकृमे, ओकामो, उमकी 5. कमी, आओ, कौआ, कोई, कई, आऊँ, आए आएँ.

2.5.2. Transcribe the following forms into *devanāgarī* :

1. *ko*, *mī̃*, *kū̃*, *kṛ*, *mā*, *mo*; 2. *am*, *ām*, *īk*, *ṛm*, *õk*, *em*; 3. *imo*, *aimū̃*, *oki*, *ame*, *aukā*, *ṛkai*; 4. *īmīm*, *ikūk*, *omek*, *ā̃kūm*, *aikīk*, *umokā*; 5. *āī̃*, *āi*, *koe*, *kaū̃*, *maī*, *moā*.

8. The transcriptions *ai* and *au* might, in theory be confused with vowel sequences of अ plus इ and अ plus उ. Fortunately no such diphthong occurs in Hindi. The Roman notations *ai* and *au* should be interpreted in this book as standing for the vowel sounds ऐ and औ respectively. The transliterations *aī*, *āī*, *aū*, *āū*, etc., here represent diphthongs (i.e. अई, आई, अऊ, आऊ). The inherent अ *a*, included when a consonant sign is written without any *mātrā*, can constitute the first element of such a diphthong (e.g., कई *kaī* मई *maī*).

9. This reform also effected a minor change in the printed form of ऋ *ṛ* as well as several alterations of consonant characters (v. 3.2).

CHAPTER 3: THE *Devanāgarī* WRITING SYSTEM AND HINDI PRONUNCIATION (Cont.)

3.1. Introduction to the Hindi Consonant System

The consonant system of Hindi, like that of all Indo-Aryan languages is substantially more complex than that of English and other West European languages. This can be attributed both to the sheer number of Hindi consonants and to the manner in which these sounds are articulated. Nevertheless, mastery of Hindi consonants can be readily achieved once the student has learned some basic phonetic principles.

Hindi consonants can be divided into groups on the basis of the phonetic properties of their formation. These groups contain twenty stops (*k, kh, g, gh, c, ch, j, jh, ṭ, ṭh, ḍ, ḍh, t, th, d, dh, p, ph, b, bh*), five nasals (*ṅ, ñ, ṇ, n, m*), four semi-vowels (*y, r, l, v*), three *sibilants* (*ś, ṣ, s*), one "*h*-like" sound (*ḥ*), and two flaps (*R, Rh*) respectively. Many Hindi speakers employ several other sounds (*ḳ, ḳh, g, z, f*) that are not part of the indigenous inventory of consonants. These supplemental consonants have come into Hindi as a result of the borrowing of vocabulary from non-Indo-Aryan languages. The source languages possessed consonants not corresponding to native Hindi ones. When the vocabulary items were adopted, some semblance of the pronunciation of the sounds in the language of origin was also adopted.

The consonants of Hindi can be further classified as either simple or conjunct, the former standing for a single consonant and the latter for two or more consonants without an intervening vowel. Double (or "geminate") consonants are a subtype of conjunct in which the two components of the cluster are the same. Although the vast majority of conjunct consonants consist of two components, clusters with three or more elements are not uncommon.

The consonant sounds of any language result from the combination of a number of phonetic factors, of which manner of articulation, place of articulation, and the presence or absence of voicing, nasality, and aspiration are the most important from the point of view of Hindi. The above-mentioned classification of Hindi consonants as stops, semi-vowels, nasals, etc., is based upon manner of articulation. It should be noted, however, that one of these classes, the so-called "semi-vowels" is nothing more than a grab-bag of sounds of diverse formation.[1]

The primary distinction among Hindi consonants is essentially between the stop consonants and nasals on the one hand and all other consonants on the other. The

1. The *y* can be considered a true semi-vowel, being little more than a positional version of the vowel इ *i*. The *r* is a tongue tap and the *l* a lateral resonant. The *v* is variable in pronunciation, ranging from a labio-dental or bilabial fricative to a true semi-vowel *w*-like sound (i.e., a positional alternate of उ *u*).

basic stop consonants are formed with a complete blockage of the airflow at one of five locations in the oral cavity (i.e., the soft palate [or velum], the central or back portion of the hard palate [often referred to simply as the palate], the extreme front portion of the hard palate, the back of the top teeth, and the lips).[2] The same distinction in place of articulation is shared by the Hindi nasals. These sounds differ from stops in that the airflow, instead of being pent up behind the blockage, is directed out of the body through the nose.

The existence of a five-way distinction in place of articulation poses certain problems for speakers of English, in which language there is only a four-way contrast. This discrepancy results from a difference in the number of places at which stops can be formed by the tip (or apex) of the tongue making contact with the front portion of the top of the mouth. In the English *t* and *d* sounds, the tip of the tongue comes into contact with the alveolar ridge (i.e., that portion of the top gum just behind the top teeth). Hindi has no such *alveolar* sounds. Rather, it has either *dental* consonants (formed with contact at the teeth) or *retroflex* ones (formed with the tip of the tongue curled back and touching the top of the mouth anywhere from the extreme rear of the alveolar ridge to the front of the hard palate). The place of articulation of the English *t* and *d*[3] is thus midway between that of the Hindi dentals and retroflexes.

The problem of apical (i.e., formed with the apex of the tongue) consonants aside, the three remaining places of articulations exhibited by Hindi basic stops correspond nicely to those of English sounds. The labials are roughly equivalent to the *p* and *b* in *pin* and *bin*. The palatals are comparable to the initial sounds in *church* and *judge*. Velars are demonstrated by the beginning consonants of *coat* and *goat*.

A sixth place of articulation can be observed in two of Hindi's supplemental consonants(*ḳ* and *ḳh* [3. 3.]). In these sounds (referred to as *uvular*) the root of the tongue makes contact with the uvula (the back appendange of the soft palate, hanging over the rear of the mouth). A cross-sectional diagram of the articulatory tract showing the general locations of the formation of Hindi and English stop consonants is shown in Figure 6 (p. 16). English possesses stop consonants of the types 1 (*p* and *b*), 3 (*t* and *d*), 5 (*ch* and *j*) and 6 (*k* and *g*); in Hindi we find stops of the types 1 (*p, ph, b, bh*), 2 (*t, th, d, dh*), 4 (*ṭ, ṭh, ḍ, ḍh*), 5 (*c, ch, j, jh*), and 6 (*k, kh, g, gh*), as well as supplemental consonants of type 7 (*ḳ, ḳh* [3. 3.]).

The Hindi stop consonants of a single place of articulation need also be classified as aspirated (having a noticeable puff of air upon the release) or unaspirated, voiced (i.e., with simultaneous glottal vibration) or voiceless. There are four logical combinations of the features of aspiration and voicing, all of which are used in the language: voiceless non-aspirated, voiceless aspirated, voiced non-aspirated, and voiced aspirated. The mastery of this four-way distinction among speech sounds is invariably difficult for speakers of English, in which differences in meaning are conveyed by distinctions in voicing, but not aspiration. The degree of aspiration of a stop consonant depends

2. Sounds formed at these five places of articulation are referred to as *velar, palatal, retroflex, dental* and *labial* respectively.

3. The transliterations *t* and *d* are here used in referring to both the English alveolars and the Hindi dentals. The student should take care, however, to distinguish the places of articulation of these two sets of sounds.

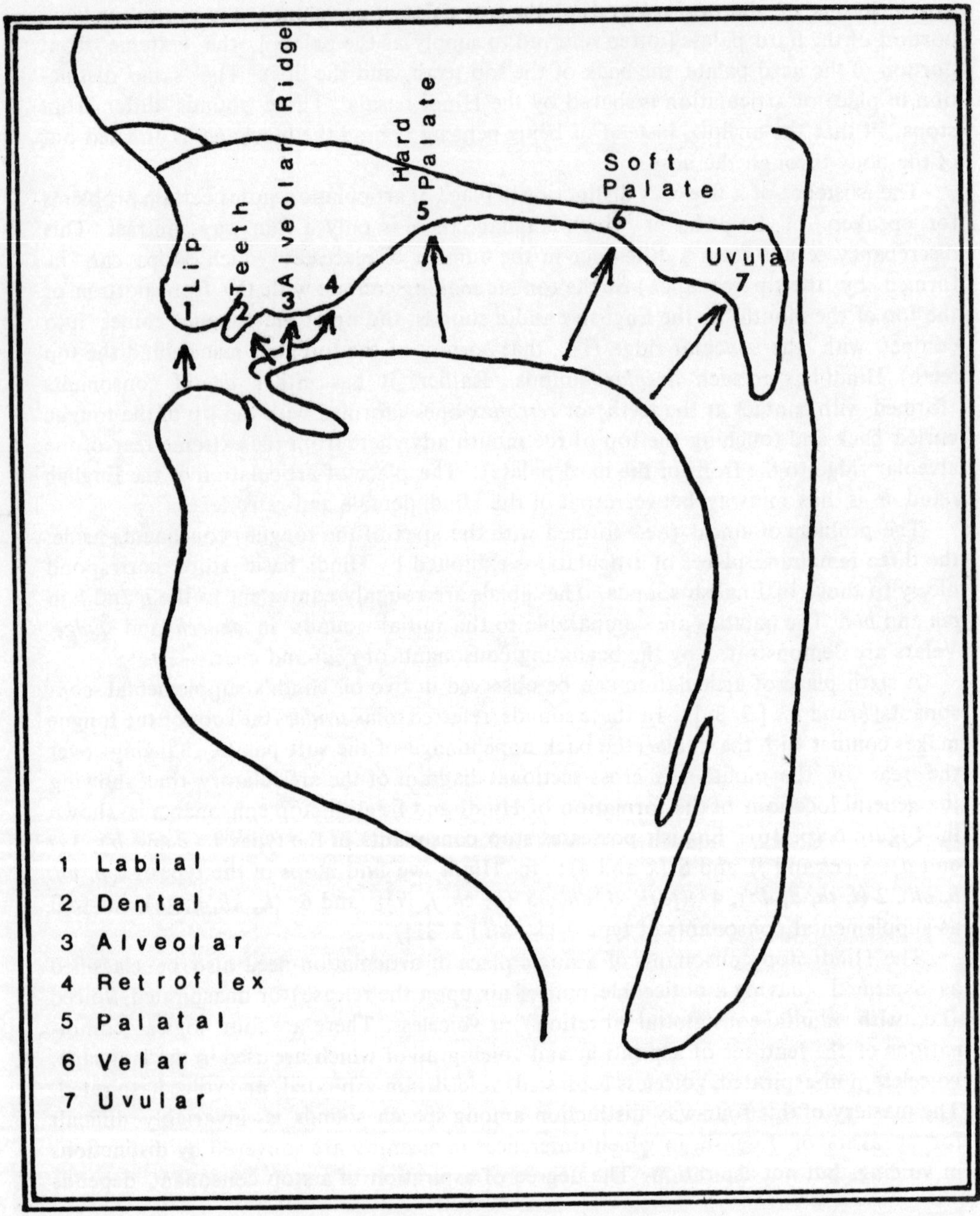

Figure 6. Places of Articulation of Stop Consonants (modified after Peter Ladefoged, *Preliminaries to Linguistic Phonetics* [Chicago and London : University of Chicago Press, 1971], 36).

to a considerable degree on whether the sound is voiceless or voiced (for example, the voiceless *t* in *Ted* is aspirated, but the voiced *d* in *dead* is not) and on the position in the word (e.g., a *t* at the beginning of a word is usually aspirated, as in *tang*, but unaspirated after an *s*, as in *sting*). There is thus a kind of linking of voicing and aspiration in English, while in Hindi the two features are fully independent of each other.

Of the four combinations of features at each place of articulation, the learning of two is quite simple for English speakers. With velars, for instance, the voiced non-aspirate corresponds closely to the *g* in *goat*. The voiceless aspirate is nearly the same as the initial sound in *coal*. The voiceless non-aspirate and the voiced aspirate are somewhat more difficult to produce. The former is uttered with an absence of glottal vibration (i.e., voicing) and without an expulsion of air upon the release of the blockage (i.e., aspiration). The latter might best be thought of as a kind of *g* combined with a breathy breathing. The proper pronunciation of this sound can be mastered through a simple exercise. The student should say a series of instances of the syllable *hā*, making sure to breathe deeply and to have the air-stream eminating from the chest. After several repetitions of the syllable, he should bring the back of the tongue up to the soft palate in order to produce a *g*. The effect of all of this is similar to "superimposing" a *g* on top of the syllable *hā*. The resulting sound should not be a sequence of *g* and *hā* elements. Rather, it should be a simple homogeneous consonant. Once the proper sound has been achieved, the vowel following the consonant can be changed from *ā* to any other Hindi vowel.

The relations among the set of voiceless non-aspirate, voiceless aspirate, voiced non-aspirate, and voiced aspirate velar stop consonants are exactly paralleled at the four other basic places of articulation (i.e., palatal, retroflex, dental, and labial). In the transliteration employed in this book the aspirates are represented as two letter sequences ending with *h* (i.e., *kh*, *gh*, *bh*, etc.). In spite of the use of such digraphic notations, however, the aspirates should be thought of and pronounced as unitary sounds.

Nasal consonants too are formed in Hindi at each of the five basic places of articulation. The labial and velar nasals (*m* and *ṅ*) correspond to the final sounds in the English *swim* and *swing* respectively. There is no sound in Hindi equivalent to the English *n* sound in *not*, *pin*, etc., this nasal, like the English *t* and *d*, being alveolar. The Hindi dental nasal *n* is formed with the tip of the tongue at the back of the teeth; the retroflex nasal *ṇ* has the tip of the tongue retracted to the same position it occupies in the formation of the retroflex stops. The retroflex nasal *ṇ* is mostly limited in Hindi to *tatsama* vocabulary items. The palatal nasal *ñ* is similar to a sequence of *n* followed by *y* (e.g., as in *vignette* or *fun year*). It is also quite close to the *ñ* sound in Spanish *piño*.

The term "semi-vowel" designates a class of four quite diverse consonantal sounds in Hindi. The *y* is quite similar to the English *y*. The Hindi *r* is nothing more than a tongue tap, formed by a rapid striking of the front of the top of the mouth anywhere from the alveolar ridge to the back of the front teeth. It also corresponds to a single unit of a tongue trill. The *l* is generally similar to the English *l*. The tip of the tongue is usually against either the gums or the top teeth. The last Hindi semi-vowel (*v*) can range in pronunciation from the [v] sound in *victory* to the [w] in *water*. It is occasionally also pronounced by bringing the lips together, as in the formation of *b*, but without enough tension in them to block completely the flow of air. This pronunciation sounds somewhat between that of [b] and a [w]. There is no significant difference in Hindi between a [w] and a [v], and no harm is brought about by the substitution of one of these sounds for the other.

The three Hindi sibilants (or "hissing" sounds) *ś*, *ṣ*, and *s*, as well as *h*, should present no difficulty in pronunciation for English speakers. The first (*ś*) and third (*s*) have the initial sounds of English *ship* and *sip* respectively. The second (*ṣ*), like the retroflex nasal (*ṇ*), is found only in *tatsama* learned borrowings from Sanskrit. For all practical purposes, there is no difference between the pronunciation of this sound and that of *ś*. The Hindi *h* is similar to the *h* sound in English.

Perhaps the most difficult sounds in Hindi to master are the flaps *R* and *Rh*. In these the tip of the tongue is curled back in the mouth to approximately the position it occupies in the enunciation of retroflex stops, but without the tip actually making contact with the top of the mouth. The tongue is then rolled (or "flapped") forward until it strikes the bottom of the mouth behind the top teeth. The motion of the tongue in forming these sounds is shown in Figure 7 below.

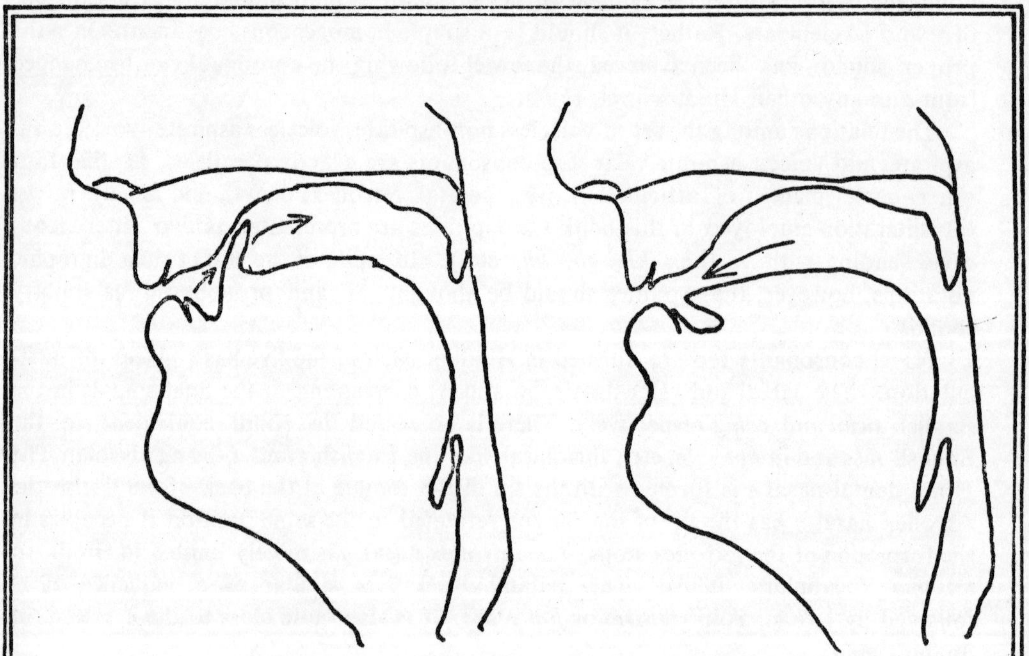

Figure 7. Formation of Hindi "Flap" Consonants.

The first of these two consonants (*R*) consists of nothing more than the tongue flap. In the second (*Rh*), the rolling motion of the tongue is superimposed upon the same kind of aspiration that is observed in the voiced aspirated stops. Correct pronunciation of the aspirated flaps can be achieved by saying a non-aspirated flap (*R*) at the same time as uttering a syllable such as *hā, he, ho, hī*, etc.

3.2. DEVANĀGARĪ SIMPLE CONSONANT SIGNS

Each of the consonants described in section 3.1. above is represented in *devanāgarī* by a distinct character. In the traditional Hindi classification of the consonants, stops at a single place of articulation are grouped together, with the voiceless sounds preceding the voiced, and the aspirates preceding the non-aspirates. The nasal consonants at a given place of articulation are also grouped together with the stops of the same place of articulation. The non-aspirated and aspirated flaps are represented by the signs for the non-aspirated and aspirated voiced retroflex stop consonants respectively, with subscript dots placed under them. A list of the signs for all of the basic Hindi vowels is given below in Figure 8.

STOPS AND NASALS					
	STOPS				NASALS
	Voiceless		Voiced		
	Non-aspirated	Aspirated	Non-aspirated	Aspirated	
Velar	क *k*	ख *kh*	ग *g*	घ *gh*	ङ *ṅ*
Palatal	च *c*	छ *ch*	ज *j*	झ(भ) *jh*	ञ *ñ*
Retroflex	ट *ṭ*	ठ *ṭh*	ड *ḍ*	ढ *ḍh*	ण *ṇ*
Dental	त *t*	थ *th*	द *d*	ध *dh*	न *n*
Labial	प *p*	फ *ph*	ब b	भ *bh*	म *m*
SEMI-VOWELS					
	य *y*	र *r*	ल *l*	व *v*	
SIBILANTS					
	श *ś*	ष *ṣ*	स *s*		
FLAPS					*h*-SOUND
	Non-aspirated	Aspirated			
	ड़ *R*	ढ़ *Rh*			ह *h*

Figure 8. Basic Hindi Consonants and their *devanāgarī* Representation

3.3. Supplemental Hindi Consonants

In addition to the basic consonantal sounds discussed in sections 3.1 and 3.2, many speakers use any or all of five additional consonants (क़ *q*, ख़ *k͟h*, ग़ *ġ*, ज़ *z*, फ़ *f*) in words of foreign origin (primarily from Persian, Arabic, English, and Portuguese). The last two of these, ज़ *z* and फ़ *f*, are the initial sounds in English *zig* and *fig* respectively. The consonant क़ *q* is a voiceless uvular stop, somewhat like क *k*, but pronounced further back in the mouth. ख़ *k͟h* is a voiceless fricative similar in pronunciation to the final sound of German *ach*. ग़ *ġ* is generally pronounced as a voiced uvular fricative, although it is occasionally heard as a stop rather than a fricative. In *devanāgarī* each of these five sounds is represented by the use of a subscript dot under one of the basic consonant signs. In practice, however, the dot is often omitted, leaving it to the reader to render the correct pronunciation on the basis of his prior knowledge of the language. Not all speakers are consistent in their use of these foreign sounds. Some employ them only in particular words; others use them in precisely those instances where they are etymologically justified; still others pronounce them not only where they are etymologically justified but in the place of the sounds that would be signified were the subscript not present. Thus, many Hindi speakers pronounce [f] not only in Persian-derived words such as हफ़्ता *haftā* but also in native Indo-Aryan forms such as फेंकना *phẽknā*.

There is one further supplemental sound occasionally encountered in Hindi. This is the *visarga*, notated in *devanāgarī* by the sign (:). This sign appears only in *tatsama* vocabulary items. In Sanskrit the *visarga* is a variant of s and r with a pronunciation somewhat like an *h* followed by a short [ə]. A word such as अतः *ataḥ* 'hence' is thus pronounced as [ətəhə]. In the traditional Indian description of speech sounds the *visarga* is considered an independent and full consonant.

3.4. Further Aspects of Hindi Pronunciation

3.4.0 Although there is an extraordinarily high degree of regularity in the relationship between Hindi speech sounds and elements of the *devanāgarī* writing system, there do exist contexts in which the rendition of Hindi sounds is anomalous. Some of these irregularities are due to the natural elisions of rapid speech. Others, however, cannot be explained by speed of pronunciation and need be considered exceptional areas in the language's phonology.

3.4.1. य *y* and व *v*

The semi-vowels य *y* and व *v* are involved in a few slight pronunciation irregularities in specific contexts. When the former of these occurs at the end of a word, but after the vowels इ *i*, ई *ī*, or ऊ *ū* (i.e., as in प्रिय *priya*, भारतीय *bhāratīya*, राजसूय *rājsūya*, an extremely short अ *a* is heard after the य *y*.[5] The य *y* is often not pronounced at all at the end of a word when preceded by अ *a*. This sequence of अ *a* plus य *y* receives a vocalization similar to that of ऐ *ai*, either in its monophthongal or diphthongal versions.

5. The inherent *a* is also retained when the य *y* is the last element in word-final consonant clusters (4.1.6). In the transliteration used here the inherent *a* is indicated after a final य *y*.

The semi-vowel व *v* likewise is often unpronounced in consonantal form at the end of a word. In its place, however, one hears an ओ *o* or उ *u* vowel-like element appended to the previous vowel, thus making it diphthongal (e.g., नाव *nāv*, गांव *gā̃v*, and पाव *pāv* are pronounced as [nāo], [gāŏ]/[gā̃o]/[gā̃ŏ], and [pāo] respectively.

3.4.2. अ *a* ADJACENT TO ह *h*

The vowel अ *a* frequently receives an irregular pronunciation when adjacent to ह *h*. In one extremely common variant the अ *a* preceding the ह *h* is realized as [ɛ] (the vowel in English *get*): e.g., *kahnā* (pronounced [kɛhəna] and *bahin* (pronounced [bɛhɪn]) More radical alterations are also heard in which the intervocalic (i.e., standing between two vowels) ह *h* is elided, with a merger or modification of the vowels to either side of the ह *h*: e.g., बहुत *bahut* and पहुँच *pahuc* pronounced [bɔt] and [pɔ̃c]; बहिन *bahin* (pronounced [bæn] in addition to [bɛhɪn]).

3.4.3. The "inherent *a*" is not pronounced in several environments other than those discussed so far. Contexts for such mute versions of the sound include the following:

a. at the end of a nominal or verbal stem before a derivational or inflectional suffix: e.g., बेचता *bectā*[6] (not *becatā*) and ख़रीदने *kharīdne*[7] (not *kharīdane*);
b. when serving as the vowel of the second syllable of what is in writing a trisyllabic nominal base, if the vowel of the third syllable is other than अ *a*: e.g., कुरसी *kursī* (not *kurasī*), सामना *sāmnā* (not *sāmanā*), but फाटक *phāṭak* (not *phāṭk*)[8];
c. when the vowel of the second syllable of a trisyllabic verbal stem, before a termination beginning with a vowel: e.g., निकला *nikalā*[9] (pronounced [nɪkla] not [nɪkəla], पिघली *pighalī* (pronounced [pɪghli] not [pɪghəli];
d. when the final sound of a nominal or verbal stem standing as the prior member of a compound: e.g., जल-पान *jal-pān* (not *jala-pān*), मिल-जुल *mil-jul* (not *mila-jul*).

3.5. EXERCISES

3.5.1. Read each of the following Hindi words aloud and then transcribe into Roman using the transliteration system shown in Figures 5 and 8 as well as described in sections 2.3, 3.2, and 3.3:

6. From the verbal root बेच- *bec-* 'to sell'.
7. From the verbal root ख़रीद- *kharīd-* 'to buy'.
8. This principle admits many exceptional forms. In ज़िंदगी *zindagī* (not *zindgī*) 'life', for instance the inherent *a* is pronounced in spite of the fact that the word satisfies all of the conditions for its deletion.
9. In this primer the inherent *a* is consistently indicated in the transliteration of verbal stems in contexts of this type. It is not represented, however, in situations of the type (a) and (d).

ऊपर, निकट, फल, गंगा, ख़तरा, गुण, ठीक, ऐसा, खाम्रो, पौना, संतरा, छोटा, झाड़ू, फलतः, जहाज़, बाज़ार, फ़ारसी, थोड़े, सड़कें, मोटी, क़दम, दिया, कलि, परदा, वग़ैर, भरना, बंगला, शिकार, सँघनी, हड़ताल, लवण, ग्रौर, मृग, घोड़ा, दंडों, ढिलाई, चांदी, बध, सुख, गाँठ, चढ़ाव, ढूँढ़ी ।

3.5.2. Transcribe each of the following Hindi words and phrases into *devanāgarī* and read aloud. In words containing nasalized vowels use the *anusvāra* unless the word is marked with an asterisk (*), in which case the *anunāsika* (*candrabindu*) is to be employed. The symbol *a* enclosed within parentheses indicates a silent *a*, and hence is not to be vocalized.

ghoṭ(a)nā, nath, ghī, rāṇā, sipāhī, bal, fidā, jholī, d̃āt (*), *k̤hud, hazār, bāt(a)cīt gābhīr, mil(a)tā, nikal(a)ne, taiyār, śeṣ, jhõkā, hathelī, khā̃ḍ, ṭhelī, chipāv, āśā, mṛdu, bhautik, kāraṇ, śobhā, bhāī, gaī, jāte hāĩ, phāĩk(a)tī thī, rukā hogā.*

CHAPTER 4: THE *Devanāgarī* WRITING SYSTEM AND HINDI PRONUNCIATION (Cont.)

4.1. Conjunct Consonants

It often happens in Hindi that a syllable, instead of consisting of a vowel standing alone or a consonant and a following vowel, is made up of a consonant cluster and subsequent vowel. There are several means in *devanāgarī* by which such consonant clusters (also called conjunct consonants) are represented. Some of these are highly productive while others are limited to combinations of particular consonants. The representation of consonant clusters normally involves the formation of special ligatures, each of which can be analyzed into elements standing for the constituent consonants of the cluster. The same consonant cluster often is represented in more than one manner, with the choice of a particular option related to factors of individual preference, aesthetics, and availability of appropriate type. A few *devanāgarī* consonant cluster signs are highly idiosyncratic and need be learned on an individual basis.

4.4.1. Combining Forms of Consonants

Conjunct characters are commonly formed by the fusing together into a single sign either all or a portion of the signs representing the individual component consonants of the cluster. The first element of the cluster is often an abbreviated version of the full character for the first consonant. This truncated (or "combining") form of the consonant is frequently built from the independent version of the consonant by the deletion of the vertical bar that appears on the right side of many *devanāgarī* characters (e.g., ग्‍ from ग *g*, न्‍ from न *n*). Letters without such vertical elements on their right sides are left unaltered or are only minimally abridged (e.g., ठ *ṭh*, घ *gh*, ढ़ *dh*, etc.). The second component of conjunct consonants is, with few exceptions, the unaltered full symbol for the second consonant. A summary of the combining forms of the basic Hindi consonants is given below in Figure 9.

There are many hundreds of conjunct consonants that can be formed by the means just described (e.g., ध्य *dhy*, प्त *pt*, क्य *ky*, ल्म *lm*, स्न *sn*, त्स्य *tsy*, etc.). In the majority of cases, however, the components of the clusters are easily recognizable. In a small number of cases the components of a consonant are strung out in a horizontal line (e.g., न्न *nn*), arranged vertically (e.g., ड्ड *ḍḍ*, ट्ट *ṭṭ*) or juxtaposed in some less regular manner (e.g., न्न *nn*, द्व *dv*, द्ध *ddh*, द्भ *dbh*). Highly irregular consonant clusters arc discussed below (4.1.4.).

4.1.2. The Use of Virāma.

As an alternative to the system detailed above, the diacritic *vīrāma* is written in conjunction with the full from of the first consonant of a cluster. This has the effect

Full Form	Short Form	Examples	Full Form	Short Form	Examples	Full Form	Short Form	Examples
क	क्	क्य *ky*	ड	ड	ड्ड *ḍḍ*	य	य्	य्य *yy*
ख	ख्	ख्य *khy*	ढ	ढ	ढ्य *ḍhy*	र	र्[b]	
ग	ग्	ग्न *gn*	ण	ण्	ण्ड *ṇḍ*	ल	ल्	ल्प *lp*
घ	घ्	घ्न *ghn*	त	त्	त्स *ts*	व	व्	व्य *vy*
ङ	ङ	ङ्ग *ṅg*	थ	थ्	थ्य *thy*	श	श्	श्क *śk*
च	च्	च्छ *cch*	द	द	द्व *dv*	स	स्	स्य *sy*
छ	छ	छ्र *chr*	न	न्	न्द *nd*	ह	ह	ह्य *hy*
ज	ज्	ज्व *jv*	प	प्	प्त *pt*			
झ/झ	[a]		फ	फ्	फ्य *phy*			
ञ	ञ्	ञ्च *ñc*	ब	ब्	ब्द *bd*			
ट	ट	ट्ट *ṭṭ*	भ	भ्	भ्य *bhy*			
ठ	ठ	ठ *ṭhy*	म	म्	म्ब *mb*			

Figure 9. Short Forms of Basic Consonants (as used as first element in conjuncts)
a. Does not occur as first element in conjuncts.
b. See 4.1.3.

of blocking the pronunciation of the inherent *a* that would normally be included in the realization of the consonant : e.g., ड्‌ड *ḍḍ*, न्‌य *ny*, ह्‌व *hv*. The *virāma* is commonly encountered in typewritten Hindi, in Hindi printed by firms without extensive supplies of type for unusual conjuncts, and in the transliteration of foreign words.

4.1.3. Conjuncts Involving *r*.

The consonant र *r* is treated unusually in consonant clusters. When serving as the second member of a cluster, it is indicated by a small diagonal slash (going in the opposite direction from that of the *virāma*) written under the sign for the first member of a conjunct : e. g., क्र *kr*, प्र *pr*, द्र *dr*, व्र *vr*. When it is the first member of a conjunct, the sound is indicated by a small hook placed on top of the *rekhā* for the second consonant : e.g., र्क *rk*, र्ह *rh*, र्ष *rṣ*, र्म *rm*. This hook is deferred until after any *mātrā* written to the right side of the character for the final component of the conjunct: e.g., र्थी *rthī*, र्मो *rmo*.

4.1.4. Irregular Conjuncts.

Several *devanāgarī* conjuncts are so irregular as to preclude the immediate recognition of their components. The most important of these are क्त *kt*, क्ष or क्ष *kṣ*, ज्ञ *jñ* (commonly pronounced [gy]), त्त *tt*, त्र *tr*, द्द *dd*, द्य *dy*, and द्म *dm*. The consonant श *ś* has a special combining form श्‍ that is often used in place of श in some clusters (e.g., श्र *śr*, श्च or श्च (*śc*). Slightly irregular but nevertheless recognizable conjuncts exist in which ह *h* stands as the first element (e.g. ह्न *hn*, ह्म *hm*, ह्य *hy*, ह्ल *hl*, ह्व *hv*.).

4.1.5. The Pronunciation of Consonant Clusters

Consonant clusters are in theory sequences of two or more consonants spoken without an intervening vowel. In practice, however, many Hindi speakers insert a short अ *a* between the consonants. Thus the word जन्म *janm* 'birth' is heard as pronounced [jənəm]. Consonant clusters beginning with स् *s* at the start of a word are often not pronounced as written. Commonly a short अ *a* or इ *i* is appended before the cluster, effectively putting the cluster in the middle of the word : स्त्री *stri* 'women' and स्कूल *skūl* 'school' pronounced as [əstri] or [Istri] and [əskul] or [Iskul] respectively. Other speakers, most often in or near the Punjab, break up these clusters by inserting an अ *a*: e.g., [sətri], [səkul].

At the end of a word clusters ending in the semi-vowels य *y*, र *r*, ल *l*, and व *v* (e.g., मनुष्य *manusya* 'man, person', पत्र *patra* 'letter', शुक्ल *śukla* 'light', महत्व *mahattva* 'importance' are variously pronounced. In careful speech they are often spoken with a clearly audible अ *a* element. In rapid speech, however, the अ *a* is often absent, with only the faintest trace of the semi-vowel discernible.

Geminate (i.e., doubled) consonants are kept distinct from non-geminates in Hindi. In the pronunciation of the geminates there is a definite prolongation of the blockage of the air flow. A word such as पन्ना *panna* 'leaf' page', for instance, should be spoken with a single drawn out न *n* rather than with a sequence of two distinct nasals. The gemination of aspirate stops in Hindi is represented as clusters of corresponding non-aspirate and aspirate consonants : e.g. च्छ *cch*, द्ध *ddh*, ब्भ *bbha*. It is not possible to form clusters containing sequences of aspirates.

4.2. *anusvāra* Before Consonants

The phonetic realization of *anusvāra* varies in Hindi according to the nature of the consonant that immediately follows it. Before stop consonants a vowel plus *anusvāra* is pronounced as a sequence of non-nasal vowel, nasal consonant, and stop consonant, with the nasal consonant having the same place of articulation as the stop :

anusvāra→ङ *ṅ* before क *k*, ख *kh*, ग *g*, and घ *gh*;
ञ *ñ* before च *c*, छ *ch*, ज *j*, and झ *jh*;
ण *ṇ* before ट *ṭ*, ठ *ṭh*, ड *ḍ*, and ढ *ḍh*;
न *n* before त *t*, थ *th*, द *d*, and ध *dh*;
म *m* before प *p*, फ *ph*, ब *b*, and भ *bh*.

This variation in the pronunciation of *anusvāra* is frequently reflected in *devanāgarī* :

अंक *ãk* can also be written as अङ्क *aṅk*;
पंजा *pãjā* can also be written as पञ्जा *panjā*;
दंड *dãḍ* can also be written as दण्ड *daṇḍ*;
हिंदी *hĩdī* can also be written as हिन्दी *hindī*;
लंबा *lãbā* can also be written as लम्बा *lambā*.

Other variations of the realization of *anusvāra* are not indicated in the orthography: before र *r*, ल *l*, and स *s* the sound is pronounced as न *n* (e.g., संरेखण *sãrekhaṇ* (pronounced [sənrekhəṇ]), संलेख *sãlekh* (pronounced [sənlekh]), हंस *hãs* (pronounced [həns])); before य *y* and श *ś* it approximates the sound *ñ* (e.g., in संयोग *sãyog*, अंश *ãś*); and before व it is pronounced as म *m* (e.g., in संवत् *sãvat*). Either vowel nasalization or the velar nasal ङ *ṅ* is heard when *anusvāra* precedes ह *h* (e.g., in संहार sãhār).

4.3. DEVANĀGARĪ NUMERALS

The following numerals are employed in *devanāgarī* : १ or १ 1; २ 2; ३ 3; ४ 4; ५ 5; ६ 6; ७ 7; ८ or ८ 8; ९ or ९ 9; ० 0. The manner of their employment is the same as with Arabic numerals. In recent years Arabic numerals have increasingly come into use.

4.4. PUNCTUATION

In traditional Hindi writing the punctuation mark *daṇḍ* (।) is used as a full stop. In older or traditional verse a double vertical line is used to mark the end of a verse, reserving the single *daṇḍ* to indicate the end of a half-verse. In more modern writing the use of western punctuation (including the period, comma, hyphen, semicolon, exclamation mark, question mark, and dash) has become common. The first of a pair of quotation marks (whether single or double) is generally inverted, as is the fashion in many European languages, but not in English.

4.5. ABBREVIATIONS

Abbreviations are formed in Hindi by the use of either a small circle or a dot after the first syllable of the word to be abbreviated:

प्रो० के० एस० शर्मा *pro. ke. es. śarmā* 'Professor K. S. Sharma';
डा० वी० बी० गुप्ता *ḍā. vī. bī. guptā* 'Doctor V. B. Gupta;
ई० पू० *ī. pū.* 'B.C.' (from ईसवी पूर्व *īsvī pūrva*).

4.6. THE ALPHABETIC ORDER OF DEVANĀGARĪ

The alphabetic order of *devanāgarī* is a model of logic and rational design, reflecting a keen understanding of the phonetic properties of the sounds designated by the various characters in the system. Vowels precede consonants, with the latter divided up into groups containing stops and nasals, semi-vowels, sibilants, and *h* respectively. The stops and nasals are arranged by place of articulation, moving from the rear of the mouth to the front. Within a given place of articulation, voiceless stops precede the voiced, with non-aspirates preceding aspirates within each of these two categories. Nasal consonants follow the stops for each of the five basic places of articulation. For purposes of alphabetization, subscript dots are disregarded; no distinction is thus made between the members of such sets of sounds as फ *ph* and फ़, *f*, ज *j* and ज़ *z*, ख *kh* and ख़ *k̤h*, ड *ḍ* and ड़ *R*, etc. Nasal vowels always precede corresponding non-nasal vowels, thus causing a word such as अंग्रेजी *ãgrezī* to be alphabetized ahead of अगला *aglā*. The *visarga* is treated as a full consonant, appearing as the last letter in the alphabet immediately after ह *h*. The full alphabetic order of *devanāgarī* as used for Hindi is as follows:

अ *a*; आ *ā*; इ *i*; ई *ī*; उ *u*; ऊ *ū*; ऋ *r̥*; ए *e*; ऐ *ai*; ओ *o*;
औ *au*; क (क़) *k* (*q*); ख (ख़) *kh* (*k̤h*); ग (ग़) *g* (*ġ*); घ *gh*;

ङ *ṅ*; च *c*; छ *ch*; ज (ज़) *j* (*z*); झ *jh*; ञ *ñ*; ट *ṭ*; ठ *ṭh*; ड (ड़) *ḍ* (*R*);
ढ (ढ़) *ḍh* (*Rh*); ण *ṇ*; त *t*; थ *th*; द *d*; ध *dh*; न *n*; प *p*; फ (फ़) *ph* (*f*);
ब *b*; भ *bh*; म *m*; य *y*; र *r*; ल *l*; व *v*; श *ś*; ष *ṣ*; स *s*; ह *h*; : *ḥ*.

In the dictionary entry for words beginning with a given consonant, the consonant followed by अ *a* precedes the consonant followed by आ *a*, which in turn precedes the consonant followed by इ *i*, etc. All consonant clusters, considered to be sequences of a consonant followed by one or more consonants, occur after sequences of consonant plus vowel. A given consonant plus क *k*, for instance, will logically precede a sequence of that consonant plus त *t*, which in turn precedes the consonant plus य *y*.

4.7. Exercises

4.7.1. Identify the components of each of the following *devanāgarī* conjunct consonants (e.g., स्क = स *s* + क *k*) :

प्र, ख्य, प्त, ल्म, ज्झ, म्ह, न्द, र्च, द्र, ष्ठ, न्त्य, र्त, त्र, स्म, ह्ल, क्ष, स्न.

4.7.2. Combine each of the following sequences of letters into single *devanāgarī* syllables (e.g., प *p* + र *r* + अ *a* = प्र *pra*; र *r* + थ *th* + ई *ī* = र्थी *rthī*) :

1. र *r* + ह *h* + आ *ā*; 2. व *v* + य *y* + ओ o; 3. म *m* + म *m* + ए *e*; 4. ण *ṇ* + ड *ḍ* + उ *u*; 5. म *m* + ल *l* + इ *i*; 6. ज *j* + ञ *ñ* + आ *ā*; 7. द *d* + ध *dh* + अ *a*; 8. द *d* + य *y* + औ *au*; 9. ट *ṭ* + ट *ṭ* + ई *ī*.

4.7.3. Rewrite the following with Arabic numerals :

३; १४; २०६; ७८९; ५०६; ७,११९; १,८४०.

4.7.4. Rewrite the numbers with *devanāgarī* numerals :

4; 8; 19; 36; 87; 405; 781; 692; 3,842.

4.7.5. Read the following Hindi sentences aloud and transliterate into Roman :

1. वह जाता है। 2. हम गये थे। 3. लड़की को घर लौटना है। 4. उसके पास तीन रुपये हैं। 5. तुम वहां क्यों गए? 6. विद्यार्थी दिल्ली का है। 7. इस स्कूल के कितने अध्यापक हैं। 8. पुष्पा को हिन्दी आती होगी। 9. मुझे पाँच टिकटें दो। 10. मेज़ पर दो पुस्तकें और तीन पैंसिलें पड़ी थीं।

4.6.6. Transliterate the following sentences into *devanāgarī* and read aloud. The transliteration of silent-*a* is enclosed within parentheses. Use *anusvāra* for nasal vowels unless the word to be transliterated is marked with an asterisk (*) :

1. *merā bhāī kal(a) katte mẽ rah(a)tā thā.* 2. *sītā rām kī patnī hai.* 3. *tumhare pās kit(a)ne phal the ?* 4. *mãĩ prati din vahā̃ (*) jātā hū̃ (*).* 5. *sūr(a)dās bahut prasiddh hindī kavi the.* 6. *us(a)ne tujhe kyā diyā ?* 7. *kuch aur samose le lījiye.* 8. *bãbaī mẽ kit(a)ne log rah(a)te hãĩ ?* 9. *kyā tum pahalī hī bār kān(a)pur ā rahe ho?* 10. *bhābhī ko kal bāzār jānā paRā.*

PART
II

CHAPTER 5

5.1. The Noun

The Hindi noun is quite simple in formation. It is somewhat more highly inflected than the English noun, but considerably less so than the nouns of German, Latin, or Greek. There are two genders in Hindi, masculine and feminine, as well as two numbers, singular and plural. Cases (i.e., nominative, accusative, dative, etc.) are by and large not indicated by word endings, but by independent words called postpositions that immediately follow the nouns. Postpositions are quite analogous to the prepositions of English. Hindi nominal forms are classified as direct or oblique. In general, Hindi nouns that are followed by postpositions are said to be in their oblique forms. Hindi nouns not followed by postpositions are said to be in their direct (or non-oblique) forms.[1] Hindi also distinguishes a vocative (address) form for all nouns in the plural and for some masculine nouns in the singular (16.4). There are no articles in Hindi, and a noun in isolation is not marked as being definite or indefinite. The noun लड़का *laRkā* may therefore be translated as 'a boy' or 'the boy' depending on context.

5.2. Masculine Nouns

There are two classes of masculine nouns in Hindi. Class I and Class II. Class I masculine nouns end in -आ *-ā* when in their singular direct, -ए *-e* in their singular oblique, -ए *-e* in their plural direct and -ओं *-õ* in their plural oblique forms :

	Singular	Plural
Direct	लड़का *laRkā* '(the/a) boy'	लड़के *laRke* '(the) boys'
Oblique	लड़के पर *laRke par* 'on the boy'	लड़कों पर *laRkõ par* 'on the boys'

The form पर *par* in the above paradigm is an example of a Hindi postposition. The words लड़के *laRke* in लड़के पर *laRke par* and *laRkõ* of लड़कों पर *laRkõ par* are said to be oblique because they are followed by postpositions.

A few Hindi class I nouns show nasal vowels throughout their declension. Other than the feature of nasalization, these nouns are similar in their formation to लड़का *laRkā* :

1. Exceptions to these definitions of *oblique* and *direct* forms of nouns are discussed in 9.2 and 10.3.

	Singular	Plural
Direct	कुआँ *kuā̃* '(the/a) well'	कुएँ *kuẽ* '(the) wells'
Oblique	कुएँ में *kuẽ mẽ* 'in the well'	कुओं में *kuõ mẽ* 'in the wells'

Masculine Class II nouns have no distinct endings in their direct singular, direct plural, and oblique singular forms. They add -ओं *-õ* to form the plural oblique :

Singular	Plural
घर *ghar* '(a/the) house'	घर *ghar* '(the) houses'
घर में *ghar mẽ* 'in the house'	घरों में *gharõ mẽ* 'in the houses'

A small number of masculine nouns ending in -आ *-ā* are declined according to the pattern of Class II.

Singular	Plural
राजा *rājā* 'king' पिता *pitā* 'father'	राजा *rājā* 'kings' पिता *pitā* 'fathers'
राजा से *rājā se* 'from the king' पिता से *pitā se* 'from the father'	राजाओं से *rajāõ se* 'from the kings' पिताओं से *pitāõ se* 'from the fathers'

Masculine Class II nouns ending in -ई *-ī* shorten this vowel to -इ *-i* and insert a -य- *-y-* before the oblique plural termination -ओं *-õ* :

	Singular	Plural
Direct	आदमी *ādmī* '(a/the) man'	आदमी *ādmī* '(the) men'
Oblique	आदमी से *ādmī se* 'from the man'	आदमियों से *ādmiyõ se* 'from the men'

Masculine Class II nouns ending in -ऊ -*ū* likewise shorten this vowel to -उ -*u* before the oblique plural termination:

Singular	Plural
चाकू *cākū* '(a/the) penknife'	चाकू *cākū* 'penknives'
चाकू पर *cākū par* 'on the penknife'	चाकुओं पर *cākuõ par* 'on the penknives'

The Vocative forms of masculine nouns are discussed in 16.4.

5.3. Postpositions

To a great extent the syntactic functions served by nouns in Hindi (i.e., direct object, indirect object, etc.) are indicated by a class of words called postpositions. These words are similar in function to English prepositions, but stand after the nouns with which they are linked. Hindi postpositions are either simple (of only one word) or compound (of two or more words). Some important simple postpositions are **में** ***mẽ*** 'in, among', **पर** *par* 'on, at', **से** *se* 'from, by, since', **तक** *tak* 'until, as far as', **को** *ko* 'to' (8.3.), and **का** *kā* 'of' (7.3). Compound postpositions are discussed in 7.4. Any postposition, whether simple or compound, requires the noun it governs to be in its oblique form.

5.4. Question Words

Questions in Hindi can be considered to be of two basic sorts. One type of question, called a *yes/no question*, is used to elicit a yes or no answer from the person addressed. "Are you my friend?", "Is Patna the capital of Bihar?", and "Have we reached Jaipur yet?" are examples of yes/no questions in English. Other Hindi questions, called *information questions*, are used to elicit spicific information other than a yes or no from the person addressed. "Who are you?", "Why have you come?", "Where has she gone?", and "What is your name?" are all English questions that elicit information other than a yes or no.

The formation of yes/no questions and informations question is fundamentally distinct in Hindi. In written Hindi, yes/no questions are indicated by an interrogative marker क्या *kyā* that appears at the beginning of the sentence :

क्या राम घर पर है ? *kyā rām ghar par hai ?*

'Is Ram at home ?"

क्या कुएँ में पानी है ? *kyā kuẽ mẽ pānī hai ?*

'Is there water in the well ?"

In colloquial Hindi the initial क्या *kyā* is frequently deleted, and a question is distinguished from a corresponding declarative sentence by intonation ;

राम घर पर है। *rām ghar par hai.*

'Ram is at home.'

राम घर पर है ? *rām ghar par hai* ?
'Is Ram at home ?'

Information questions in Hindi are indicated by any of a number of interrogative words that appear immediately before the verb of a sentence. These words all begin with be consonant क- *k*-. Some important question words of this sort are कब *kab* 'when?', कहाँ *kahā̃* 'where?', किधर *kidhar* 'in which direction?', क्यों *kyõ* 'why?', कौन *kaun* 'who?', and क्या *kyā* 'what?':

मोहन पाकिस्तान कब गया ? *mohan pākistān kab gayā*?
'When did Mohan go to Pakistan?'

ऊत्तर प्रदेश में मथुरा कहाँ है? *uttar pradeś mẽ mathurā kahā̃ hai*?
'Where in Uttar Pradesh is Mathura ?'

अब अध्यापक किधर गया ? *ab adhyāpak kidhar gayā* ?
'Which way did the teacher go now ?'

सुनीत भारत क्यों गया ? *sunīt bhārat kyõ gayā* ?
'Why did Sunit go to India?'

पानी में क्या है ? *pānī mẽ kyā hai* ?
'What is in the water ?'

N. B. : There are two distinct functions of the question word क्या *kya*. Standing initially it marks a yes/no question. Immediately before the verb it is to be translated as 'what?'.

5.5. Negative Marker नहीं *nahī̃*

There are a number of words in Hindi that are use to indicate negation. The most common of these are नहीं *nahī̃*, मत *mat*, and न *na*. Often specific grammatical constructions or verb forms require the use of a particular one of these markers in expressing the negative.

The negative marker नहीं *nahī̃* is commonly used to negate declarative sentences. It usually appears immediately before the verb of a sentence:

विद्यार्थी स्कूल में नहीं हैं। *vidyārthī skūl mẽ nahī̃ hãi*.
'The students are not in school.'

In interrogative sentences नहीं nahī̃ generally stands after the question word but before the verb :

सुनीत और राम पाकिस्तान क्यों नहीं गए ? *sunīt aur rām pakistān kyõ nahī̃ gae* ?
'Why didn't Sunit and Ram go to Pakistan?

Present tense forms of the verb 'to be' are frequently deleted when नहीं *nahī̃* is present. Thus besides

मोहन आगरे में[2] नहीं है। *mohan āgre mẽ nahī̃ hai*.
'Mohan is not in Agra.'

---

2. Many masculine place names ending in -आ *-ā* are optionally treated as Class II nouns : e.g., आगरा में *āgrā mẽ* and मथुरा में *mathurā mẽ* besides आगरे में *āgre mẽ* and मथुरे में *mathure mẽ*.

one often encounters

मोहन आगरे में नहीं। *mohan āgre mẽ nahī̃.*

This deletion is especially common in sentences in which the negative clause or phrase is followed immediately by a contrastive positive one :

मोहन आगरे में नहीं, मथुरे में है। *mohan āgre mẽ nahī̃, mathure mẽ hai.*
'Mohan is not in Agra, but in Mathura.'

5.6. है *hai* AND हैं *hãĩ*

The third person singular and plural present tense forms of the verb 'to be' are है *hai* and हैं *hãĩ* respectively. It should be noted that these forms differ from one another only by the presence of nasality in the plural :

स्कूल में विद्यार्थी है। *skūl mẽ vidyārthī hai.*
'There is a student in the school.'

स्कूल में विद्यार्थी हैं। *skūl mẽ vidyārthi hãĩ.*
'There are students in the school.'

In the above sentences the only way to determine the number of the noun विद्यार्थी *vidyārthi* is through the presence or absence of nasalization of the verb. It should also be apparent from the above examples that है *hai* and हैं *hãĩ* can be used to express the notion 'there is/are' (cf. French *il y a,* German *es gibt*). These sentences should be contrasted with.

विद्यार्थी स्कूल में है। *vidyārthī skūl mẽ hai.*

'The student (who is already known from context) is in the school. Other present tense verb forms of 'to be' are introduced in 6.4.

5.7. BASIC WORD ORDER

There are no inviolate principles of word order in Hindi. The language. particularly in its colloquial forms, demonstrates great flexibility in the order in which words and phrases are strung together to form sentences. The statements to follow should therefore be looked upon as indicating tendencies observed in large numbers of sentences, but not as exceptionless rules.

In general, the basic order of a Hindi sentence is subject-object-verb :

राम हिन्दी बोलता है। *rām hindī boltā hai.*
'Ram speaks Hindi.'

As mentioned earlier, the negative marker नहीं *nahī̃* and question words immediately precede the verb :

विद्यार्थी स्कूल में क्यों है ? *vidyārthī skūl mẽ kyõ hai ?*
'Why is the student in school ?'

विद्यार्थी स्कूल में नहीं है। *vidyārthī skūl mẽ nahī̃ hai.*
'The student is not in school ?'

The word क्या *kyā* marking yes/no questions stands at the beginning of its sentence :

क्या विद्यार्थी स्कूल में है ? *kyā vidyārthī skūl mẽ hai ?*
'Is the student in school ?'

Adverbials of various sorts tend to occur towards the beginning of a sentence, either before the subject, or immediately after it :

क्या अब मोहन आगरे में है ? *kyā ab mohan āgre mẽ hai* ? or
क्या मोहन अब आगरे में है ? *kyā mohan ab āgre mẽ hai* ?
'Is Mohan in Agra now ?'

As in English, modifiers of nouns precede the noun. Numbers, which can be considered nominal modifiers, also precede nouns :.

अच्छा आदमी *acchā ādmī* 'a/the good man'
एक अच्छा आदमी *ek acchā ādmī* 'one good man'

Further discussion of Hindi word order will be provided in several later sections, particularly 10.4 and 29.3.

5.8. Vocabulary

अध्यापक	*adhyāpak*	n.m. teacher	सब	*sab*	adj. all
आदमी	*ādmī*	n.m. man, person	है	*hai*	is (=3.s.p. of verb 'to be'
आगरा	*āgrā*	prop. m. I/II Agra (a city in Uttar Pradesh)	हैं	*haĩ*	are (=3.pl.p. of verb 'to be')
उत्तर प्रदेश	*uttar pradeś*	prop. m. Uttar Pradesh (a province in northern India)	अब	*ab*	adv. now
कमरा	*kamrā*	n.m. room	इधर	*idhar*	adv. in this direction, hither
कुआँ	*kuā̃*	n.m. well	उधर	*udhar*	adv. in that direction, thither
कुत्ता	*kuttā*	n.m. dog	नहीं	*nahī̃*	adv. neg. no, not
केला	*kelā*	n.m. banana	यहाँ	*yahā̃*	adv. here
घर	*ghar*	n.m. home, house	वहाँ	*vahā̃*	adv. there
दरवाज़ा	*darvāzā*	n.m. door	पर	*par*	post. on, at, by
पाकिस्तान	*pākistān*	prop. m. Pakistan	में	*mẽ*	post. in, among
पानी	*pānī*	n.m. water	से	*se*	post. from
फूल	*phūl*	n.m. flower	और	*aur*	conj. and
भारत	*bhārat*	prop. m. India	या	*yā*	conj. or
मथुरा	*mathurā*	prop. m. I/II Mathura (a city in Uttar Pradesh)	कब	*kab*	inter. when?
मित्र	*mitra*	n.m. friend	कहाँ	*kahā̃*	inter. where?
मोहन	*mohan*	prop. m. Mohan (man's name)	किधर	*kidhar*	inter. in which direction? whither?
राम	*rām*	prop. m. Ram (man's name)	कौन	*kaun*	inter. who?
रुपया	*rupayā*	n.m. rupee	क्या	*kyā*	inter. what?; marks yes/no question
लड़का	*larkā*	n.m. boy	क्यों	*kyõ*	inter. why?
विद्यार्थी	*vidyārthī*	n.m. student	एक	*ek*	num. one
सुनीत	*sunīt*	prop. m. Sunit (man's name)	दो	*do*	num. two
स्कूल	*skūl*	n.m. school	तीन	*tīn*	num. three
			चार	*cār*	num. four
			पाँच	*pā̃c*	num. five

5.9. Exercises :

5.9.1. Translate into English

1. भारत *bhārat*, भारत से *bhārat se*; 2. दो रुपये *do rupaye*; 3. एक घर *ek ghar*, घर पर *ghar par*; 4. लड़के से *laRke se*, लड़कों से *laRkõ se*, 5. फूलों में *phūlõ mẽ*; 6. तीन विद्यार्थियों में *tīn vidyārthiyõ mẽ* 7. दरवाज़े *darvāze*, दरवाज़े पर *darvāze par*; 8. पाँच आदमी *pā̃c ādmī*; 9. चार कुत्ते *cār kutte*; 10. आगरे से *āgre se*; 11. अध्यापकों में *adhyāpakõ mẽ* 12. कुएँ *kuẽ*, कुएँ में *kuẽ mẽ*; 13. मित्र *mitra*, मित्र से *mitra se*.

5.9.2. Translate into Hindi

1. a boy, the boys, from the boys; 2. the room, in the room, in the rooms; 3. one house, in the three houses; 4. the teachers, among all the teachers; 5. five men, from the five men, 6. a well, in the well, in the wells; 7. the king, the, kings, from the kings; 8. friend, among the friends; 9. in India; 10. from Mohan and Ram.

5.9.3. Translate into English

राम घर पर है। *rām ghar par hai.* 2. घर में क्या है? *ghar mẽ kyā hai ?* 3. पानी कुएँ में है *pānī kuẽ mẽ hai.* 4. कुएँ में पानी है। *kuẽ mẽ pānī hai.* 5. अब मोहन यहाँ नहीं है। *ab mohan yahā̃ nahī̃ hai.* 6. केले कहाँ हैं? *kele kahā̃ hãĩ ?* 7. राम और मोहन मित्र हैं। *rām aur mohan mitra hãĩ.* 8. आगरा पाकिस्तान में नहीं है। *āgrā pākistān mẽ nahī̃ hai.* 9. सब विद्यार्थी स्कूल में हैं। *sab vidyārthī skūl mẽ hãĩ.* 10. अब यहाँ कुत्ते नहीं हैं। *ab yahā̃ kutte nahī̃ hãĩ.* 11. आगरा और मथुरा उत्तर प्रदेश में हैं। *āgrā aur mathurā uttar pradeś mẽ hãĩ* 12. क्या अब सब लड़के पाकिस्तान में हैं? *kyā ab sab laRke pākistān me hãĩ ?*

5.9.4. Translate into Hindi

1. The boy is in school. 2. Where is Agra ? 3. The four friends are at home. 4. What is on the two bananas ? 5. There is a flower in the well. 6. The man is not here now. 7. Mohan is in Uttar Pradesh. 8. The boy is in India, not in Pakistan. 9. Four teachers and five students are by the door. 10. Is the man at home now ? 11. All the flowers are in the water. 12. There are three rupees in the well.

CHAPTER 6

6.1. Feminine Nouns

Hindi possesses two classes of feminine nouns, Class I and Class II. Class I feminine nouns end in -ई -ī in their singular direct, -ई-ī in their singular oblique, -इयाँ-iyā̃ in their plural direct, and -इयों-iyõ in their oblique plural forms:

	Singular	Plural
Direct	लड़की *laRkī* 'girl'	लड़कियाँ 'girls'
Oblique	लड़की को *laRkī ko* 'to the girl'	लड़कियों को *laRkiyõ ko* 'to the girls'

A small number of Class I feminine nouns show forms similar to लड़की *laRkī*, except that -इ -i or -इया -iyā appear in place of -ई -ī in the singular forms:

	Singular	Plural
Direct	शक्ति *śakti* 'power' चिड़िया *ciRiyā* 'bird'	शक्तियाँ *śaktiyā̃* 'powers' चिड़ियां *ciRiyā̃* 'birds'
Obilque	शक्ति से *śakti se* 'from the power' चिड़िया से *ciRiyā se* 'from the bird'	शक्तियों से *śaktiyõ se* 'from the powers' चिड़ियों से *ciRiyõ se* 'from the birds'

All remaining feminine nouns in Hindi belong to Class II. These nouns form their plural direct forms by means of the suffix -एँ -ẽ and their plural oblique with -ओं -õ. The singular forms, both direct and oblique, may end in virtually any sound, excepting, of course, the -ई -ī,-इ -i, and -इया -iyā characteristic of Class I Feminine nouns.

	Singular	Plural
Direct	पुस्तक *pustak* 'book' वस्तु *vastu* 'thing' माता *mātā* 'mother'	पुस्तकें *pustakẽ* 'books' वस्तुएँ *vastuẽ* 'things' माताएँ *mātāẽ* 'mothers'
Oblique	पुस्तक में *pustak mẽ* 'in the book' वस्तु पर *vastu par* 'on the thing' माता से *mātā se* 'from the mother'	पुस्तकों में *pustakõ mẽ* 'in the books' वस्तुओं पर *vastuõ par* 'on the things' माताओं से *mātāõ se* 'from the mothers'

Feminine Class II nouns having singular direct forms in -ऊ *-ū* shorten this vowel to -उ *-u* before the plural direct termination -एँ *-ẽ* and the plural oblique termination -ओं *-õ*:

	Singular	Plural
Direct	बहू *bahū* 'daughter-in-law'	बहुएँ *bahuẽ* 'daughters-in-law'
Oblique	बहू को *bahū ko* 'to the daughter-in-law'	बहुओं को *bahuõ ko* 'to the daughters-in-law'

N.B. It must be remembered that the gender of Hindi nouns cannot always be determined from the basic forms of the nouns. For example, although the ending -आ *-ā* characterizes a large number of masculine Class I nouns, it is also the terminal sound in many feminine Class II nouns, such as मित्रता *mitratā* 'friendship', छात्रा *chātrā* 'female student', and एकता *ekatā* 'solidarity, unity'. Likewise, even though Hindi nouns in -ई *-ī* tend to belong to feminine Class I, some common nouns ending in this sound are of masculine Class II, as, for example, आदमी *ādmī* 'man', पानी *pānī* 'water', घी *ghī* 'clarified butter', मोती *motī* 'pearl', and दही *dahī* 'curds, yoghurt'. Students should therefore take care to learn the gender of Hindi nouns when the words are first encountered.

6.2. ADJECTIVES

Hindi adjectives are of two basic kinds, *declinable* and *indeclinable*. Declinable adjectives agree with the nouns they modify in gender (masculine vs. feminine), number (singular vs. plural), and case (direct vs., oblique). The masculine forms of declinable adjectives end in -आ *-ā* in the singular direct, and -ए *-e* in the singular oblique, plural direct, and plural oblique cases. Declinable adjectives always show -ई *-ī* when modifying feminine nouns, whether singular or plural, direct or oblique. The paradigm of the declinable adjective खड़ा *khaRā* 'standing' is given below:

Masculine

	Singular	Plural
Direct	खड़ा लड़का *khaRā laRkā* 'standing boy'	खड़े लड़के *khaRe laRke* 'standing boys'
Oblique	खड़े लड़के को *khaRe laRke ko* 'to the standing boy'	खड़े लड़कों को *khaRe laRkõ ko* 'to the standing boys'

Feminine

	Singular	Plural
Direct	खड़ी लड़की *khaRī laRkī* 'standing girl'	खड़ी लड़कियाँ *khaRī laRkiyā̃* 'standing girls'
Oblique	खड़ी लड़की को *khaRī laRkī ko* 'to the standing girl'	खड़ी लड़कियों को *khaRī laRkiyõ ko* 'to the standing girls'

A small number of variable adjectives show nasalization throughout their paradigms; e.g. पाँचवाँ *pā̃cvā̃* (f. पाँचवीं *pā̃cvī̃*) 'fifth' (V.11.3).

Indeclinable adjectives possess but a single form when modifying nouns of different genders, numbers, or cases. These adjectives do not end in any characteristic sound or series of sounds. A small number of indeclinable adjectives end in -आ *-ā* (e.g., ज़िन्दा *zindā* 'alive', बढ़िया *baRhiyā* 'nice') and care should be taken not to treat these adjectives as declinable.

Hindi adjectives may be used either predicatively (i.e. to make a statement about some nominal entity) or attributively (i.e., to restrict or limit the meaning of some nominal entity). Examples of these two types of adjectival usage are given below:

Predicative: आदमी वहाँ खड़ा है । *ādmī vahā̃ khaRā hai.*
'The man is standing there'.

Attributive: खड़ा आदमी मदन है । *khaRā ādmī madan hai.*
'The standing man is Madan'.

Occasionally adjectives are used elliptically in place of the nouns they are understood to modify. In such cases these adjectives come to be declined as nouns. Thus besides the phrase अमीर लोगों को *amīr logõ ko* 'to the rich people' one also encounters अमीरों को *amīrõ ko* 'to the rich (people)'.

6.3. Personal Pronouns

Hindi personal pronouns distinguish three persons (first, second, and third), two numbers (singular and plural), and two cases (direct and oblique). Second person plural pronouns distinguish two different degrees of respect (familiar and polite). Third person personal pronouns may further be specified as either proximate or non-proximate.

The direct forms of the Hindi personal pronouns are as follows:

	Singular	Plural
1st Person	मैं *mãĩ* 'I'	हम *ham* 'we'
2nd Person	तू *tū* 'you (intimate)'	तुम *tum* 'you (familiar)' आप *āp* 'you (polite)'
3rd Person: proximate	यह *yah* (phonetically [ye]) 'he, she, it'	ये *ye* 'they, he/she (honorific)'
non-proximate	वह *vah* (phonetically [vo] or [wo]) 'he, she, it'	वे *ve*[1] 'they, he/she (honorific)'

The use of personal pronouns is Hindi is significantly different from the use of personal pronouns in English. The main areas of divergence are as follows:

Hindi has three second personal pronouns, whereas English has only the single form 'you'. The singular second person pronoun तू *tū* is used by Hindi speakers in situations of maximal intimacy. It is commonly used to call small children, to invoke

1. Many Hindi speakers make no distinction in the pronunciation of वह *vah* and वे *ve*, rendering both as [vo].

or address a god, to address close friends of equal status, or to express anger or disgust. It is also often used in the home by husbands to address their wives, but less often by wives addressing their husbands. तुम *tum* is employed in the home by most family members in a wide variety of contexts. In situations of social inequality it may be used to address the individual of inferior position. तुम *tum* is also commonly used by friends and colleagues in informal situations. आप *ap* is by and large used to address individuals whom the speaker wishes to accord respect. The form is therefore employed for elders, teachers, and employers. It is also generally used in situations involving a high degree of formality. In situations of social inequality आप *āp* is appropriate for addressing the superior party. The pronoun तू *tū* is grammatically singular and may be used to address only individuals. तुम *tum* and आप *āp*, by contrast, are grammatically plural, but may be used to address either individuals or groups of them. The word लोग *log* (literally 'people') is sometimes added directly after तुम *tum* or आप *āp* (i.e. तुम लोग *tum log*, आप लोग *āp log*) to specify that more than one person is indicated. Words in grammatical agreement with तू *tū* must be grammatically singular. Words in agreement with तुम *tum* or आप *āp* must be grammatically plural regardless of the actual number of persons referred to by the pronouns. In this book the pronouns तू *tū*, तुम *tum*, and आप *āp* are referred to as intimate, familiar, and polite second person pronouns respectively.

हम *ham* is the normal first person pronoun used to express the English notion 'we'. It is, however, ofter used in some varieties of colloquial Hindi in a singular sense in place of the first person singular pronoun मैं *mãĩ*. When used by females, it is not uncommon for हम *ham* to command masculine (in contrast to the expected feminine) verb forms.

The third person singular proximate pronoun यह *yah* (commonly pronounced [ye]) generally refers to a person or thing proximate to the speaker, or the most recent of a number of items mentioned in some discourse. वह *vah* (commonly pronounced [vo] or [wo] indicates a person or thing distant from the speaker or an item (among two or more) earlier specified in some discourse. When degree of proximity to the speaker is not being specifically indicated, वह *vah* tends to be preferred as the common third person singular pronouns for 'he', 'she', and 'it'.

ये *ye* and वे *ve* are third person plural pronouns, proximate and non-proximate respectively. Although grammatically plural, they can both be used to refer to either individuals or groups of them. This use of plural pronouns with singular reference is employed as a sign of respect to the person indicated by the pronoun.[2]

N.B. sentences employing third person plural pronouns are frequently ambiguous with regard to number. For example, the sentence

आज वे इलाहाबाद में हैं। *āj ve ilāhābād mẽ hãĩ.*

can be translated either as 'Today they are in Allahabad' or as 'Today he/she (polite) is in Allahabad'. The correct reading of the sentence can only be determined through context.

2. For further details on the "honorific" use of pronouns v. 7.5.

6.4. The Verb होना *honā* 'To Be'

The Hindi verb for 'to be' is होना *honā*.[3] This verb can be used as a copula in simple predicative sentences (i.e., x = y) and as an auxiliary verb in a large number of verbal constructions. There are four main sets of verbal forms of होना *honā*, the present, the past, the subjunctive, and the presumptive. Present tense forms of होना *honā* agree with their subjects in number and person :

	Singular		Plural	
1st Person	मैं *mãĩ*...... हूँ	*hũ*	हम *ham*...... हैं	*hãĩ*
2nd Person (Int.)	तू *tū*...... है	*hai*	(Fem.) तुम *tum*...... हो	*ho*
			(Pol.) आप *āp*......... हैं	*hãĩ*
3rd Person (Prox.)	यह *yah*...... है	*hai*	ये *ye*......... हैं	*hãĩ*
(Non-Prox.)	वह *vah*...... है	*hai*	वे *ve*......... हैं	*hãĩ*

Past tense forms of होना *honā* agree with their subjects in number and gender. They show था *thā* with masculine singular subjects, थे *the* with masculine plural, थी *thī* with feminine singular, and थीं *thī̃* with feminine plural :

		Masculine	Feminine
Singular :	मैं/तू/यह/वह *mãĩ/tū/yah/vah*	था *thā*	थी *thī*
Plural :	हम/तुम/आप/ये/वे *ham/tum/āp/ye/ve*	थे *the*	थीं *thī̃*

Subjunctive and presumptive forms of होना *honā* are discussed in 7.1.

6.5. बहुत *bahut* and बड़ा *baRā*

The word बहुत *bahut* 'very' is commonly used as an adverb immediately before adjectives to indicate an augmented degree of the quality of the adjective, e.g., बहुत अच्छा मित्र *bahut acchā mitra* 'very good friend'. The adjective बड़ा *baRā* 'large, great' may also be used adverbially in the same capacity as बहुत *bahut*, e.g., बड़ा अच्छा मित्र *baRā acchā mitra*. In this usage *baRā* is declined to agree with the head noun in number, gender, and case: बड़े अच्छे मित्र को *baRe acche mitra ko* 'to the very good friend'; बड़ी अच्छी पुस्तक *baRī acchī pustak* 'the very good book'.

3. The form *honā* is the infinitive of the verb 'to be'. For further discussion of the infinitive in Hindi v. 21.1.

6.6. VOCABULARY

अंग्रेज़ी	*ãgrezī*	prop. f. English language; adj. English	हिन्दी	*hindī*	prop. f. the Hindi language
अमर	*amar*	prop.m. Amar (man's name)	अच्छा	*acchā*	adj. good
			काला	*kālā*	adj. black
इमारत	*imārat*	n.f. building	खड़ा	*khaRā*	adj. standing
इलाहबाद	*ilāhābād*	prop. m, Allahabad (a city in Uttar Pradesh)	खुला	*khulā*	adj. open
			छोटा	*choṭā*	adj. small, younger
			ताज़ा	*tāzā*	adj. fresh
कुर्सी	*kursī*	n.f. chair	पुराना	*purānā*	adj. old (of things, not people)
खिड़की	*khiRkī*	n.f. window	बड़ा	*baRā*	adj. large, great, elder; adv. very
चिड़िया	*ciRiyā*	n.f. bird			
दिल्ली	*dillī*	prop.f. Delhi	बंद	*bãd*	adj. closed
दुकान	*dukān*	n.f. store, shop	बैठा	*baiṭhā*	adj. seated, sitting
नदी	*nadī*	n.f. river	भारतीय	*bhāratīya*	adj. Indian
पुस्तक	*pustak*	n.f. book.	मीठा	*mīṭhā*	adj. sweet
बंबई	*bãbaī*	prop. f. Bombay	लाल	*lāl*	adj. red
बहू	*bahū*	n.f. daughter-in-law	सफ़ेद	*safed*	adj. white
मदन	*madan*	prop. m. Madan (man's name)	साफ़	*sāf*	adj. clean, clear, pure
			आज	*āj*	adv. today
माता	*mātā*	n.f. mother	तब	*tab*	adv. then
मिठाई	*miṭhāī*	n.f. sweet, sweetmeat	बहुत	*bahut*	adv. very; adj. much many
मेज़	*mez*	n.f. table			
रानी	*rānī*	n.f. queen; prop.f. Rani (a woman's name)	लेकिन	*lekin*	conj. but
			छः	*chaḥ* (pronounced [che]	num. six
लड़की	*laRkī*	n.f. girl			
लोग	*log*	n.m.pl. people	सात	*sāt*	num. seven
वस्तु	*vastu*	n.f. thing	आठ	*āṭh*	num. eight
सीता	*sītā*	prop. f. Sita (a woman's name)	नौ	*nau*	num. nine
			दस	*das*	num. ten

6.7. EXERCISES

6.7.1. Translate into English

1. मिठाई *miṭhāī*, छः मिठाइयाँ *chah mithāiyā̃*, ताज़ी मिठाइयाँ *tāzī miṭhāiyā̃*; 2. पुरानी इमारत *purānī imārat*, बहुत इमारतें *bahut imāratẽ*; 3. खिड़कियों पर *khiRkiyõ par*, खुली खिड़की *khulī khiRkī*; 4. बड़ी अच्छी लड़की *baRī acchī laRkī*. बैठी लड़कियों से *baiṭhī laRkiyõ se*; 5. काली पुस्तकें *kālī pustakẽ*, बहुत अच्छी पुस्तकों में *bahut acchī pustakõ mẽ*; 6. सात खड़े लड़के *sāt khaRe laRke*; 7. सफ़ेद और काले कुत्ते *safed aur kāle kutte*; 8. भारतीय नदियों में *bhāratīya nadiyõ mẽ*; 9. छोटी मेज़ों पर *choṭī mezõ par*; 10. आठ साफ़ कमरे *āṭh sāf kamre*.

6.7.2. Translate into Hindi

1. I am, I (m.) was; 2. they (m.) were, they are; 3. you (int.) are, you (int. f.) were;

4. we are, we (f.) were; 5. you (pol.) are, you (fam.) are; 6. the girls were, the boys are; 7. the red book, in the very red book; 8. ten closed stores, in the ten closed stores; 9. the sweet banana, from the sweet banana; in the five very sweet bananas; 10. three daughters-in-law, from the daughters-in-law.

6.7.3. Translate into English

1. वह लड़का स्कूल में है *vah laRkā skūl mẽ hai*. 2. तब वह वहाँ नहीं थी । *tab vah vahā̃ nahī̃ thī*. 3. तुम इलाहबाद में नहीं थे । *tum ilāhābād mẽ nahī̃ the*. 4. सीता और रानी यहाँ बैठी थीं । *sītā aur rāni yahā̃ baiṭhī thī̃*. 5. मिठाइयाँ बहुत ताजी हैं । *mithāiyā̃ bahut tāzī hãĩ*. 6. क्या पुस्तकें बहुत पुरानी हैं ? *kyā pustakẽ bahut purānī hãĩ* ? 7. नदी में कौन है ? *nadī mẽ kaun hai* ? 8. मदन और भ्रमर बड़े अच्छे मित्र हैं । *madan aur amar baRe acche mitra hãĩ*. 9. कमरा साफ़ और बड़ा है । *kamrā sāf aur baRā hai*. 10. तब तू वहाँ क्यों था ? *tab tū vahā̃ kyõ thā* ? 11. आप लोग आगरे में कब थे ? *āp log āgre mẽ kab the* ? 12. क्या वह अंग्रेजी है ? *kyā vah ā̃grezī hai* ?

6.7.4. Translate into Hindi

1. The stores are open. 2. The books were very old. 3. She is at home. 4. You (int.) are in the large river. 5. There were six dogs in the house. 6. You (pol.) were sitting in the red chair. 7. Bombay is not in Uttar Pradesh. 8. The table is very large and old. 9. We (f.) were not at home then. 10. Is the building in Bombay ? 11. I (m.) am sitting on the white chair. 12. There are many tables in the large room.

CHAPTER 7

7.1. Presumptive and Subjunctive Forms of होना *honā* 'To Be'

Presumptive forms of the verb होना *honā* agree with their subjects in gender, person, and number. These forms all show 'the sound -ग- *-g-* followed by one of the vowels -आ *-ā*, -ए *-e*, or -ई *-ī*. The choice among these three vowels is determined by the number and gender of the subject.

		Masculine	Feminine
Singular	मैं *mãĩ*	हूँगा *hũga* (होऊँगा *hoũgā*)	हूँगी *hũgī* (or होऊँगी *hoũgī*)
	तू *tū*	होगा *hogā*	होगी *hogī*
	यह *yah*/वह *vah*	होगा *hogā*	होगी *hogī*
Plural	हम *ham*	होंगे *hõge*	होंगी *hõgī*
	तुम *tum*	होगे *hoge*	होगी *hogī*
	आप *āp*	होंगे *hõge*	होंगी *hõgī*
	ये *ye*/ वे *ve*	होंगे *hõge*	होंगी *hõgī*

Presumptive forms are used to indicate a state of affairs that is *presumed*, but not known through first-hand experience, to exist.

सीता और अशोक अब तक दिल्ली में होंगे *sītā aur aśok ab tak dillī mẽ hõge.*

'Sita and Ashok must[1] be in Delhi by now.' (i.e., they are presumed to be there)

यह लड़की आपकी बहन होगी *yah laRkī āpkī bahan hogī.*

'This girl must be your sister.'

When explicit mention is made of future time (as when a word such as कल *kal* 'tomorrow' is present), presumptive forms may take on future sense :

कल मेरा भाई दिल्ली में होगा *kal merā bhāī dillī mẽ hogā.*

'My brother will (presumably) be in Delhi tomorrow.' Note, however, that even in the above sentence the line between a presumptive sense and a future sense of the

1. The word *must* is commonly employed in English in a presumptive sense. The student should bear in mind, however, that there are two senses of English *must*, one indicating obligation or necessity and the other presumption. These two senses of *must* are illustrated by "You must go home now" and "You must have met my good friend John in London" respectively. It is only the latter of these two uses of English *must* that is expressed in Hindi by the use of presumptive forms of होना *honā*.

verb 'to be' in Hindi is not clear. Sentences such as this one are always felt to embody a presumptive judgement about some state of affairs, rather than a positive assertion that this state of affairs will come to be.

Subjunctive forms of होना *honā* are identical to the presumptive forms, but with the -गा /-गे /-गी *-gā- /ge /-gī* endings removed. These forms thus agree with their subjects in number and person, but not in gender :

Singular	मैं *mãĩ*	होऊँ *hoũ*
	तू *tū*	हो *ho*
	यह *yah*/ वह *vah*	हो *ho*
Plural	हम *ham*	हों *hŏ*
	तुम *tum*	होओ *hoo* (or हो *ho*)
	आप *āp*	हों *hõ*
	ये ye/वे *ve*	हों *hõ*

Subjunctive forms of होना *honā* are generally used to indicate situations that are speculative, hypothetical, contingent, or desired in some way. For example, the English sentence "I went you to be happy" is expressed in Hindi by a sequence of words that can be literally translated as 'I want that you happy might be'. The words "might be" of this translation are realized by the Hindi second person singular subjunctive form हो *ho*. As the translations into Hindi of sentences such as "I want you to be happy" involves the use of grammatical constructions not as yet introduced, a full discussion of this use of the Hindi subjunctive is deferred until later in this text (13.1.).

Subjunctive forms of होना *honā* are also commonly used in Hindi in injunctions of the type "let there be..." and in expressions used to convey greetings and congratulations of various kinds :

आपको जन्म दिन की शुभ कामनाएँ हों । *āpko janm-din kī śubh kāmnāẽ hõ.*
'Best wishes for your birthday' (literally, 'let there be best wishes [शुभ कामनाएँ *śubh kāmnāẽ*] of the birthday [जन्म दिन *janm-din*] to you [आपको *āpko*]').

नये वर्ष की बधाई हो *naya varṣ kī badhāī ho.*
'Have a happy New Year' (literally, 'let there be greetings [बधाई *badhāī*] of the New Year [नया वर्ष *nayā varṣ*]').

7.2. Demonstrative Pronouns

The third person pronouns यह *yah* 'this', वह *vah* 'that', ये *ye* 'these' and वे *ve* 'those', in addition to serving as personal pronouns (6.3), also function as demonstrative pronouns in Hindi. In this capacity they serve as quasi-adjectives, modifying the sense of following nouns :

	Singular	Plural
Proximate	यह पुस्तक *yah pustak* 'this book'	ये पुस्तकें *ye pustakẽ* 'these books'
Non-proximate	वह पुस्तक *vah pustak* 'that book'	वे पुस्तकें *ve pustakẽ* 'those books'

Both the spelling and pronunciation of Hindi demonstrative pronouns are variable. Although the common pronunciations of the singular forms are [ye] and [ve], the spelling pronunciations [yəhə] and [vəhə] are not uncommon. In some instances no distinction is made between the pronunciation of singular and corresponding plural demonstratives (v., 6.3, n.1.). In other circumstances, no distinction is made between the spelling of singular and corresponding plural demonstratives, with यह being used for both proximate forms and वह for both non-proximate ones. As the spellings यह and वह for the singular forms ये and वे for the plural are widely accepted by Indian Hindi language authorities, they have been employed in this volume.

7.3. Possessive Constructions

Possessive constructions are formed in Hindi by means of the declinable postposition का *kā*. Possessive constructions function adjectivally in Hindi, modifying nouns with which they agree in number, gender, and case.

The general format for possessive constructions in Hindi is X *kā* Y, with Y being the noun modified and the phrase X *kā* its possessive modifier. Thus the expression "the price of the cloth" is expressed in Hindi by the phrase the कपड़े का दाम *kapRe kā dām*, with the word दाम *dām* 'price' serving as a noun and *kapRe kā* 'of (the) cloth' as a kind of adjectival modifier in agreement with दाम *dām*.

The various forms of the postposition का *kā* can be arranged into the following paradigm :

		Masculine	Feminine
Direct	Singular	का *kā*	की *kī*
	Plural	के *ke*	की *kī*
Oblique	Singular	के *ke*	की *kī*
	Plural	के *ke*	की *kī*

Examples of the use of the various forms of का *kā* are given below :

Masculine	Feminine
राम का बेटा *rām kā beṭā* 'Rām's son' राम के बेटे *rām ke beṭe* 'Ram's sons'	राम की बेटी *rām kī beṭī* 'Ram's daughter' राम की बेटियां *rām kī beṭiyā̃* 'Ram's daughters'
राम के बेटे से *rām ke beṭe se* 'From Ram's son' राम के बेटों से *rām ke beṭõ se* 'From Ram's sons'	राम की बेटी से *rām kī beṭī se* 'From Ram's daughter' राम की बेटियों से *rām kī beṭiyõ se* 'From Ram's daughters'

Because का *kā* is a postposition, it causes a noun that precedes it to be placed in its oblique form :

लड़के का भाई *laRke kā bhāī* 'the boy's brother'
लड़कों का भाई *laRkõ kā bhāī* 'the boys' brother'
लड़कों के भाई *laRkõ ke bhāī* 'the boys' brothers'

If the noun before the postposition का *kā* is preceded by an adjective, that adjective is also placed in its oblique form :

अच्छे लड़के के भाई *acche laRke ke bhāī* 'the good boy's brothers'
अच्छे लड़के की बहन *acche laRke kī bahan* 'the good boy's sister'

In the above two examples the adjective अच्छा *acchā* appears in its oblique singular form अच्छे *acche* because of the presence of the following postposition. In the first of the two examples the possessive postposition takes the form के *ke* because it is in agreement with the following plural, direct, masculine noun भाई *bhaī*. In the second example it is in the form की *kī* because it is in agreement with the following feminine noun बहन *bahan*. Often in Hindi two or more possessive phrases are linked together by means of का *kā*. Thus in order to express the English notion "Ram's brother's friend's pencil" one uses the phrase राम के भाई के मित्र की पेंसिल *rām ke bhāī ke mitra kī pẽsil*. In this expression only the last postposition (की *kī*) is in its direct case form. The other possessive forms (के *ke*) are oblique because of the presence of subsequent postpositions.

N.B. The postposition का *kā* agrees with a noun following it in number, gender, and case. It causes the noun preceding it, as well as any adjective modifying this noun, to be in its oblique case form.

Possessive constructions in Hindi are used to connect nouns standing in many different relation to each other :

नदी का पानी *nadī kā pānī* 'the water of the river'
भारत का मौसम *bhārat kā mausam* 'India's weather'
संतरे का दाम *sãtare kā dām* 'the price of the orange'

Some common specifiable uses of the possessive in Hindi the following :

1. to indicate alienable possession (e.g. मदन की क़लम *madan kī ḳalam* 'Madan's pen');

2. to indicate that the item possessed is a component of the other item (e.g., कमरे की खिड़की *kamre kī khiRkī* 'the room's window');
3. to indicate a relationship, particularly that of kinship, between two or more parties (e.g. (पिताजी का मित्र *pitā jī kā mitra* 'Father's friend', सीता की बहन *sītā kī bahan* 'Sita's sister').

Hindi possessive phrases may be used either predicatively or attributively :

राम की पेन्सिल मेज पर है। *rām kī pensil mez par hai.*
'Ram's pencil is on the table.'

वह पेन्सिल राम की है। *vah pensil rām kī hai.*
'That pencil is Ram's.'

सीता की दो बहनें अब घर में नहीं हैं। *sītā kī do bahanẽ ab ghar mẽ nahī̃ hãĩ,*
'Sita's two sisters are not in the house now.

सीता की दो बड़ी बहनें हैं। *Sītā kī do baRī bahanẽ hãĩ.*
'Sita has two elder sisters'

In the first of the above two sentences the phrase राम की *rām kī* functions as an adjectival attribute of पेन्सिल *pensil.* In the second example the phrase राम की *rām kī* is used predicatively, making a statement about the noun subject पेन्सिल *pensil.*

7.4. Compound Postpositions

The vast majority of Hindi postpositions are *compound* (in contrast to the *simple* postpositions discussed in 5.3) and consist of two or more words. These postpositions are used for many different functions, ranging from the specification of case relations (e.g., 'for X', 'towards X', 'because of X') to the description of temporal and spatial relations of different kinds (e.g., after X', 'before X', 'to the left of X', 'under X', etc.). They also are employed for a wide variety of miscellaneous other relations, e.g., in spite of X, in exchange for X, in comparison to X, concerning X).

The first element of compound postpositions is almost always के *ke* or की *kī,* with the former much more common than the latter. A small sample of these postpositions includes X के लिए X *ke lie* 'for X, for the benefit of X', X के बारे में X *ke bāre mẽ* 'concerning X', X के सामने X *ke sāmne* 'in front of X', X के बाद X *ke bād* 'after X', X की तरह X *kī tarah* 'like X, in the manner of X', and X की तरफ़ X *kī taraf* 'towards X'. From time to time compound postpositions are found in which *se* appears in place of के *ke* or की *kī* as the first member. The construction X से पहले X *se pahle* 'before X (in time)', for instance, is sometimes used in a similar sense to X के पहले X *ke pahle*.

7.5. Honorific Usages

In Hindi honor or respect towards an individual is indicated by the use of plural forms to refer to that individual :

मदन के भाई अब पटना में हैं। *madan ke bhāī ab paṭnā mẽ hãĩ.*
'Madan's brother (honorific) is in Patna now'. (or 'Madan's brothers are in Patna now'.)

Pronouns referring to individuals being accorded respect are also plural :

वे शिवनाथ के भाई हैं। *ve śivnāth ke bhāī hãĩ.*

'He is Shiv Nath's brother' (or 'They are Shiv Nath's brothers'.)

The particle जी *jī* is commonly used in conjunction with proper names in order to accord respect :

शर्माजी स्कूल के अध्यापक हैं। *śarmājī skul ke adhyāpak hãĩ.*

'Mr. Sharma is the teacher of the school'.

The form जी *jī* is also frequently used following kinship terms, particularly in addressing or referring to members of the family :

कल पिताजी मथुरा में थे। *kal pitājī mathurā mẽ the.*

'Father was in Mathura yesterday'.

7.6. कुछ *kuch* AND कोई *koī*

The Hindi indefinite pronoun कुछ *kuch* is used to indicate a portion or quantity of some entity :

कुएँ में कुछ पानी है। *kuẽ mẽ kuch pānī hai.*

'There is some water in the well'.

गाँव में कुछ लोग थे *gā̃v mẽ kuch log the.*

'There were some people in the village'.

With countable entities कुछ *kuch* indicates an unspecified quantity:

कमरे में कुछ कुर्सियाँ थीं। *kamre mẽ kuch kursiyā̃ thī̃.*

'There were some chairs in the room'.

कुछ *kuch* also designates an unspecified portion of non-countable entities :

मेज पर कुछ चावल पड़ा था। *mez par kuch cāval paRā thā.*

'There was some rice lying on the table'.

The negative construction कुछ नहीं *kuch nahī̃* indicates the absence of a portion or quantity of some entity :

मुझे कुछ नहीं चाहिये। *mujhe kuch nahī̃ cāhiye.*

'I don't need anything'.

[कुछ नहीं *kuch nahī̃* 'nothing']

The indefinite pronoun कोई *koī* is used to signify some one person or thing:

सीता के घर में कोई खड़ा था। *sītā ke ghar mẽ koī khaRā thā.*

'Someone was standing in Sita's house'.

The combination of कोई *koī* with the negative marker नहीं *nahī̃* indicates the absence of even one person or thing:

दुकान में कोई आदमी नहीं था। *dukān mẽ koī ādmī nahī̃ thā.*

'There was no one in the store' (i.e., not even one person).

आज आगरे में कोई दुकान खुली नहीं है। *āj āgre mẽ koī dukān khulī nahī̃ hai.*

'No stores are open in Agra today' (i.e., not even one store).

7.7. Vocabulary

आम	*ām*	n.m. mango
कपड़ा	*kapRā*	n.m. cloth, material
कपड़े	*kapRe*	n.m. pl. clothes
क़लम	*kalam*	n.f. pen
किरण	*kiraṇ*	prop.f. Kiran (woman's name)
गांव	*gā̃v*	n.m. village
ताजमहल	*tāj mahal*	prop.m. Taj Mahal
दाम	*dām*	n.m. price, cost
पटना	*paṭnā*	prop. m.I/II. Patna (the capital city of Bihar)
पिता	*pitā*	n.m.II. father
पेन्सिल	*pensil*	n.f. pencil
बहन	*bahan*	n.f. sister (also बहिन *bahin*)
बाज़ार	*bāzār*	n.m. market, bazaar
बेटा	*beṭā*	n.m. son
बेटी	*beṭī*	n.f. daughter
भाई	*bhāī*	n.m. brother
मध्य प्रदेश	*madhya pradeś*	prop.m. Madhya Pradesh (a province in central India)
मौसम	*mausam*	n.m. season, weather
लाल क़िला	*lāl ḳilā*	prop.n. the Red Fort (a famous Mughal fort in Delhi)
संतरा	*sā̃tarā*	n.m. orange
संसार	*sā̃sār*	n.m. world
सेब	*seb*	n.m. apple
हाथ	*hāth*	n.m. hand
कुछ	*kuch*	pron. and adj. some, a few, an amount of; adv. somewhat, a little, a bit
कोई	*koī*	pron. and adj. some one (person or thing)
कच्चा	*kaccā*	adj. unripe, shoddy, built of mud or clay, raw
गरम	*garam*	adj. hot, warm
ठंडा	*ṭhā̃ḍā*	adj. cold
ठीक	*ṭhīk*	adj. correct, right
पका	*pakā*	adj. ripe
पक्का	*pakkā*	adj. substantial, built of brick (as opposed to clay), solid
प्रसिद्ध	*prasiddh*	adj. famous
सस्ता	*sastā*	adj. cheap, inexpensive
सारा	*sārā*	adj. all, entire
सुन्दर	*sundar*	adj. beautiful
हरा	*harā*	adj. green
आजकल	*ājkal*	adv. nowadays
कल	*kal*	adv. yesterday, to-morrow
लगभग	*lagbhag*	adv. approximately
का/के/की	*kā/ke/kī*	post. (v. 7.3)
को	*ko*	post. marking both direct and indirect objects (v. 8.3)
तक	*tak*	post. as far as, up to, until, by
इसलिये	*isliye*	conj. therefore
कितना	*kitnā*	inter. adj. how much?, how many?
कैसा	*kaisā*	inter. adj. what kind of?, what sort of?
ग्यारह	*gyarah*[2]	num. eleven
बारह	*bārah*[2]	num. twelve
तेरह	*terah*[2]	num. thirteen
चौदह	*caudah*[2]	num. fourteen
पंद्रह	*pā̃drah*[2]	num. fifteen

7.8. Exercises

7.8.1. *Translate into English.*

1. यह मेज़ *yah mez,* वे मेजें *ve mezẽ,* ये तेरह काली मेजें *ye terah kāli mezẽ*; 2. अमर की बेटी *amar kī beṭī,* अमर की सुन्दर बेटियाँ *amer kī sūndar beṭiyā̃,* अमर की सात सुन्दर बेटियों से *amar kī sāt sundar beṭiyõ se*; 3. कोई आदमी *koi ādmī,* कुछ आदमी *kuch ādmī,* कुछ अच्छे और

2. The final ह *h* in the written forms of many Hindi numbers is not ordinarily pronounced. These words are spoken as though ending with the vowel आ *-ā* (e.g., as if *gyārā, bārā, terā*, etc.).

पके संतरे *kuch acche aur pake sãtare*; 4. सस्ते सेब *saste seb*, सस्ते सेबों में *saste sebõ mẽ*, कुछ सस्ते सेबों में *kuch saste sebõ mẽ*; 5. दिल्ली का लाल क़िला *dillī kā lāl ḳilā*, दिल्ली के लाल क़िले में *dillī ke lāl ḳile mẽ*; 6. राम की बहन *rām kī bahan*; राम की बहन के कपड़े *rām kī bahan ke kapRe*, राम की बहन के कपड़ों का दाम *rām kī bahan ke kapRõ kā dām*; 7. दिल्ली की पुरानी इमारतें *dillī kī purānī imāratẽ*, संसार के छोटे गाँव *sãsār ke choṭe gãv*; 8. वह होगा *vah hogā*, तुम होगे *tum hoge*, आप होंगी *āp hõgī*, लड़की होगी *laRkī hogī*; 9. चौदह सेब *caudah seb*, चौदह लाल सेब *caudah lāl seb*, चौदह लाल और ताजे सेबों में *caudah lāl aur tāze sebõ mẽ*; 10. कैसा कपड़ा *kaisā kapRā*, कैसी दुकानें *kaisī dukānẽ*, कैसे कुएँ में *kaise kuẽ mẽ*.

7.8.2. *Translate into Hindi.*

1. this village, these thirteen villages, those very small villages; 2. that orange, those oranges, these good oranges; 3. some villages, some village (or other), those fifteen villages; 4. the entire world, in the entire world; 5. the sister, Ram's sister, Ram's six sisters, Ram's six very beautiful sisters; 6. this cloth, the price of the cloth, the price of all the clothes; 7. the weather in (i.e., of') Madhya Pradesh, the villages of Uttar Pradesh; 8. he must be, you (int. f.) must be, she must be; we (m) must be; 9. Father's (hon.) friends, Mother's (hon.) sweets, the teacher's (hon.) students; 10. Patna's well built houses, the village's shoddy buildings.

7.8.3. *Translate into English.*

1. राम का भाई अब पटना में होगा । *rām kā bhaī ab paṭnā mẽ hogā.* 2. पिताजी के विद्यार्थी इलाहाबाद में होंगे । *pitājī ke vidyārthī ilāhābād mẽ hõge.* 3. मध्य प्रदेश के आम बहुत अच्छे और सस्ते हैं । *madhya pradeś ke ām bahut acche aur saste hãī.* 4. सारे संसार में आगरे का ताज महल बहुत प्रसिद्ध है । *sāre sãsār mẽ āgre kā tāj mahal prasiddh hai.* 5. सीता की बेटियां बहुत सुन्दर हैं । *sītā kī beṭiyã bahut sundar hãī.* 6. हरे कपड़े का दाम दस रुपये है । *hare kapRe kā dām das rupaye hai.* 7. कल मौसम बहुत ठंडा था लेकिन कल गरम होगा *kal mausam bahut ṭhãḍā thā lekin kal garam hogā.* 8. यह स्कूल बहुत छोटा है, इसलिए यहां बहुत विद्यार्थी नहीं हैं । *yah skūl bahut choṭā hai, is liye yahã bahut vidyārthī nahī̃ hãī.* 9. आज पाकिस्तान में सब दुकानें बन्द हैं । *āj pākistān mẽ sab dukānẽ band hãī.* 10. कल किरण के घर में कितने लोग थे ? *kal kiraṇ ke ghar mẽ kitne log the?*

7.8.4. *Translate into Hindi.*

1. The girl must be in Mathura now. 2. Some pencils and pens were on the two tables. 3. Pakistan's weather was not very good yesterday. 4. What is the price of the mangos? 5. What kind of oranges are those? 6. There were approximately fifteen people in the rooms. 7. The beautiful clothes must be in the old market. 8. Some man (or other) is standing in the room. 9. There were red pencils and black pens on the chair. 10. Mr. Sharma [शर्माजी *śarmājī*] has two sons and one daughter· 11. Mr Gupta [गुप्ताजी *guptā jī*] has three very beautiful sisters.

CHAPTER 8

8.1. THE OVERALL STRUCTURE OF THE HINDI VERB

The verbal system of Hindi is not overly complex in nature. A high percentage of Hindi verb forms arise through the combination of basic components by regular principles. Exceptions to the major verbal paradigms of the language are few and easily learned. In comparison with the highly inflected verbal systems of Classical Greek, Latin, or Sanskrit, the verbal system of Hindi is relatively simple and clear.

The major grammatical categories that structure the verbal system of Hindi are those of aspect and tense. A large number of Hindi verbal forms exhibit markings for both of these categories. The term aspect is to be understood as indicating the nature of the action of a verb as to its beginning, duration, completion, or repetition, but without reference to its position in time. Hindi displays three grammatical aspects, the habitual, the progressive (oı ɔontinuous), and the perfective. Each of these aspects is expressed by the explicit marking of verbal stems. Verbal forms indicating one of these aspects are usually further specified for one of four tenses, i.e., the present, past, presumptive, and subjunctive. The combination of one of the three aspects with one of the four tenses leads to the production of one of twelve aspectual-tenses (e.g., present-perfective, past-habitual, presumptive-progressive etc.). In addition, the Hindi verbal system also permits simple-perfective forms, in which a specification is given for aspect (i.e., perfective), but not for tense. A number of "non-aspectual" verb forms are also found in Hindi. In these no specification is given as to whether a verbal action is habitual, progressive, or perfective. The most important of these non-aspectual forms are the future, the root subjunctive, various imperative (command) forms, and the infinitive. A summary of these members of the Hindi verbal system is given below[1]:

NON-ASPECTUAL

Future Root Subjunctive Imberatives Infinitive

1. This inventory of Hindi verbal forms is not complete. Other distinctions of the Hindi verbal system (e.g., active vrs. passive, simple vrs, compound, simple vrs. conjunct) and constructions (e.g., conjunctive, conditional, participles) are treated at appropriate places later in the text.

ASPECTUAL

	Habitual	*Progressive*	*Perfective*
Simple			Simple-Perfective
Present	Present-Habitual	Present-Progressive	Present-Perfective
Past	Past-Habitual	Past-Progressive	Past-Perfective
Presumptive	Presumptive-Habitual	Presumptive-Progressive	Presumptive-Perfective
Subjunctive	Subjunctive-Habitual	Subjunctive-Progressive	Subjunctive-Perfective

The various aspectual tenses of Hindi are formed by the addition of suffixes and verbal auxiliaries to verb stems. The stem may be obtained by removing the -ना *-nā* suffix with which the infinitive (21.1) ends. The desired aspect is indicated by the addition of explicit markers of some kind to the stem. The tense portion of an "aspectual-tense" is indicated by the presence of one of the basic forms of होना *honā* 'to be' (i.e., present, past, presumptive, subjunctive) enumerated in 6.4. and 7.1. The होना *honā* element follows the combination of stem and one or more suffixes.

8.2. Habitual Verb Forms

The habitual aspect in Hindi is primarily used to indicate that an action occurs on a regular or repeating basis. It can also be used to specify a general action not viewed as a series of discrete events. The various Hindi habitual aspectual-tenses are formed by the addition of the suffix -त- *-t-* to the verbal stem. This -त- *-t-* is itself immediately followed by one of the three vowels -आ *-ā*, -ए *-e*, or -ई *-ī*, with the choice among them determined by the number and gender of the subject of the verb. The stem +-त- *-t-*+ vowel combination is in turn followed by one of the simple forms of the verb होना *honā* 'to be'. In order to form the present-habitual, past-habitual, presumptive-habitual, and subjunctive-habitual aspectual-tenses, the present, past, presumptive, and subjunctive simples forms of होना *honā* are used respectively. A summary of the habitual verb forms of the verb जाना *jānā* 'to go' is given below:

Present-Habitual

Singular		Plural	
मैं जाता/जाती हूँ	*mā̃ī jātā/jātī hū̃*	हम जाते/जाती हैं	*ham jāte/jātī hā̃ī*
तू जाता/जाती है	*tū jātā/jātī hai*	तुम जाते/जाती हो	*tum jāte/jātī ho*
यह/वह जाता/जाती है	*yah/vah jātā/jātī hai*	आप जाते/जाती हैं	*āp jāte/jātī hā̃ī*
		ये/वे जाते/जाती हैं	*ye/ve jāte/jātī hā̃ī*

Past-Habitual

Singular		Plural	
मैं जाता था/जाती थी	*mãĩ jātā thā/jātī thī*	हम जाते थे/जाती थीं	*ham jāte the/jātī thĩ*
तू जाता था/जाती थी	*tū jātā thā/jātī thī*	तुम जाते थे/जाती थीं	*tum jāte the jātī thĩ*
यह/वह जाता था/जाती थी	*yah/vah jātā thā/jātī thī*	आप जाते थे/जाती थीं	*āp jāte the/jātī thĩ*
		ये/वे जाते थे/जाती थीं	*ye/ve jāte the/jātī thĩ*

Presumptive-Habitual

मैं जाता होऊँगा/जाती होऊँगी	*mãĩ jātā hõngā/jāti hoũgī*	हम जाते होंगे/जाती होंगी	*ham jāte hõge/jātī hõgī*
तू जाता होगा/जाती होगी	*tū jātā hogā/jāti hogī*	तुम जाते होगे/ जाती होगी	*tum jāte hoge/jātī hogī*
यह/वह जाता होगा/जाती होगी	*yah/vah jātā hogā/jātī hogī*	आप जाते होंगे/जाती होंगी	*āp jāte hõge/jātī hõgī*
		ये/वे जाते होंगे/जाती होंगी	*ye/ve jāte hõge/jātī hõgī*

Subjunctive-Habitual

मै जाता/जाती होऊं	*mãĩ jātā/jātī hoũ*	हम जाते/जाती हों	*ham jāte/jātī hõ*
तू/जाता/जाती हो	*tū/jātā/jātī ho*	तुम जाते/जाती हो	*tum jāte/jātī ho*
यह/वह जाता/जाती हो	*yah/vah jātā/jātī ho*	आप जाते/जाती हों	*āp jāte/jātī hõ*
		ये/वे जाते/जाती हों	*ye/ve jāte/jāti hõ*

Present-habitual forms are used to designate habitual actions or states of affairs reported from the vantage point of the present :

वह प्रति दिन दुकान जाता है। *vah prati din dukān jātā hai.*
'He goes to the store every day'.

उसकी माताजी घर में पंजाबी ही बोलती हैं *uskī mātājī ghar mẽ pãjābī hī boltī hãĩ.*
'His mother speaks only Panjabi at home'.

The present-habitual, particularly in conjunction with the adverb अभी *abhī* 'right away', is often also used to indicate that an action is to be carried out in the near future :

मैं अभी आती हूँ। *mãĩ abhī ātī hũ.*
'I'll come right away' (said by a female).

In the negative of present-habitual verbs, the present tense form of होना *honā* is usually deleted :

यहाँ हम चपातियां नहीं खाते। *yahā̃ ham capātiyā̃ nahĩ khāte.*
'We don't eat chapatis here'.

Past-habitual forms are used to indicate an habitual action or state of affairs viewed from the perspective of the past. Occasionally past-habitual verb forms simply indicate that an action or state of affairs took place in the distant past :

उसके मित्र बहुत पुराने गाने गाते थे। *uske mitra bahut purāne gāne gāte the.*
'His friends used to sing very old songs'

Presumptive-habitual forms are used to indicate that an action or state of affairs is both habitual and presumed, but not known through direct knowledge to take place:

उसका छोटा भाई वाराणसी जाता होगा। *uskā choṭā bhāī vārāṇasī jātā hogā.*

'His younger brother must (presumably) go to Benaras (regularly)'.

Subjunctive-habitual forms are used to indicate actions that are both habitual and hypothetical, contingent, imaginary, or speculative. Examples and discussion of subjunctive-habitual forms are deferred until 13.1.

8.3 Some Uses of को *ko*

The Hindi postposition को *ko* is used in a number of distinct senses and syntactic functions. Two of its most important uses are in the marking of direct and indirect objects :

एकता उस लड़की को नहीं मारती। *ektā us laRkī ko nahī̃ mārtī.*
'Ekta doesn't hit that girl' [एकता *ektā* prop. f. a woman's name'; मारना *mārnā* v.t. to hit, strike]

उस लड़के को तीन रुपये दीजिये। *us laRke ko tīn rupaye dījiye.*
'Please give three rupees to that boy'.

In the first of the above two examples को *ko* is used to mark the direct object (वह लड़की *vah laRkī*) of the verb मारती *mārtī* Because को *ko* is a postposition, it causes the direct object to be in its oblique form उस लड़की *us laRkī* (8.4. below). In the second example, को *ko* is used to mark the indirect object (वह आदमी *vah ādmī* 'that man') of the command form दीजिये *dījiye* 'please give'(12.1).

Note, however, that not all direct objects in Hindi are marked with को *ko*. In many instances the direct object appears in Hindi in its direct case form, devoid of any following postposition. For example, in the second of the above two sentences the direct object तीन रुपये *tīn rupaye* 'three rupees' is not followed by को *ko*. In general, को *ko* is used to mark the direct object in the following instances :

1. When the object is human and specific in reference. When the direct object is human but not specific in reference, however, को *ko* is normally not used. Thus किरण को बुलाओ *kiraṇ ko bulāo* 'call Kiran' and दर्जी को बुलाओ *darzī ko bulāo* 'call the tailor' [with a specific tailor intended], but दर्जी बुलाओ *darzī bulāo* 'call a tailor [i.e., any tailor].

2. When the direct object is inanimate, but made emphatic : इसी पुस्तक को देखिये *isī pustak ko dekhiye* 'please look at this very book (and no other), but यह पुस्तक देखिये *yah pustak dekhiye* 'please look at this book'.

8.4. Oblique Forms of Pronouns

Like nouns, many pronouns appear in special oblique forms when followed by postpositions. The oblique forms of Hindi personal pronouns, given in conjunction with the example postposition पर *par*, 'on, upon', are as follows :

Singular Direct		Singular Oblique		Plural Direct		Plural Oblique	
मैं	*mãĩ*	मुझ (पर)	*mujh (par)*	हम	*ham*	हम (पर)	*ham (par)*
तू	*tū*	तुझ (पर)	*tujh (par)*	तुम	*tum*	तुम (पर)	*tum (par)*
				आप	*āp*	आप (पर)	*āp (par)*
यह	*yah*	इस (पर)	*is (par)*	ये	*ye*	इन (पर)	*in (par)*
वह	*vah*	उस (पर)	*us (par)*	वे	*ve*	उन (पर)	*un (par)*

The third person pronouns यह *yah*, वह *vah*, ये *ye*, and वे *ve* also show the oblique forms इस *is*, उस *us*, इन *in*, and उन *un* respectively when serving as demonstrative pronouns :

इस मेज पर कुछ किताबें पड़ी थीं। *is mez par kuch kitabẽ paRī thī.*
'There were some books lying on this table'.

उन कमरों में बहुत लोग खड़े थे। *un kamarõ mẽ bahut log khaRe the.*
'Many people were standing in those rooms'.

Sequences of Hindi personal pronouns followed by the postposition को *ko* may optionally be replaced by single word contractions :

मुझ	*mujh*	+	को ko	becomes	मुझे	*mujhe*;
तुझ	*tujh*	+	को ko	becomes	तुझे	*tujhe*;
इस	*is*	+	को ko	becomes	इसे	*ise*;
उस	*us*	+	को ko	becomes	उसे	*use*;
हम	*ham*	+	को ko	becomes	हमें	*hamẽ*;
तुम	*tum*	+	को ko	becomes	तुम्हें	*tumhẽ*;
इन	*in*	+	को ko	becomes	इन्हें	*inhẽ*;
उन	*un*	+	को ko	becomes	उन्हें	*unhẽ*;

Thus the sentence

उसको[2] कुछ पैसे दीजिये। *usko kuch paise dījiye.*
'Please give him some money'.

is equivalent to

उसे कुछ पैसे दीजिये। *use kuch paise dījiye.*

There is no contraction of आप *āp* + को *ko*.

The pronoun कोई *koī* 'someone person or thing' (7.6) has the oblique form किसी *kisī*: e.g., कोई आदमी *koī ādmī* 'some one person or other', but किसी आदमी से *kisī ādmī se* from someone (or other)'. By contrast, the pronoun कुछ *kuch* does not have a special oblique form (e.g., कुछ लोग *kuch log* 'some people'; कुछ लोगों को *kuch logõ ko* 'to some people').

2. In careful written Hindi a sequence of a pronoun plus either a single-word postposition or the first word of a multi-word postposition is written together as a single word, e.g., मुझपर *mujhpar*, इसके लिये *iske liye*. This practice is followed in this volume.

8.5. **ही** ***hī*** **and भी** ***bhī***

The Hindi particles ही *hī* and भी *bhī* are each used in a number of distinct syntactic functions, and can affect significant semantic alterations in the sentences in which they are employed. Although these words are not technically postpositions—they do not cause the words that precede them to be placed in the oblique case—they nevertheless are reminiscent of postpositions by forming tightly fused phrases with the words immediately preceding them.

The particle भी *bhī* is used in Hindi to include the referent of the word that precedes it in some specified group. This sense is often translated into English by any of the words *too*, *also*, or *even*:

राम भी हिन्दी बोलता है। *rām bhī hindī boltā hai.*
'Ram also speaks Hindi'

वह उस लड़की को भी देखता है। *vah us laRkī ko bhī dekhtā hai.*
'He sees that girl also'.

In the first of these two examples भी *bhī* serves to include Ram in the set of people who speak Hindi. In the second example the word includes "that girl" in the set of people whom the subject sees.

By contrast, ही *hī* is employed to exclude some person or entity from some set or other. This sense of exclusion is often rendered into English by the word 'only', although other words may be more appropriate in some contexts:

अमर ही माताजी को रुपये देता है। *amar hī mātājī ko rupaye detā hai.*
'Only Amar gives Mother money'.

घर में वे हिन्दी ही बोलते हैं। *ghar mẽ ve hindī hī bolte hãĩ.*
'They speak only Hindi at home'.

The contrast between भी *bhī* and ही *hī* can be clearly seen in the following two sentences:

आगरे में दुकानदार भी साड़ियां बेचते हैं। *āgre mẽ dukāndār bhī sāRiyā̃ becte hãĩ.*
'In Agra even shopkeepers sell saris'.

आगरे में दुकानदार ही साड़ियां बेचते हैं *āgre mẽ dukāndār hī sāRiyā̃ becte hãĩ.*
'In Agra only shopkeepers sell saris'.

Further uses of Hindi भी *bhī* and ही *hī* are discussed in 21.3, 23.4, and 30.4.

8.6. VOCABULARY

उर्दू	*urdū*	prop.f. the Urdu language
कमीज़	*kamīz*	n.f. shirt
कुरता	*kurtā*	n.m. kurta (a kind of loose fitting upper garment)
खाना	*khānā*	n.m. food
गाना	*gānā*	n.m. song
गाहक	*gāhak*	n.m. customer
चपाती	*capātī*	n.f. chapati (a kind of simple, thin fried bread, made from whole wheat flour)
दाल	*dāl*	n.f. lentils
दुकानदार	*dukāndār*	n.m. shopkeeper
धोती	*dhotī*	n.f. dhoti (a man's garment wrapped around the waist and covering the bottom half of the body
पंजाबी	*pãjābī*	prop. f. the Panjabi language; adj. Panjabi
पैसा	*paisā*	n.m. 1/100 of a rupee; money
पैसे	*paise*	n.m. pl. money, wealth
फल	*phal*	n.m. fruit
फलवाला	*phalvālā*	n.m. fruitseller
लखनऊ	*lakhnaū*	prop. m. Lucknow (the capital of Uttar Pradesh)
वाराणसी	*vārāṇasī*	prop. f. Varanasi (= Benaras)
नया	*nayā*	adj. new (f. नई *naī*)
नीला	*nīlā*	adj. blue
पीला	*pīlā*	adj. yellow
महंगा	*mahãgā*	adj. expensive
शुद्ध	*śuddh*	adj. pure, refined, Sanskritized (as in the expression शुद्ध हिंदी *śuddh hĩdī* 'Sanskritized/pure Hindi')
आना	*ānā*	v.i. to come
ख़रीदना	*kharīdnā*	v.t. to buy
खाना	*khānā*	v.t. to eat
गाना	*gānā*	v.t. to sing
जाना	*jānā*	v.i. to go
जानना	*jānnā*	v.t. to know
देखना	*dekhnā*	v.t. to look, see
देना	*denā*	v.t. to give
पहनना	*pahannā*	v.t. to put on, wear
बेचना	*becnā*	v.t. to sell
बोलना	*bolnā*	v.t. to speak, say
लेना	*lenā*	v.t. to take
होना	*honā*	v.i. to be
दोपहर को	*dopahar ko*	adv. in the afternoon
प्रति दिन	*prati din*	adv. every day
रात को	*rāt ko*	adv. at night
शाम को	*śām ko*	adv. in the evening
सुबह	*subah*	adv. in the morning
हाँ	*hā̃*	adv. yes
कितने में	*kitne mẽ*	inter. for how much ?
भी	*bhī*	partl. indicating inclusion (v.8.5)
ही	*hī*	partl. indicating exclusion (v.8.5)
सोलह	*solah*[3]	num. sixteen
सत्तरह	*sattrah*[3]	num. seventeen
अठारह	*aṭhārah*[3]	num. eighteen
उन्नीस	*unnīs*	num. nineteen
बीस	*bīs*	num. twenty

8.7. EXERCISES

8.7.1. *Translate into English.*

1. मुझपर *mujhpar*, तुझसे *tujhse*, हमपर *hampar*; 2. इस साड़ी पर *is sāRī par*, उस गाहक को *us gāhak ko*, उन फलों पर *un phalõ par*; 3. लाल कुरते पर *lāl kurte par*, उन पीली साड़ियों पर *un pīlī sāRiyõ par*; 4. राम ही *rām hī*, सीता भी *sītā bhī*, उसकी बहिन ही *uskī bahin hī*, उसके पिता के मित्र भी *uske pitā ke mitra bhī*; 5. दुकानदारों को भी *dukāndārõ ko bhī*, आगरे के गानों में ही *āgre ke gānõ mẽ hī*; 6. उस गाने में *us gāne mẽ*, इन अच्छे गानों में *in acche gānõ mẽ*, उन पंजाबी गानों में *un pãjābī gānõ mẽ*;

---

3. V.7.7, n. 2.

7. फलवाले के फल *phalvāle ke phal*, उन फलवालों के फल *un phalvālõ ke phal*, वाराणसी के फलवालों के सब फल *vārāṇasī ke phalvālõ ke sab phal*; 8. मैं आता हूँ *mãĩ ātā hū̃*, वह बेचता है *vah bectā hai*, हम देते हैं *ham dete hãĩ*, तुम जानती हो *tum jāntī ho*; 9. वह जाती थी *vah jātī thī*, दुकानदार जाता था *dukāndār jātā thā*, वे बोलती थीं *ve boltī thī̃*; 10. तू जाता होगा *tū jātā hogā*, वह ख़रीदती होगी *vah ḳharīdtī hogī*, वह पहनता होगा *vah pahantā hogā*, हम खाती हैं *ham khātī hãĩ*.

8.7.2. *Translate into Hindi.*

1. In it, from them, to me, on you (fam.); 2. on this dhoti, in these fruit, from these customers; 3. from these girls, to those very good girls, on those expensive saris; 4. Madan too, only in Varanasi, only three songs, those blue kurtas also; 5. I (m.) buy, you (int.) come, she eats, they (m.) speak; 6. she used to take, he used to wear, they used to sell, I (f.) used to give; 7. he must (psmt.) know, they (f.) must (psmt.) eat, we (m.) must (psmt.) be, you (pol., f.) must (psmt.) sell; 8. how many saris?, how many blue kurtas?, on how many dhotis?; 9. eighteen customers and nineteen shirts, in the fifteen fresh and inexpensive chapatis; 10. very clean shirts, on those clean shirts, on those twenty very beautiful shirts.

8.7.3. *Translate into English.*

1. वाराणसी में लोग हिन्दी बोलते हैं। *vārāṇasī mẽ log hindī bolte hãĩ*. 2. वह दुकानदार बहुत सुन्दर साड़ियां बेचता है। *vah dukāndār bahut sundar sāRiyā̃ bectā hai*. 3. भारत में बहुत आदमी धोतियां पहनते हैं। *bhārat mẽ bahut ādmī dhotiyā̃ pahante hãĩ*. 4. घर में वह अंग्रेजी ही बोलता था। *ghar mẽ vah ãgrezī hī boltā thā*. 5. वह फलवाला कितने में फल बेचता है? *vah phalvālā kitne mẽ phal bectā hai*. 6. पिताजी पुराने गाने जानते होंगे। *pitājī purāne gāne jānte hõge*. 7. उसकी बेटी नये कुरते पहनती होगी। *uskī beṭī naye kurte pahantī hogī*. 8. क्या आप उस दाल का दाम जानते हैं? *kyā āp us dāl kā dām jānte hãĩ*. 9. शाम को वह कितनी चपातियां खाता है? *śām ko vah kitnī capātiyā̃ khātā hai*? 10. वे प्रति दिन भारतीय गाने गाते थे। *ve prati din bhāratīya gāne gāte the*.

8.7.4. *Translate into Hindi.*

1. Rani used to wear very beautiful saris. 2. He eats some lentils in the afternoon. 3. This girl used to come here from Pakistan. 4. These people must be very good friends. 5. Why don't they know Panjabi? 6. You (pol.) go (hab.) to school in the afternoon. 7. How many saris does she wear every day? 8. Mother gives us some lentils in the evening. 9. Many people speak Urdu in Lucknow. 10. The teacher gives the students books and pens. 11. They must (psmt.) buy food from that shop. 12. Why don't you speak Hindi at home?

CHAPTER 9

9.1. Progressive Verb Forms

The progressive (or continuous) aspect in Hindi is primarily employed to indicate actions or states of affairs that are thought of as drawn out or extended through time. The use of this aspect generally expresses the elongation or continuation of single actions or state of affairs rather than a series of discrete events of some kind.

Progressive verb forms in Hindi are formed by the addition of two verbal auxiliaries immediately after a verbal stem. The first auxiliary consists of the root रह– *rah*–followed by one of the three vowels –आ –*ā*, –ए –*e*, or –ई –*ī*. The choice among these three vowels is determined by the number and gender of the subject of the verb (i.e., –आ –*ā* with masculine singular subjects, -ए -*e* with masculine plural, and -ई -*ī* with feminine singular and feminine plural). The second auxiliary consists of a member of one of the sets of simple verb forms of होना *honā* 'to be' (v. 6.4, 7.1), The selection of a present, past, presumptive and subjunctive form of होना *honā* leads to the formation of present-progressive, past-progressive, presumptive-progressive, and subjuctive-progressive verb forms respectfully. A synopsis of the various Hindi progressive aspectual-tenses, using forms of the verb जाना *jānā* 'to go as examples, is given below.

Present-Progressive

		Masculine	Feminine
Singular	मैं *mãĩ*	जा रहा हूं *jā rahā hũ*	जा रही हूँ *jā rahī hũ*
	तू/यह/वह *tū/yah/vah*	जा रहा है *jā rahā hai*	जा रही है *jā rahī hai*
Plural	हम/आप/ये/वे *ham/āp/ye/ve*	जा रहे हैं *jā rahe hãĩ*	जा रही हैं *jā rahī hãĩ*
	तुम *tum*	जा रहे हो *jā rahe ho*	जा रही हो *jā rahī ho*

Past-Progressive

		Masculine	Feminine
Singular	मैं/तू/यह/वह *mãĩ/tu/yah/vah*	जा रहा था *jā rahā thā*	जा रही थी *jā rahī thī*
Plural	हम/तुम/आप/ये/वे *ham/tum/āp/ye/ve*	जा रहे थे *jā rahe the*	जा रही थीं *jā rahī thī*

Presumptive-Progressive

		Masculine	Feminine
Singular	मैं *mãĩ* तू/यह/वह *tū/yah/vah*	जा रहा होऊँगा *jā rahā hoũgā* जा रहा होगा *jā rahā hogā*	जा रही होऊँगी *jā rahī hoũgī* जा रही होगी *jā rahī hogī*
Plural	हम/आप/ये/वे *hām/ap/ye/ve* तुम *tum*	जा रहे होंगे *jā rahe hõge* जा रहे होंगे *jā rahe hoge*	जा रही होंगी *jā rahī hõgī* जा रही होगी *jā rahī hogī*

Subjunctive-Progressive

		Masculine	Feminine
Singular	मैं *mãĩ* तू/यह/वह *tū/yah/vah*	जा रहा होऊँ *jā rahā hoũ* जा रहा हो *jā rahā ho*	जा रही होऊं *jā rahī hoũ* जा रही हो *jā rahī ho*
Plural	हम/आप/ये/वे *ham/āp/ye/ve* तुम *tum*	जा रहे हों *jā rahe hõ* जा रहे हो *jā rahe ho*	जा रही हों *jā rahī hõ* जा रही हो *jā rahī ho*

Present-progressive verb forms are used to represent actions or states of affairs that are conceptualized as being extended in time and taking place in the present:

वाजपेयी जी उस कमरे में समाचारपत्र पढ़ रहे हैं। *vājpeyi jī us kamre mẽ samācārpatra paRh rahe hãĩ.*
'Mr. Vajpeyi is reading a newspaper in that room'.

लड़के गाने गा रहे हैं। *laRke gāne gā rahe hãĩ.*
'The boys are singing songs'.

Present-progressive forms also are frequently employed in Hindi with future sense:[1]

कल मैं दिल्ली जा रहा हूँ। *kal mãĩ dillī jā rahā hū̃.*
'I am going to Delhi tomorrow'.

Notice that the English translation of the above example also uses a progressive verb form (*am going*) to express the future. The use of progressive verb forms with future sense is analagous in Hindi and English.

The verb होना *honā* 'to be', when in the progressive, is used in the sense of the English verb 'to happen':

अब उसके घर में क्या हो रहा है ? *ab uske ghar mẽ kyā ho rahā hai?*
'What is happening in his house now?'

Past-progressive verb forms are used to represent actions or states of affairs that are conceptualized as being extended or drawn out in time and occurring in the past:

कल शाम को आपका भाई क्या कर रहा था ? *kal śām ko āpkā bhāī kyā kar rahā thā?*
'What was your brother doing yesterday evening?

1. This is not, however, the only way to express future time in Hindi. Other means for indicating the future in Hindi are described in 8.2, 10.1, 12.2, and 13.2.

पुराने बाज़ार में बड़ा तमाशा हो रहा था। *purāne bāzār mẽ baRā tamāśā ho rahā thā.*

'There was a big event/spectacle going on in the old market'

[तमाशा *tamāśā* n. m. spectacle, big event]

Presumptive-progressive verb forms are used to indicate that an action or state of affairs is extended in time and presumed, but not directly known, to take place:

उसकी छोटी बहन नीला आगरे से आ रही होगी। *uski choṭī bahan nīlā āgre se ā rahī hogī.*

'His younger sister Nila must be coming from Agra'. [नीला *Nīlā prop* f.]

Subjunctive-progressive verb forms are discussed in 7.1 and 13.1.

9.2. Objects of Verbs of Motion

Hindi differs from English in an important way in its treatment of the objects of verbs of motion. Normally such objects are marked in English with the preposition *to* (e.g., "he is going *to* the store/ *to* Delhi, *to* John's house, etc.'). In Hindi, when the object of a verb of motion refers to a place, it is ordinarily not marked by any word analogous to an English preposition. Thus where English would say "I am going to Delhi", Hindi says मैं दिल्ली जा रहा हूँ। *mãĩ dillī jā rahā hũ.* If the object of the verb of motion is a masculine Class I noun, it often is found in its oblique singular form, even though it is not followed by a postposition. Thus corresponding to the English sentence "I am going to Agra" one encounters both:

मैं आगरे जा रहा हूँ। *mãĩ āgre jā rahā hũ.*

and

मैं आगरा जा रहा हूँ। *mãĩ āgrā jā rahā hũ.*

If the object of the verb of motion is not a place, but rather a person, then the postposition के पास *ke pās* is employed :

वह दोपहर को स्कूल से राम के पास जाता है। *vah dopahar ko skūl se rām ke pās jātā hai.*

'He goes from school to Ram (i.e., Ram's presence) in the afternoon'.

The postposition तक *tak* is employed with objects of verbs of motion in the sense of "as far as, up to." This postposition clearly marks a limit or terminus of the act of motion.

मैं नये बाजार तक जा रहा हूँ। *mãĩ naye bāzār tak jā rahā hũ.*

'I am going as far as the new market'.

9.3. Oblique Forms of क्या *kyā* and कौन *kaun*

The interrogative pronous क्या *kyā* 'what' and कौन *kaun* 'who', when followed by postpositions, occur in special oblique forms. These pronouns, distinct in their direct case, share identical oblique case forms. The oblique singular form of both क्या *kyā* and कौन *kaun* is किस *kis* and the oblique plural form is किन *kin*:

वह आदमी किसपर बैठा है? *vah ādmī kispar baiṭhā hai?*

'On what is that man sitting?'

पिताजी पैसे किसको दे रहे हैं? *pitājī paise kisko de rahe hãĩ?*

'To whom is Father giving the money?'

वे लोग किन भाषाओं में बोल रहे हैं? *ve log kin bhāṣāõ mẽ bol rahe hãĩ?*

'In what languages are those people speaking?'

हम किन लोगों को देख रहे हैं ? *ham kin logõ ko dekh rahe hãĩ?*
'At whom are we looking?'

The oblique singular form किस *kis* followed immediately by को *ko* may optionally be replaced by the contraction किसे *kise*. Likewise, the oblique form किन *kin* immediately followed by को *ko* may be replaced by किन्हें *kinhẽ*:

वह किसको/किसे पैसे देता है ? *vah kisko/kise paise detā hai?*
'To whom (s.) does he give the money?'

वह किनको/किन्हें पैसे देता है ? *vah kin ko/kinhẽ paise detā hai?*
'To whom (pl.) does he give the money?'

9.4. ही *hī* WITH DEMONSTRATIVE PRONOUNS

The particle ही *hī* [8.5] may be used with emphatic force immediately following demonstrative pronouns. This particle combines with various demonstrative pronouns to form a series of special contractions:

यह *yah*	+ ही *hī*	becomes	यही	*yahī*
वह *vah*	+ ही *hī*	becomes	वही	*vahī*
ये *ye*	+ ही *hī*	becomes	यही	*yahī*
वे *ve*	+ ही *hī*	becomes	वही	*vahī*
इस *is*	+ ही *hī*	becomes	इसी	*isī*
उस *us*	+ ही *hī*	becomes	उसी	*usī*
इन *in*	+ ही *hī*	becomes	इन्हीं	*inhī̃*
उन *un*	+ ही *hī*	becomes	उन्हीं	*unhī̃*

यही आदमी मेरा बहुत अच्छा मित्र है। *yahī ādmī merā bahut acchā mitra hai.*
'This very man is my very good friend'.

लड़कियां इसी कमरे में बैठी थीं। *laRkiyā̃ isī kamre mẽ baiṭhī thī̃.*
'The girls were sitting in this very room'.

किशोर उन्हीं लड़कियों को देख रहा था। *kiśor unhī̃ laRkiyõ ko dekh rahā thā.*
'Kishor was looking at those very girls' [किशोर *kiśor* prop.m.].

9.5. THE PRONOUN कई *kaī*

The indefinite pronoun कई *kaī* 'several, a number of, some' is used to refer to an unspecified number of discrete entities: e.g., कई लोग *kaī log* 'several people; कई कुत्ते *kaī kutte* 'several dogs'. In contrast to कुछ *kuch* 'some' (7.6.), कई *kaī* is limited to countable entities; and unlike many other pronominal form of Hindi, कई *kaī* has no special oblique case forms. Thus the language shows the phrases कई पुस्तकों में *kaī pustakõ mẽ* 'in several books' and कई लोगों को *kaī logõ ko* 'to several people' alongside the direct case phrase कई लोग *kaī log* 'several people'.

N.B. The three indefinite pronouns कोई *koī*, कुछ *kuch*, and कई *kaī* are easily confusable and the student should take care to distinguish them from one another. कोई *koī* is grammatically singular and always refers to some one unspecified person or thing. कुछ *kuch* may be grammatically either singular or plural, with the former case used to refer to an unspecified quantity of some non-countable entity (i.e., rice, water, etc.) and the latter to an undifferentiated group of countable entities (e.g., some men, some apples, etc.). कई is always grammatically plural and specifies a number of discrete entities that are not viewed as a collective group (e.g., several women, a number of children, etc.).

9.6. Expressions Using कुछ kuch and कोई koī

There are in Hindi several expressions containing कुछ *kuch* and कोई *koī* (7.6.). Included among these are the following :

सब कोई	*sab koī*	'everybody'
कोई नहीं	*koī nahī̃*	'no one'
और कोई	*aur koī*	'someone else, some other person or thing'
कोई और	*koī aur*	
सब कुछ	*sab kuch*	'everything'
और कुछ	*aur kuch*	'some more, some additional'
कुछ और	*kuch aur*	
बहुत कुछ	*bahut kuch*	'a lot of, much, a large amount of'
कुछ नहीं	*kuch nahī̃*	'none, no'

9.7. The Indefinite Adverb कभी kabhī

The adverb कभी *kabhī* 'at some time' is used in Hindi to indicate an indefinite or unspecified time.

मैं कभी दिल्ली जाऊँगा। *mãī kabhī dillī jāū̃gā.*[1]

'I will go to Delhi sometime'.

कभी *kabhī* also is used in a number of important Hindi expressions, namely कभी-कभी *kabhī-kabhī* 'occasionally, sometimes, from time to time' and कभी नहीं *kabhī nahī̃* 'never'.

मैं कभी-कभी उसके घर जाता हूं। *mãī kabhī-kabhī uske ghar jātā hū̃.*

'I go to his house from time to time'.

हम घर में पंजाबी कभी नहीं बोलते। *ham ghar mẽ pãjābī kabhī nahī̃ bolte.*

'We never speak Panjabi at home'.

The two instances of the word कभी *kabhī* in the compound कभी-कभी *kabhī-kabhī* are often broken up and distributed in different phrases or clauses.

घर में वह कभी हिन्दी बोलता है, कभी उर्दू। *ghar mẽ vah kabhī hindī boltā hai, kabhī urdū.*

'Sometimes he speaks Hindi at home, sometimes Urdu'.

1. V. 13.2, for the formation of the future tense.

9.8. VOCABULARY

कहानी	*kahānī*	n.f. story, tale	पीना	*pīnā*	v.t. to drink, smoke
कौआ	*kauā*	n.m. crow	X को Y मिलना	X *ko* Y *milnā*	v.i. for X to get/find Y
गाय	*gāy*	n.f. cow	रहना	*rahnā*	v.i. to live, dwell, remain
चावल	*cāval*	n.m. [often pl.] rice, boiled rice	रोना	*ronā*	v.i. to cry, weep
चीनी	*cīnī*	n.f. sugar	लाना	*lānā*	v.t. to bring
दूध	*dūdh*	n.m. milk	लिखना	*likhnā*	v.t. to write
पत्र	*patra*	n.m. letter	सोचना	*socnā*	v.t. to think
बग़ीचा	*bagīcā*	n.m. garden	अंदर	*ãdar*	adv. inside
भाषा	*bhāṣā*	n.f. language	आगे	*āge*	adv. straight ahead, forward
भोपाल	*bhopāl*	prop.m. Bhopal (the capital of Madhya Pradesh)	ऊपर	*ūpar*	adv. above
मांस	*mā̃s*	n.m. meat	नीचे	*nīce*	adv. below
मोर	*mor*	n.m. peacock	पीछे	*pīche*	adv. behind
रस	*ras*	n.m. juice	साथ-साथ	*sāth-sāth*	adv. all together
राजधानी	*rājdhānī*	n.f. capital city	X के ऊपर	X *ke ūpar*	post. on top of X, above X
शहर	*śahar*	n.m. city	X के नीचे	X *ke nīce*	post. below/under X
सब्ज़ी	*sabzī*	n.f. vegetable	X के बारे में	X *ke bāre mẽ*	post. concerning/ about X
समाचारपत्र	*samācār-patra*	n.m. newspaper	X के लिए	X *ke lie*	post. for X, for the benefit of X
ऊँचा	*ū̃cā*	adj. high	X के साथ	X *ke sāth*	post. together with X, in the presence of X
और	*aur*	adj. additional	किधर से	*kidhar se*	inter. from which direction?
और भी	*aur bhī*	adj. additional, even more	कहाँ से	*kahā̃ se*	inter. from where? whence?
गुलाबी	*gulābī*	adj. rose colored, pink	इक्कीस	*ikkīs*	num. twenty-one
नीचा	*nīcā*	adj. low	बाईस	*bāīs*	num. twenty-two
लंबा	*lãbā*	adj. long, tall	तेईस	*teīs*	num. twenty-three
करना	*karnā*	v.t. to do	चौबीस	*caubīs*	num. twenty-four
कहना	*kahnā*	v.t. to say	पच्चीस	*paccīs*	num. twenty-five
खेलना	*khelnā*	v.i/t. to play			
पढ़ना	*paRhnā*	v.t. to study, read			
पहुँचना	*pahũcnā*	v.i. to reach, arrive			

9.9. EXERCISES

9.9.1. *Translate into English.*

1. कुछ और मोर *kuch aur mor*, दो और पत्र *do aur patra*, और कोई कहानी *aur koī kahānī*; 2. किसी शहर में *kisī śahar mẽ*, कई गायों से *kaī gāyõ se*, कुछ समाचारपत्रों में *kuch samācārpatrõ mẽ*; 3. उन मेज़ों के ऊपर *un mezõ ke ūpar*, लंबे पत्र के नीचे *lãbe patra ke nīce*, इन पच्चीस नीची कुर्सियों के नीचे *in paccīs nīcī kursiyõ ke nīce*; 4. इस कहानी के बारे में *is kahānī ke bāre mẽ*, मध्य प्रदेश की राजधानी भोपाल के बारे में *madhya pradeś kī rājdhānī bhopāl ke bāre mẽ*; 5. सीता की बेटी के लिये *sītā kī beṭī ke liye*, उनके भाइयों के लिये *unke bhāiyõ ke liye*; 6. उन चौबीस आदमियों के

साथ *un caubīs ādmiyõ ke sāth,* वाराणसी के फलवालों के साथ *vārāṇasī ke phalvālõ ke sāth*; 7. वही बग़ीचा *vahī bagicā,* उसी पुस्तक में *usī pustak mẽ,* यही सब्जियां *yahī sabziyā̃*; 8. मैं ला रहा हूं *mãī lā rahā hū̃,* यह बोल रहा है *yah bol rahā hai,* हम लिख रही हैं *ham likh rahī hãĩ*; 9. तू सोच रही थी *tū soc rahī thī,* आप रो रहे थे *āp ro rahe the,* वे पी रहे थे *ve pī rahe the*; 10. वह खा रहा होगा *vah khā rahā hogā,* तुम सोच रही होगी *tum soc rahī hogī,* वे पढ़ रहे होंगे *ve paRh rahe hõge.*

9.9.2. *Translate into Hindi.*

1. Some additional pencils, several boys, even more peacocks; 2. from some city (or other), together with someone, on some pink flower; 3. on top of the rice, on top of the newspaper; 4. under the table, under these twenty-one long tables; 5. concerning Bhopal, concerning Bhopal's beautiful gardens; 6. for the red birds, for these very good teachers; 7. together with the student, together with her friends, together with the school's students; 8. she is writing, you (in.m.) are reading, they are writing; 9. I (f.) was doing, they (m) were reading, you (fam.m.) were bringing; 10. we must be bringing, they (f.) must be drinking, you (pol.m.) must be buying.

9.9.3. *Translate into English.*

1. उसका मित्र एक नई कहानी लिख रहा है। *uskā mitra ek naī kahānī likh rahā hai.* 2. वे लोग किधर से आ रहे थे? *ve log kidhar se ā rahe the?* 3. वे लड़के साथ-साथ पुस्तकें पढ़ रहे थे। *ve laRke sāth-sāth pustakẽ paRh rahe the.* 4. रानी की बहन उस दुकान से क्या ला रही है? *rānī kī bahan us dukān se kyā lā rahī hai?* 5. उन बच्चों को प्रतिदिन ताज़ा दूध मिलता है। *un baccõ ko prati din tāzā dūdh miltā hai.* 6. वह उस कमरे में पढ़ रहा होगा। *vah us kamre mẽ paRh rahā hogā.* 7. माताजी सीता के लिये दाल और चपातियां ला रही हैं। *mātā jī sītā ke liye dāl aur capātiyā̃ lā rahī hãĩ.* 8. स्कूल के विद्यार्थी उस शहर के बग़ीचे में पढ़ रहे थे। *skūl ke vidyārthī us śahar ke bagīce mẽ paRh rahe the.* 9. उन बाईस लोगों के साथ एक आदमी और भी है। *un bāīs logõ ke sāth ek ādmī aur bhī hai.* 10. तब आप क्या कर रहे थे? *tab āp kyā kar rahe the?* 11. उनके मित्र उस दुकान से मांस ला रहे होंगे। *unke mitra us dukān se mā̃s lā rahe hõge.*

9.9.4. *Translate into Hindi.*

1. From where was she coming? 2. I (f.) was reading some old stories in this book. 3. The small boy is not crying now. 4. They (m.) were eating vegetables and lentils. 5. They were singing those songs all together. 6. He gets (hab.) good food everyday in the evening. 7. The crows were drinking the well's water. 8. He drinks orange juice everyday in the morning. 9. You (m. pol.) are speaking very pure Hindi. 10. Bhopal is not in Uttar Pradesh; it is the capital of Madhya Pradesh. 11. What language were those girls speaking? 12. He was thinking about that book.

CHAPTER 10

10.1. Perfective Verb Forms

The perfective aspect is employed in Hindi in order to characterize a verbal activity or state of affairs as having been completed. There are five sets of perfective forms in Hindi, the simple-perfective, the present-perfective, the past-perfective, the presumptive-perfective, and the subjunctive-perfective. Each of these five sets of aspectual-tense contains a form known as the perfective participle, derived by the modification of a verbal stem through the addition of one of a number of vowel suffixes. The perfective participle is made to agree in gender and number with the subject of the clause in which it appears. In forms of the simple-perfective, the participle appears without any verbal auxiliary. In forms of the present, past, presumptive, and subjunctive perfective, the present, past, presumptive, and subjunctive forms of होना *honā* 'to be' respectively are employed as auxiliaries.

The perfective participle is formed by the addition of one of the four "adjectival" endings –आ *-ā*, –ए *-e*, –ई *-ī*, and –ईं *-ī̃* directly after the verbal stem. The choice of one of those vowels is determined by the number and gender of the subject of the clause [i.e., -आ *-ā* with m.s. subjects, -ए *-e* with m.pl., -ई *-ī* with f.s., and -ईं *-ī̃* with f.pl.] . Thus from the verb गिरना *girnā* 'to fall' can be formed गिरा *girā* (m.s.), गिरे *gire* (m.pl.) गिरी *girī* (f.s.), and गिरीं *girī̃* (f.pl.) as alternate versions of the perfective participle.

A full paradigm of the various perfective forms of गिरना *girnā* 'to fall' is given below :

Simple-Perfective

	Masculine	Feminine
Singular	गिरा *girā*	गिरी *girī*
Plural	गिरे *gire*	गिरीं *girī̃*

Present-Perfective

		Masculine	Feminine
Singular	मैं *mãī*	गिरा हूँ *girā hū̃*	गिरी हूँ *girī hū̃*
	तू *tū*/ यह *yah*/ वह *vah*	गिरा है *girā hai*	गिरी है *girī hai*
Plural	हम *ham*/आप *āp*/ ये *ye*/ वे *ve*	गिरे हैं *gire hãī*	गिरी हैं *girī hãī*
	तुम *tum*	गिरे हो *gire ho*	गिरी हो *girī ho*

Past-Perfective

	Masculine		Feminine	
Singular	गिरा था	*girā thā*	गिरी थी	*girī thī*
Plural	गिरे थे	*gire the*	गिरी थीं	*girī thī̃*

Presumptive-Perfective

		Masculine		Feminine	
Singular	मैं *mãĩ*	गिरा होऊँगा	*girā hoū̃gā*	गिरी होऊंगी	*girī hoū̃gī*
	तू *tū*/यह *yah*/वह *vah*	गिरा होगा	*girā hogā*	गिरी होगी	*girī hogī*
Plural	हम *ham*/आप *āp*/ये *ye*/वे *ve*	गिरे होंगे	*gire hõge*	गिरी होंगी	*girī hõgī*
	तुम *tum*	गिरे होगे	*gire hoge*	गिरी होगी	*girī hogī*

Subjunctive-Perfective

		Masculine		Feminine	
Singular	मैं *mãĩ*	गिरा होऊँ	*girā hoū̃*	गिरी होऊँ	*girī hoū̃*
	तू *tū*/यह *yah*/वह *vah*	गिरा हो	*girā ho*	गिरी हो	*girī ho*
Plural	हम *ham*/आप *āp*/ये *ye*/वे *ve*	गिरे हों	*gire hõ*	गिरी हों	*girī hõ*
	तुम *tum*	गिरे हो	*gire ho*	गिरी हो	*girī ho*

There are several peculiarities with regard to the formation and use of the perfective aspect in Hindi. The treatment of transitive verbs in this aspect (11.1) is distinct from that of intransitives in a number of regards. There are a few verbs whose perfective participles are irregular and need to be memorized by students. And, lastly, there are a number of minor spelling adjustments that are employed in the written versions of some perfective verb forms.

The spelling irregularities observed in the formation of Hindi perfectives concern verbs whose stem end in vowels. In cases where the stem ends in any of the vowels -आ-*ā*, -ए-*e*, or -ओ-*o*, the glide -य- -*y*- is inserted before the masculine singular ending -आ-*ā*. This -य- -*y*- is also optionally employed before the masculine plural termination -ए- -*e*. The various forms of the perfective participles of आना *ānā* 'to come', खेना *khenā* 'to row' and सोना *sonā* 'to sleep, to go to sleep' are thus as follows :

आना *ānā*: आया *āyā*/आए *āe* or आये *āye*/आई *āī*/आईं *āī̃*;

खेना *khenā*: खेया *kheyā*/ खेये *kheye*[1]/ खेई *kheī*/ खेईं *kheī̃*;

1. The form *खेए *khee* is not however, permitted. This is most likely due to an avoidance of the sequence -ए -*e* + ए *e*.

सोना *sonā*: सोया *soyā*/ सोए *soe*/ or सोये *soye*/सोई *soī*/सोईं *soī̃*.

Stems ending in -ई *-ī* form their perfective participles on the following model :

पीना *pīnā* 'to drink, to smoke' : पिया *piyā*/पिए *pie* or पिये *piye*/पी *pī*/पीं *pī̃*

सीना sīnā 'to sew': सिया *siyā*/सिए *sie* or सिये *siye*/सी *sī*/सीं *sī̃*.

Stems ending in -ऊ *-ū* shorten this vowel to उ- *u-* before the vowel terminations of the perfective participle :

चूना *cūnā* 'to leak, ooze': चुआ *cuā*/चुए *cue*/चुई *cuī*/चुईं *cuī̃*.

A small number of Hindi verbs have irregular perfective participles. Among intransitive verbs the most important irregular forms are as follows :

जाना *jānā* 'to go' : गया *gayā*/गए *gae* or गये *gaye*/गई *gaī*/गईं *gaī̃*;
होना *honā* 'to be, come to be, happen' : हुआ *huā*/हुए *hue*/हुई *huī*/हुईं *huī̃*.

One last peculiarity concerning the Hindi perfective is to be observed in the feminine plural forms of the present, past, presumptive, and subjunctive perfectives. It was stated earlier that the feminine plural form of the perfective participle shows the termination -ईं *-ī̃*. Note, however, that when followed by a form of होना *honā* in which plurality is overtly indicated by nasalization (i.e., as in हैं *haĩ*, थीं *thī̃*, होंगी *hõgī*, or हों *hõ*), the termination loses its nasality and becomes ई *ī*. This tendency to mark 'feminine plurality' by nasalization only once in a multi-word verb form is observed in many other places throughout the grammar of Hindi.

The simple-perfective is used to indicate an action that is conceptualized as having been completed.

मैं कल ही बंबई गई। *maĩ kal hī bãbaī gaī.*
'I went to Bombay only yesterday'.

शर्माजी पिताजी के साथ घर से निकले। *śarmājī pitājī ke sāth ghar se nikale.*
'Mr. Sharma came out of the house together with Father'.

As most completed actions are assumed to have taken place in the past, the simple perfective often functions as a simple past tense :

आपने तब क्या किया ? *āpne tab kyā kiyā ?*
'What did you do then ?'

वह घर पहुंचा। *vah ghar pahũcā.*
'He arrived home'.

The simple-perfective is occasionally used to indicate a future action that is conceptualized as, for all practical purposes, already completed :

अभी आया। *abhī āyā.*
'I'm coming/I'll come right away'.

The present-perfective is used in Hindi to indicate an action or state of affairs that has already been completed, but whose effect is still felt in the present :

लक्ष्मणजी दुकान से आये हैं। *lakṣmaṇjī dukān se āye haĩ.*
'Lakshman *has* come from the store'.

सुरेन्द्र बच्चों के लिए मिठाइयाँ ले आया है। *surendra baccõ ke liye miṭhāiyā̃ le āyā hai.*

'Surendra *has* brought sweets for the children'.

The past-perfective is used in Hindi to indicate an action or state of affairs that has already been completed, but whose effect is no longer felt to be present :

उसकी सहेली बहुत जल्दी उठी थी। *uskī sahelī bahut jaldī uṭhī thī.*

'Her friend *had* gotten up very early/quickly'.

सीता रानी के घर में ठहरी थी। *sītā rānī ke ghar mẽ ṭhaharī thī.*

'Sita had stayed in Rani's house'.

The presumptive-perfective represents an action or state of affairs that is viewed as completed and presumed, but not directly known, to have occurred :

अध्यापकजी अब तक स्कूल पहुँचे होंगे। *adhyāpakjī ab tak skūl pahũce hõge.*

'The teacher must have reached school by now'.

पुस्तक उसी मेज़ से गिरी होगी। *pustak usī mez se girī hogī.*

'The book must have fallen from that very table'.

The use of the subjunctive perfective is taken up in 13.1.

10.2. Possessive Pronouns

Some Hindi personal pronouns, namely मैं *mãĩ*, तू *tū*, हम *ham*, and तुम *tum*, have special possessive forms. A list of the possessive forms of all Hindi personal pronouns is given below:

Singular		Plural	
Direct	Possessive	Direct	Possessive
मैं *mãĩ*	मेरा *merā*	हम *ham*	हमारा *hamārā*
तू *tū*	तेरा *terā*	तुम *tum*	तुम्हारा *tumhārā*
यह *yah*	इसका *iskā*	आप *āp*	आपका *āpkā*
वह *vah*	उसका *uskā*	ये *ye*	इनका *inkā*
		वे *ve*	उनका *unkā*

The above-listed possessive forms behave very much like adjectives, agreeing with nouns in number, gender, and case :

मेरा केला *merā kelā* 'my banana' vrs. मेरे केले *mere kele* 'my bananas'

उसका भाई *uskā bhāī* 'his/her brother' vrs. उसकी बहन *uskī bahan* 'his/her sister'

तुम्हारा कमरा *tumhārā kamrā* 'your (fam.) room. vrs. तुम्हारे कमरे में (*tumhāre kamre mẽ* 'in your (fam.) room'.

When a personal pronoun is followed by a multi-word postposition beginning with one of the forms of the possessive postposition का/के/की *kā/ke/kī* (e.g., के लिए *ke liye*, के साथ *ke sāth*, के बारे में *ke bāre mẽ*), the first word of the postposition combines with the personal pronoun to form an appropriate possessive pronoun. Thus मैं *mãĩ*+के लिये *ke liye* becomes मेरे लिये *mere liye* 'for me', तुम *tum*+के साथ *ke sāth* becomes तुम्हारे साथ *tumhāre sāth* 'along with you, together with you'; हम *ham* +के बारे में *ke bāre mẽ* becomes हमारे बारे में *hamāre bāre mẽ* 'about, concerning us'.

10.3. Adverbs

Adverbs can be defined as words that qualify or modify verbs, adjectives, or other adverbs. Hindi adverbs can be divided into adverbs of time, place, manner, degree, affirmation or negation. In this chapter the first four of these types are discussed.

Adverbs of time specify the time at which a verbal activity or state of affairs takes place. Some common adverbs of time already encountered are कल *kal* 'tomorrow, yesterday', आज *āj* 'today', तभी *tabhī* 'just then', सुबह *subah* 'in the morning', प्रति दिन *prati din* 'every day', etc. Some Hindi adverbs of time consist of a postpositional phrase, that is, some word or words followed by a postposition, e.g., बुधवार को *budhvār ko* 'on Wednesday', सोमवार के बाद *somvār ke bād* 'after Monday'. The postposition को *ko* is especially common in adverbs of time, occurring in a wide variety of expressions such as शाम को *śām ko* 'in the evening', दिन को *din ko* 'in the day, by day', and रात को *rāt ko* 'in the night, by night'. Occasionally, Hindi adverbs of time may consist of a noun in its oblique singular form, not followed by a postposition (e.g., सवेरे *savere* 'in the morning' [cf., सवेरा *saverā* n.m. the morning, उस दिन *us din* 'on that day']).

Adverbs of place specify the location at which verbal actions or states of affairs take place. They may be either single words (e.g., यहाँ *yahā̃* 'here', इधर *idhar* 'in this direction') or longer postpositional phrases (e.g., वहाँ से *vahā̃ se* 'from there', *bāzār mẽ* 'in the market', उनके मित्रों के घरों में *unke mitrõ ke gharõ mẽ* 'in their friends' houses'.

Adverbs of manner specify the manner in which some activity is carried out. They may consist of a single word (e.g. जल्दी *jaldī* 'quickly, early') or a lengthier postpositional phrase (e.g., देर से *der se* 'late'). The postposition से *se* 'with' is used in conjunction with preceding nouns in a large number of adverbs of manner (e.g., देर से *der se* 'late' [literally 'with a delay'], मुश्किल से *muśkil se* 'with difficulty' [cf., मुश्किल *muśkil* n.f., 'difficulty']).

Adverbs of degree specify the extent to which some adjectival quality pertains to a qualified noun. Thus in the expression बहुत अच्छा केला *bahut acchā kelā* 'very good banana' the adverb of extent बहुत *bahut* describes the extent to which the banana in question can be said to be good.

10.4. Word Order (Continued)

It is now possible to make a fuller statement about Hindi word order than was possible in sec. 5.7. The principles describing basic Hindi word order can now be modified as follows:

1. The preferred word order in the language is Subject-Object-Verb.
   (e.g., वह लड़की को देखता है *vah laRkī ko dekhtā hai* 'He sees the girl'.)
2. Where both a direct object and an indirect object are present, the latter precedes the former.
   (e.g., मैं लड़की को खाना देता हूँ। *mãĩ laRkī ko khānā detā hũ.*
   'I give the food to the girl'.)
3. Attributive adjectives precede the nouns they modify. Adverbs modifying adjectives precede the adjectives.
   (e.g. बहुत छोटी इमारत *bahut choṭī imārat* 'very small building'.)

4. Adverbs of time, place, or manner may occur either before the subject of a sentence or immediately after it.

मैं कल वहाँ गया।	*māĩ kal vahā̃ gayā.*	'I went there yesterday'.
कल मैं वहां गया।	*kal māĩ vahā̃ gayā.*	

Once again, it should be emphasized that all statements about Hindi word order must be considered only rough approximations. Any number of factors can cause Hindi sentences to exhibit patterns of word order considerably different from what has been stated here. Nevertheless, the above principles can be seen to describe the word order of a significant number of sentences of the standard language, particularly in its written form.

10.5. VOCABULARY

औरत	*aurat*	n.f. woman
गली	*galī*	n.f. a small street, lane
देर	*der*	n.f. delay, interval
लक्ष्मण	*lakṣmaṇ*	prop. m. Lakshman (a man's name)
लक्ष्मी	*lakṣmī*	prop. f. Lakshmi (a woman's name)
सहेली	*sahelī*	n.f. female friend (of a female)
सुरेन्द्र	*surendra*	prop. m. Surendra (a man's name)
रविवार	*ravivār*	prop. m. Sunday
इतवार	*itvār*	prop. m. Sunday
सोमवार	*somvār*	prop. m. Monday
मंगलवार	*māgalvār*	prop. m. Tuesday
बुधवार	*budhvār*	prop. m. Wednesday
बृहस्पतिवार	*bṛhaspativār*	prop. m. Thursday
गुरुवार	*guruvār*	prop. m. Thursday
शुक्रवार	*śukravār*	prop. m. Friday
शनिवार	*śanivār*	prop. m. Saturday
शनीचर	*śanīcar*	prop. m. Saturday
सीधा	*sīdhā*	adj. straight
उठना	*uṭhnā*	v.i. to rise, get up
उड़ना	*uRnā*	v.i. to fly
गिरना	*girnā*	v.t. to fall
जल्दी करना	*jaldī karnā*	v.t. to hurry
ठहरना	*ṭhaharnā*	v.i. to wait, stay
निकलना	*nikalnā*	v.i. to come out (of something), emerge
भागना	*bhāgnā*	v.i. to flee, escape
ले आना	*le ānā*	v.t. to bring (something or someone) from someplace
ले जाना	*le jānā*	v.t. to take (something or someone) to someplace
हंसना	*hãsnā*	v.i. to laugh
अभी	*abhī*	adv. right now [=अब *ab*+ही *hī*]
जल्दी	*jaldī*	adv. early, quickly, swiftly
तभी	*tabhī*	adv. just then [=तब *tab*+ही *hī*]
देर से	*der se*	adv. late
परसों	*parsõ*	adv. the day before yesterday, the day after tomorrow
पहले	*pahle*	adv. before, earlier, previously
बाद में	*bād mẽ*	adv. afterwards
बाहर	*bāhar*	adv. outside
सामने	*sāmne*	adv. in front, opposite
सीधे	*sīdhe*	adv. straight
X के अंदर	*X ke ãdar*	post. inside X
X के आगे	*X ke āge*	post. ahead of X
X के पहले/ से पहले	*X ke pahle/ X se pahle*	post. earlier than
X के पीछे	*X ke piche*	post. behind X
X के बाद	*X ke bād*	post. after X
X के बाहर	*X ke bāhar*	post. outside X
X के बीच (में)	*X ke bic (mẽ)*	post. in the middle of X
X के सामने	*X ke sāmne*	post. opposite X, in front of X
छब्बीस	*chabbhīs*	num. twenty-six
सत्ताईस	*sattāīs*	num. twenty-seven
अट्ठाईस	*aṭṭhāīs*	num. twenty-eight
उन्तीस	*untīs*	num. twenty-nine
तीस	*tīs*	num. thirty

10.6. EXERCISES

10.6.1 *Translate into English.*

1. उसकी सहेली *uskī sahelī*, हमारे पिताजी *hamāre pitājī*, तुम्हारी बहनें *tumhārī bahan͂e*, तेरे बेटे को *tere beṭe ko*; 2. शनिवार को *śanivār ko*, बुधवार शाम को *budhvār śām ko*, परसों सुबह *parsõ subah*; 3. घर के अंदर *ghar ke ãdar*, उनके घरों के सामने *unke gharõ ke sāmne*, बगीचे के बाहर *bagīce ke bāhar*; 4. सुरेन्द्र के आगे *surendra ke āge*, लक्ष्मी की माताजी के पीछे *lakṣmī kī mātājī ke pīche*; 5. इतवार के पहले *itvār ke pahle*, आज से पहले *āj se pahle*, शुक्रवार के बाद *śukravār ke bād*; 6. वह उठा *vah uṭhā*, मैं रही *mãī rahī*, हम गिरे *ham gire*, वे ले गईं *ve le gaī̃*; 7. तू आई है *tū āī hai*, वह उड़ी है *vah uRī hai*, तुम गए हो *tum gae ho*; 8. वह ले गया था *vah le gayā thā*, वे ठहरी थीं *ve ṭhaharī thī̃*, मैं निकला था *mãī nikalā thā*; 9. वे भागे होंगे *ve bhāge hõge*, आप हंसी होंगी *āp hãsī hõgī*, वह रोई होगी *vah roī hogī*.

10.6.2. *Translate into Hindi.*

1. My brother, our lane, your (fam.) very tall chairs; 2. from your (pol.) friend (f.), on my new clothes, concerning our expensive saris; 3. on Monday, on Sunday in the afternoon, tomorrow night; 4. inside the rooms, inside those very large rooms, outside their rooms; 5. in front of the teachers, ahead of this school's students, behind the closed door; 6. before the day after tomorrow, after tomorrow, after Tuesday; 7. I (m.) cried, they (f.) fled, we (m.) emerged, you (int. f.) laughed; 8. he has fallen, you have gone, we (f.) have arrived, it (f.) has flown; 9. they (f.) had gone, she had arrived, I (m.) had fled, you (int. m.) had fallen; 10. he must have arrived, they (m.) must have fled, we (f.) must have emerged, she must have gotten up.

10.6.3. *Translate into English.*

1. कल सुबह मेरे पिताजी बहुत जल्दी उठे। *kal subah mere pitājī bahut jaldī uṭhe.* 2. शुक्लाजी सीता के लिए कुछ ताजी मिठाइयाँ ले आए। *śuklājī sītā ke liye kuch tāzī miṭhāiyā̃ le āe.* 3. परसों सब बच्चे बहुत देर से स्कूल आए। *parsõ sab bacce bahut der se skūl āe.* 4. वही छब्बीस आदमी उस देश से भागे थे। *vahī chabbīs ādmī us deś se bhāge the.* 5. उसका छोटा भाई अब तक वाराणसी पहुँचा होगा। *uskā choṭā bhāī ab tak vārāṇasī pahũcā hogā.* 6. बाद में लक्ष्मी की सहेलियाँ सुरेन्द्र के घर आईं। *bād mẽ lakṣmī kī saheliyā̃ surendra ke ghar āī̃.* 7. अब सब विद्यार्थी स्कूल के बाहर गए हैं। *ab sab vidyārthī skūl ke bāhar gae hãĩ.* 8. दुकानदार यहाँ पहले क्यों ठहरता था ? *dukāndār yahā̃ pahle kyõ ṭhahartā thā?* 9. वह सब गायों को शहर से गाँव ले गया था। *vah sab gāyõ ko śahar se gā̃v le gayā thā.* 10. पिताजी का समाचारपत्र कुरसी से गिरा होगा। *pitājī kā samācārpatra kursī se girā hogā.* 11. घर के बाहर कई छोटी चिड़ियां उड़ रही थीं। *ghar ke bāhar kaī choṭī ciRiyā̃ uR rahī thī̃.* 12. तब राम और उसके सारे मित्र वहाँ से भागे *tab rām aur uske sāre mitra vahā̃ se bhāge.*

10.6.4. *Translate into Hindi.*

1. Those men had fled from the city with Sita. 2. Why did you bring these beautiful flowers from the market? 3. How many books did you take to school yesterday? 4. You (pol. f.) must have gone to Agra before. 5. Lakshmi had come out of my friend's house. 6. Afterwards we went to the store very quickly. 7. How many women had come there from Allahabad? 8. Many people used to live outside those cities. 9. When did those books fall from the table? 10. Rani arrived in the village before Madan. 11. Why did you bring his brother here? 12. When did the peacocks come out of the garden?

SUPPLEMENTARY READING PASSAGES

A. बातचीत *bātcīt*

मनोजः तुम्हारा क्या नाम है ?
अशोकः मेरा नाम अशोक है।
मनोजः तुम कहाँ रहते हो ?
अशोकः मैं गाँव में रहता हूँ। मेरे गांव में हिन्दू और मुसलमान दोनों रहते हैं। वहां ईसाई भी रहते हैं। पाठशाला में सब साथ-साथ पढ़ते हैं। पाठशाला में हम हिसाब सीखते हैं।
मनोजः तुम सबेरे कितने बजे उठते हो ?
अशोकः मैं छः बजे उठता हूँ। फिर मैं और मेरी बहन टहलते हैं। फिर हम सामाचारपत्र पढ़ते हैं। हम दस बजे पाठशाला पहुँचते हैं। हमें गुरुजी अच्छी तरह पढ़ाते हैं। हम रात को नौ बजे सोते हैं।
(adapted from *SHP* (P), pp. 36-37)

manoj : tumhāra kyā nām hai ?
aśok : merā nām aśok hai.
manoj : tum kahā̃ rahte ho ?
aśok : mãĩ gā̃v mẽ rahtā hū̃. mere gā̃v mẽ hīdū aur musalmān donõ rahte hãĩ. vahā̃ īsāī bhī rahte hãĩ. pāṭhśālā mẽ sab sāth-sāth paRhte hãĩ. pāṭhśālā mẽ ham hisāb sīkhte hãĩ.
manoj : tum savere kitne baje uṭhte ho?
aśok : mãĩ chaḥ baje uṭhtā hū̃. phir mãĩ aur merī bahan ṭahalte hãĩ. phir ham samācārpatra paRhte hãĩ. ham das baje pāṭhśālā pahũcte hãĩ. hamẽ gurujī acchī tarah paRhāte hãĩ. ham rāt ko nau baje sote hãĩ.

Vocabulary

बातचीत *bātcīt* n.f. conversation
नाम *nām* n.m. name
गाँव *gā̃v* n.m. village
हिंदू *hīdū* n.m. Hindu
मुसलमान *musalmān* n.m. Muslim
दोनों *donõ* pro. adj. both
ईसाई *īsāī* n.m. Christian
पाठशाला *pāṭhśālā* n.f. grade school
हिसाब *hisāb* n.m. arithmetic
सीखना *sīkhnā* v.t. to learn
सवेरे *savere* adv. in the morning
कितने बजे *kitne baje* inter. when? at what time?
छः बजे *chaḥ baje* adv. six o'clock (v., 22.2.)
फिर *phir* adv. then
टहलना *ṭahalnā* v.i. to go for a stroll
गुरुजी *guru jī* n.m. teacher.
अच्छी तरह *acchī tarah* adv. well
पढ़ाना *paRhānā* v. tr. to teach

B. हिन्दी *hindī*

हिन्दी अच्छी भाषा है। यह भारत की राष्ट्रभाषा है। महात्मा सूरदास और तुलसीदास हिन्दी के बड़े कवि हैं। तुलसीदास की रामायण बहुत प्रसिद्ध है। उसे बहुत लोग पढ़ते हैं। उत्तर में लोग सूरदास के पद गाते हैं। दक्षिण में महात्मा त्यागराज के कीर्तन गाते हैं।

hindī acchī bhāṣā hai. yah bhārat kī rāṣṭrabhāṣā hai. mahātmā sūrdās aur tulsīdās hindī ke baRe kavi hãĩ. tulsīdās kī rāmāyaṇ bahut prasiddh hai. use bahut log paRhte hãĩ. uttar mẽ log sūrdās ke pad gāte hãĩ. dakṣiṇ mẽ mahātmā tyāgarāj ke kīrtan gāte hãĩ.

भारत हमारा देश है। हम इसकी संतान हैं। यह हमें खाने को देता है। इसी के अनाज से हमारा शरीर बनता है। हम इसको प्रणाम करते हैं।

bhārat hamārā deś hai. ham iskī sãtān hai. yah hamẽ khāne ko detā hai. isī ke anāj se hamārā śarīr bantā hai. ham isko praṇām karte hãĩ.

यह ऋषि-मुनियों का देश है। यहीं हमारे पवित्र तीर्थ हैं। पवित्र गंगा नदी इसी देश में बहती है। सब से ऊंचा हिमालय पहाड़ भी यहीं है।	yah ṛsi-muniyõ kā deś hai. yahī̃ hamāre pavitra tīrth hãī. pavitra gãgā nadī isī deś mẽ bahtī hai. sab se ũcā himālay pahāR bhī yahī̃ hai.
हम अपने देश को प्यार करते हैं।	ham apne deś ko pyār karte hãī.

(adapted from *HKPP*, pp. 7-8)

Vocabulary

राष्ट्रभाषा *rāṣṭrabhāṣā* n.f. national language
महात्मा *mahātmā* n.m. saint, sage
सूरदास *sūrdās* prop. m
तुलसीदास *tulsīdās* prop. m
कवि *kavi* n.m. poet
रामायण *rāmāyaṇ* prop. m. the great epic on the life of Rāma
उत्तर *uttar* n.m. north
पद *pad* n. m. a particular genre of short poem
दक्षिण *dakṣiṇ* n.m. south
त्यागराज *tyāgarāj* prop. m.
कीर्तन *kīrtan* n.m. a kind of devotional song
देश *deś* n.m. nation, country
संतान *sãtān* n.f. progeny, offspring
खाने को *khane ko* food to eat
अनाज *anāj* n.f. grain
शरीर n.f. *śarīr* n.m. body
बनना *bannā* v.i. to be/get devoloped
प्रणाम करना *praṇām karnā* v.t to salute
ऋषि *ṛsi* n.m. sage
मुनि *muni* n.m. sage
यहीं *yahī̃* adv. right here[=यहां *yahā̃*+ही *hī*]
पवित्र *pavitra* adj. sacred, holy
तीर्थ *tīrth* n.m. pilgrimage site
गंगा *gãgā* Prop. f. the Ganges River
बहना *bahnā* v.i. to flow
सबसे ऊंचा *sabse ũcā* highest of all
हिमालय पहाड़ *himālay-pahāR* prop. m. the Himalayas
अपना *apnā* refl. adj. one's own
प्यार करना *pyār karnā* v.t. to love

C. लालच बुरी चीज़ है *lālac burī cīz hai*

एक आदमी के पास एक मुर्ग़ी थी। वह रोज़ एक सोने का अंडा देती थी। वह अंडा बेचकर खाने की चीज़ें ख़रीदता था। इस तरह वह बहुत दिनों तक सुख से रहा।	ek ādmī ke pās ek murgī thī. vah roz ek sone kā ãḍā detī thī. vah ãḍā beckar khāne kī cīzẽ kharīdtā thā. is tarah vah bahut dinõ tak sukh se rahā.
एक दिन उसने सोचा—"मुर्ग़ी के पेट में बहुत अंडे होंगे। आज उसका पेट चीर कर मैं सब अंडे निकाल लूंगा। उन्हें बेचने से बहुत-से रुपये मिलेंगे। तब मैं बड़ा धनवान हो जाऊंगा।"	ek din usne socā—"murgī ke peṭ mẽ bahut ãḍe hõge. āj uskā peṭ cīrkar mãī sab ãḍe nikāl lũgā. unhẽ becne se bahut-se rupaye milẽge. tab mãī baRā dhanvān ho jāũgā."
यह सोचकर उसने एक तेज चाकू से उस बेचारी मुर्ग़ी का पेट चीर डाला। मुर्ग़ी मर गयी। उसके पेट से एक भी अंडा न निकला।	yah sockar usne ek tez cākū se us becārī murgī kā peṭ cīr ḍālā. murgī mar gayī. uske peṭ se ek bhī ãḍā na nikalā.
लालच बुरी चीज़ है।	lālac burī cīz hai.

(adapted from HKPP, pp. 13-14)

Vocabulary

लालच *lālac* n.m. greed, avarice
बुरा *burā* adj. bad
चीज़ *cīz* n.f. thing
X के पास *X ke pās* post. here 'in X's possession'
मुर्ग़ी *murgī* n.f. hen, chicken
रोज़ *roz* adv. daily
सोना *sonā* n.m. gold
अंडा *ãḍā* n.m. egg

बेचकर *beckar* would sell and...
इस तरह *is tarah* adv. in this manner
बहुत दिनों तक *bahut dinõ tak* for many days
सुख से *sukh se* adv. happily
उसने सोचा *usne socā* he thought
पेट *peṭ* n.m. stomach
चीरकर *cīrkar* will rip open and...
निकाल लूंगा *nikāl lū̃gā* (I) will remove
बेचने से *becne se* from selling
बहुत-सा *bahut-sā* adj. very much/many
मिलेंगे *milẽge* will be obtained
यह सोचकर *yah sockar* thinking this
धनवान *dhanvān* adj. rich, wealthy
हो जाना *ho jānā* v.i. to become
उसने चीर डाला *usne cīr ḍālā* he ripped open
तेज़ *tez* adj. sharp
चाकू *cākū* n.m. penknife
बेचारा *becārā* adj. poor, helpless
मर जाना *mar jānā* v.i to die
एक भी...न *ek bhī...na* not even one

PART
III

CHAPTER 11

11.1 The Perfective of Transitive Verbs

As was mentioned in the previous chapter, the use of the perfective aspect with intransitive verbs in Hindi differs from the use of the aspect with transitive verbs. These differences appear not in the perfective verb forms themselves, but in syntactic properties of the entire sentences in which the perfective forms are employed. It will be recalled that in the case of perfective forms of intransitive verbs the perfective participle and various forms of the auxiliary verb होना *honā* 'to be' stand in grammatical agreement with the subject of the verb. This is not likewise true in the case of transitive verbs. When transitive verbs are employed in any of Hindi's perfective aspectual-tenses (viz., the simple-perfective, the present-perfective, the past-perfective, the presumptive-perfective, and the subjunctive-perfective), a special postposition ने *ne* is employed directly after the subject, thereby causing the subject to appear in its oblique case form. The verb itself stands in grammatical agreement not with the subject of the sentence, but with the object. This holds true for both the perfective participle itself and any following auxiliary form of होना *honā*. These principles are illustrated in the following sentences:

उस बच्चे ने मेज़ पर एक पुस्तक देखी। *us bacce ne mez par ek pustak dekhī.*
'That boy saw a book on the table'.

शर्माजी ने कुछ नये कपड़े ख़रीदे होंगे। *śarmājī ne kuch naye kapRe kharīde hõge.*
'Mr. Sharma must have bought some new clothes'.

उन लोगों ने हमें दो सौ रुपये दिये। *un logõ ne hamẽ do sau rupaye diye.*
'Those people gave us two hundred rupees'.

In each of the above sentences the postposition ने *ne* is employed immediately following the subject. This has caused the subjects of these sentences to appear in their oblique forms. The verbs of these sentences देखी *dekhī*, ख़रीदे होंगे *kharīde hõge*, and दिये *diye* stand in grammatical agreement with the direct objects एक पुस्तक *ek pustak*, कुछ नये कपड़े *kuch naye kapRe*, and दो सौ रुपये *do sau rupaye* respectively.

In those cases where the direct object is followed by the postposition को *ko*, or is a contraction equivalent to a pronoun plus को *ko* (e.g., मुझे *mujhe*, उसे *use* etc.), the verbal construction appears in its masculine singular form:

उस लड़के ने मेरी बहन को देखा। *us laRke ne merī bahan ko dekhā.*
'That boy saw my sister'.

सीता की सहेलियों ने उसे देखा होगा। *sitā kī saheliyõ ne use dekhā hogā.*
'Sita's friends must have seen him/her'.

In the above two sentences the verb forms देखा *dekhā* and देखा होगा *dekhā hogā* are masculine singular because of the marking of the respective direct objects with को *ko* (with subsequent contraction in the latter instance).

Sequences of some personal pronouns plus ने *ne* are irregular. Two of the pronouns (ये *ye* and वे *ve*) have special forms when followed by this postposition. Five other personal pronouns (मैं *mãĩ*, तू *tū*, हम *ham*, तुम *tum*, and आप *āp*) do not change at all before ने *ne*. The remaining two personal pronouns (यह *yah* and वह *vah*) appear in the normal oblique case forms before ने *ne*. A summary of the form of all personal pronouns when occurring before ने *ne* is given below:

Singular		Plural	
Direct Form	Form with ने *ne*	Direct Form	Form with ने *ne*
मैं *mãĩ*	मैंने *mãine*	हम *ham*	हमने *hamne*
तू *tū*	तूने *tūne*	तुम *tum*	तुमने *tumne*
		आप *āp*	आपने *āpne*
यह *yah*	इसने *isne*	ये *ye*	इन्होंने *inhõne*
वह *vah*	उसने *usne*	वे *ve*	उन्होंने *unhõne*

The sequence of interrogative pronoun कौन *kaun* 'who' plus ने *ne* appears as किसने *kisne* in the singular and किन्होंने *kinhõne* in the plural:

उस आदमी को पैसे किसने दिये ? *us ādmī ko paise kisne diye ?*
'Who (s.) gave the money to that man?'

उस आदमी को पैसे किन्होंने दिये ? *us ādmī ko paise kinhõne diye ?*
'Who (pl.) gave the money to that man?'

N.B. The plural forms इन्होंने *inhõne*, उन्होंने *unhõne*, and किन्होंने *kinhõne* are only employed to replace sequences in which ने *ne* immediately follows a pronoun. They are not used when the pronoun and ने *ne* are separated by an intervening word :

उन्होंने ताज़ी रोटी खाई। *unhõne tāzī roṭī khāī.*
'They ate (the) fresh bread'.

उन लोगों ने ताज़ी रोटी खाई। *un logõ ne tāzī roṭī khāī.*
'Those people ate (the) fresh bread'.

In the second of the above examples the subject noun phrase वे लोग *ve log* appears in the oblique form उन लोगों *un logõ* because of the presence of the following postposition ने *ne*. No contraction is possible in this sentence because the words उन *un* and ने *ne* are separated by the nominal form लोगों *logõ*.

The perfective participles of some common transitive verbs, namely करना *karnā* 'to do', लेना *lenā* 'to take', देना *denā* 'to give', and पीना *pīnā* 'to drink, smoke', are irregular. The forms of the perfective participles of these verbs are as follows :

करना *karnā* 'to do': किया *kiyā*/ किए *kie* or किये *kiye*/ की *kī*/ कीं *kī̃*
लेना *lenā* 'to take': लिया *liyā*/लिए *lie* or लिये *liye*/ ली *lī*/ लीं *lī̃*
देना *denā* 'to give': दिया *diyā*/दिए *die* or दिये *diye* / दी *dī* / दीं *dī̃*
पीना *pīnā* 'to drink, smoke': पिया *piyā* / पिए *pie* or पिये *piye* /पी *pī*/पीं *pī̃*

The irregular perfective forms of intransitive verbs whose stems end in -ई *-ī* have already been described in 10.1.

There are a few common Hindi verbs that are syntactically transitive (i.e., that have direct objects), but that do not occur in the ने *ne* construction. Some of the most frequent of these verbs are लाना *lānā* 'to bring', भूलना *bhūlnā*, to forget', डरना *ḍarnā* 'to fear, be afraid', and बोलना *bolnā* 'to speak' :

रमेश की माता जी दुकान से खाना लाई। *rameś kī mātā jī dukān se khānā lāī.*
'Remesh's mother brought (some) food from the market'.

वह मेरा नाम नहीं भूला था। *vah merā nām nahī̃ bhūlā thā.*
'He had not forgotten my name'.

In the case of the verb समझना *samajhnā* 'to understand', the use of the ने *ne* construction is optional in the perfective :

मैं आपकी बात नहीं समझा। *mãĩ āpkī bāt nahī̃ samajhā.*
or मैंने आपकी बात नहीं समझी। *mãĩne āpkī bāt nahī̃ samajhī.*
'I didn't understand what you said'.

The compound verbs ले जाना *le jānā* 'to take someone or something somewhere' and ले आना *le ānā* 'to bring someone or something from somewhere' likewise prohibit the use of the ने *ne* construction in the perfective :[1]

हम (not हमने) बाज़ार से कुछ कपड़े ले आए। *ham* (*not hamne*) *bāzār se kuch kapRe le āe.*
'We brought some clothes from the market'.

Several other Hindi verbs may occur either with or without the ने *ne* construction in the perfective. Often such verbs are to be construed as transitive when occurring with the ने *ne* construction, but intransitive without it. Thus बदलना *badalnā* with the construction has the sense 'to change something', but the same verb without the construction has the sense 'to be/get changed'. Likewise भरना *bharnā* with the ने *ne* construction has the sense 'to fill' while without it it can be glossed as 'to become full'.

Some verbs representing activities that in English are considered intransitive are treated as transitive in Hindi. A common example of this phenomenon is छींकना *chī̃knā* 'to sneeze' (e.g., उसने छींका *usne chī̃kā* 'he/she sneezed'). Note, however, that the semantically analogous verb खांसना *khā̃snā* 'to cough' is intransitive (e.g., वह खांसा *vah khā̃sā* 'he coughed').

11.2. Cardinal Numbers

The cardinal numbers from one to thirty have already been introduced in the vocabulary sections of Chapters 5-10. The remaining cardinal numbers in Hindi are as

1. For a discussion of the use of the ने *ne* construction with other compound verbs v. Chapters 19 and 20.

follows :[2]

31	इकत्तीस	*ikattīs*	57	सत्तावन	*sattāvan*			
32	बत्तीस	*battīs*	58	अट्ठावन	*aṭṭhāvan*	83	तिरासी	*tirāsī*
33	तैंतीस	*tāĩtīs*	59	उन्सठ	*unsaṭh*	84	चौरासी	*caurāsī*
34	चौंतीस	*cāũtīs*	60	साठ	*sāṭh*	85	पचासी	*pacāsī*
35	पैंतीस	*pāĩtīs*	61	इकसठ	*iksaṭh*	86	छियासी	*chiyāsī*
36	छत्तीस	*chattīs*	62	बासठ	*bāsaṭh*	87	सतासी	*satāsī*
37	सैंतीस	*sāĩtīs*	63	तिरसठ	*tirsaṭh*	88	अठासी	*aṭhāsī*
38	अड़तीस	*aRtīs*	64	चौसठ	*causaṭh*	89	नवासी	*navāsī*
39	उन्तालीस	*untālīs*	65	पैंसठ	*pāĩsaṭh*	90	नब्बे	*nabbe*
40	चालीस	*cālīs*	66	छियासठ	*chiyāsaṭh*	91	इक्यानवे	*ikyānve*
41	इक्तालीस	*iktālīs*	67	सड़सठ	*saRsaṭh*	92	बानवे	*bānve*
42	बयालीस	*bayālīs*	68	अड़सठ	*aRsaṭh*	93	तिरानवे	*tirānve*
43	तैंतालीस	*tāĩtālīs*	69	उन्हत्तर	*unhattar*	94	चौरानवे	*caurānve*
44	चवालीस	*cavālīs*	70	सत्तर	*sattar*	95	पचानवे	*pacānve*
45	पैंतालीस	*pāĩtālīs*	71	इकहत्तर	*ikahattar*	96	छियानवे	*chiyānve*
46	छयालीस	*chayālīs*	72	बहत्तर	*bahattar*	97	सत्तानवे	*sattānve*
47	सैंतालीस	*sāĩtālīs*	73	तिहत्तर	*tihattar*	98	अट्ठानवे	*aṭṭhānve*
48	अड़तालीस	*aRtālīs*	74	चौहत्तर	*cauhattar*	99	निन्यानवे	*ninyānve*
49	उन्चास	*uncās*	75	पचहत्तर	*pacahattar*	100	सौ	*sau*
50	पचास	*pacās*	76	छिहत्तर	*chihattar*	0	शून्य	*śūnya*
51	इक्यावन	*ikyāvan*	77	सतहत्तर	*satahattar*	*thousand*	हज़ार	*hazār*
52	बावन	*bāvan*	78	अठहत्तर	*aṭhahattar*	*hundred thousand*	लाख	*lākh*
53	तिरपन	*tirpan*	79	उनासी	*unāsī*	*ten million*	करोड़	*karoR*
54	चौवन	*cauvan*	80	अस्सी	*assī*	billion	अरब	*arb*
55	पचपन	*pacpan*	81	इक्यासी	*ikyāsī*	(= thousand million)		
56	छप्पन	*chappan*	82	बयासी	*bayāsī*			

Numbers above 100 are fully regular :

पांच सौ ग्यारह *pā̃c sau gyārah* 'five hundred and eleven'

इक्कीस हज़ार नौ सौ बीस *ikkīs hazār nau sau bīs*
'twenty-one thousand nine hundred and twenty'

There are a number of peculiarities in the above set of numbers from the point of view of speakers of European languages. First of all, the numbers though 100 are quite irregular. Whereas mastery of the cardinal numbers of a European language generally requires memorization of the forms through the teens, the numbers for twenty, thirty, forty, etc., and the words for higher numbers (hundred, thousand, million, etc.), in the Hindi system all of the numbers from one to one hundred need be individually learned. Moreover, the Hindi words for two higher numbers (i.e., लाख *lākh* 'one hundred thousand' and करोड़ *karoR* 'ten million' stand for numerical concepts that are not expressed by single words in European languages. Conversely, some single-word numerical concepts in European languages must find expression in Hindi by multi-word phrases. Thus, for example, the western concept of a million is conceptualized as "ten lakhs" in Indian reckoning.

2. Hindi cardinal numbers are not fully standardized, and variants can be found for many of the above forms. The versions given above are those advocated by the Central Hindi Directorate, Government of India, Ministry of Education and Social Welfare (*BGMH*, pp. 64-5).

11.3. Ordinal Numbers

The formation of ordinal numbers in Hindi is considerably more regular than the formation of the cardinals. Ordinal numbers are obtained by the addition of the declinable adjectival suffix -वां *-vā̃* to an appropriate cardinal number. Thus from the cardinal numbers तीस *tīs* 'thirty' and हज़ार *hazār* can be formed the ordinals तीसवां *tīsvā̃* 'thirtieth' and हज़ारवां *hazārvā̃* 'thousandth'. These ordinals function as adjectives and agree with the nouns they modify in number, gender, and case :

तीसवीं पुस्तक	*tīsvī̃ pustak*	'the thirtieth book'
हज़ारवें आदमी को	*hazārvẽ ādmī ko*	'to the thousandth man'

The ordinals for first, second, third, fourth, sixth, and ninth are irregular. A list of the Hindi ordinals from first through tenth is as follows :

1st	पहला	*pahlā*	6th	छटा	*chaṭā*
2nd	दूसरा	*dūsrā*	7th	सातवां	*sātvā̃*
3rd	तीसरा	*tīsrā*	8th	आठवां	*āṭhvā̃*
4th	चौथा	*cauthā*	9th	नवां	*navā̃*
5th	पांचवां	*pā̃cvā̃*	10th	दसवां	*dasvā̃*

Ordinals beyond that for tenth proceed regularly by the affixation of -वां *-vā̃*. In standard literary Hindi the Sanskrit ordinal numbers (i.e., प्रथम *pratham* 'first', द्वितीय *dvitīya* 'second', तृतीय *tṛtīya* 'third', etc.,) are often employed in the place of the Hindi ordinals cited above: e.g., प्रथम स्थान *pratham sthān* 'first place'; द्वितीय पाठ *dvitīya pāṭh* 'second chapter/lesson'.

11.4. Vocabulary

आकाश	*ākāś*	n.m. the sky
गरमी	*garmī*	n.f. heat, warmth
गरमियाँ	*garmiyā̃*	n.f. pl. the hot season, summer
घंटा	*ghãṭā*	n.m. hour
जूता	*jūtā*	n.m. shoe
दिन	*din*	n.m. day
धोबी	*dhobī*	n.m. washerman
पौधा	*paudhā*	n.m. small plant, seedling
बात	*bāt*	n.f. matter, discussion
बादल	*bādal*	n.m. cloud
बिल्ली	*billī*	n.f. cat
बुढ़िया	*buRhiyā*	n.f. old woman
बूढ़ा	*būRhā*	n.m. old man; adj. old, ancient (of living creatures)
महीना	*mahīnā*	n.m. month
मिनट	*minaṭ*	n.m. minute
मैदान	*maidān*	n.m. field
मोची	*mocī*	n.m. cobbler
वर्ष	*varṣ*	n.m. year
सरदी	*sardī*	n.f. cold
सरदियाँ	*sardiyā̃*	n.f. pl. cold season, winter
हफ़्ता	*haftā*	n.m. week
उदास	*udās*	adj. sad
ख़ुश	*khuś*	adj. happy
गंदा	*gãdā*	adj. dirty
चौड़ा	*cauRā*	adj. wide
दुबला-पतला	*dublā-patlā*	adj. thin, skinny
मोटा	*moṭā*	adj. fat
संकरा	*sãkarā*	adj. narrow
साफ़-सुथरा	*sāf-sutharā*	adj. neat and clean
उठाना	*uṭhānā*	v.t. to lift up
खोलना	*kholnā*	v.t. to open
धोना	*dhonā*	v.t. to wash, clean
नहलाना	*nahalānā*	v.t. to bathe (someone else)
नहाना	*nahānā*	v.i. to bathe
नाचना	*nācnā*	v.i. to dance
निकालना	*nikālnā*	v.t. to remove, take out
पकाना	*pakānā*	v.t. to cook
पूरा करना	*pūrā karnā*	v.t. to complete
बंद करना	*bãd karnā*	v.t. to close
बनाना	*banānā*	v.t. to make
X से बात करना	*X se bāt karnā*	v.t. to converse with X
X की मदद करना	*X kī madad karnā*	v.t. to help X
लगाना	*lagānā*	v.t. to install, place, plant
समझना	*samajhnā*	v.i./t. to understand, consider
सीना	*sīnā*	v.t. to sew
हो जाना	*ho jānā*	v.i. to become, happen, occur
आपस में	*āpas mẽ*	adv. among themselves
X के कारण	*X ke kāraṇ*	post. because of X, on account of X
X के यहाँ	*X ke yahā̃*	post. at X's place
पर	*par*	conj. but
परन्तु	*parantu*	conj. but

11.5. Exercises

11.5.1. *Translate into English*

1. मैं नहाया *mãĩ nahāyā*, तुमने पकाया *tumne pakāyā*, उन्होंने धोया *unhõne dhoyā*, उसने निकाला *usne nikālā*; 2. हमने दिया है *hamne diyā hai*, इन्होंने लिया है *inhõne liyā hai*, आपने खोला है *āpne kholā hai*, तूने सिया है *tūne siyā hai*; 3. आपने पिया था *āpne piyā thā*, राम ने पकाया था *rām ne pakāyā thā*, औरत ने बनाया था *aurat ne banāyā thā*, गुप्ताजी ने कहा था *guptājī ne kahā thā*; 4. धोबी ने कहा होगा *dhobī ne kahā hogā*, मोची ने बनाया होगा *mocī ne banāyā hogā*, बुढ़ियों ने खाया होगा *buRhiyõ ne khāyā hogā*, बेटी ने खोला होगा *beṭī ne kholā hogā*; 5. उसने पुस्तक देखी *usne pustak*

dekhī, उसने पुस्तकें देखी थीं *usne pustakẽ dehkī thī*, उसने बादल देखे होंगे *usne bādal dekhe hõge*, उसने लड़कों को देखा *usne laRkõ ko dekhā*; 6. उसने देखा *usne dekhā*, उस बेटे ने देखा *us beṭe ne dekhā*, उन अच्छे लड़कों ने देखा *un acche laRkõ ne dekhā*, उन चालीस बहुत अच्छे मित्रों ने देखा *un cālīs bahut acche mitrõ ne dekhā*; 7. सैंतीस *sãītīs*, पचपन *pacpan*, एक सौ ग्यारह *ek sau gyārah*, चार सौ सतहत्तर *cār sau satahattar*, नौ हजार छ: सौ अस्सी *nau hazār chaḥ sau assī*; 8. चार लाख चौसठ हज़ार तीन सौ उन्सठ *cār lākh causaṭh hazār tīn sau unsaṭh*, दो करोड़ साठ लाख चार सौ एक *do karooR sāṭh lākh cār sau ek*; 9. चौथा दिन *cauthā din*, सातवीं साड़ी पर *sātvī sāRī par*, बीसवें घर के अंदर *bīsvẽ ghar ke ãdar*, सौवें वर्ष के पहले *sauvẽ varṣ ke pahle*.

11.5.2. *Translate into Hindi*

1. He ate, we took, you (fam.) bought, they opened; 2. You (pol.) have drunk, we have given, she has said, they have become; 3. She had lifted, they had completed, I had closed, you (fam.) had bought; 4. She must have taken, he must have seen, they must have given, you (pol.) must have planted; 5. he gave a book, they gave some bananas, they saw those girls, he made a shoe; 6. they saw those cats, the man made, this man made, those forty-two men made; 7. Sixty-one, ninety-seven, three hundred and fifty-nine, one thousand and eighty-seven; 8. forty-three thousand six hundred and twenty-nine, fifty-nine million six hundred and eighty-one thousand four hundred and nine; 9. the sixth week, the third fat man, the nineteenth minute, the hundred and third day of this year.

11.5.3. *Translate into English*

1. लड़कों ने तीन छोटे पौधे बग़ीचे में लगाए। *laRkõ ne tīn choṭe paudhe bagīce mẽ lagāe*. 2. सब लोगों ने वे काले बादल देखे थे। *sab logõ ne ve kāle bādal dekhe the*. 3. उसकी माताजी ने हमारे लिए बड़ी अच्छी रोटियां पकाईं। *uskī mātājī ne hamāre liye baRī acchī roṭiyā̃ pakāī̃*. 4. घर के बाहर एक मोची राम से बात कर रहा था। *ghar ke bāhar ek mocī rām se bāt kar rahā thā*. 5. उसके बाद कुछ बच्चे खुश हो गए और कुछ उदास। *uske bād kuch bacce khuś ho gae aur kuch udās*. 6. मोची ने आपके जूते कब पूरे किये ? *mocī ne āpke jūte kab pūre kiye*? 7. पिताजी ने तभी घर के सब दरवाजे बन्द किये। *pitājī ne tabhī ghar ke sab darvāze band kiye*. 8. इलाहाबाद में सुरेन्द्र ने बहुत संकरी गलियां देखी होंगी। *ilāhābād mẽ surendra ne bahut sãkrī galiyā̃ dekhī hõgī*. 9. लक्ष्मी और उसकी सहेलियां मैदान में नाच रही थीं। *lakśmī aur uskī saheliyā̃ maidān mẽ nāc rahī thī*. 10. सरदियों में मेरे माता-पिता[3] बंबई से यहां आए थे। *sardiyõ mẽ mere mātā-pitā bābaī se yahā̃ āe the*. 11. उस दिन[4] मदन पिताजी की मदद कर रहा था। *us din madan pitājī kī madad kar rahā thā*. 12. आपने उन बच्चों के साफ-सुथरे कमरे देखे होंगे। *āpne un baccõ ke sāf-suthare kamre dekhe hõge*.

11.5.4. *Translate into Hindi*

1. Why did she give those books to you? 2. How many dhotis did he buy in the market? 3. The old woman must have taken the money from my friend. 4. They had cooked some very good vegetable dishes. 5. The shopkeeper must have closed the store on Saturday. 6. Did the cobbler complete the shoes before yesterday? The weather had become very warm in that month. 8. His son is fat, but his daughter is thin. 9. Mother bathed the children yesterday in the morning. 10. How many plants did she plant in the garden? 11. The children were dancing at Kiran's [किरण *kiraṇ*] place. 12. They sang some very beautiful Indian songs.

---

3. माता-पिता 'parents'. The form is a compound formed by adjoining the elements *mātā* माता and पिता *pitā*.

4. V. 10.3. for the use of oblique case forms not followed by postposition in time adverbs.

CHAPTER 12

12.1. IMPERATIVES

In contrast to English, Hindi possesses a larger number of imperative verb forms for the issuing of commands and making of requests of various kinds. These imperative forms differ among themselves in the degree of respect accorded the individual addressed and in whether the desired activity is to be carried out immediately or deferred until some future time.

Intimate imperative forms are used in issuing orders to all those who would normally be addressed with the intimate second person pronoun तू *tū*. These imperatives consist of nothing more than the uninflected verbal stem:

(तू) यहाँ से जा ! *(tū) yahā̃ se jā !* 'Get out of here!'

कपड़ा यहीं मेज पर रख ! *kapRā yahī̃ mez par rakh !*
'Put the clothes right here on the table'.

Familiar imperatives are employed in issuing commands to all those normally addressed with the familiar second-person pronoun तुम *tum*. These commands are formed by the addition of the suffix -ओ *-o* immediately after the verbal stem. Thus from ख़रीदना *kharīdnā* 'to buy' and आना *ānā* 'to come' are formed ख़रीदो *kharīdo* and आओ *āo*;

बाजार जाकर बच्चों के लिए मिठाई खरीदो । *bāzār jākar baccõ ke lie miṭhāī ḳharīdo.*
'Go to the market and buy some sweets for the children'.

कल बच्चों के साथ हमारे यहाँ आओ । *kal bacchõ ke sāth hamāre yahā̃ āo.*
'Come to our place tomorrow with your children.'

Stems ending in long -ई *-ī* shorten this vowel to -इ *-i* and optionally insert the glide -य *-y* before the termination -ओ *-o*. Thus from पीना *pīnā* 'to drink' is formed पियो *piyo* (or पिओ *pio*).

The verbs लेना *lenā* 'to take' and देना *denā* 'to give' have the irregular familiar commands लो *lo* and दो *do* respectively.

Polite imperatives are used for making requests of those whom one normally addresses with the polite second person pronoun आप *āp*. These commands are formed by the addition of the suffix –इए *–ie* (alternately –इये *–iye* immediately after the verb stem. Thus from निकालना *nikālnā* 'to remove' and धोना *dhonā* 'to wash' stem the polite com- (आप) निकालिए *(āp) nikālie* 'please remove' and (आप) धोइए *(āp) dhoie* 'please wash' respectively:

(आप) बड़े भाई को उस घर से निकालिए ।
(āp) baRe bhāī ko us ghar se nikālie.
'please remove big brother from that house'.

(आप) उन गंदे कपड़ों को धोइए।
(āp) un gãde kapRõ ko dhoie.
'Please wash those dirty clothes'.

The verbs करना *karnā* 'to do', देना *denā* 'to give', लेना *lenā* 'to take', and पीना *pīnā* 'to drink, smoke' show the irregular polite imperatives कीजिए *kījie*, दीजिए *dījie*, लीजिए *lījie* and पीजिए *pījie*, respectively. The irregular command form हूजिए *hūjie*, from होना *honā* 'to be', is occasionally found in place of the regular होइए *hoie*.

N. B. It is not common in Hindi to use independent words corresponding to the English word "please." The polite command form alone, because of its association with the respect-bestowing pronoun आप *āp*, is sufficient to convey the degree of politeness conveyed by the word "please."

Occasionally, a *deferential* command form is also employed in Hindi. This form indicates an even greater degree of politeness, formality, or deference towards the person being addressed than does the polite imperative. The form may also be employed for ironic effect. Deferential commands are formed by the addition of the invariable suffix -गा *-gā* directly after the polite command form in -इए *-ie*. Thus from लिखना *likhnā* 'to write' and देना *denā* 'to give' are obtained the deferential commands लिखिएगा *likhiegā* and दीजिएगा *dījiegā*:

उसकी सहेली को पत्र लिखिएगा। *uskī sahelī ko patra likhiegā.*
'Please be so kind as to write a letter to his/her friend'.

उनको मेरा उत्तर दीजिएगा। *unko merā uttar dījiegā.*
'Please be so kind as to give him/her/my answer'.

Deferred command forms are employed when the desired action is not to be immediately carried out, but is to be deferred, postponed, or carried out subsequent to some other activity. The infinitive (i.e., the verbal stem plus the suffix –ना *–nā*) is used to indicate deferred commands:

दिल्ली जाकर शुक्लाजी से बात करना।
dillī jākar śuklājī se bāt karnā.
'Go to Delhi and speak to Mr. Shukla'.
यह काम कल दोपहर तक पूरा करना।
'Finish this work by tomorrow afternoon.'

Note that in the first of the above examples the subject's speaking to Mr. Shukla is not to take place until after his going to Delhi. In the second example the subject's completion of the work need not occur immediately, but can be deferred for as much as a day.

The infinitive may also on occasion be used to issue warnings or to make informal requests:

उस पानी को न पीना। *us pānī ko na pīnā.*
'Don't drink that water.'

एक और चपाती ले आना। *ak aur capātī le ānā.*
'Will you bring another capati.'

In the negative, the markers मत *mat* and न *na* are employed with various commands:

उस मैदान में मत खेलो। *us maidān mẽ mat khelo.*

'Don't play in that field'.

बच्चों की मदद न कीजिए। *baccõ kī madad na kījie.*

'Please don't help the children'.

Of these two markers, मत *mat* is considered the less polite. Thus the sentence वहाँ मत जाओ। *vohā̃ mat jāo* 'don't go there' is somewhat brusquer than वहाँ न जाओ। *vahā̃ na jāo*.

One of the most common means in Hindi for making requests is the use of subjunctive verb forms. These usages are taken up in 13.1.

12.2. USES OF -वाला *-vālā*

The ubiquitous suffix -वाला *-vālā* is employed in a number of different senses and functions. In combination with preceding words and phrases it can serve to form constructions having nominal, adjectival, or verbal sense.

One common use of -वाला *-vālā* is in constructions of the form noun plus -वाला *-vālā*. The noun element is frequently placed in its oblique form. This is particularly evident if the noun belongs to masculine class I. The entire construction is nominal in sense, and is used to refer to a person who in some way is associated with the entity indicated by the prior element. Thus from फल *phal* 'fruit' and कपड़ा *kapRā* 'cloth' can be formed फलवाला *phalvālā* 'fruitseller' and कपड़ेवाला *kapRevālā* 'clothseller'. Likewise, from दिल्ली *dillī* 'Delhi' can be formed the class I masculine noun दिल्लीवाला *dillivāla* 'man from Delhi' and the class I feminine noun दिल्लीवाली *dillīvālī* 'woman from Delhi'.

Expressions using -वाला *-vālā* are often used adjectivally to modify nouns of various sorts. The -वाला *-vālā* element is encountered adjoined to words and phrases of diverse kinds, e.g. लाल कुरतेवाली लड़की *lāl kurtevālī laRkī* 'the girl with the red kurta', बड़े कानोंवाला बच्चा *baRe kānõvālā baccā* 'the boy with big ears', and लाल क़िले के पास वाली इमारतें *lāl ķile ke pās vālī imāratẽ* 'the buildings near the Red Fort'.

Other common uses of -वाला *–vālā* occur in conjunction with a form of the infinitive in which the suffix -ना *-nā* has changed to -ने *-ne*. The construction often is used predicatively to indicate the imminence of a verbal activity :

पंकज और राजू जाने वाले हैं *pãkaj aur rājū jāne vāle hãi.*

'Pankaj and Raju are about to go'.

राहुल बोलने वाला था *rāhul bolne vālā thā.*

'Rahul was about to speak'.

In a version of this construction, the particle ही *hī* stands between the infinitive and the -वाला *–vālā* element, and the entire formation is followed by the conjunction कि *ki* 'when'. The sense of this sequence is that some verbal activity was just at the point of occurring when something else happened:

मैं खाने ही वाला था कि उसके मित्र मेरे यहाँ पहुँचे।

mãĩ khāne hī vālā thā ki uske mitra mere yahā̃ pahũce.

'I was just about to eat when his friends arrived at my place'.

The -ने *-ne* form of the infinitive plus -वाला *-vālā* also is used as a nominal substantive denoting an individual associated with the activity represented by the infinitive.

वसंत विहार में/का रहनेवाला · *vasãt vihār mẽ/kā rahnevālā*
'a/the person living in Vasant Vihar'
फ़ोन पर बोलने वाले *fon par bolne vāle*
'People speaking on the telephone'

12.3. Conjunctive (कर kar) Construction

The primary use in Hindi of conjunctive constructions is in the formation of sentences in which there are two verbal activities sharing the same subject, and in which one of the activities is treated as a temporal antecedent of the other. In the English sentence "John went home and went to sleep," two sentences, "John went home" and "John went to sleep," have been conjoined. These sentences share a common subject, John, and describe events understood as occurring in a specific sequence, i.e., John's going home precedes his going to sleep. The linking of these two sentences in English is accomplished by the use of the conjunction "and," the deletion of the subject of the temporally subsequent clause, and the arrangement of the two clauses in a particular sequence.

In Hindi, sentences analagous to the above English example are formed by means of conjunctive constructions. In this usage the verb of the temporally prior clause appears in its stem form and is immediately followed by the element कर *kar*. The verb of the temporally subsequent clause receives the conjugation for the entire sentence. Thus in order to express the sense of the English "Father reached the city and bought some fruit in the market" Hindi uses the sentence

पिताजी ने शहर पहुँच कर बाज़ार में कुछ फल ख़रीदे।
pitājī ne śahār pahũc kar bāzār mẽ kuch phaḷ kharīde.

The subject phrase (पिताजी ने *pitājī ne*) in the above example appears only once. It may appear at the beginning of the entire sentence (as above) or at the beginning of the subsequent clause :

शहर पहुंच कर पिताजी ने बाजार में कुछ फल ख़रीदे।
śahar pahũc kar pitājī ne bāzār mẽ kuch phal kharīde.

With the verb करना *karnā* 'to do', either by itself or in compounds (e.g., मदद करना *madad karnā* 'to help'), the form के *ke* is used in place of कर *kar*.

घर में काम करके वह दफ़्तर गया।
ghar mẽ kām karke vah daftar gayā.

'He finished his work in the house and went to the office'.

In colloquial Hindi the form के *ke* is often used in place of कर *kar* in the conjunctive constructions (as in जा के *jā ke*, बेच के *bac ke*, etc.). This usage is to be avoided, however, in the standard written language.

On occasion, the verbal stem by itself appears in the place of the stem plus कर *kar*:

उसे पैसे दे (कर) आओ। *use paise de (kar) āo.*
'Give him/her the money and come'.

Often clauses appearing in their conjunctive forms take on adverbial sense :

वह हँस कर बोला *vah hā̃s kar bolā...*
'He said happily...'
कृपा करके उससे कहिए...' *kṛpā karke usse kahie...*
'Kindly tell him...'
वे दौड़ कर पहुँचे *ve dauR kar pahũce.*
'They arrived running'.

Some conjunctive locutions are highly idiosyncratic and should be considered fixed expressions. Examples of these include the following :

विशेष कर *viśeṣ kar* or खास कर *khās kar* 'especially'
एक-एक करके *ek ek karke* 'one by one'
X (से) हो कर *X (se) ho kar* 'via X' (e.g., बंबई (से) होकर *bābaī (se) hokar* 'via Bombay')

In the negative, न *na* is used with conjunctive forms :

आप किसी से बात न करके यहाँ आइए।
āp kisīse bāt na karke yahā̃ āie.
'Please come here without speaking to anyone'.

12.4. THE CONJUNCTION कि KI

The conjunction कि *ki* (pronounced [*ki*] or [*ke*]) is used to introduce a wide veriety of dependent clauses. Some important usages of this conjunction include the following :

1. to introduce the objects of verbs of thinking, speaking, hearing, knowing, etc.

वह {सोचता है / कहता है / सुनता है / जानता है} कि... *vah {soctā hai / kahtā hai / suntā hai / jāntā hai} ki...*

'He thinks/says/hears/knows that...'

2. as a substitute for the conjunction या *yā* 'or'

मैं नहीं जानता कि वह आया कि नहीं।
mā̃ī nahī̃ jāntā ki vah āyā ki nahī̃.
'I don't know if he came or not'.

3. as a substitute for जब *jab* (v., 22.1)

मैं जाने ही वाला था कि वह मेरे पास आई।
mā̃ī jāne hī vālā thā ki vah mere pās āī.
'I was just about to go when she came to me'.

Often the कि *ki* element appears merged together with other material in the formation of subordinating conjunctions (e.g., क्योंकि *kyõki* 'because', इसलिए कि *islie ki* 'because', हालाँकि *hālā̃ki* 'even though'). Subordinating conjunctions are taken up in greater detail in 23.1.

12.5. VOCABULARY

आंख	*ā̃kh*	n.f. eye	ऐसा	*aisā*	adj. of this kind/sort
उत्तर	*uttar*	n.m. answer, reply	कम	*kam*	adj. few, little; adv. on few occasions, seldom
कान	*kān*	n.m. ear	पिछला	*pichlā*	adj. last, previous
कानपुर	*kānpur*	prop. m. Kanpur (a city in Uttar Pradesh)	वैसा	*vaisā*	adj. of that kind/sort
काम	*kām*	n.m. work, task	काम करना	*kām karnā*	v.t. to work
घी	*ghī*	n.m. clarified butter	चलना	*calnā*	v.i. to go, move, progress
तरह	*tarah*	n.f. manner, way, kind, sort	दौड़ना	*dauRnā*	v.i. to run
दफ़्तर	*daftar*	n.m. office	X से पूछना	*X se pūchnā*	v.t. to ask X
दही	*dahī*	n.m. yoghurt	X की प्रतीक्षा करना	*X kī pratīkṣā karnā*	v.t. to wait for X
दादा	*dādā*	n.m.II. paternal grandfather	बनना	*bannā*	v.i. to be/get made
दादी	*dādī*	n.f. paternal grandmother	रखना	*rakhnā*	v.t. to place, put keep, store
नाक	*nāk*	n.f. nose	X की सेवा करना	*kī sevā karnā*	v.t. to serve X
नाना	*nānā*	n.m.II. maternal grandfather	ऐसे	*aise*	adv. in this manner
नानी	*nānī*	n.f. maternal grandmother	न	*na*	adv. neg. no, not
पता	*patā*	n.m. address, information	मत	*mat*	adv. neg. no, not
परिवार	*parivār*	n.m. family	यहीं	*yahī̃*	adv. right here, at this very place [=यहाँ *yahā̃*+ही *hī*]
पहाड़	*pahāR*	n.m. mountain, mountain range	वहीं	*vahī̃*	adv. right there, at that very place [=वहाँ *vahā̃*+ही *hī*]
प्रश्न	*praśn*	n.m. question	वैसे	*vaise*	adv. in that manner
भजन	*bhajan*	n.m. devotional hymn	X के पास	*X ke pās*	post. near X, in X's possession
मुंह	*mũh*	n.m. mouth	कि	*ki*	conj. that, or if (often pronounced *ke*)
रंग	*rãg*	n.m. color	कितने बजे	*kitne baje*	inter. when ? (=at what time ?)
शरीर	*śarīr*	n.m. body	कैसे	*kaise*	inter. how? in what manner?
सिर	*sir*	n.m. head			
सेवा	*sevā*	n.f. service, aid			
स्त्री	*strī*	n.f. woman			
हाथ	*hāth*	n.m. hand			
अगला	*aglā*	adj. next, coming			
इतना	*itnā*	adj. this much, this many			
उतना	*utnā*	adj. that much, that many			

12.6. EXERCISES

12.6.1. *Translate into English.*

1. तू पूछ *tū pūch*, तू रख *tū rakh*, तू काम कर *tū kām kar*, तू गा *tū gā*; 2. तुम प्रतीक्षा करो *tum pratīkṣā karo*, तुम दो *tum do*, तुम दौड़ो *tum dauRo*, तुम पढ़ो *tum paRho*; 3. आप लीजिए *āp lījie*,

आप नाचिए *āp nācie*, आप बोलिए *āp bolie*, आप कीजिए *āp kijie*; 4. आप जाइएगा *āp jāiegā*, आप दीजिएगा *āp dījiegā*, आप धोइएगा *āp dhoiegā*; 5. मत बोलो *mat bolo*, न चलना *na calnā*, न समझिए *na samajhie*; 6. मोची के पास *mocī ke pās*, मेरे दफ़्तर के पास *mere daftar ke pās*, दादीजी के पास *dādījī ke pās*; 7. फलवाला *phalvālā*, कपड़ेवाला *kapRevālā*, मिठाईवाला *miṭhāīvālā*, दिल्लीवालियां *dillīvāliyā̃*; 8. लाल कुरतेवाला आदमी *lāl kurtevālā ādmī*, बड़ी नाकवाली लड़की *baRī nākvālī laRkī*, सौ रूपयेवाली साड़ी *sau rupayevālī sāRī*; 9. मैं जानेवाला हूं *mãī jānevālā hū̃*, वह भागनेवाली थी *vah bhāgnevālī thī*, वे उठनेवाले होंगे *ve uṭhnevāle hõge*; 10. ऐसी औरतें *aisī auratẽ*, ऐसे स्कूलों में *aise skūlõ mẽ*, वैसा मौसम *vaisā mausam*, वैसे बाज़ारों में *vaise bāzārõ mẽ*.

12.6.2. *Translate into Hindi.* Use intimate command forms in no.1. familiar in no.2, polite in no.3, and deferential in no.4. Use various forms of वाला *vāla* in numbers 7,8, and 9.

1. Wait!, sew!, write!, eat!; 2. you take!, you bring!, you drink!, you say!; 3. please come, please sell, please remove, please wear; 4. please be so kind as to go, please be so kind as to sing, please be so kind as to write; 5. don't go!, don't buy!, please don't get up, please be so kind as not to drink; 6. near the city, near those stores, in Mr. Sharma's possession; 7. the flower sellers, the fruit seller, the women of Varanasi, with the man from Lucknow; 8. the man with the red shirt. the woman writing a letter, in the market with many stores; 9. you (int., m.) were about to arrive, they (f.) are about to sing, the girls must be about to dance; 10. this kind of friend, in that kind of food, near cities of this kind, on books of that kind.

12.6.3. *Translate into English.*

1. बाज़ार जाकर उन्होंने बच्चों के लिए ताजी मिठाइयाँ खरीदीं। *bāzār jākar unhõne baccõ ke liye tāzī miṭhāiyā̃ kharīdī*. 2. दिल्ली जाकर आप किन लोगों के यहाँ ठहरे ? *dillī jākar āp kin logõ ke yahā̃ ṭhahare*. 3. माताजी की मदद करके सब बच्चे बाहर खेलने (के लिए) गए। *mātājī kī madad karke sab bacce bāhar khelne [ke lie] gae*. 4. दरवाज़ा बंद करके किसी से मत बोलो। *darvāzā bãd karke kisī se mat bolo*. 5. तुम परसों तक घर न आना। *tum parsõ tak ghar na ānā*. 6. माताजी खाना पकाने ही वाली थीं कि पिताजी दफ़्तर से घर आए। *mātājī khānā pakāne hī vālī thī ki pitājī daftar se ghar āe*. 7. वाजपेयीजी, कल दोपहर को हमारे यहाँ आइएगा। *vājpeyījī, kal dopahar ko hamāre yahā̃ āiegā*. 8. उनके परिवार में माता-पिता, दादा-दादी, और सात बच्चे भी हैं। *unke parivār mẽ mātā-pitā, dādā-dādī, aur sāt bacce bhī hãī*. 9. आप उनके प्रश्नों के उत्तर क्यों नहीं देते ? *āp unke praśnõ ke uttar kyõ nahī̃ dete*? 10. तुम इस तरह के भजन यहां मत गाओ। *tum is tarah ke bhajan yahā̃ mat gāo*. 11. खाने के साथ वह दही और घी खाता था। *khāne ke sāth vah dahī aur ghī khātā thā*. 12. दुकान जाकर उसने पाँच सौ रुपये दुकानदार के सामने रखे। *dukān jākar usne pā̃c sau rupaye dukāndār ke sāmne rakhe*.

12.6.4. *Translate into Hindi.*

1. He went into the garden and planted the flowers. 2. My sister gets up in the morning and goes to school. 3. She goes to the city everyday and buys food. 4. Please go to Mr. Sharma's house and bring some good cloth. 5. Please be so kind as to sing those beautiful Panjabi songs. 6. I was just about to buy the book when the shopkeeper gave me a different (i.e., second) book. 7. In his hands there were some mangos and oranges. 8. The (maternal) grandfather and grandmother don't live near the old city now. 9. Very beautiful clothes are made in villages of this sort. 10. All of her friends were running in the green fields. 11. Don't give that old man any more money! 12. I very seldom go to the office in the afternoon.

CHAPTER 13

13.1. THE SUBJUNCTIVE

Subjunctive forms can be constituted in Hindi by the addition of certain suffixes directly after the verbal stem. These suffixes are -ऊँ– ū̃ in the first person singular, -ए –e in the second and third persons singular, –ओ -o in the second person plural familiar, and -एं -ẽ in the first and third persons plural and in the second person plural polite. Thus from आना ānā 'to come' and कहना kahnā 'to say' can be formed the following subjunctive forms :

1. sg.	मैं mãi	आऊँ āū̃	कहूँ kahū̃		1. pl.	हम ham	आएँ āẽ	कहें kahẽ
2. sg.	तू tū				2. pl.fam.	तुम tum	आओ āo	कहो kaho
3. sg.	यह yah	आए āe	कहे kahe		pol.	आप āp		
	वह vah				3. pl.	ये ye	आएँ āẽ	कहें kahẽ
						वे ve		

In the subjunctive होना honā 'to be', लेना lenā 'to take', and देना denā 'to give' show the following irregular forms :

			होना honā	लेना lenā	देना denā
	मैं	mãi	होऊँ hoū̃ (or हूँ hū̃)	लूँ lū̃	दूँ dū̃
	तू	tū			
Sing.	यह	yah	हो ho	ले le	दे de
	वह	vah			
	हम	ham	हों hõ	लें lẽ	दें dẽ
Plural	तुम	tum	हो ho	लो lo	दो do
	आप	āp			
	ये	ye	हों hõ	लें lẽ	दें dẽ
	वे	ve			

Stems ending in -ई –ī and -ऊ –ū shorten these vowels to -इ –i and -उ –u before the various vowel endings of the subjunctive (e.g., पिऊँ piū̃, पिए pie, etc. from पीना pīnā 'to drink/smoke'; छुऊँ chuū̃, छुए chue, etc. from छूना chūnā 'to touch'). Occasionally, the endings -य -y and -यं -yẽ are seen in written Hindi instead of -ए -e and -एं -ẽ (e.g. जाय jāy and जायं jāyẽ for जाए jāe and जाएं jāẽ). In addition, the element –व– -v- is at times inserted between a stem final vowel and the subjunctive endings -ए -e and -एं -ẽ (e.g., आवे āve and आवें āvẽ for आए āe and आएं āẽ). All of these usages are, however, considered archaic or dialectal and are avoided in the standard written language.

The primary function of the subjunctive is to represent activities or states of affairs as hypothetical, imaginary, desired, contingent, or speculative, but not directly asserted to take place. Examples of such usages are given below :

मैं चाहती हूँ कि हम उसके साथ जाएं। *mãĩ cāhti hũ̄ ki ham uske sāth jāẽ.*
'I want us to go with him/her'.

हो सकता है कि वे हम पर आक्रमण करें। *ho saktā hai ki ve hampar ākramaṇ karẽ*
'It's possible that they will attack us'.

यह संभव है कि वह दूसरी कक्षा में पढ़े। *yah sãbhav hai ki vah dūsrī kakṣā mẽ paRhe.*
'It's possible that he/she will study in the second grade'.

मेरी इच्छा है कि आप उसकी पुस्तक पढ़ें। *meri icchā hai ki āp uskī pustak paRhẽ.*
'I want you to read his/her book'. (literally/'my wish is that you might read his/her book').

Subjunctive verb forms are particularly common in 'if... then' constructions:
यदि/अगर तुम मेरी मदद करो तो मैं तुमको अपना मित्र समझूंगा।
yadi/agar tum merī madad karo to mãĩ tumko apnā mitra samajhũgā.
'If you help me I will consider you my friend'.

The use of the subjunctive is correlated in Hindi with the presence of certain words, phrases, or constructions. For instance, the conjunctions जैसे *jaise* 'as if' and मानों *mānõ* 'as if' tend to be followed by clauses showing subjunctive verb forms:

वह बोलता है जैसे/मानों उसके शत्रु इसी शहर में हों। *vah boltā hai jaise/mānõ uske śatru isī śahar mẽ hõ.*
'He speaks as if his enemies were in this very city'.

The conjunction कहीं...न *kahī̃...na* 'lest' similarly occurs in conjunction with subjunctive verb forms:[1]

देखना कहीं तुम भी एक दिन बीमार न हो जाओ।
dekhnā kahī̃ tum bhī ek din bīmār na ho jāo.
'Watch out lest you fall sick yourself some day'.

The subjunctive is also commonly employed in Hindi in order to make requests and exhortations of various kinds :

चलें। *calẽ.* 'Let's go'.
कुछ काफ़ी पिएँ। *kuch kāfī piẽ* ? 'Would you like some coffee?'

Another important use of the subjunctive is in indicating the obligation or necessity to do something. Thus usage is exceedingly common in questions :

मैं क्या करूँ ? *mãĩ kyā karũ*? 'What should I do?'
वह कब आए ? *vah kab āe*? 'When should he/she come ?'
हम क्या कहें ? *ham kyā kahẽ*? 'What should/can we say ?'

1. The marker न *na* (rather than नहीं *nahī̃*) is used in expressing the negative in virtually all subjunctive expressions.

The subjunctive is also to be found in statements of congratulations and greeting, as well as in formulaic expressions of different kinds :

(आपको) नये वर्ष की बधाई हो। (*āpko*) *naye varṣ kī badhāī ho* !
'Happy New Year (to you) ! [cf. बधाई *badhāī* n.f. greeting]

भारत की जय हो। *bhārat kī jay ho*!
'Victory to India !' [cf. जय *jay* n.f. victory]

As was mentioned in earlier chapters (8.1, 8.2, 9.1, 10.1, 11.1), the subjunctive forms of the copula होना *honā* are employed together with other suffixes or auxiliaries in forming subjunctive-habitual, subjunctive-progressive, and subjunctive-perfective aspectual tense. Illustrations of the use of these constructions are given below.

Subjunctive-Habitual:

हो सकता है कि वह बंगाली समझती हो। *ho saktā hai ki vah bãgālī samajhtī ho.*
'It is possible that she understands Bengali'.

ऐसा लगता है कि वह किसी बड़े शहर में रहता हो।
aisā lagtā hai ki vah kisī baRe śahar mẽ rahtā ho.
'It seems that he lives in some large city or other'.

Subjunctive-Progressive:

अगर वह खेत में काम कर रहा हो तो उससे मत बोलो।
agar vah khet mẽ kām kar rahā ho to usse mat bolo.
'Don't speak to him if he is working in the field'.

Subjunctive-Perfective:

संभव है कि वह अभी पटना से पहुंचा हो।
sãbhav hai ki vah abhī paṭnā se pahũcā ho.
'It is possible that he has just arrived from Patna'.

In the first two of the above examples the verbs refer to general or characteristic activities and so are placed in the habitual aspect. Because these activities are only possible and apparent, as opposed to actual or definite, subjunctive forms of the copula होना *honā* are employed. In the third example the activity of working is conceptualized as both in progress and hypothetical, hence the subjunctive-progressive is used. In the last example the action of arriving is viewed as complete, but only in a hypothetical or possible world. In this example the use of the subjunctive, as opposed to present, past, or presumptive, perfective has been dictated by the presence of the phrase संभव है कि... *sãbhav hai ki....*

13.2. The Future

Future verb forms in Hindi are identical to subjunctive forms, but with the addition of the suffix –गा/–गे/–गी *-gā/-ge/-gī*. The choice among the alternates of this suffix is determined by the number and gender of the subject (i.e., –आ *–ā* with m.s. subjects, –ए *-e* with m. pl., and –ई *-ī* with feminine, whether s. or pl.). Thus from आना *ānā* 'to come' and कहना *kahnā* 'to say' can be formed the following paradigms:

		Masculine	Feminine
Singular	मैं *mãī*	आऊंगा *āũgā* कहूंगा *kahũgā*	आऊंगी *āũgī* कहूंगी *kahũgī*
	तू *tū* / यह *yah* / वह *vah*	आएगा *āegā* कहेगा *kahegā*	आएगी *āegī* कहेगी *kahegī*

		Masculine		*Feminine*	
	हम *ham*	आएंगे *ā̃ẽge*	कहेंगे *kahẽge*	आएंगी *ā̃ẽgī*	कहेंगी *kahẽgī*
	तुम *tum*	आओगे *āoge*	कहोगे *kahoge*	आओगी *āogī*	कहोगी *kahogī*
Plural	आप *āp* ये *ye* वे *ve*	आएंगे *ā̃ẽge*	कहेंगे *kahẽge*	आएंगी *ā̃ẽgī*	कहेंगी *kahẽgī*

Examples of the use of future verb forms are as follows:

कल मैं आपके साथ दिल्ली जाऊंगा । *kal mā̃ī āpke sāth dillī jāū̃gā.*
'I will go to Delhi with you tomorrow'.

वहाँ हम दो-तीन कुरते ख़रीदेंगे । *vahā̃ ham do-tīn kurte k̲harīdẽge.*
'We will buy two or three kurtas there'.

अगर तुम उसके घर जाओ (जाओगे) तो हम भी तुम्हारे साथ जाएंगे ।
agar tum uske ghar jāo (or *jāoge*) *to ham bhī tumhāre sāth jā̃ẽge.*
'If you go to his/her house then I'll go with you'.

The futures of होना *honā* 'to be', लेना *lenā* 'to take', and देना *denā* 'to give' are based on the irregular subjunctives of these verbs (i.e., होऊंगा *hoū̃gā* [or हूंगा *hū̃gā*], होगा *hogā*, etc.; दूंगा *dū̃gā*, देगा *degā*, etc.; लूंगा *lū̃gā*, लेगा *legā*, etc.).

13.3. The Reflexive Possessive Form अपना *apnā*

The reflexive form अपना *apnā* is used in place of other possessive constructions (i.e., those showing का/के/की *kā/ke/kī*) when the "possessor" in the possessive phrase refers to the same person or entity as another noun in the clause. The word अपना *apnā* functions adjectivally, and agrees with the noun it modifies in number, gender, and case. Illustrations of these usages are given below:

उन्होंने अपने घरों को छोड़ दिया । *unhõne apne gharõ ko choR diyā.*
'They deserted their own homes'.

हम अपनी सहेलियों से बात करेंगी । *ham apnī saheliyõ se bāt karẽgī.*
'We will speak with our own friends'.

राजा ने अपने शत्रुओं पर आक्रमण किया । *rājā ne apne śatruõ par ākramaṇ kiyā.*
'The king attacked his own enemies.

Bear in mind that the two instances of the same nominal entity must occur in the same clause for अपना *apnā* to be employed. Thus in the sentence

मैंने कहा कि मेरा भाई (not अपना भाई) अब बिहार में रहता है ।
mā̃īne kahā ki merā bhāī (not *apnā bhāī*) *ab bihār mẽ rahtā hai.*
'I said that my brother lives in Bihar now'.

the possessive form मेरा *merā* is used instead of अपना *apnā* because the two references to मैं *mā̃ī* occur in different clauses (i.e., as the subject of the main clause and as the "possessor" of *brother* in the dependent clause). अपना *apnā* is likewise not used if the two instances of the noun are in coordinate elements of the same syntactic component of a sentence:

सीता और उसकी (not अपनी) बहनें दादीजी की मदद करेंगी।
sītā aur uskī bahanẽ (not *apnī bahanẽ*) *dādijī kī madad karẽgī.*
'Sita and her sisters will help Grandmother'.

सीता अपनी बहनों की मदद करेगी।
sītā apnī bahanõ kī madad karegī.
'Sita will help her sisters'.

Notice that in the first of the two above examples सीता *sītā* and उसकी बहनें *uskī bahanẽ* are coordinate subjects, but in the second सीता *sītā* is the subject of the clause while sisters constitute the object of the activity of helping.

A number of other uses of अपना *apnā* are to be found in Hindi. It is used intensively after other possessive forms:

यह मेरी अपनी पुस्तक है। *yah merī apnī pustak hai.*
'This is my very own book'.

यह आपकी अपनी दुकान है। *yah āpkī apnī dukān hai*
'This is your very own store'.

It is also used in sentences in which there is ellipsis of one of the instances of the repeated noun or pronoun :

अपना काम स्वयं करो। *apnā kām svayā̃ karo.*
'Do your own work' (with ellipsis of तुम *tum*). [स्वयं *svayā̃* adv. refl. 'by oneself']

13.4. MULTIPLICATIVES

The declinable adjectival suffix -गुना *-gunā* is used after the cardinal numbers to indicate a given number multiple of some entity: e.g., दसगुना कपड़ा *dasgunā kapRā* 'ten times as much cloth', बीसगुने पैसे *bīsgune paise* 'twenty times as much money', दसगुनी स्त्रियों से *dasgunī striyõ se* 'from ten times as many women'. The following multiplicative forms for small integers are irregular:

दुगुना	*dugunā*	'twice as much/many'
दुगना	*duganā*	
दूना	*dūnā*	
तिगुना	*tigunā*	'three time as much/many'
चौगुना	*caugunā*	'four times as much/many'
पचगुना	*pacgunā*	'five times as much/many'
सतगुना	*satgunā*	'seven times as much/many'
अठगुना	*aṭhgunā*	'eight times as much/many'

13.5. THE SUFFIX-हरा *-harā*

The declinable adjectival suffix -हरा *-harā* is used to indicate that some entity has a multi-layered or multi-leveled nature: e.g., दसहरा पुरस्कार *dasaharā puraskār* ten-fold reward',

तिहरे आक्रमण में *tihare ākramaṇ mẽ* 'in the three-fold (i.e., three-pronged) attack'. The following irregular forms using हरा- *harā* are to be noted.

इकहरा / एकहरा	*ikharā* / *ekharā*	'single-fold, thin'
दुहरा / दोहरा	*duharā* / *doharā*	'double, two-fold, thick'
तिहरा	*tiharā*	'three-fold'
चौहरा	*cauharā*	'four-fold'
पचहरा	*pacharā*	'five-fold'

13.6. THE SUFFIXES -ओं -õ AND -इयों -iyõ

The suffix -ओं -õ is used with some cardinals in the sense of 'all two, both', 'all three', 'all four', etc. Thus from तीन *tīn*, चार *cār*, and दस *das* can be formed तीनों *tīnõ* 'all three', चारों *cārõ* 'all four', दसों *dasõ* 'all ten', etc. The irregular form दोनों *donõ* 'both' is extremely common throughout the language.

The same suffix is also used to indicate an indefinite quantity of some number or unit of measure: हज़ारों *hazārõ* 'thousands', लाखों *lākhõ* 'lakhs', दरजनों *darjanõ* 'dozens', महीनों *mahīnõ* 'months', दिनों *dinõ* 'days'. The form सैकड़ों *sãikaRõ* is used to indicate the concept 'hundreds'.

With a few numbers –इयों –*iyõ* is used in place of -ओं -õ to indicate an indefinite quantity of the number: e.g., बीसियों वर्ष *bīsiyõ varṣ* 'scores of years', दसियों लोग *dasiyõ log* 'several tens of people'. Note that whereas बीसों *bīsõ* is to be translated as 'all twenty', बीसियों *bīsiyõ* indicates several twenties, i.e., scores.

13.7. INDEFINITE NUMBERS

There are a number of means in Hindi for expressing; indefinite or approximate numbers.

1. The independent words लगभग *lagbhag*, क़रीब *karīb* or कोई *koī* can be used immediately before a cardinal number:

{लगभग / क़रीब / कोई} पंद्रह लोग आए । {*lagbhag* / *karīb* / *koī*} *pãdrah log āe.*

'Approximately fifteen people came'.

2. The number एक *ek* can be appended as a suffix immediately after another cardinal number: दस-एक लड़के *das-ek laRke* 'ten or so boys'; दो-एक पेंसिलें *do-ek pensilẽ* 'one or two pencils, a very few pencils'.

3. Two numbers can be compounded without any intervening connecting word: आठ-दस दिन *āṭh-das din* 'eight or ten days, approximately eight to ten days'.

13.8. FRACTIONS

There are diverse means in Hindi for denoting different fractions. These include single words that designate specific numerical ratios and a number of longer grammatical constructions. Single Hindi words for specific fractions include the following :

आध/आधा *ādh/ādhā* '$\frac{1}{2}$' (e.g., आध/आधा घंटा *ādh/ādhā ghãṭā* 'half hour')
चौथाई *cauthāī* '$\frac{1}{4}$' (eg., एक चौथाई दाल *ek cauthāī dāl* 'a quarter of the lentils')
तिहाई *tihāī* '$\frac{1}{3}$' (e.g., एक तिहाई दाल *ek tihaī dāl* 'a third of the lentils')
पौन/पौना *paun/paunā* '$\frac{3}{4}$' (e.g., पौन/पौना घंटा *paun/paunā ghãṭā* 'three quarters of an hour')
सवा *savā* '$1\frac{1}{4}$' (e.g., सवा घंटे *savā ghãṭe* $1\frac{1}{4}$ hours')
डेढ़ *ḍeRh* '$1\frac{1}{2}$' (e.g. डेढ़ घंटे *ḍeRh ghãṭe* '$1\frac{1}{2}$' hours')
ढाई *ḍhāī* '$2\frac{1}{2}$' (e g. ढाई घंटे *ḍhāī ghãṭe* '$2\frac{1}{2}$' hours')

Some of the above words join in combination with other words to form yet other fractions :

सवा *savā* plus a number indicates a quarter unit more than the number: e.g., सवा दो *savā do* '$2\frac{1}{4}$', सवा चार लाख *savā cār lākh*, 425,000';

पौने *paune* plus a number indicates a quarter unit less than the number: e.g., पौने चार *paune cār* '3 3/4', पौने छः घंटे *paune chaḥ ghãṭe* '5 3/4 hours'.

The word साढ़े *saRhe* followed by a number indicates a half unit more than the number : e.g., साढ़े तीन घंटे *saRhe tīn ghãṭe* '$3\frac{1}{2}$ hours', साढ़े ग्यारह *sāRhe gyārah* '$11\frac{1}{2}$'. N.B. डेढ़ *deRh* and ढाई *dhāī* are used to express the specific numbers $1\frac{1}{2}$ and $2\frac{1}{2}$. साढ़े *saRhe* is used only for $3\frac{1}{2}$, $4\frac{1}{2}$ and beyond.

It is quite common to use the word बटा *baṭā* 'over, divided by' in expressing numerical ratios : e.g., तीन बटा चार *tīn baṭā cār* '3/4'. It is also possible to use ordinal numbers in conjunction with the words हिस्सा *hissā* 'part, share, portion' or भाग *bhāg* 'part, share, portion' for the same purpose :

दो पांचवें भाग *do pā̃cvẽ bhāg* '2/5' (literally 'two fifth portions')
आठ नौवें हिस्से *āṭh nauvẽ hisse* '8/9'.

Larger mixed numbers can be formed with the use of the word सही *sahī* (literally 'correct, whole, complete' :

नौ सही चार बटा पांच *nau sahī cār baṭā pā̃c* '9 4/5'.

13.9. Vocabulary

अवसर	*avsar*	n.m. occasion, opportunity
इच्छा	*icchā*	n.f. wish, desire
कक्षा	*kakṣā*	n.f. grade, class
किसान	*kisān*	n.m. farmer
गंगा	*gãgā*	prop. f. the river Ganges
देश	*deś*	n.m. country, nation
प्रदेश	*prades*	n.m. state, province
बदन	*badan*	n.m. body
बर्फ़	*barf*	n.f. snow, ice
बारिश	*bāriś*	n.f. rain
बीज	*bīj*	n.m. seed
यमुना	*yamunā*	pro p.f. the river Jamuna
युद्ध	*yuddh*	n.m. war
राजा	*rājā*	n.m.II. king
शत्रु	*śatru*	n.m. enemy
समुद्र	*samudra*	n.m. ocean
सैनिक	*sainik*	n.m. soldier
अपना	*apnā*	adj. refl. one's own
उचित	*ucit*	adj. proper, correct
निश्चित	*niścit*	adj. definite
प्रसन्न	*prasann*	adj. happy
बीमार	*bīmār*	adj. sick
संभव	*sãbhav*	adj. possible
(X पर) आक्रमण करना	*(X par) ākramaṇ karnā*	v.t. to attack X
चाहना	*cāhnā*	v.t. to want, desire
छोड़ना	*choRnā*	v.t. to give up, abandon, renounce
पड़ना	*paRnā*	v.i. to lie, full
बर्फ़ गिरना	*barf girnā*	v.i. to snow
बारिश होना	*bāriś honā*	v.i. to rain
बीमार पड़ जाना	*bīmār paR jānā*	v.i. to fall sick
बोना	*bonā*	v.t. to sow (seeds)
मरना	*marnā*	v.i. to die
अवश्य	*avaśya*	adv. certainly
ज़रूर	*zarūr*	adv. certainly
सचमुच	*sacmuc*	adv. truly
X के किनारे (पर)	*X ke kināre (par)*	post. on the banks of X, by the side of X
X के भीतर	*X ke bhītar*	post. inside X
अगर...तो	*agar...to*	conj. if...then
कहीं...न	*kahī...na*	conj. lest
जैसे	*jaise*	conj. as if
मानों (also मानो)	*mānõ (also māno)*	conj. as if
यदि...तो	*yadi...to*	conj. if...then
ऐसा लगता है कि...	*(aisā lagtā hai ki...*	it seems that...
हो सकता है कि...	*ho saktā hai ki ...*	it is possible that...

13.10. Exercises

13.10.1. *Translate into English.*

1. (हम) चलें *(ham) calẽ*, (मैं) ख़रीदूं *(mãī kharīdũ*, (आप) देखें *(āp) dekhẽ*, (तू) दे *(tū) de*; 2. वह जाएगा *vah jāegā*, तुम दोगे *tum doge*, वे लेंगी *ve lẽgī*, हम छोड़ेंगे *hum choRẽge*, मैं चाहूंगा *mãī cāhũgā*; 3. वह क्या कहे ? *vah kyā kahe*? हम कब आएं ? *ham kab āẽ*? मैं क्या करूँ *mãī kyā karũ* ? वे क्या खाएं ? *ve kyā khāẽ* ? 4. वे आक्रमण करेंगे *ve ākramaṇ karẽge*, बर्फ़ गिरेगी *barf giregī*, लड़की मदद करेगी *laRkī madad karegī*, बच्चे बीमार पड़ जाएंगे *bacce bīmār paR jāẽge*; 5. दुगुना काम *dugunā kām*, चौगुने पैसे *caugune paise*, बीसगुना खाना *bīsgunā khānā*, तिगुनी स्त्रियों से *tigunī striyõ se*; 6. दुहरे काग़ज़ पर *duhare kāgaz par* इकहरे कपड़े में *ikahare kapRe mẽ*, इकहरे बदन पर *ikahare badan par*; 7. दोनों लड़कियां *donõ laRakiyā̃*, पांचों शहरों से *pācõ śaharõ se*, उसके तीनों कुत्तों को *uske tīnõ kūttõ ko*, दसों सैनिकों के साथ *dasõ sainikõ ke sāth*; 8. बीसियों वर्षों के बाद *bīsiyõ varṣõ ke bād*, हज़ारों लोग *hazārõ log*, लाखों रुपये

lākhõ rupaye, सैंकड़ों बच्चे *sãikaRõ bacce;* 9. पौने चार *paune cār*, सवा दस *savā das*, साढ़े आठ *sāRhe āṭh*, ढाई *ḍhaī*, दो तिहाई *do tihāī*; 10. पौने चार घंटे तक *paune cār ghãṭe tak*, सवा तीन हफ़्ते *savā tīn hafte*, डेढ़ सौ रुपये *ḍeRh sau rupaye*.

13.10.2. *Translate into Hindi.*

Use subjunctive verb forms in numbers 1 and 2 and future verb forms in 3 and 4. Forms containing the suffix -हरा *-harā* should be employed in number 6.

1. he should sell, we should eat, they should take, you (fam.) should renounce; 2. what should I say? what should she do? why should they go? where should we live?; 3. it will rain, she will want, they will attack, you (int.) will die; 4. he will fall sick, we (f.) will give, you (int.m.) will give, I (f.) will take; 5. four times as many apples, triple the rupees, twice as many children, from the triple work; 6. two-fold work, on the single-fold paper; 7. both cobblers, all three answers, all eight of my childern, on all seven occasions; 8. lakhs of rupees, his hundreds of friends, for scores of years (use तक tak), dozens of oranges; 9. one and a quarter, one quarter, nine and three fourths, two hundred and fifty, four and a half, six and a quarter; 10. after three and a half weeks, two hundred and fifty thousand years, for those three hundred and fifty people, five and three quarters hours.

13.10.3. *Translate into English.*

1. ऐसे युद्ध में हमारे शत्रु हमपर आक्रमण अवश्य करेंगे। *aise yuddh mẽ hamāre śatru hampar ākramaṇ avaśya karẽge* 2. गांव के सब किसान परसों तक खेतों में बीज बोएंगे। *gãv ke sab kisān parsõ tak khetõ mẽ bīj boẽge*. 3. उसकी छोटी लड़की कमलेश अगले वर्ष पहली कक्षा में पढ़ेगी। *uskī choṭī laRkī kamleś agle varṣ pahlī kakṣā mẽ paRhegī*. 4. उसी अवसर पर राजा अपने सैनिकों को सब कुछ देंगे। *usī avsar par rājā apne sainikõ ko sab kuch dẽge*. 5. हो सकता है कि (मैं) परसों अपने बच्चों के साथ लखनऊ जाऊं। *ho saktā hai ki mãĩ parsõ apne baccõ ke sāth lakhnaū̃ jāū̃*. 6. अपना देश छोड़कर वह यहां आएगा। *apnā deś choRkar vah yahā̃ āegā*. 7. मैं चाहती हूं कि आप सचमुच ख़ुश हों। *mãĩ cāhtī hū̃ ki āp sacmuc khuś hõ*. 8. यह उचित है कि हम माता-पिता की सेवा करें। *yah ucit hai ki ham mātā-pitā kī sevā karẽ*. 9. उसने गरम कपड़े पहने कहीं वह बीमार न पड़ जाए। *us ne garam kapRe pahane kahĩ vah bīmār na paR jāe*. 10. यदि आप मेरे साथ वहां चलें तो मैं बहुत प्रसन्न हो जाऊंगा। *yadi āp mere sāth vahā̃ calẽ to mãĩ bahut prasann ho jaū̃gā*. 11. हो सकता है कि वे अब तक वाराणसी पहुंचे हों। *ho saktā hai ki ve ab tak vārāṇasī pahū̃ce hõ*. 12. आगरा यमुना नदी के किनारे (पर) है। *āgrā yamunā nadī ke kināre (par) hai*.

13.10.4. *Translate into Hindi.*

1. Many people will die in that war. 2. Their friends will definitely come. 3. How many people from that province will come to Delhi ? 4. We will give the books to our students. 5. It is certain that it will rain tomorrow. 6. I want you (fam.m) to go to the market. 7. It is possible that they have gone into that building. 8. The children were playing along (i.e., 'on') the banks of the Ganges (River). 9. It is proper for you to speak to that woman. 10. Why does the king give so much money to his enemies? 11. If you (pol.) wish, I will certainly help you. 12. It is definite that he will bring his children here from Allahabad.

CHAPTER 14

14.1. The Auxiliaries सकना saknā, पाना pānā and चुकना cuknā

14.1.1. The verb सकना *saknā* is used as an auxiliary immediately after a verbal stem to indicate the capability of carrying out an action :

मैं वहां नहीं जा सका। *mãĩ vahā̃ nahī̃ jā sakā.*
'I wasn't able to go there'.

वह इलाहाबाद जा सकेगा। *vah ilāhābād jā sakegā.*
'He will be able to go to Allahabad'.

The सकना *saknā* element in such constructions may be fully conjugated except that it is not generally found in any of the continuous aspectual-tenses :

आप अभी उसको देख सकती हैं। *āp abhī usko dekh saktī hãĩ.*
(not * देख सक रही हैं *dekh sak rahī hãĩ*).
'You can see him/it/her right now'.

In the various perfective aspectual-tenses the marker ने *ne* is not used if सकना *saknā* is also employed. This is true whether or not the main verb would require ने *ne* if सकना *saknā* were not present :

मैंने वह खाना नहीं खाया। *mãĩ ne vah khānā nahī̃ khāyā.*
'I didn't eat that food'.

but मैं वह खाना नहीं खा सका। *mãĩ vah khānā nahī̃ khā sakā.*
'I couldn't eat that food'.

14.1.2. The verb पाना *pānā* is also used as an auxiliary in a capabilitive sense immediately after a verbal stem. Unlike सकना *saknā*, पाना *pānā* is almost always employed in this manner only if the sentence has a negative sense :

उस रात को सुमित्रा नहीं सो पाई। *us rāt ko sumitrā nahī̃ so pāī.*
'Sumitra couldn't sleep that night'.

हम उस होटल में नहीं ठहर पाएंगे। *ham us hoṭal mẽ nahī̃ ṭhahar pāẽge.*
'We will not be able to stay in that hotel'.

Usually, the use of पाना *pānā* (in the negative) as an auxiliary indicates that the subject wishes to carry out the action of the main verb, but is prevented from doing so by external circumstances.

As is the case with सकना *saknā*, the use of पाना *pānā* as a verbal auxiliary normally prevents the marking of the subject by means of ने *ne*. Instances where this prohibition is not in force can on occasion be found, but they are quite uncommon:

वह उनके प्रश्नों के उत्तर नहीं दे पाया। *vah unke praśnõ ke uttar nahī̃ de pāyā.*
उसने उनके प्रश्नों के उत्तर नहीं दे पाए। *usne unke praśnõ ke uttar nahī̃ de pāe.* (rarely)
'He wasn't able to answer their questions'.

14.1.3. The auxiliary चुकना *cuknā* is used directly after verbal stems to indicate the prior completion of the activity of the main verb. The sense of चुकना *cuknā* in this construction is often best expressed in English by the word 'already':

अनुराधा चावल ख़रीद चुकी है। *anurādhā cāval k͟harīd cukī hai.*
'Anuradha has already bought rice'.

वे वहाँ पहुंच चुके होंगे। *ve vahā̃ pahũc cuke hõge.*
'They must have already arrived there'.

The use of the ने *ne* construction is prohibited in conjunction with चुकना *cuknā*:

हम (not हमने) खाना खा चुके थे। *ham* (not हमने *hamne*) *khānā khā cuke the.*
'We had already eaten the food'.

14.2. Deictic Uses of रहना *rahnā* and होना *honā*

The simple perfective forms of रहना *rahnā* are often employed deictically (i.e., in pointing out or motioning towards some object) in conjunction with the demonstrative pronouns यह *yah*, वह *vah*, ये *ye*, or वे *ve*:

यह रहा आपका मित्र। *yah rahā āpkā mitra.*
'Here's your friend'.

वे रहीं बाएँ हमारी किताबें। *ve rahī̃ bāẽ hamārī kitābẽ.*
'There are our books to the left'.

In this construction the form of रहना *rahnā* agrees in number and gender with the noun indicating item or items being pointed out.

The simple present tense forms of होना *honā* are likewise employed with deictic sense:

यह है तुम्हारी बहन। *yah hai tumhārī bahan.*
'Here's your sister'.

वे हैं उसके भाई। *ve hãĩ uske bhāī.*
'There are his/her brothers'.

14.3. Comparative and Superlative Degrees of Adjectives

The comparative degree of adjectives is formed by adding the postposition से *se* immediately after the word that indicates the fixed reference point in the comparison. This latter word is consequently placed in the oblique case. Unlike English, the adjective itself normally bears no inflection:

यह फूल उस फूल से लाल है। *yah phūl us phūl se lāl hai.*
'This flower is redder than that flower'.

उसका खाना इससे अच्छा है। *uskā khānā isse acchā hai.*
'His/her food is better than this'.

मालती उससे तिगुना काम करती है। *mālti usse tigunā kām karti hai.*
'Malti does three times as much work as he/she'.

The postpositional phrases X से बढ़कर X *se baRhkar* 'better than X, superior to X, and X से घटकर X *se ghaṭkar* 'less than X, inferior to X' are occasionally encountered in place of से *se* in comparative construction:

उससे बढ़कर और कोई नहीं। *usse baRhkar aur koī nahī̃.*
'There is no one/nothing better than he/she/it'.

वह तुमसे बढ़कर अमीर है। *vah tumse baRhkar amīr hai.*
'He/she is richer than you'.

यह क़लम आपकी क़लमों से घटकर है। *yah ḳalam āpkī ḳalmõ se ghaṭkar hai.*
'This pen is inferior to your pens'.

The words और *aur* 'more, additional', और भी *aur bhī* 'even more', अधिक *adhik* 'more, additional', ज़्यादा *zyādā* 'more, additional', and कम *kam* 'less, little, few' may be employed in comparative expressions in order to make them explicit.

राम अपने भाई से अधिक/ज़्यादा/और/ *rām apne bhaī se adhik/zyādā/aur/*
और भी अमीर है। *aur bhī amīr hai.*
'Ram is richer than his brother'.

किरण पुष्पा से कम समझती है *kiraṇ puṣpā se kam samajhtī hai.*
'Kiran understands less than Pushpa'.

The superlative degree of adjectives is commonly formed by adding the word सब *sab* 'all' immediately before the postposition से *se* used in the comparative. In effect, the superlative construction can be viewed as a special sub-case of the comparative in which सब *sab* has replaced the form that served as the fixed reference point in the comparative:

सीता का सबसे छोटा भाई *sītā kā sabse choṭā bhāī*
'Sita's youngest brother'

यह उसकी सबसे पुरानी साड़ी है। *yah uskī sab se purānī sāRī hai.*
'This is her oldest sari'.

The postposition में *mẽ* or the sequence of postpositions में से *mẽ se* is often used to mark the set of entities among which a comparison is being made:

उसके भाइयों में (or में से) विजय सबसे बड़े हैं।
uske bhāiyõ mẽ (or *mẽ se*) *vijay sabse baRe hãĩ.*
'Vijay is the oldest of his/her brothers'.

Possessive constructions with का/के/की *kā/ke/kī* are likewise also used to specify the domain within which a ranking in terms of some adjectival quality is taking place:

भारत का सबसे बड़ा शहर कलकत्ता है। *bhārat kā sab se baRā śahar kalkattā hai.*
'The largest city in India is Calcutta'.

Superlative forms of adjectives can also be constructed through the repetition of the adjective, with the postposition से *se* standing between the two instances:

मैं अच्छी-से-अच्छी हिन्दी पुस्तकें पढ़ता हूं। *mãĩ acchī-se-acchī hindī pustakẽ paRhta hū̃.*
'I read the very best Hindi books'.

The expression कम-से-कम *kam-se-kam*, although a superlative construction of the type just described, has the idiomatic sense 'at least:

वह प्रति दिन कम-से-कम चार रोटियां खाता था। *vah prati din kam-se-kam cār rotiyā̃ khātā thā.*
'He used to eat at least four bread loaves every day'.

In Sanskritized Hindi comparatives and superlatives are often employed showing the Sanskrit adjectival suffixes -तर *-tar* (for the comparative) and –तम *–tam* (for the superlative) : e.g.,

उच्चतर	*uccatar*	'higher';	उच्चतम	*uccatam*	'highest'
प्रियतर	*priyatar*	'dearer';	प्रियतम	*priyatam*	'dearest'
कठिनतर	*kaṭhintar*	'more difficult';	कठिनतम	*kaṭhintam*	'most difficult'

Sanskrit superlative forms ending in -इष्ठ *-iṣṭh* (which becomes -एष्ठ *-eṣṭh* under certain circumstances) are also found in Sanskritized Hindi. Some common words of this type include ज्येष्ठ *jyeṣṭh* 'eldest' कनिष्ठ *kaniṣṭh* 'youngest', and श्रेष्ठ *śreṣṭh* 'best'. Occasionally forms of this type are used in Hindi without their original superlative sense (e.g., स्वादिष्ट *svādiṣṭ* 'savoury, tasty').

14.4. Expressions of Greeting

Hindi, as indeed all languages, has a number of formulaic expressions that are employed as salutations or in extending greetings.

The most common expressions of greeting in Hindi are नमस्ते *namaste* and नमस्कार *namaskār*, these both said with the hands held together in front of the chest in a posture of respect.

Among Muslims the salutations आदाब अर्ज़, *ādāb arz* and सलाम अलैकुम *salām alaikum* are common. All of these expressions may be employed at the beginning of a social encounter or at the close of one. Often salutations of the above kinds are combined with honorific titles or respect markers of various kinds:

नमस्ते, पण्डितजी *namaste, paṇḍit jī.*
आदाब अर्ज़, डाक्टर साहब *ādāb arz, ḍākṭar sāhab.*
नमस्कार, वाजपेयी जी *namaskār, vājpeyī jī.*

For salutations of welcome, the word स्वागत *svāgat* is commonly used:

स्वागत, रस्तोगी जी *svāgat, rastogī jī* ! 'Welcome, Mr. Rastogi !'

Often polite commands, which may be combined with honorific terms of addres , are used in initiating conversations:

कहिए, शर्मा जी, *kahie, śarmā jī* 'Excuse me, Mr. Sharma'
(literally 'Please say, Mr. Sharma')

सुनिए, शुक्ला जी *sunie, śuklā jī* 'Excuse me, Mr. Shukla'
(literally, 'Please listen, Mr. Skukla')

14·5. Further Honorific Usages

The word साहब *sāhab* is commonly employed in non-Sanskritized styles of Hindi and Urdu in terms of address. It is combined with surnames to add to them the sense of English 'Mister':

गुप्ता साहब *guptā sāhab* 'Mr. Gupta'; इकबाल साहब *ikbāl sāhab* 'Mr. Ikbal'. All names containing the element साहब *sāhab* are grammatically plural. All words standing in agreement with names containing साहब *sāhab* must therefore also be grammatically plural.

तिवारी साहब बाजार के पास रहते हैं । *tivārī sāhab bāzār ke pās rahte hãĩ.*
'Mr. Tiwari lives near the market'.

The honorific markers जी *jī* and साहब *sāhab* are combined with religious or occupational terms for use in referring to or addressing different kinds of individuals:

मास्टर जी	*māsṭar jī*	'a teacher'
डाक्टर साहब	*ḍākṭar sāhab*	'a doctor'
लाला जी	*lālā jī*	'a shopkeeper'
सरदार जी	*sardār jī*	'a Sikh'

Some of other common polite terms of address employing जी *jī* or साहब *sāhab* are as follows:

देवी जी	*devī jī*	a term of address used for women [cf. देवी *devī* n. f. 'goddess']
भाई साहब	*bhāī sāhab*	used to address men previously unknown to the addresser. Also used to address male friends and relatives in informal situations.
बहन जी	*bahan jī*	'a female teacher'. The term is also used in addressing younger women in general.

In Sanskritic Hindi the terms श्री *śrī* (or श्रीमान *śrīmān*), श्रीमती *śrīmatī*, and कुमारी *kumārī* are used in the senses of Mr., Mrs., and Miss respectively:

श्री (or श्रीमान) गोपाल	*śrī* (or *śrīmān*) *gopāl*	'Mr. Gopal'
श्रीमती इन्दिरा गांधी	*śrimatī indirā gāndhī*	'Mrs. Indira Gandhi'
कुमारी जैन	*kumārī jain*	'Miss Jain'.

The terms श्रीमान *śrīmān* and श्रीमती *śrīmatī* may themselves be combined with जी *jī*:

श्रीमान जी *śrīmān jī* 'Sir'; श्रीमती जी *śrīmatī jī* 'Madame'

The particle जी *jī* is frequently found combined with the words हाँ *hã* 'yes' and नहीं *nahī̃* 'no' to form respectful positive and negative replies to questions:

जी हाँ	*jī hã*;	हाँ जी	*hã jī*	'yes'
जी नहीं	*jī nahī̃*;	नहीं जी	*nahī̃ jī*	'no'

The above examples in which the जी *jī* element precedes the other word are slightly more polite than the examples with the order of words reversed.

The particle जी *jī* is by itself often employed as a response to being addressed or called:

सीता जी, सुनिए ।	*sītā ji, sunie.*	'Excuse me, Sita.'
जी ।	*jī.*	'Yes' [this response indicates that the speaker awaits further conversation]. 'What?'

14.6. VOCABULARY

आबादी	*ābādī*	n. f. population	X को Y पसंद होना	*X ko Y pasãd honā*	v.i. for X to like Y
आया	*āyā*	n. f. nursemaid	पिलाना	*pilānā*	v. t. to give to drink
चपरासी	*caprāsī*	n. m. peon	बताना	*batānā*	v. t. to tell
नाम	*nām*	n. m. name	भूल जाना	*bhūl jānā*	v. i. to forget
पंडित	*pãḍit*	n. m. pandit	X को Y मालूम होना	*X ko Y mālūm honā*	v. i. for X to know Y
पति	*pati*	n. m. husband, lord	लेटना	*leṭnā*	v. i. to lie down
पत्नी	*patnī*	n. f. wife	अंत में	*ãt mẽ*	adv. finally, in the end
पेड़	*peR*	n. m. tree	अधिकतर	*adhiktar*	adv. mostly, generally
बस्ती	*bastī*	n. f. colony, a residential community	इधर-उधर	*idhar-udhar*	adv. here and there, everywhere
भूल	*bhūl*	n. f. error, mistake	ज्यादातर	*zyādātar*	adv. mostly, generally
मज़दूर	*mazdūr*	n. m. worker, laborer	दाएं	*dāẽ*	adv. to the right
लेख	*lekh*	n. m. written article	दाहिने	*dāhine*	adv. to the right
लेखक	*lekhak*	n. m. writer, author	फिर (से)	*phir (se)*	adv. again
अधिक	*adhik*	adj. much, more; adv. much, excessively	बाएं	*bāẽ*	adv. to the left
अमीर	*amīr*	adj. rich	X के अलावा	*X ke alāvā*	post. besides X, in addition to X
कठिन	*kaṭhin*	adj. difficult	X की तरह	*X kī tarah*	post. like X, in the manner of X
ख़राब	*kharāb*	adj. bad, spoiled	X के दाहिने हाथ पर	*X ke dāhine hāth par*	post. to the right side of X
ग़रीब	*garīb*	adj. poor	X से बढ़कर	*X se baRh kar*	post. more than X, superior to X, better than X
ज़्यादा	*zyādā*	adj. much, more; adv. much, excessively	X के बाएं हाथ पर	*X ke bāẽ hath par*	post. to the left side of X
तेज़	*tez*	adj. quick, swift, sharp; adv. quickly	नहीं तो	*nahī̃ to*	conj. otherwise
दिलचस्प	*dilcasp*	adj. interesting			
मशहूर	*maśhūr*	adj. famous			
मुश्किल	*muśkil*	adj. difficult			
सफल	*saphal*	adj. successful			
खिलाना	*khilānā*	v. t. to feed, to give to eat			
जलना	*jalnā*	v.i. to burn, be ignited, be jealous			
जलाना	*jalānā*	v. t. to burn, ignite			
दुहराना	*duharānā*	v. t. to repeat			

14.7. EXERCISES

14.7.1. *Translate into English.*

1. मैं आ सकता हूं । *mãĩ ā saktā hū̃,* वह जा सकेगी *vah jā sakegī,* हम दुहरा सके *ham duharā sake,* आप बता सकते थे *āp batā sakte the.* 2. हम नहीं सो पाए *ham nahī̃ so pāe,* मैं नहीं जा पाती

mãĩ nahĩ jā pātī, वह न भूल पाया *vah na bhūl pāyā,* तू न छोड़ पाएगा *tū na choR pāegā.* 3. हम खा चुके हैं *ham khā cuke hãĩ,* वह खिला चुकेगी *vah khilā cukegī,* तुम जला चुके थे *tum jalā cuke the,* वे बता चुके होंगे *ve batā cuke hõge.* 4. यह रही आया *yah rahī āyā,* वह रही उसकी पत्नी *vah rahī uskī patnī,* वह रहा संतरा *vah rahā sãtarā,* वे रहे तुम्हारे मित्र *ve rahe tumhāre mitra.* 5. इससे बड़ा *isse baRā,* उनसे छोटे *unse choṭe,* उस कहानी से दिलचस्प *us kahānī se dilcasp,* हिंदी से कठिन *hindī se kaṭhin* 6. उन लोगों से ग़रीब *un logõ se garīb,* हमसे सफल *hamse saphal,* पंडितजी से प्रसिद्ध *pãḍitjī se prasiddh,* इससे दुगुना अमीर *isse dugunā amīr.* 7. सब से तेज़ *sab se tez,* सबसे ग़रीब *sabse garīb,* यहाँ का सबसे अच्छा लड़का *yahā̃ kā sabse acchā laRkā.* 8. उस लेखक के अलावा *us lekhak ke alāvā,* मेरे माता-पिता की तरह *mere mātā-pitā kī tarah,* हमारे विद्यार्थियों की तरह *hamāre vidyārthiyõ kī tarah.* 9. स्कूलों के दाहिने हाथ पर *skūlõ ke dāhine hāth par,* उसके कमरे के बाएं हाथ पर *uske kamre ke bāẽ hāth par.* 10. उसकी माता के खाने से बढ़कर *uskī mātā ke khāne se baRhkar,* यहाँ के लोगों से बढ़कर *yahā̃ ke logõ se baRhkar.*

14.7.2. *Translate into Hindi.* Use सकना *saknā* in no. 1, पाना *pānā* in no 2, चुकना *cuknā* in no. 3. and रहना *rahnā* in no. 4.

1. you (int. m.) can speak, they (f.) could give, we (m.) will be able to ignite (t.), he isn't able to tell; 2. I couldn't sing, we aren't able to dance, you (pol. f.) weren't able to buy, he isn't able to tell; 3. she has already drunk, we have already seen, I will have already given, we (f.) have already bought; 4. here's the book, there's the woman, here's the workman, there are the tall buildings; 5. sweeter than the mango, taller than that tree, bigger than their house, older than Madan; 6. riper than these oranges, faster than those children, more beautiful than her sister, more difficult than Panjabi: 7. the smallest apple, the poorest pandit, the most famous writer, the worst fruit (pl.); 8. in addition to your friends, in addition to Hindi, in addition to both those girls; 9. like the nursemaid, like those rich men, like the beautiful birds; 10. to the left of the dog, to the right of those books, on top of these very people; 11. superior to these fruit, superior to his story, superior to his articles.

14.7.3. *Translate into English.*

1. उसकी माता जी भूल गई थीं कि मैं इस तरह का खाना नहीं खा सकता। *uskī mātā jī bhūl gaī thī ki maĩ is tarah kā khānā nahī̃ khā saktā.* 2. यहाँ के पंडित जी को मेरे सब लेख बहुत पसन्द होते हैं। *yahā̃ ke pãḍit jī ko mere sab lekh bahut pasand hote hãĩ.* 3. उस शहर की सारी आबादी उन नई बस्तियों में नहीं रह पाई। *us śahar kī sārī ābādī un naī bastiyõ mẽ nahī̃ rah pāī.* 4. उसके सबसे बड़े भाई इस काम में बहुत सफल हुए। *uske sab se baRe bhāī is kām mẽ bahut saphal hue.* 5. वह अपने सब प्रश्न दूसरों के लिए नहीं दुहरा सका। *vah apne sab praśn dūsrõ ke liye nahī̃ duharā sakā.* 6. उनकी कहानियों से बढ़कर और कुछ नहीं (है) *unkī kahāniyõ se baRhkar aur kuch nahī̃ (hai).* 7. वह मज़दूर तुमसे तिगुना काम करता है। *vah mazdūr tumse tigunā kām kartā hai.* 8. उनके सब लेखों के नाम मुझे मालूम नहीं (हैं)। *unke sab lekhõ ke nām mujhe mālūm nahī̃ (hãĩ).* 9. हो सकता है कि हम उनकी मदद नहीं कर सकें। *ho saktā hai ki ham unkī madad nahī̃ kar sakẽ.* 10. अधिकतर वहाँ के लोग मेरी हिन्दी नहीं समझते। *adhiktar vahā̃ ke log merī hindī nahī̃ samajhte.* 11. आप इतनी कठिन पुस्तकें क्यों पढ़ते हैं ? *āp itnī kaṭhin pustakẽ kyõ paRhte hãĩ ?* 12. आपकी बहन के अलावा वहां और कौन रहता है ? *apkī bahan ke alāvā vahā̃ aur kaun rahtā hai ?*

14.7.4. *Translate into Hindi.*

1. Those people are poorer than the people of this village. 2. She is sadder than you (pol.). 3. I have already told you the name of that nursemaid. 4. Finally he looked here and there and went outside the room. 5. How many errors did you see in his letter ? 6. I know three Indian languages in addition to Hindi. 7. The farmer wasn't able to set fire to the chair. 8. She had already given her children milk (to drink). 9. They speak Hindi like students. 10. His daughter runs more quickly than his son. 11. The peon wasn't able to bring the food from the market. 12. How many women are standing to the left of that building ?

CHAPTER 15

15.1 Indirect Verb Constructions

There is in Hindi a set of grammatical constructions referred to generically as "indirect verb constructions." These formations are used to represent psychological states or conditions, physical sensations, judgements and perceptions, as well as other predicates of diverse kinds. There are grammatical properties shared by all indirect verb constructions. The noun indicating the animate being or beings having the psychological state, feeling the physical sensation, etc., is placed in its oblique case form and followed by the postposition को *ko*. The noun referring to the psychological state, physical sensation, etc. is made the subject of the sentence. The verb of the clause is intransitive, and generally is, one of होना *honā*, लगना *lagnā*, पड़ना *paRnā*, मिलना *milnā*, or आना *ānā*.

One of the most common types of indirect verb construction is used to express such psychological states as wishes, desires, wants, fears, happiness, and sadness:

प्रमोद को आशा है कि वह परीक्षा में पास हो जाएगा ।
pramod ko āśā hai ki vah parīkṣā mẽ pās ho jāegā.
'Pramod hopes that he passes the examination'.

महेश्वर को आने की इच्छा थी पर वह न आ पाया ।
maheśvar ko āne kī icchā thī par vah na ā pāyā.
'Maheshvar wanted to come, but he was unable to'.

नाज़िरा (prop. f.) को नई किताब लिखने से बड़ा डर लग रहा था ।
nāzirā ko naī kitāb likhne se baRā ḍar lag rahā thā.
'Nazira was experiencing quite a lot of fear about writing a new book'.

मुझे बड़ी प्रसन्नता हुई कि वाजपेयी जी हमारे यहां आए ।
mujhe baRī prasannatā huī ki vājpeyījī hamāre yahā̃ āe.
'I was very pleased that Mr. Vajpeyi came to our place.'

Indirect verb constructions are also quite common in indicating physical sensations or the incurring of afflictions or diseases:

उसको प्यास लग रही थी । *usko pyās lag rahī thī.*
'He/she was thirsty'.

तब उस मोची को ठंड लग रही थी । *tab us mocī ko ṭhā̃ḍ lag rahī thī.*
'That cobbler was very cold then'.

उसको बुख़ार आया । *usko bukhār āyā.*
'He she/came down with a fever.'

आना *ānā* is often used in indirect verb constructions to indicate the mastery of some learned skill:

उसको कम हिन्दी आती है। *us ko kam hindī ātī hai.*
'He/she knows little Hindi'.

राम को उर्दू पढ़ना नहीं आता। *rām ko urdū paRhnā nahī̃ ātā.*
'Ram does't know how to read Urdu'.

मिलना *milnā* is employed in the ubiquitous indirect verb construction X को Y मिलना X *ko* Y *milnā* 'for X to get/find Y' :

बाजार में आपको क्या मिला ? *bāzār mẽ āpko kyā milā ?*
'What did you get/find in the market ?'

मुझे तीन नए खिलौने मिले। *mujhe tīn nae khilaune mile.*
'I got/found three new toys'.

Indirect verb constructions are extremely prevalent in sentences indicating a judgement about the appearance or nature of some object or situation :

उस को लगता है कि उसकी बहन नहीं आएगी।
us ko lagtā hai ki uskī bahan nahī̃ āegī.
'It seems to him/her that his/her sister will not come'.

हमारे गाने उन्हें अच्छे नहीं लगे।
hamāre gāne unhẽ acche nahī̃ lage.
'They didn't like our songs'. [cf., X को Y Z लगना X *ko* Y Z *lagnā* 'for Y to strike X as being Z']

उसको जान पड़ा कि उसका बच्चा अंग्रेज़ी कभी नहीं सीख सकेगा।
us ko jān paRā ki uskā baccā ãgrezī kabhī nahī̃ sīkh sakegā.
'It seemed to him/her that his/her son will never be able to learn English'.

Some other common indirect verb constructions are the following:

X को Y पसन्द होना	X *ko* Y *pasand honā* 'for X to like Y'
X को Y पसन्द आना	X *ko* Y *pasand ānā* 'for X to like Y'
X को हंसी आना	X *ko hãsī ānā* 'for X to laugh, smile'
X को Y मालूम होना	X *ko* Y *mālūm honā* 'for X to know Y'
X को Y पता होना	X *ko* Y *patā honā* 'for X to know Y'
X को पता चलना कि	X *ko patā calnā ki* 'for X to find out/learn that...'
X को जल्दी होना	X *ko jaldī honā* 'for X to be in a hurry'
X को देर होना	X *ko der honā* 'for X to be late, to be delayed'
X को काम होना	X *ko kām honā* 'for X to have work (to do)'
X को चोट लगना	X *ko coṭ lagnā* 'for X to get injured'
X को Y नज़र आना	X *ko* Y *nazar ānā* 'for Y come into X's sight, for X to see Y'
X को मौक़ा मिलना	X *ko mauḳā milnā* 'for X to get an/the opportunity'
X को चक्कर आना	X *ko cakkar ānā* 'for X to become dizzy'

15.2. Sets of Related Adverbs and other Forms

It is possible to arrange a number of the most common Hindi adverbial forms into a highly systematic paradigm. The four columns of this paradigm contain forms of the following types : (1) proximate forms (i.e., referring to closeness in either space or time); (2) non-proximate forms (i.e., specifying distance in either space or time); (3) interrogative forms; and (4) relative forms. This paradigm may also be extended to include a number of sets of related adjectival pronouns (e.g., ऐसा *aisā*, इतना *itnā*).

Proximate	*Non-Proximate*	*Interrogative*	*Relative*[1]
अब *ab* 'now'	तब *tab* 'then'	कब *kab* 'when ?'	जब *jab* 'when'
इधर *idhar* 'in this direction, hither'	उधर *udhar* 'in that direction, thither'	किधर *kidhar* 'in which direction, whither?'	जिधर *jidhar* 'in which direction, whither'
यहां *yahā̃* 'here'	वहां *vahā̃* 'there'	कहां *kahā̃* 'where ?'	जहां *jahā̃* 'where'
यह *yah* 'this one'	वह *vah* 'that one'	कौन *kaun* 'who ?' क्या *kyā* 'what'	जो *jo* 'who, that, which'
इस *is* 'obl.s of यह *yah*'	उस *us* 'obl.s. of वह *vah*'	किस *kis* 'obl.s. of कौन/क्या *kaun/kyā*'	जिस *jis* 'obl.s. of जो *jo*'
इन *in* 'obl. pl. of ये *ye*'	उन *un* 'obl. pl. of वे *ve*'	किन *kin* 'obl. pl. of कौन/क्या *kaun/kyā*'	जिन *jin* 'obl. pl. of जो *jo*'
ऐसा *aisā* 'of this sort'	वैसा *vaisā* 'of that sort'	कैसा *kaisā* 'of what sort ?'	जैसा *jaisā* 'of which sort'
ऐसे *aise* 'in this way, thus'	वैसे *vaise* 'in that way/manner, thus'	कैसे *kaise* 'in what way, how ?'	जैसे *jaise* 'as, as if, for instance'
इतना *itnā* 'this much/many'	उतना *utnā* 'that much/many'	कितना *kitnā* 'how much/many?'	जितना *jitnā* 'as much/many'

It will be noted that all of the interrogative forms in the above chart begin with the sound क- *k*- and the relative forms with ज- *j*-. Furthermore, with the exception

1. The use of Hindi relative forms is discussed in 21.4 and 22.1.

of तब *tab*, the non-proximate forms all show the initial sounds उ- *u-* or व- *v-*. The proximate forms show the initial sounds अ– *a–*, य– *y–*, इ- *i-*, and ऐ- *ai–*.

15.3. Relationship between Certain Adjectives and Adverbs

Certain forms in Hindi (viz., ऐसा *aisā*, वैसा *vaisā*, कैसा *kaisā*, and जैसा *jaisā*) can be used either adjectivally or adverbially, this difference in usage being associated with a difference in inflection. It is quite important to keep these two usages distinct.

When the form in question modifies a noun, either explicit or implied, it is being used adjectivally. In such cases it agrees with the modified noun in number, case, and gender:

ऐसा लड़का *aisā laRkā* 'this sort of boy'
वैसे लड़के को *vaise laRke ko* 'to that sort of boy'
कैसी लड़कियों को *kaisī laRkiyõ ko* 'to what sort of girls?'

When the form is not modifying a noun, but rather modifying the verb of the entire clause, the usage is said to be adverbial. In these instances the form shows the invariable ending –ए *–e* (i.e., ऐसे *aise* 'in this manner, thus', वैसे *vaise* 'in that manner', कैसे *kaise* 'in which manner?', जैसे *jaise* 'as if'):

ऐसे मत बोलो *aise mat bolo.* 'Don't speak in this manner'.
तुम वहाँ कैसे पहुंचे ? *tūm vahā̃ kaise pahũce?* 'How did you arrive there?'

वह बोल रहा था जैसे वह मेरा मित्र न हो।
vah bol rahā thā jaise vah merā mitra na ho.
'He was speaking as if he weren't my friend'.

Several other grammatical forms of Hindi, particularly perfective and imperfective participles (cf. 27.1, 24.1) show this same distinction between adjectival and adverbial usages.

15.4. Some Expressions of Thanks

Explicit expressions of thanks are not as commonly employed in Hindi as they are in English. In general, these forms are not used as mechanical markers of politness, but as genuine indications of thanks for significant favours received.

The most frequent expressions of thanks are धन्यवाद *dhanyavād* in Sanskritized Hindi and शुक्रिया *śukriyā* in Urdu and colloquial Hindi. The feminine nouns कृपा *kṛpā* and मेहरबानी *meharbānī*, both having the literal sense 'favor, kindness', are often employed in slightly more discursive expressions of thanks:

आपकी बड़ी कृपा है। *āpkī baRī kṛpā hai.*
आपकी बड़ी मेहरबानी है। *āpkī baRī meharbānī hai.*
'Thank you very much'.

The adjectives आभारी *ābhārī* 'grateful, obliged' and अनुगृहीत *anugṛhīt* 'grateful, obliged' are sometimes employed in the expression of gratitude:

मैं आपकी सेवा के लिए बहुत आभारी/अनुगृहीत हूं ।
mãĩ āpkī sevā ke lie bahut ābhārī/anugṛhīt hū̃.
'I am very grateful for your service'.

15.5. Inceptive Expressions

The verb लगना *lagnā* is employed immediately after the oblique infinitive (i.e., the infinitive showing the ending –ने *-ne* instead of -ना *-nā*) to indicate the inception of an action or state of affairs :

वह जाने लगा । *vah jāne lagā.*
'He began to go'.

हम पढ़ने लगेंगे । *ham paRhne lagẽge.*
'We will begin to read/study'.

वह हंसने लगी । *vah hãsne lagī.*
'She began to laugh'.

Sentences showing this inceptive use of लगना *lagnā* never use the ने *ne* construction, even though the main verb may be transitive and the entire predicate be in one of the perfective aspectual-tenses :

मैंने खाना खाया । *mãĩne khānā khāyā.*
'I ate the food'.

but मैं खाना खाने लगा । *mãĩ khānā khāne lagā.*
'I began to eat the food'.

The transitive verbs शुरू करना *śurū karnā* 'to begin, start' and आरम्भ करना *ārambh karnā* 'to begin, start', can also be used to indicate the inception of activities :

उसने अपना काम शुरू किया । *usne apnā kām śurū kiyā.*
'He began his work'.

अध्यापक ने परीक्षा आरम्भ की होगी । *adhyāpak ne parīkṣā ārambh kī hogī.*
'The teacher must have started the examination'.

These two verbs may take infinitives as their direct objects :

उसने पढ़ना शुरू किया । *usne paRhnā śurū kiyā.*
'He/she began to study/read'.

उन्होंने उर्दू सीखना आरम्भ किया होगा । *unhõne urdū sīkhnā ārambh kiyā hogā.*
'They must have begun to learn Urdu'.

15.6. VOCABULARY

अफ़सोस	*afsos*	n.m. sorrow, grief, pity
आशा	*āśā*	n.f. hope
ओर	*or*	n.f. direction
कोट	*koṭ*	n.m. coat
ख़ुशी	*ḳhuśī*	n.f. happiness, pleasure
चक्कर	*cakkar*	n.m. dizziness
छात्रवृत्ति	*chatravṛtti*	n.f. scholarship
ठंड	*ṭhãḍ*	n.f. cold
डर	*ḍar*	n.m. fear
दु:ख	*duḥkh*	n.m. grief, sadness
परीक्षा	*parīkṣā*	n.f. examination
प्यास	*pyās*	n.f. thirst
प्रसन्नता	*prasannatā*	n.f. happiness, pleasure
बुख़ार	*bukhār*	n.m. fever
भूख	*bhūkh*	n.f. hunger
मौक़ा	*mauḳā*	n.m. opportunity, occasion
संतोष	*sãtoṣ*	n.m. satisfaction
सड़क	*saRak*	n.f. street
सरकार	*sarkār*	n.f. government
सुख	*sukh*	n.m. happiness, contentment
हंसी	*hãsi*	n.f. laughter
दूर	*dūr*	adj. distant; adv. far, far away
X को अफ़सोस होना	X *ko afsos honā*	v.i. for X to regret, feel sorry
X को आशा होना	X *ko āśā honā*	v.i. for X to hope
X को ख़ुशी होना	X *ko ḳhuśī honā*	v.i. for X to be happy, glad
X को गरमी लगना	X *ko garmī lagnā*	v,i. for X to be/feel warm/hot
X को चक्कर आना	X *ko cakkar ānā*	v.i. for X to become dizzy
X को ठंड लगना	X *ko ṭhãḍ lagnā*	v.i. for X to feel cold
X को डर लगना	X *ko ḍar lagnā*	v.i. for X to be/feel afraid
X को दु:ख होना	X *ko duḥkh honā*	v.i. for X to be sad/unhappy
X को देर होना	X *ko der honā*	v.i. for X to be delayed, for X to be late
X को प्यास लगना	X *ko pyās lagnā*	v.i. for X to be thirsty
X को प्रसन्नता होना	X *ko prasa-nnatā honā*	v.i. for X to be happy, for X to be pleased
X को बुख़ार आना	X *ko bukhār ānā*	v.i. for X to get/have a fever
X को भूख लगना	X *ko bhūkh lagnā*	v.i. for X to be hungry
X को मौक़ा मिलना	X *ko mauḳā milnā*	v.i. for X to get the chance, opportunity
X को संतोष होना	X *ko sãtoṣ honā*	v.i. for X to get pleasure, satisfaction
X को सुख होना	X *ko sukh honā*	v.i. for X to be happy, for X to get satisfaction, contentment
X को हंसी आना	X *ko hãsī ānā*	v.i. to laugh
केवल	*keval*	adv. only, just
बिलकुल	*bilkul*	adv. completely
सिर्फ़	*sirf*	adv. only, just
हमेशा	*hameśā*	adv. always
X के अनुसार	X *ke anusār*	post. according to X
X की ओर	X *kī or*	post. in the direction of X, towards X
X की ओर से	X *kī or se*	post. from X, from the direction of X
X से दूर	X *se dūr*	post. far from X
X के समान	X *ke samān*	post. like X, the same as X, equal to X
क्योंकि	*kyõkī*	conj. because
तथा	*tathā*	conj. and
फिर भी	*phir bhī*	conj. nevertheless, still
किस लिए	*kis lie*	inter. why?

15.7. Exercises

15.7.1. *Translate into English.*

1. मौक़ा *maukā*, जाने का मौक़ा *jāne kā maukā*, उसके साथ जाने का मौक़ा *us ke sāth jāne kā maukā*; 2. डर *ḍar*, बोलने का डर *bolne kā ḍar*, उर्दू में बोलने का डर *urdū mẽ bolne kā ḍar*; 3. इच्छा *icchā*, अमीर होने की इच्छा *amīr hone kī icchā*, उनकी अमीर होने की सब इच्छाएं *unkī amīr hone kī sab icchāẽ*; 4. हमको हंसी आई *hamko hãsī āī*, उसको बुख़ार आएगा *usko bukhār āegā*, मुझे मौक़ा मिला था *mujhe maukā milā thā*, सीता को आशा है *sītā ko āśā hai*; 5. तुझे प्रसन्नता हुई *tujhe prasannatā huī*, उन्हें दुःख हुआ *unhẽ duḥkh huā*, तुम्हें संतोष होगा *tumhẽ sãtoṣ hogā*, उसे सुख हो रहा है *use sukh ho rahā hai*; 6. इतने मित्र *itne mitra*, उतने कच्चे आम *utne kacce ām*, कितनी ताजी मिठाइयां *kitnī tāzī miṭhāiyā̃*; 7. केवल दो लड़कियां *keval do laRkiyā̃*, केवल यही पुस्तकें *keval yahī pustakẽ*, सिर्फ़ दो घंटे *sirf do ghãṭe*; 8. उसके लेखों के अनुसार *uske lekhõ ke anusār*, भारत (की) सरकार के अनुसार *bhārat* (*kī*) *sarkār ke anusār*; 9. शहर की ओर *śahar kī or*, उस गांव की ओर *us gā̃v kī or*, माताजी की ओर से *mātājī kī or se*; 10. दिल्ली से दूर *dillī se dūr*, यमुना नदी से बहुत दूर *yamunā nadī se bahut dūr*, एक रुपये के समान *ek rupaye ke samān*, एक छात्रवृत्ति के समान *ek chātravṛtti ke samān*.

15.7.2. *Translate into Hindi.*

1. hope, hope of going, hope of learning Panjabi; 2. thirst, very great thirst, those three men's very great thirst; 3. I regret, he hopes, they are happy, she liked; 4. we have gotten the opportunity, he must have gotten the opportunity, you (fam.) have the opportunity; 5. you (int.) have a fever, we feel cold, they feel warm; 6. we are hungry, they are thirsty, I was hungry; 7. completely ripe oranges, completely correct answers; 8. according to Indian newspapers; according to their desires; 9. (use X की ओर X *kī or* or X की ओर से X *kī or se*) towards the street, towards her friend, from your (pol.) brother; 10. far from the village, very far from the tall buildings, equal to his fear, equal to five rupees.

15.7.3. *Translate into English.*

1. मुझे बहुत ख़ुशी हुई कि उस मौक़े पर किरण आपके साथ आ सकी। *mujhe bahut khuśī huī ki us mauke par kiraṇ āp ke sāth ā sakī.* 2. पिताजी को डर लग रहा था कहीं बड़े भाई को बुख़ार न आए। *pitājī ko ḍar lag rahā thā kahī̃ baRe bhāī ko bukhār na āe.* 3. श्रीवास्तव जी को संतोष हुआ कि उनका लड़का प्रमोद परीक्षा में पास हो गया। *śrīvāstav jī ko sãtoṣ huā ki unkā laRkā pramod parīkṣā mẽ pās ho gayā.* 4. हमें आशा है कि तुम अपने परिवार के साथ हमारे यहां आओगे। *hamẽ āśā hai ki tum apne parivār ke sāth hamāre yahā̃ āoge.* 5. उसके लेख तुम्हें पसन्द क्यों नहीं आते? *uske lekh tumhẽ pasand kyõ nahī̃ āte?* 6. उसे अफ़सोस है कि राम ने आपकी किताब नहीं पढ़ी है। *use afsos hai ki rām ne āpkī kitāb nahī̃ paRhī hai.* 7. बच्चे को बुख़ार आया क्योंकि वह कोट न पहनकर खेलने (के लिए) बाहर गया। *bacce ko bukhār āyā kyõki vah koṭ na pahankar khelne* (*ke lie*) *bāhar gayā.* 8. वह अमीर है। फिर भी अमीर होने से उसे कम सुख होता है। *vah amīr hai. phir bhī amīr hone se use kam sukh hotā hai.* 9. उस सरदार जी के केवल दो बच्चे थे। *us sardārjī ke keval do bacce the.* 10. उनके बच्चों को छात्रवृत्ति मिलने के कारण श्री तथा श्रीमती शर्मा को अधिक प्रसन्नता हुई। *unke baccõ ko chātravṛtti milne ke kāraṇ śrī tathā śrīmatī śarmā ko adhik prasannatā huī.* 11. सरकार उनको इतने पैसे किस लिए दे रही है? *sarkār un ko itne paise kis lie de rahī hai?* 12. अधिकतर यहां लोग ऐसे नहीं बोलते। *adhiktar yahā̃ log aise nahī̃ bolte.*

15.7.4. *Translate into Hindi.*

1. That girl had gotten a fever. 2. She is very happy that all the children could come to your house. 3. We hope that he will arrive in Agra by evening. 4. Why weren't you able to help Amar on that occasion? 5. I sleep outside because it is very hot inside (अन्दर *andar*). 6. She used to live right here. 7. They were very afraid that the children would die of (i.e., from) hunger. 8. She didn't receive (मिलना *milnā*) any letters from you (आपकी ओर से *āpkī or se*) (use से *se*) for months. 9. Her friends will certainly like her new sari. 10. He will always live in that house with his children. 11. Agra is not very far from Delhi. 12. According to today's newspaper thousands of people are dying of hunger.

SUPPLEMENTARY READING PASSAGES

A. बुढ़िया के बेटे

किसी गांव में एक बुढ़िया रहती थी। वह बहुत कमज़ोर थी। वह चल-फिर नहीं सकती थी। उसके दो बेटे थे।

एक बार उस गांव में आग लगी। सब लोग अपनी-अपनी चीजें लेकर भागने लगे। राह में एक जंगल था। बड़ा बेटा अपना सब सामान लेकर भागा जा रहा था। डाकुओं ने उसे पकड़ लिया और उसका सब माल लूट लिया।

छोटे लड़के ने सोचा, "मां के आगे धन-दौलत क्या चीज़ है?" यह सोचकर वह बूढ़ी मां को अपने कंधे पर लेकर भागा। राह में उसे भी डाकुओं ने आ घेरा। एक डाकू ने पूछा—"बोलो, तुम्हारे पास कितना धन है?" लड़के ने जवाब दिया—"मेरी यह बूढ़ी मां मेरा धन है। मेरे पास दूसरा कोई धन नहीं है?"

यह सुनकर डाकुओं का सरदार आश्चर्य में आ गया। उसने सोचा, "यह छोटा-सा लड़का अपनी मां को कितना प्यार करता है?" लड़के से सरदार बहुत खुश हुआ। उसने उसे बहुत-सा धन दिया और अपने दो साथियों के साथ उसे जंगल के बाहर भेज दिया।

(from *HKPP*, pp. 15-16)

buRhiyā ke beṭe

kisī gā̃v mẽ ek buRhiyā rahtī thī. vah bahut kamzor thī. vah cal-phir nahī̃ saktī thī. uske do beṭe the.

ek bār us gā̃v mẽ āg lagī. sab log apnī-apnī cīzẽ lekar bhāgne lage. rāh mẽ ek jā̃gal thā. baRā beṭā apnā sab sāmān lekar bhāgā jā rahā thā. ḍākuõ ne use pakaR liyā aur uskā sab māl lūṭ liyā.

choṭē laRke ne socā, "mā̃ ke āge dhan-daulat kyā cīz hai?" yah sockar vah buRhī mā̃ ko apne kā̃dhe par lekar bhāgā. rāh mẽ use bhī ḍākuõ ne ā gherā. ek ḍākū ne pūchā—"bolo, tumhāre pās kitnā dhan hai?" laRke ne javāb diyā—"merī yah būRhī mā̃ merā dhan hai. mere pās dūsrā koī dhan nahī̃ hai."

yah sunkar ḍākuõ kā sardār āścarya mẽ ā gayā. usne socā, "yah choṭā-sā laRkā apnī mā̃ ko kitnā pyār kartā hai!" laRke se sardār bahut ḳhuś huā. usne use bahut-sā dhan diyā aur apne do sāthiyõ ke sāth use jā̃gal ke bāhar bhej diyā.

Vocabulary

कमज़ोर *kamzor* adj. weak

चलना-फिरना *calnā-phirnā* v.i. to wander, walk

बार *bār* n.f. time, occasion

आग (n.f.) लगना *āg lagnā* v.i. for a fire to be started/ignited

चीज़ *cīz* n.f. thing

राह *rāh* n.f. way, passage, route

राह में *rāh mẽ*, on the way

सामान *sāmān* n.m. possessions, baggage

भागा जाना *bhāgā jānā* v.i. to flee

डाकू *ḍākū* n.m. thief, robber

पकड़ लेना *pakaR lenā* v.t. to capture, seize
माल *māl* n.m. possessions
लूट लेना *lūṭ lenā* v.t. to rob
X के आगे X *ke āge* here 'in comparison to X'
धन-दौलत *dhan-daulat* n.m. riches, wealth
मां *mā̃* n.f. mother
कंधा *kā̃dhā* n.m. shoulder
आ घेरना *ā ghernā* v.t. to encircle
धन *dhan* n.m. wealth, fortune
जवाब *javāb* n.m. answer, reply
सरदार *sardār* n.m. leader
आश्चर्य *āścarya* n.m. wonder, surprise
आश्चर्य में आ जाना v.i. *āścarya mẽ ā jānā* v.i. to become surprised
छोटा-सा *choṭā-sā* adj. rather small
X को प्यार करना X *ko pyār karnā* v.t. to love X
बहुत-सा *bahut-sā* adj. quite a bit
साथी *sāthī* n.m. companion
जंगल *jā̃gal* n.m. jungle, woods, forest
भेज देना *bhej denā* v.t. to send

B. मेरी बिटिया सो जा, सो जा
कुत्ता तबला बजा रहा है,
नाच रही है बिल्ली।
कुत्ता जाएगा कलकत्ता,
बिल्ली जाए दिल्ली।
घोड़ा बाबू ढोल बजाएं,
बछड़ा जी सारंगी।
बन्दर बाबू काम न करते,
खाते हैं नारंगी।
मेरी बिटिया सो जा, सो जा
ब्रजकिशोर नारायण
(From *BKSK*, p. 63)

merī biṭiyā so jā, so jā
kuttā tablā bajā rahā hai,
nāc rahī hai billī.
kuttā jāegā kalkattā,
billī jāe dillī.
ghoRā bābū ḍhol bajāẽ.
bachRā jī sārā̃gī.
bā̃dar bābū kām na karte,
khāte hā̃i nārā̃gī.
merī biṭiyā so jā, so jā
Brajkiśor Nārāyaṇ

Vocabulary

बिटिया *biṭiyā* n.f, little daughter (diminutive of बेटी *beṭī* 'daughter')
सो जाना *so jānā* v.i. to go to sleep
तबला *tablā* n.m. a kind of drum
बजाना *bajānā* v.tr. to play, to make sound
घोड़ा *ghoRā* n.m. horse
बाबू *bābū* n.m. a term of address used for educated and upper-class men as well as for clerks; here used for humorous effect.
ढोल *ḍhol* n.m. a kind of large drum
बछड़ा *bachRā* n.m. calf
सारंगी *sārā̃gī* n. f. a kind of stringed musical instrument
बंदर *bā̃dar* n.m. monkey
नारंगी *nārā̃gī* n.f. orange

C. बोलनेवाला तोता

एक आदमी के पास एक तोता था। उसने उस तोते को एक ही बात बोलना सिखाया था, "इसमें क्या शक है ?" इसके सिवा वह और कुछ नहीं बोल सकता था।

bolnevālā totā

ek ādmī ke pās ek totā thā. usne us tote ko ek hī bāt bolnā sikhāyā thā, "is mẽ kyā śak hai?" iske sivā vah aur kuch nahī̃ bol saktā thā.

एक दिन वह आदमी उस तोते को बेचने के लिए बाजार ले गया। बाजार में पहुंचकर वह चिल्ला-चिल्ला कर कहने लगा, "कोई तोता लेगा ? कोई तोता लेगा ?"

इतने में एक अमीर आदमी वहां आया। उसने तोतेवाले से पूछा, "इस तोते का क्या दाम है ? " तोतेवाले ने जवाब दिया, "महाराज, एक सौ रुपया।"[1]

अमीर ने कहा, "दाम तो बहुत है"।

तोतेवाले ने जवाब दिया, "महाराज, विश्वास न हो, तो इस तोते ही से पूछ लीजिये ?"

यह सुनकर अमीर ने तोते से पूछा, "क्यों जी, तुम्हारा दाम सौ रुपया है ?"

तोता बोला, "इसमें क्या शक है ?"

तोते का जवाब सुनकर अमीर बड़ा ख़ुश हुआ। उसने तोतेवाले को सौ रुपये दिये और तोता लेकर अपने घर चला गया।

(From *HKPP*, pp. 17-19)

ek din vah ādmī us tote ko becne ke lie bāzār le gayā. bāzār mẽ pahũckar vah cillā-cillākar kahne lagā, "koī totā legā? koī totā legā?"

itne mẽ ek amīr ādmī vahā̃ āyā. usne totevāle se pūchā, "is tote kā kyā dām hai?" totevāle ne javāb diyā, "mahārāj, ek sau rupayā."

amīr ne kahā, "dām to bahut hai."

totevāle ne javāb diyā, "mahārāj, viśvās na ho, to is tote hī se pūch lījiye."

yah sunkar amīr ne tote se pūchā, "kyõ jī, tumhārā dām sau rupayā hai?"

totā bolā, "is mẽ kyā śak hai?"

tote kā javāb sunkar amīr baRā k̤huś huā. usne totevāle ko sau rupaye diye aur totā lekar apne ghar calā gayā.

तोता *totā* n.m. parrot

सिखाना *sikhānā* v.t. to teach, instruct

शक *śak* n.m. doubt

X के सिवा X *ke sivā* (*y*) post. except for X

चिल्ला-चिल्लाकर *cillā-cillākar* adv. screaming, shouting out

महाराज *mahārāj* n.m. literally 'great king', here used as a slightly ironic term of address

विश्वास *viśvās* n.m. trust, confidence

विश्वास न हो तो... *viśvās na ha to*...if you don't believe me (then)...

पूछ लेना *pūch lenā* v.t. to ask, inquire

क्यों जी *kyõ jī* pardon me, excuse me.

चला जाना *calā jānā* v.i. to leave, depart

1. Terms for units of money and time are often used in their singular forms even though they have plural reference.

PART
IV

CHAPTER 16

16.1. INFINITIVES+चाहना

The verb चाहना is commonly employed in Hindi in the sense of 'to wish, desire'. This verb appears in conjunction with preceding infinitives when that which is wanted or desired is the carrying out of some activity or the attainment of some state or condition :

मैं उसके साथ बाजार जाना चाहता हूँ ।
'I want to go to the market with him/her'.
वह अमीर होना चाहती थी ।
'She wanted to be rich'.
बच्चे उस पेड़ पर चढ़ना चाहेंगे ।
'The children will want to climb up that tree'.

In the event that the चाहना form appears in one of the perfective aspectual-tenses, then it as well as the infinitive agree in number and gender with the direct object of the infinitive :

उसने अपनी माता की मदद करनी चाही ।
'He wanted to help his mother'.
उस स्त्री ने ताजे फल ख़रीदने चाहे ।
'That woman wanted to buy fresh fruit'.

If the direct object of the infinitive is followed by को, or if the infinitive is that of an intransitive verb (and hence lacks a direct object), then the infinitive and the चाहना element occur in their singular masculine forms:

उसने राजा की सुन्दर लड़की को देखना चाहा ।
'He wanted to look at the beautiful daughter of the king'.
मैंने आपके यहां आना चाहा था ।
'I had wanted to come to your place'.

In cases where the subject of the act of wishing and the subject of the desired activity are different, the clause indicating the desired activity is transposed to a position following चाहना. This clause is introduced by the conjection कि. In such instances the verb of the transposed clause is likely to be in the subjunctive:

मैं चाहती हूँ कि वह हमारे साथ बाजार जाए ।
'I want him/her to go to the market with us'.
वह चाहती थी कि उसका बच्चा ख़ुश हो ।
'She wanted her child to be happy'.

16.2. Uses of मिलना

The verb मिलना is used in several very common Hindi expressions. The construction X को Y मिलना has the sense 'for X to get, obtain, find Y':

उस दुकान में आपको क्या मिला ?
'What did you get in that store?'

कानपुर की सबसे अच्छी मिठाइयां उसी दुकान पर मिलेंगी ।
'You can get the best sweets in Kanpur, in that very shop'.

हमें आशा है कि आपको अधिक प्रसन्नता मिलेगी ।
'We hope that you will get great pleasure'.

The expression X Y से मिलना has the sense 'for X to meet, encounter Y':

मंगलवार को तुम शहर में किन लोगों से मिले ?
'Whom did you meet in the city on Tuesday?'

मैं उनसे मिलना जरूर चाहती हूँ ।
'I certainly want to meet them'.

Often the मिलना element of this last expression is converted to the oblique infinitive मिलने and followed by जाना or आना. The locutions so formed have the senses 'for X to go to meet Y' and 'for X to come to meet Y' respectively:

वह आपके माता-पिता से मिलने कलकत्ते गया ।
'He went to Calcutta to meet your parents'.

तुम तब किससे मिलने आए ?
'Whom did you come to meet at that time?'

In conjunction with such expressions as चेहरे से 'in face, appearance' [cf. चेहरा n.m. face, countenance, appearance] or शक्ल से 'in form, appearance [cf. शक्ल n.f. form, appearance]' *milnā* has the meaning 'to resemble'. In sentences showing this usage the person who is resembled is marked with the postposition से :

लोग कहते हैं कि वह चेहरे से अपने भाई से मिलता है ।
'People say he resembles his brother'.

Occasionally मिलना is linked to the semantically empty verbal element जुलना, with the entire locution so formed roughly equivalent to one or another of the basic senses of मिलना :

छोटे गांवों में हम कई प्रकार के लोगों से मिलते-जुलते हैं ।
'We encounter several kinds of people in the small villages'.

The verb मिलाना functions in Hindi as the transitive analogue to the intransitive मिलना. Having the general sense of 'to bring together, to mix', this verb appears in a wide range of Hindi verbal constructions of which the following are examples :

X Y से हाथ मिलाना	'for X to shake hands with Y'
X Y को Z से मिलाना	'for X to introduce Y to Z'
X में Y मिलाना	'to mix Y into X' (as in cooking)

राम ने मुझसे हाथ मिला दिया ।

'Ram shook hands with me'.

मैं आपको अपनी बहिन पुष्पा से मिलाना चाहती हूँ ।

'I want to introduce you to my sister Pushpa'.

आधे सेर आटे में एक अंडा और पौन सेर दूध मिला दीजिए ।

'Mix one egg and 3/4 of a ser of milk in one half ser of whole wheat flour'.

A small sample of lexical items using मिलना or मिलाना includes the following:

X और Y के दिल मिलना	'for X and Y to be in sympathy with one another, for X and Y to be in love'
X ख़ाक में मिलना	'for X to be reduced to ashes, for X to fall to the ground'
सब मिलकर	'all together'
सब/कुल मिलाकर	'all in all, in toto' [cf. कुल adv. 'all in all, in sum, in toto']

16.3 Expressions for 'To Seem/Appear'

By far the most common expression in Hindi corresponding to the English verbs 'to seem' and 'to appear' involves the verb लगना. The general scheme for this locution is Y X को Z लगना, literally 'for Y to strike X as (being) Z'. By the use of this construction the Hindi speaker signifies that some party (X) perceives or judges some entity (Y) to be (Z):

उसके कपड़े मुझे नए लगे ।

'His clothes seemed new to me.' (i.e., 'struck me as [being] new'.)

अश्क़ की नई पुस्तक आपको कैसी लगी ?

'How did you like Ashk's new book?'

[cf. अश्क़ prop. m. the contemporary Hindi writer Upendranath 'Ashk'].

काफ़ी अच्छी लगी ।

'I liked it very much'. (i.e., 'it struck me [literally 'seemed to me'] as [being] very good'.)

लगना can also be used in sentences in which the clause indicating the perception or judgement is transposed to after the main verb of the sentence :

यह लगता है कि अश्क़ की नई पुस्तक काफ़ी अच्छी है ।

'It seems/appears that Ashk's new book is quite good'.

उस अध्यापक को लगा कि उसके विद्यार्थी सब कुछ सीख रहे हैं ।

'It seemed to that teacher that his students were learning everything'.

Note that in the last example the postposition को is used to mark the noun indicating the person making the judgement or having the perception. It should also be observed that the semantically empty elements यह and ऐसा are often used anticipatorily in sentences of seeming or appearing:

यह/ऐसा लगता है कि वह नहीं आएगा।
'It seems he won't be coming' (literally 'this seems/[it] thus seems that he won't come')
उनको ऐसा लगा कि प्रभाकर की आवाज कमज़ोर हो रही थी।
'It seemed to them that Prabhakar's voice as becoming weaker' (literally, 'to them thus it seemed that...') [cf. कमज़ोर adj. weak].

Several other Hindi constructions are encountered in the senses of 'to seem' and 'to appear'. Some of the most frequent of these are X को दिखना, X को जान पड़ना, X को प्रतीत होना, and X को मालूम होना (in the habitual):

मुझे { दिखता है / जान पड़ता है / प्रतीत होता है / मालूम होता है } कि उस युद्ध में बहुत सैनिक मरेंगे।
'It seems to me that many soldiers will die in that war'.

16.4. Vocative Forms of Nouns

Vocative forms of nouns are those employed in addressing or calling the individuals signified by those nouns. Hindi nouns of both genders have special vocative forms in the plural, and masculine Class I nouns have special vocative forms in the singular.

Masculine Class I singular nouns in the vocative display the termination -ए. For other masculine singular nouns, as well as for all feminine singular nouns, the vocative is the same as the direct singular forms:

हे बेटे, इधर आ!	'Son, come here!'
ओह फल वाले	'Oh, fruitseller!'
हे लड़की	'Oh, girl!'
पुत्र	'Son!'

The vocative forms of all plural nouns (whether masculine or feminine) are the same as their oblique plural, except that termination ends in the non-nasal -ओ in place of the nasal -ओं:

हे लड़को	'Oh, boys!'
ओह आदमियो	'Oh, men!'
हे लड़कियो	'Oh, girls!'
भाइयो और बहनो	'Brothers and sisters!'

16.5. Interjections

Interjections are words interposed in the flow of speech to indicate strong emotions or feelings. They are often used in invoking or addressing individuals. In these last functions, interjections often occur in conjunction with nouns in their vocative forms. There are many interjections found in Hindi, and they cover a wide range of emotions and psychological states. Some common Hindi interjections include the following:

In addressing or invoking: हे ! ओह !
In expressing appreciation: वाह ! वाह-वाह ! शाबाश !
In expressing surprise: आह! ओहो ! क्या !
In expressing disgust: छिः ! थू !
In expressing grief, shock or distress: हाय ! बाप रे बाप !

The frequent interjection राम-राम ! is used to express a number of distinct emotional states, ranging from surprise to hate and anger.

16.6 The Expressions चला जाना and चला आना

The important verbal expressions चला जाना 'to go, depart, set off' and चला आना 'to depart, set off' are somewhat irregular in their formation. It should be observed that these two expressions are verbal compounds formed of two verbal elements, चला and either जाना or आना. The चला element is declinable and agrees with the subject of the verb in number and gender (-आ m.sg., -ए m.pl., –ई f.sg. and f. pl.). चला जाना is used when the act of setting off or departing involves motion directed away from the speaker whereas चला आना is used when the motion is directed towards the speaker:

अपनी बहन से बात करके वह चला गया।
'After he talked to his sister he departed'.

अपनी बहन से बात करके वह घर चली आई।
'She came home after she talked to her sister'.

बेटे, तू वहाँ से चला जा!
'Child, leave that place !' (i.e., depart from that place)

बेटे, तू यहाँ चला आ !
'Child, come here!'

भाग जाना 'to flee, escape, set off in flight' and भाग आना 'to flee, escape, set off in flight' show the same grammatical irregularities as चला जाना and चला आना :

डर के कारण वह अपने गांव से भाग गया।
'He fled from his village out of fear'. (motion away from speaker)

बच्चा रोते-रोते यहां भाग आया।
'The child fled here in tears'. (motion towards speaker)
[cf. रोते-रोते adv. 'crying all the while, in tears'].

16.7. Vocabulary

अंधेरा	n.m. darkness
आवाज़	n.f. voice, sound, noise
ईद	prop. f. Id (a Muslim festival)
ईदगाह	n.m. a place of assembly for offering Id prayers
ईसाई	n.m. Christian
खेत	n.m. field
चांद	n.m. moon
चांदी	n.f. silver
चूड़ी	n.f. bangle
चेहरा	n.m. face
थैला	n.m. bag, sack
दीपक	n.m. earthen lamp
दीवाली	prop. f. Diwali (a Hindu festival)
धरती	n.f. earth, land
नमाज़	n.f. prayer (of Muslims)
पाठशाला	n.f. elementary/grade school (of traditional style)
पीपल	n.m. pipal tree
पूजा	n.f. prayer (of Hindus)
पूजाघर	n.m. place for doing पूजा, place of worship
भेड़	n.f. sheep
मंत्री	n.m. minister (of a state), secretary (of a government or organization)
मुसलमान	n.m. Muslim
शादी	n.f. wedding, marriage
समय	n.m. time, occasion
सूरज	n.m. the sun
सोना	n.m. gold
हिंदू	n.m. Hindu
गीला	adj. wet, moist
पवित्र	adj. holy, sacred
बुरा	adj. bad
चढ़ना	v.i. to rise, ascend, climb up
चढ़ाना	v.t. to raise, offer cause to ascend, elevate, to place on a fire (for cooking)
देख लेना	v.t. to take a look
नमाज़ पढ़ना	v.t. (for Muslims) to pray, to do नमाज़
पकड़ना	v.t. to grasp, catch, seize
पाना	v.t. to find
पूजा करना	v.t. (for Hindus, Jains, or Sikhs) to pray
फूल चढ़ाना	v.t. to make an offering of flowers (as part of a religious ceremony)
रुकना	v.i. to stop (of one's own accord)
रोकना	v.t. to stop (something else)
Y से X की शादी करना	v.t. to marry X to Y
हटना	v.i. to pull back, to desist, retreat
हटाना	v.t. to cause to pull back or retreat
इस समय	adv. now, at this time
उस समय	adv. then, at that time
काफ़ी	adv. quite; adj. enough, sufficient
किस समय	inter. when? at what time?

16.8. Exercises

16.8.1. *Translate into English*

1. वह ख़रीदना चाहता है, हम जाना चाहते थे, तुम बोलना चाहोगे, मैंने खाना चाहा; 2. हे लड़को, हे बच्ची, हे औरतो; 3. वह चढ़ने लगा, हम रोने लगे थे, तू जाने लगा होगा, लड़के हटने लगेंगे; 4. वह खेलना शुरू करता है, उसने गाना शुरू किया, उन्होंने पूजा करना आरम्भ किया; 5. उसको थैला मिला, हमको चीनी मिलेगी, उसको सुख मिला; 6. हम उनसे मिलेंगे, मैं तुझसे मिली, तू उससे मिलती है; 7. आम, आम का पेड़, आम के पेड़ों पर, पीपल के पेड़ से; 8. शादी, उषा की शादी, उन दो लड़कों की शादियाँ; 9. खाना अच्छा लगा, जूते अच्छे लगेंगे, लेख बुरे लगे; 10. मुझे जान पड़ता है, हमको दिखता है, बच्चे को मालूम होता था.

16.8.2. *Translate into Hindi*

1. She wants to laugh, we wanted to dance, you (int.) will want to flee, he wanted to die; 2. Cobblers! child! friends (f.)! boys!; 3. (use लगना) she began to rise, he had begun to come out, you (fam. f.) will begin to run, he must have begun to fall; 4. (use शुरू करना or आरम्भ करना) we began to study, you (pol. f.) will begin to do, she had begun to sew; 5. he got the opportunity, they got some water, she got several saris, the boy got a scholarship; 6. I (m.) met him, he will meet her, you (pol. m) meet (hab.) me, I had met them; 7. tree, tall tree, seven tall apple trees, on those forty tall apple trees; 8. Ram's wedding, Ram's very beautiful wedding; 9. The garden seems large, the sari seems beautiful, the book seemed good; 10. her voice seemed sweet, the shoes seemed too small, the river seemed holy to us.

16.8.3. *Translate into English*

1. मैं आपके साथ नमाज़ पढ़ने ईदगाह जाना चाहता हूँ। 2. सुरेश ने अपनी बेटी की शादी एक मित्र के लड़के से की थी। 3. वहां के लोग गंगा नदी को पवित्र समझते हैं। 4. बहुत देर तक बारिश होने के बाद सूरज निकलने लगा। 5. संतोष की पत्नी प्रमिला चांदी और सोने की ही चूड़ियां पहनती हैं। 6. हिन्दू लोग अधिकतर पूजाघर में फूल चढ़ाते हैं। 7. वह चेहरे से अपने दादा जी से मिलता-जुलता है। 8. हमें जान पड़ा कि वहां के लोग सिनेमा बहुत कम जाते हैं। 9. दीवाली पर सब बच्चों ने दीपक जलाए। 10. वह पीपल के पेड़ के नीचे ही सोने लगी। 11. अंधेरे में वे घर जाने का रास्ता नहीं पा सके। 12. पंजाब और कश्मीर के पहाड़ आपको कैसे लगे?

16.8.4. *Translate into Hindi*

1. He wanted to offer flowers in the pujaghar. 2. We were not able to hear her voice at that time. 3. We had met his sisters in that garden. 4. How much money did you get on that occasion? 5. He wanted (pt. hab.) to catch some small birds for his children. 6. People consider the cow the holiest animal in India. 7. Why did they marry their daughter to that fat boy? 8. He keeps (use रखना) his shoes in that sack. 9. Boys! Are you going to the pujaghar to offer flowers? 10. What room of that elementary school did they look in? How did those people like the Divali festival? 12. It seems to them that the land was completely wet from the rain.

CHAPTER 17

17.1. चाहिए CONSTRUCTIONS

The verbal marker चाहिए (var. spelling चाहिये) is used in a frequent indirect verb construction that has a number of distinct, albeit related, senses. The schema for this construction is X को Y चाहिए and the Y element of this formula may stand for either a simple noun phrase or an entire infinitival clause.

When the Y element of the above formula stands for a noun phrase, the construction has the sense 'X wants/needs/lacks/desires Y' :

उसको ठंडा पानी चाहिए ।
'He wants/needs some cold water'.

आपको क्या चाहिए?
'What do you want/need ?'

पिताजी को आपकी मदद चाहिए ।
'Father needs your help'.

If the noun indicating that which is desired or required is grammatically plural, then the form चाहिएं is used in place of चाहिए.[1]

लक्ष्मी को कुछ नई साड़ियां चाहिएं ।
'Lakshmi needs some new saris'.

नया घर बनाने के लिए कितने मज़दूर चाहिएं ?
'How many people are required to build a new house ?'

चाहिए also occurs in conjunction with simple past tense forms of होना to indicate a lack, desire, requirement, etc., of some entity (or entities) in the past. This होना element agrees in number and gender with the noun signifying the item (or items) lacking or desired :

उसको कुछ दाल चाहिए थी ।
'He/she needed/wanted (some) lentils'.

उनको क्या चाहिए था ?
'What did they want/need'.

When the Y element of the formula X को Y चाहिए stands for an infinitival clause (i.e., a verbal infinitive with or without its various objects), the entire construction indicates that X ought to carry out the activity indicated by the infinitive:

प्यारेलाल को दिल्ली जाना चाहिए ।
'Pyarelal ought to go to Delhi'.

1. For many Hindi speakers, however, चाहिए is treated as unchangeable, regardless of whether the preceding noun is singular or plural.

इस महीने में कैसा मौसम होना चाहिए ?
'What sort of weather ought there to be in this month ?'

तुमको प्रति दिन संस्कृत में कुछ-न-कुछ लिखना चाहिए ।
'You ought to read something or other in Sanskrit every day'.
[cf. कुछ-न-कुछ 'something or other'.]

उसको अपने परिवार के साथ यहाँ आना चाहिए ।
'He/she ought to come here with his/her family'.

Here too चाहिए can be expanded with a following simple past tense form of होना. When this occurs the entire construction signifies that X ought to have carried out the activity denoted by the infinitive. This usage presupposes that X did not, in fact, carry out the activity :

उनको यहाँ आना चाहिए था ।
'They ought to have come here'.

तुम्हें इतना खाना नहीं खाना चाहिए था ।
'You ought not to have eaten so much food'.

In cases where the infinitive has a direct object, the infinitive is made to agree in number and gender with that direct object. The चाहिए element likewise agrees in number with the direct object. If there is a past tense simple form of होना also present, it agrees in number and gender with the direct object, but the चाहिए element invariably appears in its non-nasalized form :

उसको कुछ पुस्तकें ख़रीदनी चाहिएं ।
'He ought to buy some books'.

उसको कुछ नई पुस्तकें ख़रीदनी चाहिए थीं ।
'He ought to have bought some new books'.

उनको इतने पपीते नहीं खाने चाहिए थे ।
'They shouldn't have eaten so many papayas'.

If the direct object of the infinitive is followed by the postposition को, the infinitive and the past tense form of होना are masculine singular, while the चाहिए element is in its singular (i.e., non-nasalized) form :

राम को इन लड़कियों को नहीं देखना चाहिए था ।
'Ram ought not to have looked at these girls'.

Occasionally, चाहिए sentences are encountered in which the phrases denoting the desired action is transposed after the चाहिए element. The verb of the transposed clause, instead of being in its infinitival form, is generally in the subjunctive:

यह चाहिए कि वह आपसे मिलने जाए ।
'He/she ought to go to meet you'.

This last sentence is roughly synonymous with उसे आपसे मिलने जाना चाहिए ।

17.2. INFINITIVE+होना

Very similar to the construction X का Y चाहिए is another construction having the form X को Y होना, where the variable Y stands for an infinitive or infinitival phrase

The entire construction signifies that X has to, as opposed to ought to, carry out the activity referred to by the infinitive. Examples of the use of this construction are given below :

मोहन को कलकत्ते जाना है ।
'Mohan has to go to Calcutta'.

उसे बाज़ार से खाना लाना था ।
'He/she had to bring the food from the market'.

यहाँ के विद्यार्थियों को प्रतिदिन पढ़ना होता है ।
'The students there have to study every day'.

As was the case in the चाहिए construction, the infinitive may agree with its direct object in number and gender, unless that direct object is followed by को. When that occurs, the होना element of this construction also stands in grammatical agreement with the direct object of the infinitive :

मुझे पिता जी की मदद करनी है ।
'I have to help Father'.

धोबी को उनके सब कपड़े धोने होंगे ।
'The washerman must have to wash all of their clothes'.

माता जी को दोनों बच्चियों को नहलाना था ।
'Mother had to bathe both girls'.

17.3. INFINITIVE+पड़ना

Where the necessity for carrying out some activity is specifically due to force of circumstances or external compulsion, the above construction is used with पड़ना substituted for होना :

उनको अपना घर बेचना पड़ा ।
'They had to sell their house (because of lack of money, a transfer in employment, etc.)'.

तुमको वहाँ कितनी देर (तक) रहना पड़ेगा ?
'How long will you have to stay there ?'

The infinitive and पड़ना element show the same features of grammatical agreement with a direct object of the infinitive as were seen in the infinitive+चाहिए and infinitive+होना constructions :

मुझे ढाई घंटे तक उसकी प्रतीक्षा करनी पड़ी ।
'I had to wait for him/her for two and a half hours'.

उनको अपने देश छोड़ने पड़ेंगे ।
'They will have to leave their countries'.

आपको उन्हीं पुस्तकों को पढ़ना पड़ेगा ।
'You will have to read those very books'.

17.4. ANOTHER CONSTRUCTION INDICATING OBLIGATION OR NECESSITY

The feminine nouns आवश्यकता and जरूरत may be employed in an indirect verb construction X को Y की आवश्यकता/जरूरत होना in the sense 'X needs or requires Y'. The Y of this construction may be either a noun (with or without modifiers) or an entire infinitival clause :

राम को पैसे की बड़ी आवश्यकता/जरूरत है ।
'Ram very much needs money'.

उनपर आक्रमण करने की क्या जरूरत है ?
'What need is there to attack them ?'

मुझे दोपहर को शहर जाने की जरूरत थी ।
'I had to go to the city in the afternoon.'

17.5. THE PASSIVE

A passive construction is found in Hindi in which the logical object of a transitive verb is made the grammatical subject of the sentence. The verb itself appears in its simple perfective form[2] and is followed by the auxiliary जाना, which can be freely conjugated :

उस विश्वविद्यालय में अंग्रेज़ी पढ़ी जाती है ।
'English is studied at that university'.

उस दफ़्तर में कैसा काम किया जा रहा था ?
'What kind of work was being done in that office ?'

मेरे यहां बहुत सुंदर गाने जरूर गाए जाएंगे ।
'Very beautiful songs will certainly be sung at my place'.

उस मौक़े पर कैसे कपड़े पहने जाने चाहिएं ?
'What kind of clothes ought to be worn on that occasion ?'

कहा जा सकता है कि लता से बढ़कर कोई गाने वाली नहीं ।
'It can be said that there is no better singer than Lata'.
[Cf. लता pn. f. Lata Mangeshkar, a famous Hindi film singer]

Normally, sentences containing transitive verbs in the passive do not provide a specification of the person or persons who actually carried out the action. On those occasions when such information is provided, however, the noun designating this party (or, these parties) is marked with से, के हाथ (alternate के हाथों) or, in Sanskritized Hindi, के द्वारा:

वह अपने भाई से/के हाथ/के द्वारा मारा गया ।
'He was killed by his brother'.

Occasionally, passive sentences are encountered in which the logical subject is marked with को and the passive verb is masculine singular. Thus the sentence

2. Except that the simple perfective feminine plural termination ईं is denasalized to ई before the auxiliary जाना. Thus साड़ियां बेची गई appears instead of the hypothetical *साड़ियां बेचीं गईं ।

अंधेरे में लड़की को नहीं देखा जा सकता था ।

'The girl couldn't be seen in the darkness'.

is an acceptable alternate of अंधेरे में लड़की नहीं देखी जा सकती थी ।

Passive sentences in which the जाना auxiliary is placed in its subjunctive form are exceedingly common in Hindi. These constructions offer a polite means of making requests or offers of various kinds :

कुछ चाय पी जाए ?

'Would you like some tea ?' (literally 'should some tea be drunk ?') [cf. चाय n.f. tea]

कुछ संतरे खाए जाएं ?

'Would you like some oranges ?'

The passive subjunctive sentence क्या किया जाए ! 'What is to be done?' is commonly used rhetorically to indicate one's helplessness in unpleasant or difficult circumstances.

N.B. The passive in Hindi is not to be considered functionally equivalent to the English passive, particularly with regard to the specification of the party who carries out the verbal activity. The Hindi passive tends to be frequent where specification of location, time, or manner are also present (e.g., in expressing the senses of the English sentences 'Hindi is spoken in the market/on such occasions/very carefully', etc.). When to this is added the specification of the doer of the action, the resulting sentence has a forced quality to it. This additional information tends to be given only for emphatic or stylistic purposes, or in responding to questions that are themselves posed in the passive voice.

There is to be found in Hindi another use of passive verb forms that is quite distinct from the use outlined above. This construction is not limited to transitive verbs, and is, indeed, often found with intransitive verbs in the negative. This usage indicates the inability of some party (marked by से) to carry out some verbal activity:

कल रात को उससे सोया नहीं गया ।

'He couldn't sleep last night'.

यह देखकर उससे नहीं रहा गया ।[3]

'When he/she saw this he/she was beside him/herself (in anger)'.

यह बड़ी अफ़सोस की बात है कि उनसे आया नहीं जाएगा ।

'Unfortunately, they will not be able to come'.

When जाना is used as the main verb in this construction it appears in the form जाया in place of the expected simple perfective form गया :

मुझसे नहीं जाया गया ।

'I was not able to go'.

---

3. रहना when appearing in this construction has the idiomatic sense of 'to be beside oneself in anger, frustration, or disgust'.

17.6. VOCABULARY

अजनबी	n.m. stranger
आंगन	n.m. courtyard
आलू	n.m. potato
खादी	n.f. home-spun cloth
चप्पल	n.f. sandal
चीज़	n.f. thing
जगह	n.f. place
तरफ़	n.f. direction
ध्यान	n.m. concentration, attention, care
नमक	n.m. salt
नौकर	n.m. servant
नौकरानी	n.f. female servant
पड़ोसी	n.m. neighbor
पुलिस	n.m. police
प्रकार	n.m. kind, sort, variety, manner
बार	n.f. time, occasion
मटर	n.f. pea, peas
मसाला	n.m. spice, spices
मिट्टी	n.f. clay, earth, dust
रसोई	n.f. kitchen
वस्तु	n.f. thing
विद्वान	n.m. scholar, learned person
स्थान	n.m. place, location
जरूरी	adj, important, necessary
थोड़ा,	adj. a little, some
थोड़ा-बहुत	adj. some, somewhat, a little
देशी	adj. native, indigenous
घूमना	v.i. to wander, meander, stroll
घूमना-फिरना	v.i. to wander, meander, stroll
डालना	v.t. to put in, place, insert, to pour
फिरना	v.i. to turn, revolve, wander
फेंकना	v.t. to throw, throw away, hurl
फैलना	v.i. to spread out
बचना	v.i. to escape, be left over, remain, survive
बचाना	v.t. to save, protect, retain
मारना	v.t. to strike, hit
मार डालना	v.t. to kill
सहना	v.t. to endure, tolerate
तुरन्त	adv. immediately
ध्यान से	adv. carefully, attentively
निरन्तर	adv. continuously
बार-बार	adv. time and again, over and over
X की तरफ़	post. towards X
कितनी बार	inter. how often ? how many times ?
किस तरफ़	inter. in which direction ?
किस तरह	inter. in what manner? how?
किस तरह का	inter. of what kind ?
किस प्रकार का	inter. of what kind ?

17.7. EXERCISES

17.7.1. *Translate into English*

1. उसको पानी चाहिए, मुझे चप्पलें चाहिए, आपको क्या चाहिए ?; 2. मसाला चाहिए था, कितनी चीजें चाहिए थीं ?, दो नौकर चाहिए थे; 3. मुझे जाना चाहिए, विद्वान को बोलना चाहिए, पुलिस को घूमना चाहिए, रानी को बेचना चाहिए था; 4. उसको कपड़े बेचने चाहिएं, हमको पुस्तकें पढ़नी चाहिएं, तुझे मदद करनी चाहिए, पड़ोसी को फल ख़रीदने चाहिए थे; 5. हमको जाना है, प्रमोद को सहना था, लक्ष्मी को देना होगा, बच्चे को उठना है, उसको बहुत चीजें लानी होंगी; 6. उसको भागना पड़ा, पुलिसवालों को यहां से जाना पड़ा, उनको अपने घर बेचने पड़े, मदन को उठना पड़ा; 7. थोड़ी हिन्दी, थोड़ी देर के लिए, थोड़ा-बहुत काम; 8. पंजाबी बोली जाती थी, साड़ियां बेची गईं, आक्रमण किया गया, मदद की जाएगी; 9. मुझसे सोया नहीं गया, हमसे नहीं ठहरा गया; 10. क्या पिया जाए ? थोड़ा खाया जाए ? कुछ गाने गाए जाएं ?; 11. किस प्रकार का काम, किस तरह के कपड़े, किस तरह की दाल ।

17.7.2. *Translate into Hindi*

1. He needs food, she needs money, we need those clothes; 2. the pandit

needed the book, the female servant needed the salt, rain was needed here, the neighbor needed the help; 3. I ought to cook, you (pol.) ought to be happy, they ought to speak Hindi, she ought to flee; 4. he ought not to have spoken, I ought to have drunk, we ought to have cooked, Father ought to have repeated; 5. (use infinitive+होना) he has to laugh, we had to speak, people have to wear, she must have to work; 6. (use infinitive+पड़ना) I will have to flee, she had to abandon, they (hab.) have to tell, you (fam.) will have to close; 7. a little water, a little bit of Panjabi, with (use से) a little bit of attention; 8. the book is (hab.) read, Hindi was (hab.) taught, food will be given, these clothes were cleaned; 9. (use passive) we couldn't see, he couldn't get up, the children couldn't understand; 10. (use passive subjunctive) what should be seen ? what ought to be done ? what questions should be asked ?; 11. this kind of mango, that kind of important work, that sort of spice.

17.7.3. *Translate into English*

1. हिंदी भारत के बड़े-बड़े[4] शहरों में बोली जाती है। 2. उस अवसर पर सब प्रकार के अच्छे खाने पकाए गए । 3. वह पुस्तक ध्यान से पढ़ी जानी चाहिए। 4. वहां पहुंच कर तरह-तरह[5] के जरूरी काम किए जाएंगे। 5. नौकरानी को मिट्टी की कितनी चीज़ें चाहिएं ? 6. आलू अच्छी तरह पकाने के लिए किस तरह का मसाला चाहिए ? 7. कहा जाता है कि कश्मीर भारत का सबसे सुन्दर स्थान है। 8. आपको उनकी बातें[6] कितनी बार सुननी पड़ीं ? 9. उनके सारे काग़ज़ खिड़की के बाहर फेंके गए। 10. भारत के बारे में अच्छी तरह सीखने के लिए उसकी पुरानी सड़कों मर घूमना-फिरना चाहिए। 11. उस बाज़ार में सब वस्तुओं की दुकानें देखी जा सकती हैं। 12. कल रात को बुख़ार लगने के कारण उससे सोया नहीं गया। 13. कमलेश को सब्ज़ी में इतना नमक नहीं डालना चाहिए था।

17.7.4. *Translate into Hindi*

1. You (pol.) should speak only Hindi when you go to India (use कर and चाहिए). 2. Mr. Vajpeyi had to take his children to Calcutta last week. 3. In Pakistan the native fruit are considered the best (use passive of समझना). 4. How many potatoes did the female servant need ? 5. You (fam.) ought not use (i.e., put) so much (use इतना) salt in your food. 6. He ought to have worn his sandals on that occasion. 7. The shopkeepers were compelled to sell their stores. 8. She had to work at the office over and over again. 9. What kind of sandals used to be sold in that market ? 10. Much clarified butter was eaten with the bread. 11. Those people were seen in the market of the old city. 12. Panjabi has begun to be understood in those colonies (use बस्तियां) 13. It is inappropriate to do so much work in the hot season (i.e., so much work ought not be done in the hot season). 14. He couldn't come last week (use passive) because he had to go to the village.

---

4. बड़े-बड़े, 'very large'. For a discussion of the functions of the repetition (or 'reduplication') of linguistic forms v. 28.2.

5. तरह-तरह का 'all kinds of'.

6. उनकी बातें 'what they have to say'.

CHAPTER 18

18.1 Conjunct Verbs

A conjunct verb may be defined as a sequence of either a noun or an adjective and a following verb that constitutes a tightly knit conceptual and syntactic unit. Such sequences are often used to express notions that in other languages or in other circumstances might be expressed by a unitary verb. Conjunct verbs are to be found in all styles of Hindi, although they are especially prevalent in Sanskritic Hindi and in literary Urdu. By far the most common conjunct verbs in Hindi are those showing करना or होना as their verbal components, although others with different verbs are by no means infrequent.

18.2. Conjunct Verbs With करना

A very large number of Hindi conjunct verbs consist of a noun or an adjective followed by करना. Examples showing adjectives include बंद करना v. tr. 'to close' [cf. बंद adj. 'closed'] and प्रकाशित करना v.t. 'to publish' [cf. प्रकाशित adj. 'published'], and साफ़ करना v.t. 'to clean':

शेखर ने उस कमरे का दरवाज़ा बंद किया ।
'Shekhar [prop. m.] closed the door to that room'.

अगले वर्ष में यह पुस्तक प्रकाशित करूंगा ।
'I will publish this book next year'.

नौकर को दोनों कमरे साफ़ करने चाहिएं ।
'The servant ought to clean both rooms'.

Conjuncts consisting of a noun plus करना are far more numerous than those with adjectives plus करना. These 'nominal' conjuncts can be divided into two broad classes according to some syntactic properties they display. In conjucts of the first type the noun element is "linked" to its object by means of the postposition का/के/की.[1] Examples of conjuncts of this kind include X की सेवा करना v.t. 'to serve X, to attend to X', X की प्रतीक्षा करना v.t. 'to wait for X', and X का प्रयोग करना v.t. 'to employ, use X':

दोनों लड़कों ने पिताजी की सेवा की थी ।
'Both boys had aided (i.e., provided assistance/service for) Father'.

मुझे बहुत देर तक आपकी प्रतीक्षा करनी पडी ।
'I had to wait for you for a long time'.

1. If the noun element of the conjunct is masculine, का is the linking postposition, while की is used if the noun is feminine.

वे इस प्रकार की वस्तुओं का प्रयोग क्यों करते हैं ?
'Why do they use things of this kind?'

There are some important syntactic peculiarities to be observed in the above sentences. Notice that in the first sentence even though the sequence सेवा करना is a conceptual whole, one whose logical direct object is the noun पिता जी (i.e., it is Father who is being attended to), the feminine noun सेवा functions as the grammatical direct object of करना. This explains why करना (as well as the following auxiliary) appears in a feminine singular form. Likewise, in the second example प्रतीक्षा (n.f.) functions as the grammatical direct object of करना. Hence both the infinitive and the पड़ना element are in their feminine singular forms. Note too that in passive sentences involving this kind of "linked" conjunct it is the nominal element of the conjunct that serves as the grammatical subject of the sentence:

यहाँ पिता जी की सेवा की जाती है ।
'Father is always attended to here'.

उस समय इन वस्तुओं का प्रयोग किया जा रहा था ।
'These things were being used at that time'.

In the second large class of conjuncts (consisting of a noun plus करना) the noun element is not linked to the direct object of the entire conjunct. Examples of conjuct verbs of this type include काम करना v. tr. 'to work', स्वीकार करना 'to accept', and माफ़ करना 'to excuse, pardon':

वह नई दिल्ली के एक दफ्तर में काम करता है ।
'He works in an office in New Delhi'.

वह आपकी बातें नहीं स्वीकार कर सका ।
'He couldn't accept what you said'.

माफ़ कीजिये, शुक्ल साहब । आप अपनी बात दुहराइये ।
'Pardon [me], Mr. Shukla. Will you please repeat what you said?'

When the direct object of this last type of conjunct verb is animate, and under certain other defined conditions (8.3.), the direct object may be followed by को :

गांव के लोग मुझे माफ़ करना नहीं चाहते थे ।
'The people of the village didn't want to forgive me'.

Some conjunct verbs may be treated alternately as linking or non-linking, as, for example, (X का) अनुभव करना v.t, 'to experience (X),' (X की) तलाश करना v.t. 'to look for, search for (X)', and X (का) ख़र्च करना v.t. 'to spend (X)':

मीना (prop. f.) और रत्न (prop. f.) ने पहाड़ों की सुन्दरता अनुभव की थी ।
मीना और रत्न ने पहाड़ों की सुन्दरता का अनुभव किया था ।
'Mina and Ratna had experienced the beauty of the mountains'.

अरुण (prop. m.) और दीनदयाल (prop. m.) बच्चों को तलाश कर रहे थे ।
अरुण और दीनदयाल बच्चों की तलाश कर रहे थे ।
'Arun and Dindayal were looking for the children'.

उस दिन आपने कितना पैसा ख़र्च किया ?
उस दिन आपने कितने पैसे का ख़र्च किया ?
'How much money did you spend that day?'

18.3. Conjunct Verbs With होना

The very same nouns and adjectives that appear in conjunct verbs with करना generally also appear in conjunct verbs with होना. Whereas the conjuncts with करना are grammatically transitive—as demonstrated by the fact that they require the ने construction in the perfective—, those with होना are grammatically intransitive. Thus where बंद करना and प्रकाशित करना can be glossed as 'to close' and 'to publish', बंद होना and प्रकाशित होना have the senses 'to be closed' and 'to be published' respectively:

अब उस कमरे का दरवाजा बंद है ।
'The door to that room is closed now'.
अगले वर्ष मेरी पुस्तक दिल्ली में प्रकाशित होगी ।
'My book will be published next year in Delhi'.

Those nouns that are linked to their objects with का/के/की when appearing together with करना are also so linked to these objects when occurring with होना *honā*:

उस समय उन वस्तुओं का प्रयोग हो रहा था ।
'Those things were being used at that time'.
ऐसे लोगों के घरों में बूढ़ों की सेवा नहीं होती ।
'Elderly people aren't attended to in the homes of such people'.

Many conjunct verbs with होना are employed in indirect verb constructions having the general form X को noun होना. The noun element in this construction type is used to represent psychological states or conditions, physical sensations or afflictions, and judgements and perceptions of various kinds; the noun followed by को *kō* indicates the person or persons perceiving, experiencing, undergoing, etc., the specified state, perception, affliction, etc.:

मुझे त्रिपाठी जी से मिलने की इच्छा है ।
'I want to meet Mr. Tripathi'.
मीना और रत्न को पहाड़ों की सुन्दरता का अनुभव हुआ था ।
'Mina and Ratna had experienced the beauty of mountains'.
परसों शाम को पटेल साहब को बहुत काम था ।
'Mr. Patel had much work [to do] the day before yesterday in the evening'.

It should be observed that many of the indirect verb constructions described in 15.1. contain conjunct verbs of the sort being discussed here.

18.4. Relationship Between Conjunct Verbs With करना and Those With होना

Conjunct verbs consisting of a noun or adjective followed by करना and conjuncts consisting of the same noun or adjective followed by होना stand in a close syntactic relationship to one another. Indeed, the two sorts of conjuncts can be looked upon as transitive and intransitive counterparts of one another.

Consider the abstract noun अनुभव 'experience, perception'. This noun can appear in conjuncts with either करना or होना. If one wishes to make the person (or persons) who experiences something (as, for example extreme grief) the grammatical subject of the sentence, then अनुभव occurs together with करना:

उसने अत्यन्त दुःख का अनुभव किया।
'He experienced great grief'.

If, by contrast, one wishes to make the experience or perception itself of the grief the topic of the sentence, then the noun अनुभव is linked to होना. The noun indicating the person or persons having this experience assumes a subsidiary status and is marked with the postposition को:

उसको अत्यन्त दुःख का अनुभव हुआ।

It cannot be said that there is any denotative difference between the two last example sentences. In both sentences it is the same party who perceives and the same emotion that is perceived. The sentences differ, however, in whether it is the perceiver who is the primary focus of the sentence or the act of experiencing or perceiving itself.

18.5. Conjunct Verbs not Employing करना or होना

Conjunct verbs employing verbal elements other than करना or होना although not as frequent as those using करना and होना, are nevertheless common throughout Hindi. Verbs often encountered in conjuncts include देना (e.g., X को Y का परिचय देना v.t. 'to introduce Y to X'), लेना (e.g., साँस लेना v.t. 'to breathe'), डालना (e.g., X की आदत डालना v.t. 'to form the habit of X'), उठाना (e.g., X का फ़ायदा उठाना v. 'to take advantage of X'), खाना (e.g. मार खाना v.t. 'to get beaten'), रखना (e.g, याद रखना v.t. 'to bear in mind, remember'), and आना (e.g., वापस आना v.i. 'to return, come back'). Often conjunct verbs display quite idiosyncratic combinations of noun or adjective with verbal elements, thus requiring that they be learned as idioms (e.g., तस्वीर खींचना v.t. 'to take/draw a picture', हल जोतना v.t. 'to plough' and X का मज़ाक़ उड़ाना v.t. 'to make fun of X').

18.6. Postpositions Other Than का/के/की in Conjunct Verbs

In the conjunct verbs examined so far any linkage of the conjunct with its direct object has been carried out by means of the postposition का/के/की. There are, however, many conjunct verbs in Hindi in which the nominal or adjectival component of the conjunct is linked to other nouns in the sentences by means of postpositions other than का/के/की. Common postpositions so employed include में, पर, से, के ऊपर, की तरफ (or की ओर), and others: e.g., X से सवाल पूछना v.t. 'to ask a question of X', X में/पर विश्वास करना v.t. 'to place trust in X, to trust X', X पर/के ऊपर क्रोध करना v.t. 'to get angry with/at X', and X की तरफ़/ ओर मुंह करना v.t. 'to turn one's face towards X'.

18.7. VOCABULARY

ख़र्च	n.m. expense, expenditure	X को Y का परिचय देना	v.t. to introduce Y to X
गाड़ी	n.f. cart, train, vehicle	प्रकाशित करना/होना	v.t./i. to publish/to be published
चोर	n.m. thief	X की प्रतीक्षा करना/होना	v.t./i. to wait for X/for X to be waited for
जंगल	n.m. woods, forest, jungle	X का प्रयोग करना/होना	v t./i. to use X/for X to be used
जनता	n.f. populace, the people	X से प्रश्न पूछना	v.t. to inquire of X, to ask X
जीवन	n.m. life, existence	X का/से फ़ायदा/ उठाना	v.t. to derive benefit from X
झूठ	n.m. lie, falsehood	X का मजाक़ उड़ाना	v.t. to ridicule X
तस्वीर	n.f. picture	माफ़ करना	v.t. to excuse, pardon
पत्थर	n.m. stone, rock	मार खाना	v.t. to get a beating, to be beaten up
परिचय	n.m. familiarity, acquaintance	X की तरफ़/की ओर मुंह करना	v.t. to turn one's face towards X
फ़ायदा	n.m. benefit	याद रखना	v.t. to bear in mind, remember
बरतन	n.m. (cooking) utensil	वापस आना	v.i to return, come back
भवन	n.m. residence, house, home	X में/पर विश्वास करना/होना	v.t./i. to trust X
भीड़	n.m. crowd, multitude, throng	सांस लेना	v.t. to breathe, to take a breath
भोजन	n.m. food	साफ़ करना	v.t. to clean
हल	n.m. plough	स्वीकार करना/ होना	v.t./i. to accept/to be accepted
ग़लत	adj. incorrect, wrong	हल जोतना	v.t. to plough
गहरा	adj. deep, dark, profound	अत्यन्त	adv. extremely, excessively
हलका	adj. light (in color and weight)	धीरे	adv. slowly
X की आदत डालना	v.t. to form the habit to X	सदा	adv. always
X की इच्छा करना/होना	v.t/i. to wish, desire X		
X को उत्तर देना	v.t. to reply to X		
X पर/के ऊपर क्रोध करना/आना	v.t./i. to get angry/be angry with X		
X (का) ख़र्च करना/होना	v.t./i. to spend X/for X to be spent		
X (की) तलाश करना/होना	v.t/i. to look for X/for X to be looked for		
तस्वीर खींचना	v.t. to take/draw a picture		

18.8. EXERCISES

18.8.1. *Translate into English*

1. उस प्रदेश की जनता को भी पक्के घरों में रहने की इच्छा है। 2. वह श्री के० पी० गोपाल को आपका परिचय देना चाहता था। 3. मुझे बहुत देर तक आपकी प्रतीक्षा करनी पड़ी। 4. तुम इतनी किताबें पढ़ने से क्या फ़ायदा उठा सकोगे ?. 5. सब देशों में बच्चे अपने भाई-बहिनों का मजाक़ उड़ाते हैं। 6. याद रखिए कि दिल्ली जानेवाली गाड़ी इस गांव में नहीं रुकती। 7. हिन्दुस्तान जाने में आपने कितना पैसा ख़र्च किया ? 8 माफ़ कीजिए, रहमान साहब, क्या आप मेरे साथ लखनऊ वापस आएंगे ? 9. शीला ने अपने खाने में बहुत मसाला खाने की आदत डाली थी। 10. चोर जंगल में अपने दोस्तों की तलाश कर रहा था। 11. यहां इन बरतनों का प्रयोग किस लिए किया जाता है ? 12. पिताजी को मेरे मित्रों पर अत्यन्त क्रोध आता है। 13. आपकी अगली पुस्तक कब प्रकाशित होगी ? 14. मैं उनकी बातों पर विश्वास नहीं कर पाता क्योंकि वे कभी-कभी झूठ बोलते हैं। 15. उसने कहा था कि आपकी सारी बातें बिलकुल ग़लत हैं।

18.8.2. *Translate into Hindi*

1. How many times did you (pol.) have to clean those utensils? 2. The thief turned his face towards those people. 3. Those animals were ploughing [in] the fields. 4. I want to ask what (use कि) the weather will be tomorrow. 5. My father took seven pictures of Mr. and Mrs. Gupta, 6. Why do you always get angry at what he says (उसकी बातें)? 7. We will want to go to the store with you (pol.). 8. What kinds of stones were used in building this house? 9. I will not be able to reply to you until Thursday. 10. Why do those girls always ridicule their teachers? 11. He waited for Father outside the house because it was too warm inside. 12. How much money did you spend in the market yesterday? 13. I will certainly introduce you to my friends on that occasion. 14. Our enemies will certainly want to attack us. 15. All of their friends began to come home yesterday afternoon.

18.8.3. Transform the following sentences using conjunct verbs with करना into sentences using conjunct verbs with होना (e.g., वह राम पर क्रोध करता है→उसे राम पर क्रोध आता है; उसने कल बाज़ार में बहुत पैसे ख़र्च किये→कल बाजार में बहुत पैसे ख़र्च हुए):

1. हम उसकी पुस्तक प्रकाशित करेंगे। 2. मैं उसकी बातों पर विश्वास नहीं करता। 3. वहाँ लोग पिता जी की सेवा करते हैं। 4. हम आपसे बात करेंगे। 5. अगले हफ़्ते मोहनलाल रामनाथ की बेटी से शादी करेगा।

18.8.4. Transform the following sentences using intransitive conjunct verbs with होना into sentences using conjuncts with करना. Wherever necessary, supply appropriate grammatical subjects: e.g., मुझे उनके बच्चे पसन्द हैं →मैं उनके बच्चों को पसन्द करता हूं; उसका कमरा साफ़ हुआ→राम ने अपना कमरा साफ़ किया।

1. मुझे पूरा विश्वास है कि उसकी बातें ठीक हैं। 2. उसकी दुकान कब बन्द होती है ? 3. आजकल बूढ़ों की मदद क्यों नहीं होती ? 4. राम को अपनी छोटी बहिन पर क्रोध आने लगा। 5. कल सुबह स्कूल के बाहर मदन की तलाश हो रही थी।

CHAPTER 19

19.1. Compound Verbs (Introduction)

In the preceding chapters of this book it has been assumed that the Hindi sentence ordinarily contains a verbal stem to which grammatical inflections of various sorts are added. For pedagogical reasons the verbal stems treated so far have by and large been single, that is, have contained only one verbal element prior to the inflections. Now it must be revealed that Hindi stems are frequently *compound*, that is, composed of two distinct verbal elements prior to the inflections.

The general schema for the compound verb in Hindi is V_1V_2+ inflections. In this construction the V_1 element occurs in its stem form (i.e., devoid of any inflection) while the V_2 element receives the inflection for the entire compound.[1] In the vast majority of cases the meaning of a V_1V_2 compound is a modification of the general meaning of the V_1 element. These principles are illustrated in the following example sentence:

सन् १९४७ में भारत को आज़ादी मिल गई ।
'In 1947 India received [her] independence'.

In this sentence मिल गई is a compound verb form. It contains the V_1 element मिल in its uninflected stem form as well as the V_2 element गई which is the si. perf. f.s. form of जाना. The central meaning of the entire compound, namely 'received, obtained', is a modification of the lexical sense of the V_1 element मिलना, not of the V_2 element जाना.

Virtually all verbs of Hindi can occur as the V_1 member of compound verb constructions, although only a small number commonly occur as the V_2. The verbs most frequently found as V_2 components of compounds are जाना, आना, लेना, देना, रखना, बैठना, पड़ना, उठना, पहुंचना, चलना, डालना, मरना, and मारना.[2] In many cases, the meaning contributed by the V_2 element to the compound bears little or no resemblance to the literal meaning of the V_2 element when it occurs elsewhere as an independent verb of a sentence. Thus in the above example it is not possible to say that the जाना V_2 element contributes some element of 'going' to the entire compound. In fact, it is quite difficult to isolate a single semantic notion contributed by the same V_2 element to the various compounds in which it can occur. Often a V_2 element brings different semantic properties to compounds formed with V_1 elements of different types.

---

1. There are in Hindi other verbal compounds in which the V_1 elements bear some sort of inflection. These constructions are taken up in 16.6., 30.1, and 30.6.

2. Verbal stem +सकना, verbal stem+चुकना, and verbal stem+पाना constructions, classified by some grammarians as compounds, have been discussed elsewhere (17.1.).

19.2. Compounds With जाना

Compounds in which जाना appears as the V_2 element are of several distinct types. In the first of these the जाना element is used together with an intransitive verb of some sort, the whole compound indicating a change of state or condition. Thus whereas होना 'to be' by itself indicates a state (namely one of being), हो जाना 'to become' indicates a change of state. Often to the notion of change of state is added an indication of the completion or fulfillment of some intransitive verbal activity.[3]

छोटे पौधे घर के पीछे आ गए ।
'The small plants grew up behind the house'.

सुबह का खाना चूल्हे पर पक गया ।
'The morning meal got cooked on the (earthen) stove'.

घर जाकर वह तुरंत सो गई ।
'She went home and immediately went to sleep'.

Often it is not possible to isolate any denotative meaning added by the element to an intransitive V_1. This is especially true when the V_1V_2 compound occurs as the main verbal element of a sentence. In such cases the जाना element is used to mechanically expand any of a wide variety of intransitive V_1 elements:

अच्छी रोटी कहाँ मिलती है/मिल जाती है ?
'Where can [you] get good bread?'

बच्चो, तुम इधर आओ/आ जाओ ।
'Children, come here'.

समय बीत जाता है, बात रह जाती है ।
'Time passes by but the memory remains'.

ख़राब दिन किसी तरह कट गए ।
'Somehow or other the bad days were endured'.

With transitive verbs indicating ingestion, जाना adds a sense of the totality or thoroughness of the acts of ingestion. Thus from खाना 'to eat' and पीना 'to drink' are formed खा जाना 'to eat up, devour' and पी जाना 'to drink up':

काम से लौट कर वह घर का सब खाना खा जाता है ।
'He eats up all the food in the house when he comes home from work'.

In yet other compounds, जाना retains some of its literal meaning of 'to go'. In such cases जाना designates motion away from the speaker of the sentence. The constructions ले जाना 'to take someone or something somewhere' and निकल जाना 'to emerge' (with motion away from the speaker) are compounds of this sort:

वह कल दोपहर को अपने घर से निकल गया ।
'He left his home yesterday afternoon'.

---

3. हो जाना often also has the idiosyncratic sense 'to be completed'. Thus in response to a query as to the status of some project it is appropriate to respond हो गया 'it's done, finished'.

19.3. COMPOUNDS WITH आना

The primary use of आना in V_1V_2 compounds is to add a sense of motion directed towards the speaker of the sentence. In this capacity आना stands in direct opposition to the use of जाना in such compounds as ले जाना and निकल जाना. Whereas जाना designates an act of taking something or someone away from the speaker, आना signifies that the taking is directed towards the speaker :

वह अपने बच्चों को चिड़ियाघर ले गया ।
'He took his children to the zoo'.

वह अपने बच्चों को चिड़ियाघर ले आया ।
'He brought his children [here] to the zoo'.

N.B. The verbs जाना and आना are not used as the second component of V_1V_2 compounds in which the first component is the uninflected stem of चलना.[4] Rather, the expressions चला जाना and चला आना are employed, showing the inflected stem चला– (cf. 16.6).

19.4. COMPOUNDS WITH लेना

There are two main senses in which लेना is used as the second member of V_1V_2 compounds. In the first of these the verb indicates the capacity to employ some learned skill or capacity:

वह थोड़ी-बहुत हिन्दी बोल लेती है ।
'She can speak a fair amount of Hindi'.

मैं यहाँ की बोलचाल थोड़ी-थोड़ी समझ लेता हूँ ।
'I can hardly understand the style of speech here'.

The second use of लेना is to indicate that a verbal activity, almost always transitive is carried out for the benefit of its doer, or that the activity is in some way oriented or directed towards the doer :

दुकान जाकर वह नए कपड़े ख़रीद लेगा ।
'He will go to the store and buy some new clothes (for himself)'.

श्रीमान जी, कुछ ताज़े फल ले लीजिए ।
'Sir, please have some fresh fruit'.

There are a number of other instances of लेना in common compounds that do not fit the above patterns. These include हो लेना '[for work] to be completed', X के साथ हो लेना 'to accompany X', and सो लेना 'to finish sleeping'.

19.5. COMPOUNDS WITH देना

The verb देना is used in compounds in two important ways. Firstly, it is used with transitive verbs to indicate that a verbal activity is outwardly directed or carried out for the benefit of someone other than the doer. In this capacity देना stands in direct opposition to one of the uses of लेना in compounds :

4. An exception to this rule, however, is the idiomatic construction चल जाना, having the use 'to circulate falsely, to be counterfeit'.

दुकान जाकर वह नए कपड़े ख़रीद देगा ।
'He will go to the store and buy some new clothes (for someone else)'.
इस गांव के बढ़ई ने हमारे लिए तीन मेज़ें बना दी थीं ।
'This village's carpenter had made three tables for us'.

Secondly, देना is used with intransitive V_1 elements to indicate the initiation of an activity:

सात घंटे के बाद वह उस रास्ते से चल दिया ।
'After seven hours h` set off by that route'.

19.6. Syntactic Properties of V_1V_2 Compounds

There are a number of aspects of the compound verb in Hindi that are problematic for students. One of the most important of these concerns knowing when to use compounds and when to use single verbs. Unfortunately, there is no simple answer to this problem, although some general guidelines concerning this matter can be provided. As a rule, compound verbs are not employed in Hindi to indicate verbal activities or states of affairs that are anticipatory or subordinate to other verbal activities within the same sentence. For example, in the sentence

वह घर लौट कर सो गया ।
'He returned home and went to sleep'

the action of returning home is anticipatory of the main action of the sentence, that of going to sleep. For this reason, the simple stem लौट– is used instead of the compound लौट आ– before the conjunctive form कर. The action of going to sleep, being the primary predicate of the sentence, is, however, amplified by a V_2 element, here जाना. In general, verbs followed by कर (or its alternate के) or by postpositions of various kinds tend not to occur in compound form. Conversely, verbs that indicate the primary action of a sentence are very likely to be compound. This is especially the case if these verbal activities are specified as being carried through to some sort of conclusion. In negative clauses the use of compound verbs is generally avoided. Thus नहीं मिला is to be considered the negative of मिल गया, not *नहीं मिल गया.

Another aspect of the compound verb in Hindi that provides some difficulty for students is knowing when to use the ने construction in conjunction with compounds. It should be recalled that the ने construction is generally used when the verb is both transitive and in one of the perfective aspectual-tenses. This statement needs to be amplified if compound verbs are concerned. The ने construction is employed with compounds if and only if each element of the compound would itself require ने were it the unique verbal element of the sentence. For example, consider the compound बना लेना 'to make something (for oneself)'. This compound requires the ने construction in the perfective because each of its two components, बनाना and लेना, independently requires ने in the perfective. By contrast, ले जाना, and ले आना, although semantically transitive (i.e., they have direct objects), do not appear in the ने construction when they are in the perfective. This is because even though लेना independently takes ने in the perfective, जाना and आना, being intransitive, do not. Since it is not the case that both components of the compound would independently require ने, the entire compound does not appear in the constructions.

19.7. Dates According to the Western Calendar

The Hindi names of the months according to the western calender are as follows:

जनवरी	अप्रैल	जुलाई	अक्तूबर
फ़रवरी	मई	अगस्त	नवम्बर
मार्च	जून	सितम्बर	दिसम्बर

The names of the days of the week have already been provided in the vocabulary to Chapter 10.

Normally cardinal numbers are used to specify a given day of the month:

बीस दिसम्बर 'December 20th' नौ मई 'May 9th'.

An exception to this is the first (and occasionally the second) day of the month, commonly indicated by the appropriate ordinal:

पहली अक्तूबर 'October 1st'

When locating some event at some particular date the postposition को is optionally used:

आठ दिसम्बर (को) 'on the 8th of December'.

In relating years the word सन् (literally 'year') often precedes the specification of the exact year. Moreover, the word ईसवी 'Christian' (abbreviated ई०) is often found after a date. This usage corresponds to the English language abbreviation A.D. For dates prior to the birth of Christ the phrase ईसा पूर्व (abbreviated ई० पू०) is used:

सन् उन्नीस सौ पैंतीस ई० '1935 A.D.'

सन् एक सौ एक ई० पू० '101 B.C.'

The words दिनांक (abbreviated दि०) and तारीख़ (abbreviated ता०) are frequently used in conjunction with dates:

दि० पहली अप्रैल उन्नीस सौ सत्तर ई० को
'on April 1st, 1970 A.D.'

ता० छ: सितम्बर सन् अठारह सौ पचास ई० को
'on September 6th, 1850 A.D.'

अगस्त की दूसरी तारीख़ को
'on August 2nd'

दिनांक पच्चीस नवम्बर सन् उन्नीस सौ इकसठ ई० को
'on the 25th of November, 1961 A.D.'

19.8. The Expressions दिखाई देना/पड़ना and सुनाई देना/पड़ना

The verbal expressions दिखाई देना and दिखाई पड़ना are frequently employed in Hindi and have the quasi-passive sense 'for something or someone to be seen'. These formations are used in the indirect grammatical construction X को Y दिखाई देना / पड़ना in which X indicates the person to whom the object or person (Y) is made visible. In this construction the दिखाई element is invariable, always ending with the long vowel-ई. It is the देना or पड़ना element that receives the conjugation for the entire construction:

उस समय बग़ीचे के पास हमें दो कुएँ दिखाई दे सके ।
'At that time we could see two wells near the garden'.
मेज़ पर उसकी दो पुस्तकें दिखाई पड़ीं ।
'His/her two books became visible on the table'.

The expressions सुनाई देना and सुनाई पड़ना 'to be audible, to be heard' are in their formation and employment exactly analogous to दिखाई देना and दिखाई पड़ना :

मुझे उसकी मधुर आवाज सुनाई देने लगी ।
'I started to hear his/her mellifluous voice'.
लता के गाने कहाँ सुनाई दे सकते हैं ?
'Where can Lata's songs be heard'?

19.9. VOCABULARY

आज़ादी	n.f. independence, freedom	विशेष	adj. special
उत्तर	n.m. north	कटना	v.i. to be cut, for time to elapse or be spent
उम्र (often pronounced उमर)	n.f. age	काटना	v.t. to cut, to spend time
घटना	n.f. incident, event	नापना	v.t. to measure
चिड़ियाघर	n.m. zoo	बिताना	v.t. to spend time
चूल्हा	n.m. stove, hearth	बीतना	v.i. for time to elapse
जवाब	n.m. answer, reply	मांगना	v.t. to demand
तारीख़	n.f. date, day	लौटना	v.i. to return
दक्षिण	n.m. south	सो लेना	v.i. to finish sleeping
दिनांक	n.m. date, day	हो लेना	v.i. (for work) to be completed
नौजवान	n.m. young man	X के साथ हो लेना	v.i. to accompany X
पश्चिम	n.m. west		
पूर्व	n.m. east	आसानी से	adv. easily
बढ़ई	n.m. carpenter	एकदम	adv. at once, suddenly, totally
बत्ती	n.f. lamp		
बिजली	n.f. electricity, lightning	किसी तरह	adv. somehow
बोलचाल	n.f. speech, manner of speaking, conversation	थोड़े-थोड़े	adv. hardly, seldom
		पैदल	adv. on foot
मंजिल	n.f. floor or story (of a building)	प्रायः	adv. usually, generally
		यूँ ही	adv. casually, by chance, in this manner
मंदिर	n.m. (Hindu or Jain) temple		
मसजिद	n.f. mosque	X की अपेक्षा	post. in comparison to X
सवाल	n.m. question	X के आस-पास	post. near X, around X
स्वतंत्रता	n.f. independence, freedom	X के उत्तर	post. to the north of X
आज़ाद	adj. independent	X के दक्षिण	post. to the south of X
पतला	adj. thin, lean	X के पश्चिम	post. to the west of X
बलवान	adj. strong	X के पूर्व	post. to the east of X
मधुर	adj. sweet, mellifluous	X के बदले	post. in place of X, in exchange for X
मामूली	adj. ordinary, routine		

19.10. Exercises

19.10.1. *Translate into English.*

1. पहली नबम्बर, पांच मई, तीस सितम्बर ; 2. इक्कीस जून सन् उन्नीस सौ सत्तर को, दिनांक छब्बीस दिसम्बर सन् अठारह सौ इक्यावन ई० को; 3. शुक्रवार जून की नौ तारीख़ को , सोमवार अक्तूबर की दूसरी तारीख़ को; 4. चिड़ियाघर के आस-पास, उन तीन मंदिरों के आस-पास, उस बूढ़े की उम्र की अपेक्षा; 5. भारत के उत्तर, दिल्ली के पूर्व, पाकिस्तान के दक्षिण में, उत्तर प्रदेश के पश्चिम में; 6. वह समझ लेता है, हम बोल लेते हैं, तू पढ़ लेती है; 7. उन्होंने बना दिया, स्त्री ने पका लिया, (आप) दे दीजिए, (तुम) ले लो; 8. क्या हो गया है ?, वह खा गया था, वे पी गए होंगे, वह निकल गई है; 9. नौजवान ले आया है, बढ़ई निकल आए थे, शत्रु वहाँ से भाग आए; 10. क्या दिखाई पड़ा, गाने सुनाई देंगे, शहर दिखाई देंगे।

19.10.2. *Translate into Hindi.*

1. April 9th, February 29th, on the first of May, on the 28th of July; 2. on September 2nd, 1763 A.D.; on August 19th, 1912 A.D.; on December 3rd, 1538; 3. Thursday, May 16th, 1974; Saturday, January 18th, 1980; 4. surrounding those small gardens, in exchange for those kurtas, in comparison to his voice; 5. to the north of Madhya Pradesh, to the south of the village, to the west of those cities, to the east of these very tall mountains; 6. (use compound verbs with लेना as second member) he is able to write, she was able to understand, you (pol.) know how to speak, I (f.) know how to sing; 7. (use compounds with लेना or देना as second member) he made (for himself), we cooked (for others), those women gave, we took, Father bought (for himself); 8. (use compounds with जाना as second member) we (m.) will become, they ate up, that thin woman drank up, one week elapsed; 9. (use compounds with आना as second member) the women had brought, the birds emerged, they (m.) fled here, the workers arrived home; 10. (use (दिखाई देना/पड़ना or सुनाई देना/पड़ना) a young man could be seen, the man's voice began to be heard, the mosque could be seen, beautiful songs are heard (p. hab.).

19.10.3. *Translate into English.*

1. सन् उन्नीस सौ सैंतालीस ई० में भारत को स्वतंत्रता मिली। 2. आपके मित्र किस रास्ते से शहर की ओर चल दिए ? 3. उस समय पिता जी की आवाज़ सब जगहों पर सुनाई दे रही थी। 4. मेरी बहन कुछ हिन्दी समझ लेती है पर बोल नहीं पाती। 5. तुमने मेरे सब सवाल क्यों दुहरा दिए ? 6. माताजी ने पिता जी की मदद किस तरह की थी ? 7. इन घटनाओं के बाद सुरेश अपने परिवार वालों के साथ घर की ओर हो लिया। 8. पिताजी दफ़्तर से कब लौट आएंगे ? 9. प्रायः हिंदू मंदिरों में फूल चढ़ाए जाते हैं। 10. कुछ समय के बाद मोची घर की तीसरी मंजिल तक पहुंच गया। 11. आपने बग़ीचे में इतने फूल क्यों लगा दिए ? 12. उस मसजिद तक आसानी से नहीं पहुंचा जा सकता। 13. वहां के लोगों की बोलचाल की अपेक्षा वह स्त्री बहुत शुद्ध हिन्दी बोलती है। 14. बिजली की बत्तियां उस समय जल गई थीं। 15. कुत्ते को देखकर बिल्ली तुरंत पेड़ पर चढ़ गई।

19.10.4. *Translate into Hindi, using compound verbs wherever possible.*

1. What time do you (fam.) get up every day ? 2. How many years did Mr. Sharma spend in India ? 3. My children do not know how to sing Indian songs. 4. He is rather strong for (i.e., in comparison to) his age. 5. Madhya Pradesh is to the south of Uttar Pradesh. 6. The carpenter made six new chairs for us. 7. When

they read the letter they set out for Allahabad immediately. 8. Yesterday I just happened to meet your brother in the market. 9. Mother lit the clay lamps yesterday evening. 10. Animals from all over the world can be seen in Delhi's zoo. 11. That village can be reached easily on foot (use pass. of पहुँचना). 12. By what route did those young men arrive here ? 13. Please don't make any special food for us. 14. They were extremely angry with the washerman. 15. His voice could be heard in every room of the house.

CHAPTER 20

20.1. COMPOUNDS WITH रखना

The verb रखना appears as a V_2 element in compounds following many transitive and, on occasion, intransitive verbs. Unfortunately, it is not possible to isolate a consistent meaning contributed by रखना to such compounds. Indeed, although generalizations can be made about some of the behaviour of रखना in compounds, much of this behaviour must be considered idiosyncratic.

In some instances, the literal sense of रखना as an independent verb, namely 'to keep, hold' can be discerned:

माथुर जी अपने घर में दो-तीन कुत्ते पाले रखते थे ।
'Mr. Mathur used to keep two or three dogs in his home'.
उसने बड़े चमचे पाल रखे हैं ।
'He has surrounded himself with lackeys' [cf. चमचा n.m. 'lackey']

In other sentences, the use of रखना seems to paraphrase the use of the perfective participle of the main verb followed by हुआ, हुए, etc. (28.1.). Thus

जान ने ज्यादा शराब पी रखी है ।
'John has drunk too much liquor'

is equivalent to

जान ने ज्यादा शराब पी हुई है ।

Occasionally, रखना in compounds takes on the semantic properties of चुकना. Thus

मैंने यह पिक्चर दो बार देख रखी है ।
'I have already seen this picture twice'.

is equivalent to

मैं यह पिक्चर दो बार देख चुका हूँ ।

Further examples of रखना as the V_2 of a verbal compound include the following:

मैंने उसे दिल्ली न जाने को कह रखा था ।
'I had told him not to go to Delhi'.'
शर्मा जी ने अपनी जवानी में कई शेर मार रखे थे ।
'Mr. Sharma had killed many a lion in his youth'.

20.2. COMPOUNDS WITH बैठना

बैठना is employed in compound verbs designating the main verbal activity that is carried out with a lack of awareness on the part of its doer of the consequences of the action. The use of this V_2 element often implies a judgement on the part of the speaker that the action is inappropriate or undesirable:

तुम क्या पागलपन कर बैठे हो ।
'What madness you have gone and done !'
तुम उस ग़रीब बूढ़े पर क्रोध क्यों कर बैठे ?
'Why did you get so angry with that poor old man?'
वह अपना सब कुछ छोड़ बैठा ।
'He foolishly threw away everything he had'.

The combination of the stem of उठना, 'to rise, get up' and बैठना has the sense 'to jump up, to get up suddenly' :

अपनी सहेली की आवाज़ सुनकर प्रियंका (prop. f.) तुरंत उठ बैठी ।
'Priyanka immediately jumped up when she heard her friend's voice'.

20.3. Compounds With पड़ना

There are at least three distinct senses in which पड़ना is used us the V_2 element of V_1V_2 compound verbs. The verb is often encountered adding a sense of the sudden onset of a verbal activity :

बच्चा रो पड़ा ।
'The boy burst out in tears',
बच्ची हंस पड़ी ।
'The girl burst out laughing'.

The verb is also used synonymously with देना to specify the beginning of a verbal activity:

वह उस शहर की ओर चल पड़ा (=चल दिया) ।
'He set off towards the city'.

Lastly, the verb is used in compounds in a sense close to that of its independent meaning of 'to fall, befall'. This sense is most commonly found when the independent meaning of the V_1 also betrays some sense of falling :

अशोक दूसरी मंजिल की खिड़की से गिर पड़ा ।
'Ashok fell from the second floor window'.
वह गाड़ी से ज़मीन पर कूद पड़ा ।
'He jumped from the train onto the ground'.

20.4. Compounds With उठना

Like पड़ना, उठना can be used as the V_2 element in compounds to designate the suddenness or spontaneity of a verbal activity. By comparison to पड़ना, however, उठना often implies a slightly more pronounced or emphasized initiation of the verbal activity. It can also add a sense of the speaker's negative reaction towards the activity being described :

राम दयाल का चेहरा देख कर वह बोल उठा कि सारी ग़लती मेरी है ।
'When he saw Ram Dayal's face he blurted out that the entire fault was his'.
चोरों की आवाज़ सुनकर आराधना (prop. f.) कांप उठी कि कहीं वे उसको न देख लें ।
'When she heard the thieves' voices Aradhana started to tremble lest they see her'.

In compounds with V_1 elements whose literal meanings incorporate a sense of rising, उठना retains some of the lexical sense of 'to rise, get up':

उस दिन वह दूसरों के पहले जाग उठी।
'She got up before the others on that day'.

20.5. Compounds With पहुँचना

The V_2 element पहुँचना is used in compounds with verbs of motion to denote that the act or motion also constitutes an act of arrival at some terminus:

हम पिताजी के यहाँ जा पहुँचे।
'We arrived at Father's place'.
बहुत देर तक कार चलाने के बाद जोगिन्दर सिंह (prop. m.) भोपाल आ पहुँचा।
'Jogindar Singh reached Bhopal after driving for a long time'.

20.6. Compounds With चलना

चलना has a number of distinct uses as the second member of compound verbs. Firstly, it can be used synonymously with जाना to specify motion directed away from the speaker:

वह अपनी बेटी को चिड़ियाघर ले चला।
'He took his daughter to the zoo'.

Secondly, the verb can be employed to indicate the drawing out over time of a verbal activity:

सोनू (prop. m) के पिता का पेट बड़ा हो चला था।
'Sonu's father's stomach had (gradually) gotten larger'.

Lastly, चलना is used for the inception of a verbal activity or condition:

उसकी तबीयत ख़राब हो चली थी।
'His condition started to worsen'.

20.7. Compounds With डालना

When used in verbal compounds डालना, literally, 'to put, throw, place', adds a sense of violence or vehemence to the meaning of the prior verbal stem. This verb is most commonly found combined with transitive V_1 elements:

उसने यह बदमाशी क्यों कर डाली?
'Why did he do all of these evil deeds?'
बच्चे ने अपने सब नए खिलौने तोड़ डाले।
'The child broke all of his (own) new toys'.

डालना also can convey a sense of quickness or ravenousness in compounds:

उसने तुरंत जयशंकर प्रसाद की सब कविताएं पढ़ डालीं।
'He immediately read all of Jaishanker Prasad's poems'.

The compound मार डालना has the specific sense 'to kill' [cf. मारना 'to hit, strike']:

बदमाशों ने पड़ोस के तीन छोटे बच्चों को मार डाला।
'The ruffians killed three neighbourhood children'.

20.8. Compounds With मरना

In many compounds मरना indicates that a primary verbal activity results in death. This use of मरना in compounds is clearly related to the literal meaning of मरना, 'to die':

बिल्ली गली के कुत्तों के साथ लड़ मरी।
'The cat fought with the street dogs and died'.

उसका सबसे बड़ा बेटा गांव के तालाब में डूब मरा।
'His oldest son drowned in the village pond'.

Often मरना in compounds implies the unwarranted or inappropriate quality of a verbal activity :

बड़ी अफसोस की बात है कि भजन (prop. m.) उसी समय पर आ मरा।
'It is most unfortunate that Bhajan came just then'.

मरना can also be used to indicate that some verbal activity is carried through to extreme lengths :

अंत में वह कुछ-न-कुछ कर मरेगी।
'In the end she will take drastic action'.

भारत को स्वतंत्र बनाने के लिए जवाहरलाल नेहरू जी लड़ मरने के लिए तैयार थे।
'Jawaharlal Nehru was ready to fight to the death to make India free'.

इस मामले में वह कुछ-न-कुछ कर मरेगा।
'He will carry this matter through to the bitter end'.

20.9. Compounds With मारना

The transitive counterpart to मरना, मारना (literally 'to hit, strike') also is frequently found in verbal compounds. In such instances the मारना element adds the sense that force was used in carrying out the action:

उसने अचानक राम को थप्पड़ दे मारा।
'He suddenly slapped Ram'.

The verb can also be used to indicate thoughtlessness or carelessness in carrying out an activity:

तुमने उसको ऐसा पत्र क्यों भेज मारा?
'(For heaven's sake) why did you send him such a letter?'

20.10. Other Compound Verbs

The description of compound verbs provided here by no means has discussed all of the compound verbs that can be formed in Hindi. The V_2 elements treated so far have been those that are relatively productive, that is, that can occur in conjunction with a wide variety of V_1 elements. Many other verbs can serve as V_2 elements, but they are much more limited in their pattern of occurrence than the verbs already examined. For example, the verb बसना, literally 'to be located, settled' can occur in compounds, but in a relatively small number of contexts. It can occur with some semblance of its independent meaning together with verbs of motion and it can occur in the euphemistic expression चल बसना 'to die':

उस साल वे दिल्ली में आ बसे ।

'They settled in Delhi that year'.

यसमीन (prop. f.) की माता जी कल रात को चल बसीं ।

'Yasmin's mother passed away last night'.

Many other verbs similarly display limited patterns of occurrence in verbal compounds.

In 19.1. it was observed that the meaning of a compound verb in Hindi is generally a modification of the independent meaning of the V_1 element However, compound verbs are occasionally found whose meanings are essentially amplifications or modifications of the meanings of the V_2 elements. Such compounds arise through the reversal of the order of the original V_1 and V_2 elements, with the verbal endings for the entire compound attached to the stem that ultimately appears second. Thus in compounds such as

गप्पू ने हमारे दो गिलास दे तोड़े ।

'Gappu broke two of our glasses'.

We find a reversed sequence दे तोड़े in place of the expected तोड़ दिए. By this process of reversal it is possible to form compounds showing a very large number of V_2 elements.

V_1V_2 compounds are also formed in Hindi through the simplification of complex sentences in which two clauses are combined with the conjunctive form कर Through a process of deletion of the कर element, the verbs of the two clauses are brought into immediate proximity to each other, thus constituting a V_1V_2 compound. For example, from the sentence

चोर खिड़की से बाहर कूद कर निकल गया ।

'The thief jumped out of the window'.

it is possible to form

चोर खिड़की से बाहर कूद निकला ।

This has been accomplished by deleting the कर element conjoining the two clauses, and by using the form निकल (taken from the निकल गया of the second clause of the original sentence) as the V_2 of the newly formed compound कूद निकला ।

20.11. The Vikrama Dating System

In addition to the dating system based on the western calendar two dating systems based on the lunar calendar are employed in India. The Saka (शक) dating system is discussed in 21.5. The Vikrama (विक्रम), calculated from the year 57 B.C.,[1] is still widely used among traditional Hindus. Within the Vikrama system, a year is composed of twelve months, known both by Sanskrit and corresponding Hindi names :

1. The procedure by which a Vikrama year is convered into a corresponding one is quite complex. As a rule of thumb, the western year can be determined by subtracting 57 from the Vikrama year. However, for some Vikrama dates it is necessary to substract either 56 or 58 years to determine the correct western year.

Sanskrit		*Hindi*	
चैत्र	आश्विन	चैत	क्वार
वैशाख	कार्त्तिक (or कार्तिक)	बैशाख	कातिक
ज्येष्ठ	आग्रहायण	जेठ	अगहन
आषाढ़	पौष	अषाढ़	पूस
श्रावण	माघ	सावन	माघ
भाद्रपद	फाल्गुन	भादों	फागुन

Every three years an intercalary month (अधिक मास) is added to make a necessary adjustment between the solar and lunar years. The new year according to the Vikrama systems begins on the sixteenth day of Caitra, which occurs approximately at the end of the western month of February or at the beginning of March.

Each lunar month is divided into two पक्ष ('phases'). The शुक्ल पक्ष (or 'bright phase') lasts from the new moon to the full moon, whereas the कृष्ण पक्ष (or 'dark phase') lasts from the full moon to the new moon. Each phase is divided into fifteen days, consisting of either the day of the full or the new moon and fourteen other days, referred to by the Sanskrit ordinal numerals from 1-14 or by their derived Hindi equivalents:

Sanskrit				*Hindi*			
प्रथमा	1st	अष्टमी	8th	परिवा	1st	आठें	8th
द्वितीया	2nd	नवमी	9th	दूज	2nd	नौमी	9th
तृतीया	3rd	दशमी	10th	तीज	3rd	दसमी	10th
चतुर्थी	4th	एकादशी	11th	चौथ	4th	ग्यारस	11th
पंचमी	5th	द्वादशी	12th	पांचें	5th	दुआस	12th
षष्ठी	6th	त्रयोदशी	13th	छठ	6th	तेरस	13th
सप्तमी	7th	चतुर्दशी	14th	सातें	7th	चौदस	14th

With Vikrama dates, the word मिती is sometimes used in the same manner that तारीख or दिनांक are used with dates of the western calendar. In addition, the words पूर्णिमा and अमावस are used to refer to the night of the full moon and new moon respectively. In writing Vikrama dates, a number of abbreviations are often employed: शु० (= शुक्ल पक्ष); कृ० (= कृष्ण पक्ष), and वि० (= विक्रमी) 'according to the Vikrama system'). Sample citations of dates according to the Vikrama system are given below :

मिती कार्त्तिक शुक्ल एकादशी, संवत् दो हजार तीस विक्रमी
'the 11th day of the light phase of Kārttik, 2030 Vikrama'

मिती चैत्र कृ० ३, सं० १९९६ वि० को
'on the 3rd day of the dark phase of Caitra, 1996 Vikrama'.

श्रावण की अमावस, सं० २००० वि० को
'on the new moon of Śrāvaṇ, 2000 Vikrama'

20.12. VOCABULARY

आटा	n.m. whole wheat flour
इतिहास	n.m. history
ऊन	n f. wool
कवि	n.m. poet
कविता	n.f. poem
गला	n.m. throat
ग़लती	n.f. mistake, error
ज़मीन	n.f. earth, ground
तबीयत	n.f. disposition, condition
तालाब	n.m. pond, tank
थप्पड़	n.m. slap
पड़ोस	n.f. neighbourhood
पागलपन	n.m. madness
पूरी	n.f. puri (a kind of bread made from आटा and fried in hot oil
पेट	n.m. stomach
बदमाश	n.m. hooligan
बदमाशी	n.f. hooliganism
बहाना	n.m. excuse, pretext
मामला	n.m. affair, matter
मालिक	n.m. boss, employer, master
मुसीबत	n.f. calamity, hardship
मैदा	n.m. white (bleached) flour
रेशम	n.m. silk
संबंध	n.m. relationship, connection
कुछ-न-कुछ	pron. and adj. something or other
ग़लत	adj. incorrect, wrong
तैयार	adj. ready, prepared
पागल	adj. mad, crazy
सूती	adj. cotton
स्वतंत्र	adj. independent, free
कांपना	v.i. to tremble, shake
कूदना	v.i. to jump
ख़रीद लाना	v.i. to buy and bring back
गले मिलना	v.i. to embrace [literally 'for the necks to meet']
चल बसना	v.i. to die
जगाना	v.t. to wake someone up, awaken
जा बैठना	v.i. to go and sit down
जागना	v.i. to wake up, arise
डूबना	v.i. to drown, sink
तोड़ना	v.t. to break
थप्पड़ देना	v.t. to slap
दिखाना	v.t. to show (something to someone)
पालना	v.t. to protect, keep, raise
भेजना	v.t. to send
लड़ना	v.i. to fight
अचानक	adv. suddenly
असल में	adv. in fact
चुपचाप	adv. silently, quietly
दिन-भर	adv. all day
मन ही मन	adv. inwardly, to oneself
वास्तव में	adv. in fact
X के प्रति	post. towards X, with regard to X, as concerns X
X के बहाने	post. on the pretext of X
X के संबंध में	post. concerning X, on the matter of X

20.13. EXERCISES

20.13.1. *Translate into English.*

1. मिती फाल्गुन शुक्ल नवमी, संवत् दो हज़ार ग्यारह विक्रमी; मिती वैशाख की पूर्णिमा, संवत् उन्नीस सौ सत्तानवे विक्रमी को; मिती ज्येष्ठ कृष्ण १, सं० २०१४ वि० को; 2. खादी का कुरता, ऊन के कपड़े, रेशम की साड़ियां, नीले रेशम की तीन सुन्दर साड़ियां; 3. तबीबत, उसकी तबीबत, पिताजी की तबीयत; 4. घर का मालिक, उसके दफ़्तर का मालिक; 5. आटे की रोटी, मैदे की रोटी, आटे की पूरियाँ; 6. भारत की स्वतंत्रता के प्रति, उनकी कविताओं के प्रति, भारत के प्रसिद्ध कवियों के प्रति; 7. तैयार, खाने के लिए (or को) तैयार, पानी में कूदने के लिए तैयार; 8 वहाँ जाने के बहाने, बीमार होने के बहाने से, अमीर न होने के बहाने से; इसके संबंध में, उनकी कविताओं के संबंध में, भारत के इतिहास के संबंध में।

20.13.2. *Translate into Hindi*

1. the fourth day of the dark phase of Āśvin, 1984 Vikrama; on the second day of the light phase of Kārtik, 2001 Vikrama; on the night of the full moon of Māgh, 1942 Vikrama. 2. silk clothes, three cotton saris, several woolen shirts; 3. Father's disposition, Ram's bad disposition, those peoples' disposition; 4. ready to study, ready to buy some whole wheat flour, ready to go to the market with you; 5. on the pretext of studying, on the pretext of not understanding Hindi, on the pretext of going to see Father; 6. concerning these questions, concerning the south of India, concerning those matters; 7. (use रखना or बैठना, in verbal compounds) he put on, they (foolishly) spoke, they (f.) will jump up; 8. (use पड़ना, or उठना in compounds) he had burst out in tears, he set out, the boss burst out laughing, the boys arose; 9. (use पहुँचना, or चलना in compounds) they arrived, these men must have taken Sita there, her sisters arrived; 10. (use डालना, मरना, or मारना in compounds) he had killed, they had (unfortunately) arrived, that youth slapped.

20.13.3. *Translate into English.*

1. शीला ने अपनी सब नई साड़ियाँ एक-एक बार (once each) पहन रखी हैं। 2. पिताजी ने बड़े भाई को कह रखा था कि तुम सदा सच (n.m. the truth) बोलो। 3. एक दिन मैं तुम्हें ताजमहल दिखाने के लिए आगरा ले चलूंगा। 4. वे बंबई की किसी नई बस्ती में जा बसे थे। 5. मैंने समाचारपत्र में पढ़ा कि अशोक गंगा में कूद मरा था। 6. हम नहीं समझ सकते हैं कि उन्होंने अपने दोस्तों को क्यों मार डाला है। 7. उधर की कुरसी पर जा बैठिए। 8. दिन-भर सोने के बाद भजन तुरंत जाग बैठा। 9. लगता है कि सोनू बड़े ध्यान से अपना काम कर रहा है। असल में वह कुछ भी नहीं कर रहा है। 10. उसने मन-ही-मन सोचा कि मैं यह क्यों कर बैठा था। 11. अपने मालिक से बात करने के बहाने जगदीश दफ़्तर जा पहुंचा। 12. घर पहुंच कर कवि ने डिकंस की एक पुस्तक पढ़ डाली। 13. दो भाई एक-एक पैसे के लिए लड़ मरे। 14. यह जानकर कि उसका छोटा भाई चल बसा था बच्चा रो पड़ा। 15. वह क्रोध से जल मरी कि उन्होंने उसके बेटे को थप्पड़ दे मारा था।

20.13.4. *Translate into Hindi.*

1. Joginder's sister put on her best clothes on that occasion. 2. When he learned (use जानकर) that his sister was very sick he burst into tears. 3. The poet suddenly blurted out that all of your answers are completely incorrect. 4. What insanity you have gone and (stupidly) done! 5. The two boys woke up (i.e., got up) yesterday before noon. 6. The girls went to the side of the river and jumped into the water. 7. Shila's father passed away last Wednesday. 8. Please go into that room and sit down. 9. His friend keeps four dogs, a cat, three horses, and many birds. 10. Priyanka went into that room on the pretext of waking the child up. 11. On Id (literally 'on the day of Id') Muslims embrace in the Idgah. 12. Their boss set off towards the city. 13. All of the children of that neighbourhood were sent to the city. 14. Why did they do this hooliganism? 15. In fact, Sonu didn't answer our questions.

SUPPLEMENTARY READING PASSAGES

A. तीन मछलियाँ

एक तालाब में तीन बड़ी-बड़ी मछलियाँ रहती थीं। उनकी आपस में दोस्ती थी, लेकिन तीनों का स्वभाव अलग-अलग तरह का था।

दूसरी मछली लाल रंग की थी। वह हमेशा खुश रहती थी। वह बड़ी चतुर थी। मौक़े पर चटपट फ़ैसला करना जानती थी। यदि उसपर कोई मुसीबत आती तो फ़ौरन बचने का उपाय खोज निकालती थी।

तीसरी मछली भूरे रंग की थी। वह हर समय मुंह फुलाये रहती थी। केवल पुरानी बातें ही पसन्द करती थी। वह सोचती रहती थी कि जो होना है सो तो होगा ही। होनी को कोई नहीं टाल सकता।

एक दिन नीली मछली ने कुछ मछुओं को बातें करते सुना। एक मछुआ दूसरे से कह रहा था, "यह नीली मछली कैसी मोटी-ताज़ी है। वाह, इस तालाब में तो और भी ढेरों मछलियाँ हैं। हम कल यहाँ आकर मछली पकड़ेंगे।

नीली मछली भागी-भागी अपने दोस्तों के पास पहुँची और सारा हाल सुनाकर बोली, "हमें समझ से काम लेना चाहिए। आज ही इस तालाब को छोड़कर भाग लेना चाहिए।"

लाल मछली ने कहा, "अरे, मछुए आएं तो सही। मैं बचने का कोई-न-कोई उपाय निकाल ही लूंगी!"

भूरी मछली ने कहा, "मैं जीवन-भर इसी तालाब में रही हूँ। मैं इस जगह को केवल इसलिए नहीं छोड़ सकती कि किसी मछुए ने यहाँ मछली पकड़ने की बात कही है। जो होना है सो देखा जाएगा।"

तब नीली मछली बोली, "भई, मैं तो मछुओं के आने से पहले ही यहाँ से भाग जाना चाहती हूँ।" ऐसा कहकर नीली मछली दूसरे तालाब को चली गई।

दूसरे दिन मछुओं ने आकर तालाब में जाल डाला। जाल में बहुत-सी मछलियाँ फंस गईं। उनमें लाल और भूरी मछली भी थी।

लाल मछली ने ख़तरा देखा तो ऐसा बहाना कर दिया मानों मर गई हो। एक मछुए ने उसे मरा हुआ समझ कर ज़मीन पर फेंक दिया।

ज़मीन पर आते ही लाल मछली धीरे-धीरे रेंगते हुए तालाब के किनारे पहुंची और उचक कर तालाब में कूद पड़ी और तैर कर दूर भाग गई। इस तरह उसने अपनी जान बचा ली।

लेकिन भूरी मछली जाल में फंसी-फंसी तड़फड़ करती रही। उसे उछलता देख उसी मछुए ने एक ऐसा वार किया कि एक ही बार में उसका काम तमाम हो गया।

VOCABULARY

मछली	n.f. fish
X की आपस में	post. among X
दोस्ती	n.f. friendship
दोस्ती तो थी	there was friendship to be sure
स्वभाव	n.m. nature, character
अलग-अलग	adj. individual, distinct
सयाना	adj. cunning, clever
सोच-विचार कर लेना	v.t. to think/consider carefully
चतुर	adj. cunning, sly
मौक़े पर	adv. at the appropriate time, when the opportunity would arise
चटपट	adv. immediately, at once
फ़ैसला करना	v.t. to decide, to resolve
यदि X पर... आतीं तो	if X would suffer . . . then . . .
फ़ौरन	adv. immediately
उपाय	n.m. plan, contrivance
खोज निकालना	v.t. to seek, search for
भूरा	adj. brown
हर	adj. every, each
मुंह फुलाए	sulking, displeased
पुरानी बातें	i.e., things as they've always been, the status quo
पसन्द करना	v.t. to like
सोचती रहती थी	kept on thinking
जो होना है सो तो होगा ही	things will turn out exactly as they have to
होनी	n.f. what must be
टालना	v.t. to put off, deter
मछुआ	n.m. fisherman
X को बातें करते सुना	heard X conversing
ढेर	n.m. heap, pile
भागी-भागी	adv. fleeing, hurrying
हाल	n.m. story
समझ से	adv. carefully

X आएं तो सही	if X (pl.) should come then well and good	रेंगते हुए	creeping, crawling [cf. रेंगना to creep, crawl]
कोई-न-कोई	adj. some (thing) or other	उचकना	v.i. to stretch upwards
जीवन-भर	for (my) entire life	तैरना	v.i. to swim
मछली पकड़ने की बात कही है	has said that he is going to catch fish	जान	n.f. life
		फंसी-फंसी	entrapped
जो होना है सो देखा जाएगा	Let's see what happens [literally 'what must be, that will be seen']	तड़फड़ करना	v.i. to toss about, to writhe
		तड़फड़ करती रही	kept on tossing about
		उछलना	v.i. to leap, jump
भई	=भाई	X को उछलता	seeing X leaping
जाल	n.m. net	देख	
फंसना	v.i. to become entrapped	वार	n.m. assault,
ख़तरा	n.m. danger	वार करना	v.t. to assault, attack
उसे मरा हुआ समझ कर	believing he/she/it to be dead	X का काम तमाम हो जाना	v.i. for X to be done in, for X to be killed

B. कार पड़ी बीमार

गप्पीमल ने गप्प लड़ाई—
खुली लाटरी, भाई,
आज हमारे घर पर उससे
नई कार है आई ।
भीड़ जमा जब हुई देखने,
गप्पीजी की कार,
गप्पी बोले अस्पताल में—
कार पड़ी बीमार ।

(From *BKSK*, p. 86)

VOCABULARY

कार	n.f. car, automobile	लाटरी खुलना	v.i. for a prize to be won in a lottery
गप्पीमल	prop. m. [the name is a pun on the word 'गप्पी a gossip, chatterbox']	जमा	adj. indecl. assembled
		जब	rel. pron. when
गप्प	n.f. bit of gossip, rumor	अस्पताल	n.m. hospital
गप्प लड़ाना	v.t. to spread a rumor/gossip	देखने	= देखने के लिए

C.

एक दिन एलिस अपनी बहन के साथ नदी के किनारे बैठी थी । लेकिन थोड़ी ही देर में वह ऊबने लगी । कोई काम ही नहीं था करने को। एक-दो बार उसने झांक कर उस किताब में देखा जिसे उसकी बहन पढ़ रही थी। लेकिन उसमें न तो चित्र ही थे और न पात्रों की बातचीत ही । "ऐसी किताब किस काम की, जिसमें न चित्र हैं और न बातचीत !" एलिस ने मन-ही-मन कहा ।

इसलिए वह सोचने लगी कि अब क्या किया जाए ? वह गुलबहार के फूल चुनने और उनकी माला गूंथने के बारे में सोच रही थी कि अचानक एक सफ़ेद ख़रगोश, जिसकी आंखें गुलाबी रंग की थीं, भागता हुआ उसके पास से निकल गया ।

इस ख़रगोश में ऐसी कोई ख़ास बात नहीं थी । यहां तक कि जब ख़रगोश ने यह कहा कि, "ओह, मुझे बहुत देर हो गई," तब भी एलिस ने उसकी ओर कोई विशेष ध्यान नहीं दिया । लेकिन जब उसने देखा कि खरगोश कुछ दूर जाकर रुका और एक जेब-

घड़ी निकाल कर उसे देखने लगा, और फिर तेज़ क़दमों से वहाँ से भाग पड़ा, तो उसके आश्चर्य की सीमा न रही। उसने देखा कि ऐसा ख़रगोश तो कभी देखा नहीं था। वह फ़ौरन उठकर उसके पीछे भागी। भागते-भागते उसने देखा कि ख़रगोश एक झाड़ी के पास अपने बिल में घुस गया।

झाड़ी के पास जाकर एलिस ने देखा कि ख़रगोश का बिल काफ़ी बड़ा है। उसका मन हुआ कि ख़रगोश का पीछा करना चाहिए। फिर बिना कुछ सोचे-समझे वह भी उसके बिल में उतर गई।

(Adapted from जादूनगरी, p. 5)

Vocabulary

एलिस	prop. f.
ऊबना	v.i. to become bored
करने को	= करने के लिये
झांकना	v.i. to peer, peek
जिसे	which = obl. s. of rel. pron. जो
न (तो) . . . न (ही)	neither . . nor
चित्र	n.m. picture
पात्र	n.m. character
बातचीत	n.f. conversation
किस काम का/के/की	of what use?
जिसमें	in which
गुलबहार	n.m. group/bunch of flowers
चुनना	v.i. to choose
माला	n.f. garland
गूँथना	v.t. to braid, weave
ख़रगोश	n.m. rabbit
जिसकी	rel. pron. pos. whose
भागता हुआ	running, hurrying
X के पास से निकल गया	passed by her
ख़ास	adj. special
इस . . . बात नहीं थी	there was nothing special about . . . this rabbit
यहां तक कि	even to the point that . . .
तब भी	conj. nevertheless, still
जेबघड़ी	n.f. pocket-watch
क़दम	n.m. (foot) step
तो	conj. then; partl. blut. (v. 28.3)
आश्चर्य	n.m. wonder, surprise
सीमा	n.f. limit, border
फ़ौरन	adv. immediately
भागते-भागते	fleeing, rushing
झाड़ी	n.f. bush, thicket
बिल	n.m. burrow, hole
घुसना	v.i. to enter (into)
उसका मन हुआ कि . . .	she started to feel that . . .
X का पीछा करना	v.t. to follow after X, to trail X
बिना सोचे-समझे	without thinking or deliberating
उतरना	v.i. to descend, to go down

PART

V

CHAPTER 21

21.1. Uses of the Infinitive

The "infinitive" is the citation form of a verb, that is, the form that refers to the verbal activity in an abstract or "nominal" sense. In many languages, including Hindi, verbs are cited in dictionaries and other reference works in this "infinitive" form.

As already stated (8.1), Hindi infinitives display the termination –ना. The infinitive in –ना in many ways functions as a masculine singular Class I noun, changing its ending to –ने when followed by a postposition (e.g., जाना 'to go' but जाने में 'in/while going'). Hindi infinitives serve a wide variety of grammatical functions. It has earlier been observed that infinitives are employed to issue deferred commands (12.1) and to serve as part of indirect constructions indicating obligation and necessity (17.1—17.4). But infinitives may also serve a number of functions that stem from the fact that these forms behave in the same manner as other nouns of the language. Nouns in Hindi serve various syntactic functions, as, for example, subject, direct object, indirect object, object of a postposition, etc. Infinitives can likewise serve each of these syntactic functions:

Subject of a Clause

हर रोज़ कम-से-कम एक गिलास पानी पीना स्वास्थ्य के लिए अच्छा है ।

'It is good for one's health to drink at least one glass of water every day'.

इस रास्ते पर कार चलाना मना है ।

'It is forbidden to drive a car on this road'.

Direct Object of a Clause

वह अपनी कुरसी में बैठ कर तम्बाकू पीना पसंद करता है ।

'He likes to smoke while sitting in his chair'.

वे हिन्दुस्तान जाकर हिन्दी बोलना सीख गए ।

'They went to India and learned to speak Hindi'.

Indirect Object of a Clause

हीरा लाल डाक्टर साहब को बुलाने के लिए दरियागंज चला गया ।

'Hira Lal went to Dariya Ganj [an area of Old Delhi] to call the Doctor'.

राहुल सब लोगों की सेवा करने के लिए तैयार था ।

'Rahul was ready to assist everyone'.

Object of a Postposition

गाँव के अधिकारियों ने नया अस्पताल बनवाने का निश्चय किया ।

'The village authorities decided to have a new hospital built'.

तब तक यहाँ रहने से तुमको क्या फ़ायदा ?

'What benefit will you get from remaining here until then?'

हिंदू परिवार में न पैदा होने के कारण बचपन में मुश्ताक़ मंदिर नहीं जाता था ।

'Because he wasn't born into a Hindu family, Mushtak didn't go to temple when he was a child'.

If the subject of the nominalised verbal activity is to be present, it is often connected to the infinitive by means of the possessive position का:

शंकर लाल का समय पर न आना दूसरों को बहुत नापसंद था ।

'The others didn't like the fact that Shankar Lal didn't come on time'.

चाचाजी के चले जाने के तीन घंटे के अंदर सारा घर फिर ख़ामोश हो गया ।

'The entire house became quiet again within three hours after Uncle [father's younger brother) left'.

उनकी भतीजी का परीक्षा में फ़ेल हो जाना बड़े आश्चर्य की बात थी ।

'Their niece's [brother's daughter's] failing the examination was a great surprise'.

There are important verbal constructions in Hindi in which the oblique infinitive (i.e., the verbal stem+ —ने) plays a significant role. The use of the oblique infinitive +लगना has already been taken up in 15.5. Its use with –वाला has been discussed in 12.2. The oblique infinitive is also used in connection with देना in constructions indicating permission or allowance to carry out some verbal activity. The full scheme for this construction is X Y को oblique infinitive (= Z)+देना 'for X to allow/let Y to carry out Z':

उसने मुझे जाने नहीं दिया ।

'He/She didn't let me go'.

अध्यापक जी विद्यार्थियों को स्कूल में हिन्दी नहीं बोलने देते थे ।

'The teacher didn't let the students speak Hindi in class'.

The oblique infinitive also occurs in Hindi immediately followed by पाना in the construction X oblique infinitive +पाना :

मृदुला आपके साथ बाज़ार नहीं जाने पाई क्योंकि उसको बहुत काम था ।

'Mridula couldn't go to the market with you because she had much work to do'.

This last sentence type is a close paraphrase of the construction in which पाना immediately follows the uninflected verbal stem (e.g., नहीं जा पाया [cf. 17.1]). Like that construction type, this usage is almost always found in the negative.

It should be noted that in instances where the verbal activity of an infinitive has a direct object, and the infinitive is not itself followed by a postposition (thus causing it to show the ending -ने), many Hindi speakers allow the infinitive to agree with that direct object in number and gender:

हमने उसको हिन्दी बोलनी सिखा दी ।

'We taught him/her how to speak Hindi'.

This rule is, however, not employed by all Hindi speakers, and many individuals show the invariable ending -ना on the infinitives of examples such as that given above.

21.2. The Expression न जाने

The expression न जाने is commonly used in Hindi in conjunction with a following interrogative word or phrase with the sense of the English expressions 'who knows...' 'no one knows...,' 'God knows...,' etc.:

न जाने वे किधर से आए।
'Who knows where they came from'. (i.e., no one knows where they came from)

न जाने क्या होगा इसके बाद।
'No one knows what will happen after this'.

न जाने कहाँ से लोग अरोड़ा जी से मिलने आए थे।
'Who knows where the people came from who came to see Mr. Arora.

Often the words भगवान 'God' or ख़ुदा 'God' are used in place of न in this expressions:

'भगवान/ख़ुदा जाने उनके यहाँ क्या हो रहा था।
'God only knows what was going on at their place'.

21.3. The Construction -ते ही

The invariable verbal suffix -ते and the following particle ही are often used in Hindi immediately after a verbal stem, the entire construction having the sense 'as soon as...':

घर पहुँचते ही विनोद सो गया।
'As soon as he arrived home Vinod went to sleep'.

मालती की आवाज़ सुनते ही नीरद ख़ुशी से मुसकराने लगा।
'Nirad began to smile happily as soon as he heard Malti's voice'.

If the subject of the prior clause is different from that of the subsequent, it is often connected to the verb of the prior clause by means of the postposition के:

मेरे वहाँ पहुँचते ही पुष्पा अपने कमरे में चली गई।
'Pushpa went into her room as soon as I arrived there!

बच्चे के रोते ही माँ ने उसे दूध पिलाया।
'Mother gave the child (some) milk as soon as it started to cry'.

21.4. Relative Constructions with जो

The relative pronoun जो 'who, what, which' is commonly used in a wide variety of Hindi relative constructions. Like many other pronouns in Hindi, जो has different forms when followed by various postpositions. The declension of the relative pronoun

जो is as follows:

	Singular	*Plural*
Direct (= non-oblique)	जो	जो
Oblique	जिस	जिन
Optional Contraction for Oblique + को	जिसे	जिन्हें
Oblique + ने	जिसने	जिन्होंने

Relative clauses in Hindi may either precede or follow the clauses to which they are subordinated:

वह कौन था जो आपसे मिलने आया था ?
जो आपसे मिलने आया था वह कौन था ?
'Who was that who came to see you?'

वह दुकान किसकी है जो हलवाई की दुकान के पास ही है ?
जो दुकान हलवाई की दुकान के पास ही है वह किसकी है ?
'Whose store is that next to the sweet shop?'

The selection of an appropriate form from out of the above paradigm for use in a relative clause depends on the syntactic function that the relative pronoun serves within its own clause. This can be seen in the following example sentences:

वह कौन था जिसको (= जिसे) तुमने पत्र भेजा था ?
'Who was that to whom you sent the letter?'

वे कौन थे जिनको (= जिन्हें) तुमने पत्र भेजे थे ?
'Who were the people to whom you sent the letters?'

मुझे तीन कमरों वाला फ़्लैट चाहिए जिसमें सात लोग आराम से रह सकें।
'I need a three room apartment in which seven people can live comfortably'.

जिन घरों में हमारा स्वागत नहीं होता उनमें हम जाना नहीं चाहते।
'We don't want to go into homes where we are not welcome'.

जिस स्त्री ने उनकी सहायता की थी वह हमारे पड़ोस में रहती है।
'The lady who had helped them lives in our neighbourhood!

मैं उन लोगों को जानता हूँ जिन्होंने यह काम आपके लिए किया था।
'I know the people who had done the work for you'.

In the first two above examples the simple oblique forms of the relative pronoun are shown. These oblique forms are used because of the presence of the postposition को, in both cases indicating that the relative pronouns serve as the indirect objects of the act of sending. The singular oblique form is used in the first instance because the letter is sent to only one individual, while in the second instance the plural oblique relative pronoun is used because there are more than one individual to whom letters are sent. The forms जिसे and जिन्हें (shown parenthetically) in these examples are optional contractions of जिस or जिन plus को. The oblique forms जिस and जिन of the third and fourth examples are likewise used in place of direct case जो because of the presence of the postposition में. The forms जिसने and जिन्होंने in the fifth and sixth examples are used because the clauses in which these forms appear are of the type that ordinarily require that their objects be marked with ने (i.e., the verbs are transitive and in the perfective aspect). In the former case, जिसने is employed because it is only one woman who did the helping, whereas in the latter case जिन्होंने reflects the fact that more than one woman did the work.

It should be noted that the direct case form जो can be used in both the singular and plural. Occasionally, however, the repeated (or "reduplicated") form जो जो is also found to indicate the plural, albeit in a "distributive" sense (cf. 28.2.):

जो जो शहर मशहूर हैं केवल उन्हीं शहरों के बारे में बताइये।

'Please fell me about those cities that are famous.' (Colloquial)

जिन जिन के घरों में हम गए थे वे सब अच्छी हालत में थे।

'All the people whose homes we went into are in good condition'.

In all of the example sentences in the discussion of relative clauses so far, third person non-proximate demonstrative pronouns (i.e., वह, वे, उस, उन, etc.) have served as correlatives to the relative pronouns themselves. In colloquial usage, however, correlatives are often deleted from sentences having relative clauses:

दफ़्तर का जो काम था (उसे) मैं पूरा नहीं कर सका।

'I couldn't finish the work I had at the office yesterday'.

Occasionally, the form सो is used in place of वह, etc. as the correlative of जो. This is particularly common in idioms, adages, and dialectal styles of the language:

जो होना है सो होगा।

'What must be will be'.

जो चाहो सो करो।

'Do what you will'.

In colloquial Hindi, the order of words within a relative clause can be quite free, with the जो element (and the noun that it modifies) able to occur in any of a number of positions within the clause:

{ जो आदमी उसके साथ आया वह मेरा मित्र है।
उसके साथ आदमी जो आया....।
उसके साथ जो आदमी आया...।

'The man who came with him is my friend'.

Frequently, a semantically empty न is found added after the verb of the relative clause:

उसके साथ आदमी जो है न, वह मेरा मित्र है।

'The man who is with him is my friend'.

This use of न in relative clauses, ubiquitous in conversational Hindi, is, however, avoided in written literary Hindi.

21.5. THE SAKA DATING SYSTEM

The second dating system based on the lunar calendar that is widely used in Hindi speaking areas is the Saka (शक) system. This calendar, modified in 1957 and henceforth known as the Reformed Indian Calendar, is used for numerous official purposes. The Saka dating system is reckoned from the year 78 A.D., and it is thus necessary to add 78 to the number of a Saka year to derive the number of a corresponding western year.

In the Saka system, a year contains twelve months, seven having 30 days and the remaining five having 31 days each. The names of the months are the same as in the Vikrama system; unlike that system however, the months are not divided into phases, and individual days are referred to by ordinary cardinal numbers (except, as in the case of the western dating system, the first one or two days of each month, for which ordinals are employed). In referring to Saka dates, the words शक संवत् (abbreviated श० सं०) are used. Examples of dates according to the Saka system are given below:

ग्यारह माघ अठारह सौ दस शक संवत् को
'On the 11th of Māgh, 1810 (= 1888 A.D.) Saka'.
बीस श्रावण १८३५ श० सं०
'The 20th of Srāvaṇ, 1835 (= 1913 A.D.) Saka'.

21.6. Vocabulary

अधिकारी	n.m. authority, official
अस्पताल	n.m. hospital
आराम	n.m. comfort
आश्चर्य	n.m. surprise, astonishment
कार	n.f. car, automobile
कारख़ाना	n.m. factory
ख़ुदा	n.m. God
गिलास	n.m. glass (for drinking)
चाचा	n.m. uncle (= father's younger brother)
तंबाकू	n.m. tobacco
धर्म	n.m. dharma, righteousness, moral order/authority
पाप	n.m. sin
बचपन	n.m. childhood
भगवान	n.m God
भतीजा	n.m. nephew (= brother's son)
भतीजी	n.f. niece (= brother's daughter)
मेला	n.m. fair, festival
रिवाज़	n.m. custom
शास्त्र	n.m. sacred scripture
सामान	n.m. luggage, materials, paraphernalia
स्वागत	n.m. welcome

स्वास्थ्य	n.m. health
हलवाई	n.m. sweet seller
हालत	n.f. state, condition
ख़ामोश	adj. quiet, sad
नापसंद	adj. displeasing. disliked
पैदा	adj. indecl. born, produced, grown
बढ़िया	adj. indecl. fine, good, nice
मना	adj. indecl. forbidden
सच्चा	adj. true
X को आश्चर्य होना	v.i. for X to be surprised
घबराना	v.i. to be bothered, vexed
चलाना	v.t. to drive, cause to move, set into motion
X का निश्चय करना/होना	v.t/i. to decide X/for X to be decided
पैदा करना/होना	v.t./i. to give birth, produce/to be born, produced
बनवाना	v.t. to cause to be made
बुलाना	v.t. to call (someone)
मुस्कराना	v.i. to smile
मेहनत करना	v.t. to do hard work
X का सामना करना	v.t. to confront X, to challenge X
सिखाना	v.t. to teach
X का स्वागत करना/होना	v.t./i to welcome X/for X to be welcomed
आराम से	adv. comfortably
X के संग	post. together with X

21.7 EXERCISES

21.7.1. *Translate into English*

1. पुराने शास्त्रों के अनुसार अपने माता-पिता की सेवा न करना बड़ा पाप है। 2. उन्हें बड़ा आश्चर्य हुआ कि हमने अपने बच्चों को अंग्रेजी सिखाने का निश्चय किया था। 3. सारा दिन सोने से मेहनत करना अच्छा है। 4. हलवाई को मदद देने के बदले राजेश को ताजी मिठाइयाँ मिल गईं। 5. मोतीलाल उस प्रदेश के एक ग़रीब परिवार में पैदा हुआ। 6. भगवान जाने उनके बच्चे यह क्यों कर बैठे हैं। 7. उस कारख़ाने में जो बर्तन बनते हैं वे मिट्टी के ही होते हैं। 8. चाचाजी को जो आराम मिलता था वह बहुत कम था। 9. हिंदू लोगों के जो रिवाज़ हैं उनके बारे में मैं थोड़ा जानता हूँ। 10. मैदान में हमने उसी स्त्री को देखा जिसने पिछले हफ़्ते एक बेटे को पैदा किया। 11. दिल्ली में मेरे दो-तीन मित्र हैं जो उसका स्वागत कर सकेंगे। 12. उनकी जो तीन भतीजियां हैं वे सब कालेज में पढती हैं। 13. मेले में हम कुछ लोगों से मिले जिनके भाई आपके घर के पास ही रहते हैं। 14. यह नहीं कहा जा सकता है कि अरुण मेरा सच्चा दोस्त है। 15. सारे देश में कोई नहीं था जो राजा का सामना कर सकता।

21.7.2. *Translate into Hindi*

To work in a factory, to teach children Hindi, to welcome one's (own) parents, to have a house built; 2. 14 Māgh, 1893 Saka; 1 Phālgun, 1900 Saka; on the eighteenth of Āsvin, 1712 Saka; 3. God only knows why they were unable to meet you. 4. As soon as their niece came into the room everyone started to smile. 5. It was completely forbidden to smoke tobacco in his house. 6. They had decided to go to Bombay, but no one knows why they didn't go. 7. I have a nephew who is a student in (i.e., 'of') that school. 8. Asha (आशा prop. f.) works in a factory in which all sorts of things are made. 9. I know a cobbler who can make very good shoes for you. 10. The books that are lying on the table are hers. 11. This is the man (literally 'this is that man') who had the hospital built. 12. The people who gave them the money are not from this village. 13. Mridula (मृदुला prop. f.) was wearing (i.e., 'Mridula had put on') the sari that we brought for her from Madras (मद्रास). 14. We were very surprised to learn (use यह जानकर कि) that the woman is not from India. 15. Whoever does not help you cannot be called (use passive of कहना) your true friend.

21.7.3. Combine each of the following sets of sentences into single sentences using relative clauses. In each instance use the first sentence as the main clause and the second sentence as the relative clause:

e.g., मेज़ पर दो पुस्तकें हैं। पुस्तकें इलाहाबाद में प्रकाशित थीं।
मेज पर दो पुस्तकें हैं जो इलाहाबाद में प्रकाशित थीं।

1. मेरी एक बहन है। मेरी बहन को पूरियाँ पसंद नहीं हैं।
2. वह बचपन से एक गांव में रहता है। गांव आगरे के पास ही है।
3. उसको खाना पसंद आता है। खाने में सब तरह के मसाले हैं।
4. उस सड़क पर दो बच्चे खड़े थे। पिता जी बच्चों से बात कर रहे थे।
5. मोती (prop. m) का एक लड़का है। हम अपनी लड़की की शादी लड़के से करना चाहते हैं।
6. अमृत (prop. m) के दो मित्र हमारे यहाँ आए थे। मित्रों को माता जी का खाना बहुत अच्छा लगा।

21.7.4. Convert each of the following sentences into an infinitival phrase:

e.g. वह यहाँ आया→उसका यहाँ आना

1. हम आराम से सोते हैं। 2. वाजपेयी जी अपने बच्चों को सिखाते हैं। 3. मालती मध्य प्रदेश में पैदा हुई। 4. अधिकारियों ने तीन अस्पताल बनवाए। 5. लड़कियां ख़ुशी से मुसकराईं। 6. मदन ने बग़ीचे में पौधे लगाए।

CHAPTER 22

22.1. Other Relative Pronouns and Corresponding Correlative Pronouns

There are sets of relative pronoun and corresponding correlative in Hindi besides जो...वह. Whereas जो is used as the relative pronoun in clauses referring to people (i.e., that would begin in English with 'who') or things (i.e. that would begin in English with 'that' or 'which'), these other relative pronouns are used in clauses of place, time, quantity, quality, or manner.

22.1.1 जहाँ ..वहाँ ... and जिधर ...उधर

The pairs of forms जहाँ...वहाँ .(where...there) and जिधर...उधर (whither...thither) are used in relative clauses of place or location. The first of these sets is used when it is a specific locus that is referred to; by contrast, the second is employed with reference to directions (as opposed to specific places):

जहाँ हम रहते हैं वहाँ उनके कई रिश्तेदार भी रहते हैं ।
'Several of their relatives live where we live'.
जहाँ भी आप जाने का निश्चय करें वहाँ मैं भी जाना चाहता हूं ।
'I want to go wherever (i.e., to whatever place) you decide to go'.
जिधर मोहन जाए उधर अमर जाएगा ।
'Amar will go wherever (i.e., in whatever direction) Mohan goes'.

The pronouns used in each of these sets of forms are often combined with one or another postposition:

जहाँ का वह है वहाँ की पुष्पा भी है ।
'Pushpa is from the same place that he is from'.
जिधर से तुम आए उधर से वापस जाओ ।
'Go back the same way that you came'.

Occasionally, the form तहाँ is found in place of वहाँ as the correlative of जहाँ :

जहाँ सुमति तहाँ संपत्ति ।

'Where there is unity there is prosperity'. [cf. सुमति n.f. 'unity, concord'; संपत्ति n.f. 'prosperity']

22.1.2. जब ...तब

The relative/correlative pair जब ...तब (when...then) appears in sentences showing relative clauses of time. The elements of this pair are quite often used in conjunction with various postpositions:

एक दिन आएगा जब सब लोगों को सच्ची स्वतंत्रता मिलेगी ।
'A day will come when all men will receive true freedom'.

जब वह आया (तब)[1] मैं घर पर नहीं थी।
'I wasn't at home when he came'.
जब से मैं हिन्दुस्तान में हूँ (तब से) मैं हिन्दी सीख रहा हूँ।
'I have been learning Hindi as long as I've been in India'.
जब तक वह घर न लौटा (तब तक) पंकज को नींद नहीं आई।
'Pankaj couldn't sleep as long as he couldn't return home'.

22.1.3. जितना...उतना

The relative/correlative pair जितना... उतना (as much...so much) is used in sentences containing relative clauses of quantity. The pair is also used in sentences indicating equality in the extent to which some adjectival quality pertains to different nominal entities (i.e., X is as Y as Z):

मैं उतने समोसे नहीं खा सकता हूँ जितने आपने खाए।
'I cannot eat as many samosas as you ate'.
तुम्हारे पास जितने पैसे हैं उतने पैसे मेरे पास नहीं।
'I don't have as much money as you have'.
लता के गाने जितने प्रिय हैं उतने (प्रिय) रफ़ी के (गाने) हैं।
'Rafi's songs are as beloved as Lata's'. [cf. रफ़ी prop. m. the Hindi film singer Mohammed Rafi]
हरिद्वार उतना ही पुराना शहर है जितना कि दिल्ली।[2]
'Hardwar is as old a city as Delhi'.

N.B. Observe that the forms जितना and उतना are adjectival in nature, agreeing with some modified noun in number, gender, and case. This explains why the form उतना in the last of the above examples has the ending –आ (agreeing with the masculine, singular, direct case noun शहर), while जितनी has the ending –ई (agreeing with the feminine, singular, direct case noun दिल्ली)

22.1.4. जैसा...वैसा

In sentences having relative clauses specifying the sort or kind of some nominal entity, the relative/correlative pair brought into use is जैसा...वैसा, these forms standing in grammatical agreement in number, gender and case with the nouns they modify:

मेरे पास वैसी मूर्त्तियां हैं जैसी मैंने आन्ध्र प्रदेश में देखी थीं।
'I have the same kind of statues that I had seen in Andhra Pradesh.'
कल शाम को जैसे पकोड़े हमने खाए वैसे (पकोड़े) माँ ने आज पका दिए।
'Today mother made the same kind of pakoras that we ate yesterday evening'.
जैसा बाप वैसा बेटा।
'Like father like son'.

1. The correlative element of relative/correlative pairs is commonly deleted in colloquial usage.
2. Hindi relative/correlative structures having the sense 'just as adjective as Y, exactly as adjective as Y' often show the form ही after the उतना element and कि after the जितना correlative.

The relative form जैसा is often used immediately following oblique case nouns in the sense 'like X, similar to X'. This जैसा too is adjectival, and agrees with the noun that the sequence of oblique case noun+जैसा is modifying:

लड़के-जैसी लड़की 'a boy-like girl'
लड़की-जैसे लड़के 'girl-like boys'.

22.1.5. जैसे...वैसे

The pair of indeclinable forms जैसे...वैसे is used adverbially in sentences having the sense 'just as...so' or 'in such a manner as...so':

जैसे हम कहें वैसे करो।
'Do as we say'.

जैसे तुम बोलो वैसे ही मैं बोलूंगा।
'I will speak just as you do'.

Often the form जैसे is used by itself as a subordinating conjunction having the meaning '(just) as' or 'as if':

जैसे मैं आपको बता रहा था वह नहीं आ सकेगा।
'Just as I was telling you, he will not be able to come'.

ऐसा लगता है जैसे आज बारिश नहीं होगी।
'It appears that (i.e., it seems as if) it won't rain today'.

वह अंग्रेजी बोल रही थी जैसे वह हिन्दुस्तानी न होकर अमेरिकन हो।
'She was speaking English as if she were not an Indian but an American'.

The word जैसे also appears as part of the postposition X के जैसे 'like X, in the manner of X':

वह अपने भाई के जैसे सारा दिन नहीं पढ़ सकता।
'He cannot study all day as his brother does'.

22.1.6. The relative/correlative construction जैसे ही... वैसे ही has the special sense 'as soon as...(then)'. Care should be taken not to confuse this usage of जैसे with other uses of the form. In Sanskritized Hindi, ज्यों ही ....त्यों ही is used instead of जैसे ही...वैसे ही:

जैसे ही श्रीकांत कमरे में आया (वैसे ही) सब लोग हंसने लगे।
'Everyone started to laugh as soon as Shrikant came into the room'.

ज्यों ही राजा के शत्रुओं ने नगर पर आक्रमण किया त्यों ही वहाँ के निवासियों ने अपने घरों को सुरक्षित करने का निश्चय किया।
'As soon as the enemies of the king attacked the city, the residents of the city decided to protect their homes'.

22.1.7 ज्यों-ज्यों....त्यों-त्यों

The relative/correlative combination ज्यों-ज्यों...त्यों-त्यों is used to indicate the coordination of two ongoing activities or states of affairs:

ज्यों-ज्यों दिन लम्बे होते जाते हैं त्यों-त्यों रातें छोटी होती जाती हैं।[3]

3. For the use of the verbal construction consisting of the verbal stem+ता followed by जाना v.31.1.

'The nights get shorter as the days get longer'.

22.2. Time Expressions

The most commonly employed verb in Hindi time expressions is बजना 'to sound, (for the hour) to strike, to emit a sound'. In general, expressions of time are formed by stating that a given number (presumably of bells) has sounded. For purposes of exposition, statements of time in Hindi can be divided into those pertaining to hours, quarter hours, and times other than those falling on the quarter, half, or full hour.

Statements of the full hour are formed with the cardinal numbers 1-12:

एक बजा है।	'It's one o'clock'.
ग्यारह बजे हैं ।	'It's eleven o'clock'.
दस बजने वाले हैं।	'It's almost ten o'clock' (i.e., 'ten are about to strike').
चार बज चुके हैं।	'It's already four' (i.e., 'four have already struck').

In order to indicate quarter or half hours, the fractions सवा, डेढ़, ढाई, साढ़े, and पौन (or पौने) are used The uses of these fractions in time expressions is a logical extension of the strict mathematical sense of these forms (cf. 13.8). The word सवा ('$1\frac{1}{4}$') is used to designate 1:15 and, by extension, a quarter past later hours:

सवा बजा	'1:15'
सवा बजा है।	'It's 1:15'.
सवा चार बजे	'at 4:15'.

The fractional term डेढ़ ('$1\frac{1}{2}$') and ढाई ('$2\frac{1}{2}$') are used to refer to the specific times 1:30 and 2:30 respectively:

डेढ़ बजा	'1:30'
डेढ़ बजे	'at 1:30'
ढाई बजे हैं।	'It's 2:30'.

For half hours beyond 2 : 30, साढ़े is employed:

साढ़े तीन बजे हैं।	'It's 3:30'.
साढ़े तीन बजने के बाद	'after 3:30'.
दिन के साढ़े ग्यारह बजे	'at 11:30 a.m.'

The fraction पौन ('3/4' is) used to indicate the exact time 12:45:

पौन बजा है।	'It's 12:45'.

For a quarter to hours other than 1, the term पौने occurs in place of पौन।

रात के पौने दो बजे हैं।	'It's 1:45 a.m.'

In order to express times after the hour (but before the half hour), Hindi uses sentences that state that the hour having struck, such and such a number of minutes has elapsed:

दो बजकर चौदह मिनट हुए हैं।	'It's 2:14'.
आठ बजकर नौ मिनट पर	'at 8:09'.

For times after the half hour (but before the full hour), Hindi states that a specified number of minutes remain before (expressed by means of the postposition में) the hour strikes:

बारह बजने में तीन मिनट बाक़ी हैं।	'It's 11:57'.
दस बजने में बीस मिनट पर	'at 9:40'.

In order to express the exactness of some time expression, the word ठीक appears before the actual time expression:

रात के ठीक ग्यारह बजे	'at exactly 11:00 p.m.'

22.3. Divisions of the Day

In common usage the primary parts of the day are सुबह (alternately सवेरा or प्रातःकाल) 'morning', दोपहर 'afternoon, noon', शाम (or संध्या) 'evening', and रात 'night'. The term दोपहर designates either noon itself or that period of the time immediately following it (i.e., afternoon). In combination with the words रात को (i.e., in the phrase दोपहर रात को), however, it specifically indicates midnight. Midnight is also referred to by the phrase आधी रात.

One also finds in modern Hindi vestiges of an older time system in which the day was divided into eight intervals (पहर), each lasting three hours. This system is reflected in such modern expressions as दोपहर (see above), आठों पहर 'all day' [all eight pahars], and तीसरी पहर 'middle to late afternoon'.

22.4. Other Time Expressions

There are a number of common locutions that are used in Hindi in speaking about or inquiring about time. Some of these are listed below:

क्या समय (वक़्त/टाइम) है ?	'What time is it ?'
कितने बजे हैं ?	'What time is it ?' (literally 'how many has it struck ?')
मेरी घड़ी में तीन बजे हैं।	'It's three o'clock according to my clock/watch'.

22.5. Elapsing of Time

The verb लगना is employed to indicate that some quantity of time is involved in the carrying out or transpiring of some activity. Normally the activity during which time is involved is indicated by an oblique infinitive followed by the postposition में :

दिल्ली पहुंचने में कितना समय लगा ?
'How long did it take to reach Delhi ?'

काम पूरा करने में तीन और घंटे लगेंगे।
'It will take three more hours to finish the work'.

The oblique infinitive plus में or तक is also used to indicate the reckoning of time until the inception of an activity :

फ़िल्म शुरू होने में/तक पौन घंटा बाक़ी है।
'There are forty-five more minutes until the film starts'.

Hindi employs a special indirect verb construction to express the elapsing of time subsequent to some activity. Normally the verb subsequent to which time has elapsed is placed in its m. pl. si. perf. form and is optionally extended with हुए. The main verb of the entire construction is commonly होना. If the temporally prior verb has an animate subject, this subject is placed in the oblique and followed by the postposition को :

मुझे दिल्ली आए (हुए) दो हफ़्ते हुए हैं ।
'It's been two weeks since I came to Delhi'.

माधुरी को बी० ए० पास किए (हुए) चार साल हो चुके हैं ।
'It's already been four years since Madhuri passed (i.e., received) her B.A. (degree)'.

To express the English 'ago' Hindi uses the simple perfective of होना or the adverbs पहले and पूर्व :

फ़िल्म दो घंटे हुए/पहले/पूर्व शुरू हुई ।
'The film began two hours ago'.

मैं दो हफ़्ते हुए/पहले/पूर्व दिल्ली आया ।
'I came to Delhi two weeks ago'.

22.6. VOCABULARY

अंडा	n.m. egg	प्रिय	adj. dear, beloved
घड़ी	n.f. watch, clock	बाक़ी	adj. remaining; n.f. remainder
चाय	n.f. tea		
देखभाल	n.f. care, custody, supervision	विवाहित	adj. married
		सुरक्षित	adj. protected, safe
निवासी	n.m. resident	इकट्ठा करना/होना	v.t./i. to gather together/to be gathered
नींद	n.f. sleep, sleepiness		
पकौड़ा	n.m. pakora [a kind of fritter]	X (का) इस्तेमाल करना/होना	v.t./i. to use X/ for X to be used
पहर	n.f. a measure of time equal to three hours	उगना	v.i. to grow
		उलटना	v.t./i. to overturn/to be overturned
पीठ	n.f. back		
पैर	n.m. foot	कम करना/होना	v.t./i. to make less/to diminish, become less
प्याज़	n.m. onion		
प्रातःकाल	n.m. (early) morning, dawn	कमाना	v.t. to earn
बाँसुरी	n.f. flute	चुप करना/होना	v.t./i. to make quiet/to become quiet
बाप	n.m. father		
माँ	n.f. mother	थकना	v.i. to become tired or exhausted
मिर्च	n.f. pepper		
मूर्त्ति	n.f. statue	X की देखभाल करना	v.t. to look after/supervise X
रिश्तेदार	n.m. relative		
लहसुन	n.m. garlic	X को नींद आना	v.i. for X to feel or become sleepy
वक़्त	n.m. time, occasion		
शाम	n.f. evening	X को पहचानना	v t. to recognize X
शेष	n.m., remainder; adj. remaining	बदलना	v.t./i. to change/to be changed
संध्या	n.f. evening	पूर्व	adv. previously, ago
सप्ताह	n.m. week	वापस	adv. back
समोसा	n.m. samosa [a triangular pastry filled with vegetables or meat]	X (को) छोड़ कर	post. except for X
		X के दौरान	post. during X
		X के स्थान पर/में	post. in place of X
साल	n.m. year	न...न	conj. neither...nor
इकट्ठा	adj. frequently indecl. gathered, collected	भी...भी	conj. both...and
		या...या	conj. either...or

22.7. EXERCISES

22.7.1. *Translate into English*

1. ढाई बजे, सवा चार बजे, दिन के ढाई बजे; 2. तीन बजे हैं, सात बजने से पहले; 3. नौ बजने लगे हैं, दस बजने वाले थे, रात के ठीक ग्यारह बजे; 4. तीन बजकर पाँच मिनट हुए हैं, दिन के दस बजकर चार मिनट पर, संध्या के चार बजने में पच्चीस मिनट पर; 5. नौ बजने से दो घंटे पहले, साढ़े तीन बजने के तीन मिनट बाद, आठ बजने से ठीक पहले; 6. हमारी चप्पलें छोड़ कर, प्याज और लहसुन छोड़ कर, अपने एक भाई को छोड़ कर; 7. फिल्म के दौरान, इन खेलों के दौरान, सर्दियों के दौरान; 8. इन मूर्तियों पर, अपने रिश्तेदारों के स्थान पर, वहां के निवासियों के स्थान पर ।

22.7.2. *Translate into Hindi*

1. It's one o'clock, it's already six o'clock, it's almost ten o'clock; 2. it's one fifteen, it's three forty-five, it's eight thirty a.m.; 3. at five thirty in the evening, at exactly midnight, it must be ten o'clock; 4. it's seven minutes past nine, it's twelve twenty-eight, at eleven nineteen a.m. 5. It's seven twenty-six in the morning, at twelve minutes after five in the evening, at eleven nineteen at night; 6. two hours before noon, six minutes after striking ten, before two o'clock in the afternoon; 7. except for their friends, except for this new book, except for all their relatives; 8. during the examination, during those long songs, during that week; 9. in place of his niece, in place of that sort (प्रकार) of pepper, in place of that married woman.

22.7.3. *Translate into English*

1. हमें किसी सुरक्षित स्थान पर जाना चाहिए जहाँ कोई हमको न देख सके। 2. जहाँ वह रहता है (वहाँ) लोग अंडे, प्याज़ और लहसुन भी नहीं खाते। 3. जब तक तुम अपना कमरा न साफ़ करो (तब तक) हम तुम्हें पकौड़े, समोसे और दूसरे अच्छे खाने नहीं देंगे। 4. शेखर की चप्पलें उतनी ही पुरानी हैं जितने कि मेरे जूते। 5. जब तक उसने मुझे नाम से (by name) न बुलाया (तब तक) मैं उसे पहचान न पाया। 6. मैं वैसे कपड़े ख़रीदना चाहता हूँ जैसे विनय (prop.m.) पहनता है। 7. वर्मा जी के पास उतना पैसा नहीं है जितना कार ख़रीदने के लिए चाहिये। 8. जैसे ही किरण की माँ बोलने लगी वैसे ही किरण ने पहचान लिया कि उसकी बातें कोई नहीं सुनेगा। 9. सारा दिन दफ़्तर में काम करने से प्रभा (prop. f.) को काफी नींद आने लगी। 10. जैसे शिखा (prop. f.) गाती थी वैसे ही गाने की हम कोशिश करते थे। 11. जब से तुम मथुरा में हो तब से उस पुराने मकान में क्यों रह रहे हो ? 12. मनोज (prop. m.) न अपनी स्कूल की किताबें पढ़ता है न घर में किसी तरह का काम करता है। 13. वे या यूँ ही घर में रहेंगे या बाहर खेलने जाएँगे, पर कोई ज़रूरी काम नहीं करेंगे। 14. जिधर से वे आए उधर से ही लौट गए। 15. मोहन राकेश[4] की कहानियाँ उतनी प्रसिद्ध नहीं हैं जितनी प्रेमचन्द[5] जी की हैं।

22.7.4. *Translate into Hindi*

1. There are no wells where we live. 2. Her dog would go (i.e., used to go) wherever she went. 3. They have been speaking Punjabi as long as they've been in Delhi. 4. Mother didn't let the child play until he ate up all of his food (i.e., until he did *not* eat up his food). 5. Like mother, like daughter. 6. We cannot read as many books as you (pol.) can. 7. Hindi is as beautiful (use मीठा) a language as Marathi (मराठी n.f.). 8. I want to do the same sort of work as he does in the office. 9. The baby burst into tears as soon as Mother left the room. 10. He uses (डालना) no spices in his food except salt and pepper. 11. There is a sweet shop near where my relatives live. 12. As soon as she changed her sari she set out to catch (पकड़ना) the train (गाड़ी n.f.). 13. How many hours is it until school starts ? 14. How many days has it been since Mr. Kapur's (कपूर) relatives gathered in the village ? 15. He neither makes nor spends much money (i.e., he neither makes much money nor spends much).

---

4. मोहन राकेश (prop. m.) the contemporary Hindi writer Mohan Rakesh (1925-1972).

5. प्रेमचन्द (prop. m.) the well known Hindi and Urdu writer "Premchand" (=Dhanpat Rai [1880-1936]).

CHAPTER 23

23.1. Subordinating Conjunctions[1]

There are numerous conjunctions that are employed in Hindi to introduce subordinate clauses of various kinds. The selection of a particular subordinating conjunction to introduce a given dependent clause is based to a great extent upon the semantic relationship between the main and subordinate clause of the sentence in question. The formation of sentences involving subordinate clauses can often be quite intricate, with the subordinating conjunction of the dependent clause counterbalanced by a correlative word or phrase in the main clause.

23.1.1. *Subordinating conjunctions with the sense 'because'*

The words क्योंकि and चूँकि introduce subordinate clauses indicating reasons or causes. The former word is employed only when the subordinate clause follows the main clause:

मैं शिमला में रहना चाहता हूँ क्योंकि पहाड़ों का मौसम मुझे माफ़िक आता है।
'I want to live in Shimla because the weather in the mountains suits me'.
[cf. शिमला prop. m. Shimla (a hill station in Himachal Pradesh)]

If the subordinate clause precedes the main clause, चूँकि appears in lieu of क्योंकि, and one of the phrases इसलिए, इस कारण (से), or इस वजह (से) serves in the main clause as correlative to चूँकि :[2]

चूँकि पहाड़ों का मौसम मुझे पसंद आता है इसलिए/इस कारण (से)/इस वजह (से) मैं शिमला में रहना चाहता हूँ।
चूँकि उसके बड़े भाई कानपुर के हैं इसलिए वहाँ उनके रहने का प्रबन्ध होता है।
'He has a place to stay in Kanpur because his brother is from there'.

Frequently, the phrase इसलिए कि appears in place of either क्योंकि or चूँकि:

तुमने टायर की हवा क्यों निकाली ?
इसलिए कि कार कहीं न जा सके।
'Why did you let the air out of the tire ?
'So that the car won't be able to go anywhere'.

23.1.2. *Subordinating conjunctions with the sense 'even though'*

There are several common combinations of subordinating conjunction and corresponding correlative that express the notion of 'even though...still'. The most important

---

1. The use of subordinating conjunctions in a number of constructions of the type 'if...then' will be taken up in the following two chapters (cf. sections 24.1, 24.2, 25.1).

2. As was observed in the discussion of relative pronouns and corresponding correlatives (21.4, 22.1), correlatives are frequently deleted in colloquial usage.

of these pairs are यद्यपि...तथापि and either अगच or हालांकि and any of फिर भी, तो भी, पर, or लेकिन:

यद्यपि हम अपने कार्यों में इन वस्तुओं का प्रयोग नहीं करते, तथापि वे बहुत उपयोगी वस्तुएं हैं ।
'Those are very useful things even though we don't use them in our own work'

अगर्चे मीनू बहुत कम मिठाई खाती है फिर भी वह आपकी बर्फ़ी पसन्द करेगी ।
Minu will like your barfi even though she doesn't eat sweets very much'.
[cf. बर्फ़ी n.f. a kind of sweet made from dried milk]

हालांकि छवि यू० पी० का है तो भी/लेकिन/पर उसे हिंदी बिलकुल नहीं आती ।
'Chavi doesn't know any Hindi at all even though he is from U.P.'[3]

23.1.3. *Subordinating conjunctions with the sense 'so that'*

The subordinating conjunctions ताकि and जिससे (कि) are used to indicate that some activity (i.e., that of the main clause) is carried out so that some other activity (i.e., that of the subordinate clause) might also be carried out or brought into effect. Normally the verb of the subordinate clause introduced by ताकि or जिससे (कि) has a subjunctive inflection :

सिंह साहब बाजार में रुके ताकि खाने को[4] कुछ मिल जाए ।
'Mr. Singh stopped in the market to get something to eat' [literally 'so that something to eat might be obtained'].

हम दुगुना काम करने लगे जिससे चाचाजी का घर जल्दी तैयार हो जाए ।
'We started to do twice as much work so that uncle's house would get completed quickly'.

23.1.4. अर्थात् *and* यानी

The conjunctions अर्थात् and यानी are used to introduce paraphrases of that which has already been stated in a previous clause:

जानकी अधिक परिश्रमी स्त्री है अर्थात् वह औरत बहुत मेहनत करती है ।
'Jānaki is a most industrious woman; that is to say, she does a lot of hard work'.

अर्थात् and यानी may also be used to provide paraphrases not only of entire clauses, but also of single words or small phrases within large clauses:

राम सरन के घर वाले अर्थात्/यानी उसकी पत्नी और दो बच्चे नहीं आ सके ।
'The members of Ram Saran's, family, that is to say, his wife and two children, were not able to come'.

23.1.5. *Constructions with* चाहे

The conjunction चाहे is employed in a number of related, albeit semantically distinct, constructions. The pair चाहे...परन्तु has the sense 'regardless of the fact that. . .still'. Normally the clause in which चाहे appears is in the subjunctive :

---

3. Cf. 23.2 for a discussion of the use आना to specify the ability to use a learned skill.
4. The postposition को is used frequently as a variant of के लिए after infinitives.

चाहे वह अमरीकन हो परन्तु देखने में हिन्दुस्तानी-सा[5] लगता है[6]।
'Regardless of the fact that he is an American, he looks like an Indian'.

चाहे is often followed by one of another चाहे, या, or अथवा, the entire construction having the sense 'whether X or Y . . .still':

इस जीवन में चाहे अमीर चाहे ग़रीब स्वर्ग में सब लोग एक-से हैं।
'Whether rich or poor in this life, all people are alike in heaven !

चाहे मेरी बातें मानो या न मानो उनमें सच्चाई है।
'There is truth in what I say, regardless of whether you believe it or not'.

Occasionally the disjunctive phrase क्या . . .क्या is used synonymously with चाहे . . .चाहे/या/अथवा;

इस जीवन में क्या अमीर क्या ग़रीब स्वर्ग में सब लोग एक-से हैं।

23.2. A Further Use of आना

Yet another means for indicating the ability to carry out a learned activity is provided in Hindi by means of an indirect verb construction employing आना. The full scheme for this construction is X को Y आना 'X knows Y, is able to perform Y', where Y can stand for a noun (representing, for example, the name of a language) or an infinitive or infinitival phrase (i.e., an infinitive plus any objects it might have) :

आपको काफ़ी गुजराती आती है।
'You know Gujarati quite well'.

उसको हिंदी बोलना आता है पर लिखना-पढ़ना नहीं आता।
'He/she knows how to speak Hindi, but can't read it or write it'.

23.3. Expressions for Opinions and Intentions

The primary means in Hindi for indicating one's opinions concerning some matter or other involve a number of nouns having the sense 'opinion, judgement'. The most important of these are विचार (n.m.), ख़याल (n.m.), मत (n.m.), and राय (n.f.). Sentences illustrating the employment of these nouns include the following :

सक्सेना जी के विचार/के ख़याल/के मत/की राय में हमें नहीं जाना चाहिए था।

सक्सेना जी { का विचार/का ख़याल/ का मत/की राय } यह { था / थी } कि हमें नहीं जाना चाहिए था।

'It was Mr. Saksena's opinion that we shouldn't have gone.

To express the intention to carry out some activity, the nouns इरादा (n.m. 'intention') or उद्देश्य (n.m. 'intent, purpose, aim') are used. For expressing a wish (as opposed to an intention) to carry out an action, any of several nouns may be used, of which इच्छा (n.f.) and चाह (n.f.) are important examples. The noun मन (n.m. 'mind, inclination, disposition') is frequently also employed in either of the senses 'wish' or 'intention':

हमारा इरादा/मन/उद्देश्य/सारा दिन सोने का था।
'We intended to sleep all day'.

---

5. हिन्दुस्तानी-सा 'like an Indian' (cf. 25.5).

6. लगता 'looks like, seems like' (cf. 16.3).

हमारी इच्छा सारा दिन सोने की थी ।
'We wanted to sleep all day'.
मेरा एक दिन भारत जाने का इरादा है ।
'I intend to go to India one day'.
हमें जाने की इच्छा/चाह थी ।
'We wanted to go'.

The verb चाहना 'to want, wish' with an infinitival direct object may, of course, also be used to express wishes and desires:

वह जाना चाहता था ।
'He wanted to go'.

23.4. OBLIQUE INFINITIVE + पर भी

In 23.1.2. it was shown that यद्यपि ..तथापि and several other subordinating conjunction+correlative pairs can be used to express the notion 'in spite of...still'. The use of this pair was carried out over two clauses, one a main clause and the other a subordinate clause. However, another expression exists in Hindi for expressing this relationship between clauses. In this locution the verb of what would otherwise be the subordinate clause is placed in its oblique infinitival form and is followed by the phrase पर भी :

अमीर होने पर भी सेठ जी कम पैसे ख़र्च करते हैं ।
'Mr. Seth spends little money in spite of being rich'.
हमारे साथ खाने पर भी हमारी उनसे बातें नहीं हुईं ।
'We didn't speak to them in spite of (their) eating with us'.

If the subject of the infinitive is different from that of the main verb of the sentence and is to be explicitly stated, then it (i.e., the subject of the infinitive) may be linked to the infinitive by means of the postposition के. In the usage of some speakers, however, this के is omitted:

सिंह साहब (के) हमारे साथ खाने पर भी हमारी उनसे बातें नहीं हुईं ।
'In spite of the fact that Mr. Singh ate with us, we didn't converse with him'.

23.5. EXPRESSIONS FOR THE ENGLISH VERB 'TO HAVE'

The English verb 'to have' is used in a wide variety of ways that have little in common with one another semantically. This can easily be observed by examining the following set of sentences:

John has a cold/a brother/ a new car/ to go home/ an examination tomorrow'.

The use of the verb 'to have' in each of the above sentences conveys something quite different. In the first example, it signifies a state of affairs concerning John's physical condition. In the second, a description is given of a familial relationship to which John is a party. This third instance specifies alienable possession, that is, a right of possession that is transferable from one person to another. The sentence

'John has to go home' denotes a psychological state of obligation or necessity. The last sentence is an abbreviated version of a longer sentence 'John has to take an examination tomorrow' indicating a state of obligation or necessity.

Hindi, unlike English and several other western European languages, lacks a single verb serving the various functions of English 'have'. The senses illustrated in the above sentences are expressed in Hindi by independent linguistic means.

For sentences such as 'John has a cold' indirect verb constructions are employed (cf. 15.1):

उसको बुखार आया है ।
'He has a fever'.
शंकर लाल को सिर का दर्द है ।
'Shankar Lal has a headache'.

For familial relationships, possessive expressions in का are employed in conjunction with होना;

सीता की दो छोटी बहनें हैं
'Sita has two younger sisters'.

This last construction type is also extended to relationships among people other than familial ones:

हमारा एक नौकर था जो....!
'We had a servant who...'.
उस गांव का एक नाई है जो....!
'That village has a barber who...'.

The postposition के पास is employed commonly for alienable possession:

डिंपिल के पास नई कार है ।
'Dimple has a new car'
उनके पास काफ़ी पैसा है ।
'They have plenty of money'.

The English sentence 'John has to go' is expressed in Hindi by constructions using an infinitive plus होना or पड़ना or by an indirect verb construction with some noun such as जरूरत or आवश्यकता (cf. 17.4):

जान को जाना है/पड़ता है ।
जान को जाने की जरूरत/आवश्यकता है ।
'John has to go'.

23.6. आदि AND वग़ैरह

Either of the two forms आदि and वग़ैरह the former in Sanskritized Hindi and the latter in Urdu and non-Sanskritized Hindi, may be appended to the end of a list of entities in the sense of 'et cetera':

पार्टी में हमें खाने को नमकीन, समोसे, पकौड़े वग़ैरह मिल गया ।
'We got salty snacks, samosas, pakoras, etc. to eat at the party'.

जयशंकर प्रसाद के लेख, उपन्यास, कविताएं आदि पढ़ने से हम अधिक लाभ उठा सकते हैं।
'We can derive much benefit from studying Jay Shankar Prasad's articles, novels, poems, etc.'.
[जयशंकर प्रसाद prop. m. Jay Shankar Prasad (1889-1937), one of the major Hindi literary figures of the 20th century']

23.7. VOCABULARY

अमरीकन	n.m. American	उपयोगी	adj. useful
इरादा	n.m. intention	परिश्रमी	adj. hard working
उँगली	n.f. finger	बहुत-सा	adj. many, quite a few
उद्देश्य	n.m. purpose, aim, intention	उतरना	v.i. to descend, come down
उपन्यास	n.m. novel	जीतना	v.i. to be victorious
कार्य	n.m. work, deed, action	X का प्रबंध करना/ — होना	v.t. i. to arrange for X/ for X to be arranged
ख़याल	n.m. opinion, meaning		
गुजराती	prop. f. the Gujarati language	X की Y से बातें होना	v.i. to X to converse with Y
चाह	n.f. wish	मानना	v.t. to accept, believe
ज़ुकाम	n.m. a cold	X को Y माफ़िक आना	v.i. for Y to suit X
टांग	n.f. leg	X से लाभ उठाना	v.t. to derive benefit from X
दर्द	n.m. pain		
नमकीन	n.f. salty snack	X का सफ़र करना	v.t. to travel to X
नाई	n.m. barber	हारना	v.i. to be defeated
प्रबंध	n.m. arrangement	X के (इस/उस) पार	post. across X, on (this/that) side of X
बांह	n.f. arm	X की बाईं तरफ़/ओर	post. to the left side of X
मन	n.m. mind, inclination, intention, wish	X की दाहिनी तरफ़/ओर	post. to the right side of X
मोज़ा	n.m. sock		
याद	n.f. memory, remembrance	X के चारों तरफ़/ओर	post. all around X, surrounding X
राय	n.f. opinion	अथवा	conj. or
लाभ	n.m. benefit	इस कारण (से)	conj. therefore
वजह	n.f. reason, explanation	इस वजह (से)	conj. therefore
सच्चाई	n.f. truth	किन्तु	conj. but
सफ़र	n.m. trip, journey	तो भी	conj. still, nevertheless
साहित्य	n.m. literature	आदि	partl. et cetera
स्वर्ग	n.m. heaven	वग़ैरह	partl. et cetera

23.8. EXERCISES

23.8.1. *Translate into English*

१. इरादा, पढ़ने का इरादा, देर तक यहाँ रहने का इरादा, उन लोगों का दिल्ली में रहने का इरादा; २. उनके खयाल में, उन बूढ़ों के ख़याल में, पिता जी की राय में; ३. प्रबंध, ठहरने का प्रबन्ध, उनके उस होटल में ठहरने का प्रबंध, खाना अच्छी हालत

में रखने का प्रबंध; ४. बहुत-से उपन्यास, बहुत-सी यादें, उनके बहुत-से कार्यों में; ५. हिंदी साहित्य से लाभ उठाना, पंडितजी के साथ पढ़ने से लाभ उठाना; ६. हिन्दी, संस्कृत, पंजाबी, गुजराती आदि; जूते, चप्पलें, मोज़े वग़ैरह; ७. याद, कई यादें, उस समय की पुरानी यादें, लता और रफ़ी के गानों की यादें; ८. गंगा नदी के पार, समुद्र के इस पार, मध्य प्रदेश के उस पार; ९. मेज़ की बाईं तरफ़, उस पहाड़ की दाहिनी ओर, बग़ीचे के चारों तरफ़।

23.8.2. *Translate into Hindi*

1. Wish, intention of speaking, our intention of not remaining poor; 2. opinion, in the shopkeeper's opinion, in the opinion of those four women, his opinion concerning these matters; 3. rather a lot of opportunities, in quite a few families, in many of the answers of the servant's wife; 4. to derive benefit from attacking that country, to derive benefit from the rain, to begin to derive benefit from their actions; 5. apples, oranges, papayas, etc.; literature, languages, history, etc.; to write, read. understand, speak, etc.; 6. memories of that year, memories of their life in Mathura, memories of their childhood; 7. on the other side of that field, on this side of the Jamuna River, on the other side of India; 8. all around the city, to the left of those three windows, to the right of the tall door.

23.8.3. *Translate into English*

१. अगर्चे उसका मन राजस्थान जाने का नहीं था फिर भी उसे जयपुर जाना पड़ा। २. चूँकि कल से मुन्नू को बुख़ार आया है इसलिए हम उसे स्कूल नहीं जाने देंगे। ३. तुमको सूर (prop. m. the devotional poet Sūrdās) के कुछ पद (n.m. a genre of short poem) पढ़ने चाहिएँ जिससे तुम हिन्दी साहित्य के विषय में कुछ सीखो। ४. अगले साल वे दिल्ली, आगरे, जयपुर, कलकत्ते वग़ैरह का सफ़र करेंगे। ५. रामलाल स्टेशन आया ताकि वहाँ हमारा स्वागत करने कोई हो। ६. उसका इरादा ६ जून तक कलकत्ते जाने का था। ७. मेरी एक ही इच्छा यह थी कि इस युद्ध में हम जीतें। ८. चाहे कितनी ही मुसीबतें सहनी पड़ें पर हम अपना धर्म कभी नहीं छोड़ेंगे। ९. क्या घर में, क्या दफ़्तर में वह बकवास (n.f. twaddle, nonsense) ही करता रहता है ('keeps on saying' cf. 29.1.)। १०. तुम्हें कितनी भारतीय भाषाएँ आती हैं? ११. हिंदी साहित्य पढ़ने से आप बहुत लाभ उठा लेंगे अर्थात् आप हिंदुस्तानी लोगों के जीवन के बारे में सीख सकेंगे। १२. पिताजी की राय में हमें राजस्थान का सफ़र नहीं करना चाहिए था। १३. अश्क़ के नये उपन्यास के बारे में आपका क्या विचार है? १४ लड़ाई (n.f. war, fight) में चाहे जीते चाहे हारे परन्तु सैनिक का जीवन बहुत सख़्त (adj. hard, strenuous, difficult) है। १५. इन बातों के बारे में लोगों के बहुत-से विचार हैं।

23.8.4. *Translate into Hindi*

1. I will get off the train here because I don't want to go so far as Kanpur. 2. The barber threw the money in the street because he thought that to accept it (स्वीकार करना) is a sin. 3. We will go with her to the market even though we went there only yesterday. 4. Mother started to cook the food so that it would be ready by the time they arrive (i.e. उनके आने/पहुंचने तक). 5. Her writings (that is to say, novels, poems, and stories) are very famous in Bihar and Uttar Pradesh. 6. Whether young or old, everyone will like his stories. 7. Mr. Patel (पटेल) does not know (use आना) how to read Hindi, but he speaks it quite well. 8. Siddheshvari (सिद्धेश्वरी prop. cf.) intended to stay (ठहरना) here until next Thursday. 9. They have never come to our house in spite of being (use पर भी) our relatives. 10. Our daughter gets headaches in the evening. 11. We have three children who want to get married and live in some

big city (use कर construction). 12. I intend to read the poems, novels, etc. of Jay Shankar Prasad (जय शंकर प्रसाद). 13. How many saris and kurtas does she have? 14. Even though our village had two sweet shops, he thought that there was no one who could make good rasgullas (रसगुल्ला n.m. a kind of sweet). 15. His intention was to go to Bombay, but Father wouldn't let him go.

CHAPTER 24

24.1. Conditional Sentences

Conditional sentences are those that have the general sense 'if ... then'. These sentences normally consist of two basic components, an antecedent clause stating the conditions under which some action or state of affairs might occur, and a clause stating what might or will occur given the transpiring of the antecedent.

In formal Hindi, conditional sentences normally have the form यदि/अगर ... तो .... The verb of the antecedent clause is commonly in the subjunctive or future, less commonly in the present habitual, with the verb of the subsequent clause most generally in the future, although other verbal inflections are also encountered:

अगर सुनीता आए तो उसकी मदद करने कौन होगा ?
'If Sunita should come, who will be there to help her?'

यदि वहाँ जाने में ज़्यादा समय लगे तो हम क्या करें ?
'What will we do if it takes longer to get there?'

अगर तुम बाज़ार से ताज़े मसाले न ख़रीद लाओ तो सब्जियां कैसे पकाई जाएंगी ?
'How will it be possible to cook the vegetables if you don't bring fresh spices from the market?'

अगर आप यह उचित समझते हैं[1] तो मैं उनसे मिलने जरूर जाऊँगा ।
'I certainly will go to meet him/her if you think it appropriate'.

Often the verb of the antecedent clause is not in the simple subjunctive, but in one of the perfective aspectual-tenses:

यदि वह दिल्ली से कोई ख़ास चीज़ लाया हो तो मुझे बुला लीजिए ।
'Please call me if he has brought anything special from Delhi'.

अगर बहादुर वहाँ के किसी गांव में रहता हो तो उसका जीवन काफ़ी सख़्त होगा ।
'Bahadur's life must be very difficult if he lives in some village there'.

The relative pronoun जो is employed from time to time in place of यदि/अगर in introducing the antecedent clauses of conditional sentences:

जो तुम मेरे दोस्त हो तो मुझे गालियाँ क्यों देते हो ?
'Why do you curse me if you are my friend?'

In colloquial Hindi, verb forms of the simple perfective are often found in place of the subjunctive or future in the antecedent clause:

अगर वह यहाँ शिकायत करने आया तो बोलने नहीं दूँगा ।
'I won't let him speak if he comes here to complain'.

---

1. For this use of समझना v. 24.6.

अगले हफ़्ते अगर मौसम इससे अच्छा हुआ तो हम देहात की सैर कर सकेंगे।

'We will be able to travel to the countryside if the weather is better than this next week'.

The introductory word यदि/अगर/जो of the antecedent clause of conditional sentences is commonly deleted in colloquial usage. In such cases the existence of an 'if...then' sentence is conveyed through the sequence of tenses in the antecedent and subsequent clause as well as by the presence of तो introducing the subsequent clause:

हम उसकी मदद न करें तो क्या ?

'So what if we don't help him/her'. (Literally, 'we don't help him/her, then what?')

बच्चों को गरम दूध पिलाया जाए तो उन्हें नींद जल्दी आ जाएगी।

'If the children are given warm milk, they'll get sleepy quickly'.

24.2. Contrary to Fact Conditional Sentences

A special kind of conditional sentence is employed in Hindi in the sense 'if X had occurred then Y would have occurred'. These sentences are designated as contrary to fact because they presuppose that X did not occur. In form, contrary to fact conditional sentences contain two clauses, each of whose verb ends with one of the suffixes –ता/-ते/–ती/–तीं not followed by any auxiliary. The two clauses are connected by the conjunction तो. Although it is not technically incorrect to begin the antecedent clause with the explicit marker यदि/अगर, it is not common to do so, and the collocation of two clauses ending in –ता/–ते/–ती/–तीं in conjunction with the conjunction तो is sufficient to signal the existence of a contrary to fact conditional sentence:

मेरे पास और पैसा होता तो आपकी मदद कर पाता।

'I would be able/would have been able to help you had I more money'.

तुम इसके बारे में कुछ कहतीं तो मुझे याद आती।

'If you had said anything about this I would have remembered'.

In a majority of instances, contrary to fact conditional sentences of this sort refer to hypothetical situations in the past. They can, however, occasionally have present or future sense:

मैं भारत का प्रधान मंत्री होता तो इस स्थिति को अवश्य बदल देता।

'Were I the Prime Minister of India, I would certainly change/have changed this situation'.

In the examples presented above, as the terminations –ता/–ते/–ती/–तीं are attached directly to the verbal stems, the verbs of the two clauses cannot be said to be specified for grammatical aspect. It is possible, however, to form contrary to fact conditional sentences in which one or the other of the two clauses is specified as being progressive, habitual, or perfective:

उस समय (अगर) तुम जा रहे होते तो तुम्हें कष्ट न देता।

'Had you been going (i.e., about to go) at that time, I wouldn't have bothered you'.

उन दिनों आप नमाज़ पढ़ते होते तो हम ईदगाह में जरूर मिलते ।
'If you (habitually) used to pray those days, we certainly would have met in the Idgah'.

उसने कालेज ख़त्म किया होता तो शायद जीवन में और सफलता मिलती ।
'He/She would have had more success in life if he/she finished college'.

24.3. Some Expressions Involving याद

The feminine noun याद 'memory, recollection' appears in a number of exceedingly common idioms. Some of the more important of these are as follows:

याद करना 'to memorize, commit to memory'

मुझे कल तक सूरदास के दो पद[2] याद करने हैं ।
'I have to memorize two *pads* by Sūrdās by tomorrow'.

याद रखना 'to bear in mind, recall'

याद रखो कि उसकी वर्षगांठ आनेवाली है ।
'Bear in mind that his/her birthday is coming'.

X को Y (की) याद आना 'to come to mind, to be recalled, for X to remember Y'

मुझे कभी-कभी उसकी सुन्दर मुस्कराहट की याद आती है ।
'From time to time I remember her beautiful smile'.

X को Y की याद रहना 'for X to (continue) to remember Y'

भारतीय लोगों को पंडित जवाहरलाल नेहरू की याद हमेशा रहेगी ।
'The people of India will always remember Pandit Jawaharlal Nehru'.

24.4. Further Reflexive Forms

There are several reflexive forms and constructions in Hindi beyond the relative possessive form अपना discussed in 13.3. Unfortunately, there is considerable variation in the use of these further reflexive forms, with individual forms or constructions often having several senses and single senses of functions expressible by any of a number of distinct forms or constructions.

The forms आप, स्वयं, and ख़ुद are all used adverbially to add to some noun the sense 'by himself, herself, themselves, etc.' These reflexive forms occur immediately after the noun so modified, Often one or the other of these forms is followed by the particle ही :

राम आप (ही)/स्वयं (ही)/ख़ुद (ही) खाना खाएगा ।
'Ram will eat the food himself'.

सीता आप (ही)/स्वयं (ही)/ख़ुद (ही) दूध ख़रीदने बाज़ार गई ।
'Sita herself went to the market to buy milk'.

With following postpositions other than का/के/की (either alone or in compound postpositions such as के पास, के बारे में, etc.)[3] the oblique reflexive form अपने is used. This

2. n.m. a metrical form in which many of the poems of Sūrdās were composed.

3. The possessive pronoun is, of course, अपना (e.g., अपनी पुस्तक 'one's own book', अपने पास 'in one's possession', अपने बारे में concerning one/self' [cf. 13.3).

pronoun is frequently expanded to अपने आप with such following postpositions :

उसने अपने (आप) से पूछा कि मैं किस लिए यहाँ आया ?
'He asked himself why he had come here?'

वह अपने (आप) पर बहुत क्रोध करता था ।
'He used to get very angry with himself'.

अपने (आप) को मारना कोई नहीं चाहेगा ।
'No one wants (literally 'will want to') strike himself'.

Another oblique case reflexive form आपे (derived from the masc. noun आपा 'one's self') is occasionally found in adages, idioms, and dialectal usage:

वह गुस्से से आपे से बाहर हो गई ।
'She was beside herself with rage'.

In order to express the adverbial reflexive notion 'by oneself (i.e., of one's own accord)', अपने आप (without following postposition), आप ही and occasionally आप से आप are used :

मैंने अपने आप/आप ही/आप से आप अपना कमरा साफ़ कर दिया ।
'I cleaned my room by myself'.

The expression आप ही आप also is used adverbially in the senses 'by oneself, to oneself'. It tends, however, to be restricted to situations such as asides in stage dramas.

The adverbial reflexive expression आपस में is utilized to indicate that some activity is being carried out internally within the group of individuals denoted by the subject of the sentence:

बच्चे आपस में लड़ रहे थे ।
'The children were fighting among themselves'.

The adjectival forms आपसी or परस्पर are likewise employed to specify the mutuality or reciprocity of some abstract entity:

उन लड़कों में आपसी दोस्ती/परस्पर मित्रता दिखाई दे सकती है ।
'You can see mutual friendship among those children'.

Occasionally the form आपकी appears in this sense in place of आपसी.

The semantic notion of reciprocity, related, although not identical, to that of reflexivity, also finds expression in the idiom एक दूसरे plus a following postposition:

गुरुजी के भक्त एक दूसरे से बात कर रहे थे ।
'The devotees of the guru were speaking with each other'.

वे दोनों अलग-अलग[1] जगहों पर एक-दूसरे का इंतज़ार कर रहे थे ।
'The two of them were waiting for each other at separate places'.

24.5. Further Uses of लगना

In earlier sections of this book the use of लगना to indicate the inception of a verbal activity (15.5), seeming and appearing (16.3), and the elapsing of time (22.5) were

1. For a discussion of the use of such repeated (or "reduplicated") forms see 28.2.

discussed. The use of the verb as a component of some indirect verb constructions (15.1) has also been treated. There are, however, several other important aspects of this word.

लगना can be employed to designate the incurring of cost in carrying out some activity:

फ़िल्म देखने के लिए कितना पैसा लगता है?
'How much does it cost to see the film?'
होटल के एक दिन का (=के लिए) कितना पैसा लगता है ?
'What is the charge for one day in the hotel?'

The verb is also widely used in its etymological sense of 'to adhere to something, come in contact with something, be applied':

लिफ़ाफ़े पर दो पन्द्रह पैसे वाले टिकट लगे थे ।
'There were two fifteen paisa stamps on the envelope.'
मोहन लाल के सुन्दर बग़ीचे में तरह-तरह के फूल लगे थे ।
'All kinds of flowers were planted in Mohan Lal's beautiful garden.'

There are innumerable idioms in Hindi using either लगना or लगाना. Often an idiom with लगना and the identical idiom with लगाना substituted for लगना serve as intransitive and transitive alternates of each other:

कर लगना	'for taxes to be levied'
कर लगाना	'to levy taxes'
बाज़ी लगना	'for a bet to be wagered'
बाज़ी लगाना	'to wager a bet'

Some other common idioms with लगना and लगाना include the following:

X में Y का जी/मन/दिल लगना
'for Y to be happy/ contented in X'
सारा दिन पढ़ने में मेरा जी/मन/दिल नहीं लगता ।
'I don't like to study all day'.
मन/दिल लगाकर adv. 'diligently'

24.6. A USAGE OF समझना

The verb समझना 'to understand, comprehend' is used in a construction X Y (*ko*) Z समझना 'for X to consider Y (to be) Z':

मैं आपको अपना बड़ा अच्छा दोस्त समझता हूँ ।
'I consider you my very good friend'.
अध्यापक ने बच्चों का इस तरह बोलना अनुचित समझा ।
'The teacher considered the childern's speaking in this way improper'.

Sentences of this type may alternately be expressed with the verbal complement transposed after the verb and introduced by the conjunction कि :

मैं यह समझता हूँ कि आप मेरे बड़े अच्छे दोस्त हैं ।
अध्यापक ने यह समझा कि बच्चों का इस तरह बोलना अनुचित है ।

24.7. Vocabulary

कष्ट	n.m. inconvenience, bother	ख़त्म	adj. completed, finished
गाली	n.f. curse, abuse	ख़ास	adj. special
गुरु	n.m. spiritual master, guru, teacher	परस्पर	adj. mutual, reciprocal
ग़ुस्सा	n.m. anger, rage	सख़्त	adj. hard, arduous, harsh
जी	n.m. heart, mind, soul, will	कर लगना	v.i. for taxes to be levied
टिकट	n.m. stamp, ticket	कर लगाना	v.t. to levy taxes
दिल	n m. heart	X को कष्ट देना	v.t. to bother X, to in convenience X
देहात	n.m. countryside	ख़त्म करना/होना	v.t./i. to complete/to be completed
दोस्ती	n.f. friendship	X को गाली (गालियाँ) देना	v.t. to curse, abuse X
प्रधान मंत्री	n.m. Prime Minister	झगड़ना	v.i. to quarrel, fight
प्रशंसा	n.f. praise	X की प्रशंसा करना/होना	v.t./i. to praise X/for X to be praised
प्रेम	n.m. love, affection	बाज़ी लगाना	v.i. for a bet to be wagered
भक्त	n.m. devotee, follower	बाजी लगाना	v.t. to wager a bet
मित्रता	n.f. friendship	शिकायत करना	v.t. to complain, issue a complaint
मुस्कराहट	n.f. smile	सजना	v.i. to be decorated
रोज़	n.m. day; adv. daily, every day	सजाना	v.t. to decorate
लिफ़ाफ़ा	n.m. envelope, bag	X की सैर करना	v.t. to wander around X, to make a trip to X
वर्षगाँठ	n.f. birthday	हिलना	v.i. to stir, move, wag
बैर	n.m. hatred, hostility	हिलाना	v.t. to stir, move, wag
शिकायत	n.f. complaint	दिल लगाकर	adv. intently, earnestly, from the depths of one's heart
सफलता	n.f. success	मन लगाकर	adv. intently, diligently, conscientiously
स्थिति	n.f. situation, circumstances, condition	हर रोज़	adv. every day, daily
सैर	n.f. stroll, walk, excursion		
अनुचित	adj. improper		
अलग	adj. separate, distinct		
आपसी	adj. mutual, reciprocal		

24.8. Exercises

24.8.1. Join each of the following pairs of sentences into a single conditional sentence following the pattern of the given example. Use either subjunctive or simple perfective verb forms in the prior clause of the resultant sentences:

वह आएगी।+हम साथ-साथ खाएँगे। अगर/यदि वह आए/आई तो हम साथ-साथ खाएँगे।

1. शुक्ला साहब प्रधान मंत्री फिर बन जाएँगे। +लोग उनकी प्रशंसा करने लगेंगे।

2. हम उसको पैसा देंगे। +वह तुरन्त उसको ख़र्च करने बाज़ार चला जाएगा।
3. तुम शहर की सैर करोगे। +तुम अपनी आंखों से शहर की मशहूर जगहें देख सकोगे।
4. हम दोनों दिल्ली के हैं। +हम एक दूसरे को क्यों नहीं समझते ?
5. कोई तुमको गालियां देगा। +उसकी बातें न सुनो।

24.8.2. Join each of the following pairs of sentences into a single contrary to fact conditional sentence following the pattern of the given example:

तुमने इतनी बड़ी बाज़ी नहीं लगाई। +तुम इस बुरी हालत में नहीं हो→तुम इतनी बड़ी बाज़ी नहीं लगाते तो इस बुरी हालत में नहीं होते।

1. मेरे पास और पैसा था। +मैं उसकी मदद कर सका।
2. हम ग़रीब नहीं हैं। +हमारे पास काफ़ी खाना है।
3. तुम (f.) ने उसको गालियां दीं। +उसको गुस्सा आया।
4. सरकार ने लोगों पर अधिक कर नहीं लगाया। +लोगों का जीवन इतना सख़्त नहीं था।

24.8.3. *Translate into English*

1. अपने को देखना, अपने आपको अमीर समझना, अपने पर क्रोध करना, अपने आपको गालियां देना; 2. एक दूसरे से सवाल पूछना, एक दूसरे को मारना, एक दूसरे को कष्ट देना, एक दूसरे की प्रशंसा करना; 3. आपस में खेलना, आपसी दोस्ती, परस्पर संबंध, आपस में बात करना; 4. टिकट, एक रुपये-वाला टिकट, चार दो रुपये-वाले टिकट।

24.8.4. *Translate into Hindi*

1. to feed oneself, to teach oneself, to talk to oneself, to bathe oneself; 2. to look at one another, to speak to one another, to attack each other, to help each other; 3. to argue among oneselves, mutual love, mutual hatred; 4. trip, trip to Pakistan, Mr. Sharma's trip to Pakistan, to make a separate trip to Pakistan.

24.8.5. *Translate into English*

1. (अगर) तुम इलाहाबाद जाने का निश्चय करो तो मुझे ज़रूर बताना। 2. (अगर) आप चाहें तो हम साथ-साथ देहात की सैर कर सकेंगे। 3. (यदि) वह फिर शिकायत करे तो शायद इस बार सफलता मिलेगी। 4. (यदि) ज़्यादा ठंड लगे तो खिड़की बन्द कर लेना। 5. तुम मेरी बातें मानते तो इतनी मुसीबतें नहीं सहनी पड़तीं। 6. फ़िल्म इतनी जल्दी ख़त्म न होती तो गाड़ी पकड़ने में ज़्यादा देर न होती। 7. रमेश की इच्छा थी कि कोई उसके स्थान पर आगरे जाए, पर अंत में उसको स्वयं जाना पड़ा। 8. उनके बच्चे एक दूसरे को गालियां देते हैं। 9. राम ने उस लिफ़ाफ़े पर दो बीस पैसे-वाले टिकट लगा दिए। 10. तुम अपने को दूसरों से अच्छी क्यों समझती हो ? 11. उन तीन संतरों का (=के लिए) कितना पैसा लगेगा ? 12. सरकार हम जैसे लोगों पर इतना कर क्यों लगाती है ? 13. दिन रात पढ़ने में मेरा जी नहीं लगता। 14. उन्हें कितनी देर तक एक दूसरे की प्रतीक्षा करनी पड़ी ? 15. मैं उनकी सुन्दर मुस्कराहट न देखता तो मुझे उस समय की दोस्ती की याद नहीं आती।

24.8.6. *Translate into Hindi*

1. We will take you to the market if you say [so]. 2. If she has arrived in Varanasi by now (use subjunctive perfective), she will have already met (use presumptive perfective) with Saroj. 3. We will stay at home if it rains tomorrow. 4. If it had rained yesterday we would have stayed at home. 5. If you know how to speak Hindi you would have been able to speak with more people. 6. How long will it take to reach Bombay?

7. They are trying to teach each other Panjabi. 8. They were playing among themselves in the field when (कि) the weather started to change. 9. We don't like to study all day (use (जी लगना). 10. He learned those songs all by himself. 11. If you sell that table Father will be beside himself with rage. 12. You will always be remembered in this city. 13. They will memorize that song by Friday. 14. So what if I can't sleep. 15. Even though they might come tomorrow, we won't stay home.

CHAPTER 25

25.1. Other Contrary to Fact Constructions

In the previous chapter, the formation of conditional contrary to fact sentences was discussed. In these sentences two clauses, the verb of each ending in–ता/–ते/–ती/–तीं, are connected by the conjunction तो. Contrary to fact sentences may be formed in Hindi, however, other than in conditional structures. In general, the use of –ता/–ते/–ती/–तीं without following auxiliary is sufficient to signal the existence of a contrary to fact clause, regardless whether that clause is part of a larger 'if...then' structure:

मेरी इच्छा है कि बशीरा मेरे साथ आती ।
'I wish Bashira had come with me.'

कितना अच्छा होता कि तुम हमारे साथ सिनेमा जा सकते ।
'Oh how nice it would have been/would be if you could have gone/could go with us to the movies.

The exclamatory word काश is generally used in conjunction with a following clause having a verb ending in–ता/–ते/–ती/–तीं. The construction so formed declaims the wish for the coming to pass of some situation that did not or has not as yet come to be:

काश कि कुलदीप सिह का देहांत न होता ।
'Oh (I) wish that Kuldip Singh had not died'.
(i.e.,) 'Would that Kuldip Singh had not died'.

25.2. Narrative Uses of Verb Stem+–ता/–ते/–ती/–तीं

The verbal stem plus –ता/–ते/–ती/–तीं not followed by होना may also be employed to narrate a repeated activity in the past:

मीनाक्षी सुबह आठ बजे उठती और कुछ नाश्ता खाकर स्कूल जाती ।
'Meenakshi would wake up in the morning, eat something and go to school'.

Care should be taken not to confuse the narrative use of the verbal stem plus -ता/–ते/–ती/–तीं without following होना with the employment of such constructions in sentences with contrary to fact force.

25.3. Inverted Postpositions

A small number of Hindi postpositions show the peculiarity of allowing that portion of them following the के/की element to be transposed in front of the nouns with which they are associated. These postpositions include X के बिना and its Urdu equivalent X के बग़ैर 'without X', X के मारे 'on account of X', X के सिवा(य) 'except for X', X के अलावा 'in addition to X, apart from X', and X के बजाय 'instead of X'. Thus the members of each of the following pairs of phrases can be considered equivalent:

राम के बिना	बिना राम के	'without Ram'
रहीम के बग़ैर	बग़ैर रहीम के	'without Rahim'
ग़रीबी के मारे	मारे ग़रीबी के	'on account of poverty'
उन दो बच्चियों के सिवा	सिवा उन दो बच्चियों के	'except for those two girls'
राम के अलावा	अलावा राम के	'in addition to Ram'
हमारे दोस्तों के/की बजाय	बजाय हमारे दोस्तों के[1]	'in place of our friends'

In the event that any of the above postpositions is linked to a verbal infinitive, there are two possibilities of construction. In the first of these, the verb is placed in its oblique infinitive form and followed by the postposition:

वहाँ ठहरने के अलावा	'in addition to staying there'
खाने के सिवा	'except eating'

In the other possibility, the element after the के/की is transposed in front of the verbal form, which is converted from the infinitive to a simple perfective form with the invariable ending –ए. This verb form in –ए may then optionally be expanded by the addition of the हुए. The के/की of the original postposition is normally deleted once these transformations have occurred. Thus from खाने के बिना and यहाँ ठहरने के बिना one also finds बिना खाए (हुए) and बिना यहाँ ठहरे (हुए).

The postpositions X के बिना and X के बग़ैर behave somewhat differently from the other postpositions mentioned above. These forms do not generally occur with preceding oblique case infinitives, but rather require that the बिना or बग़ैर element be transposed before the verbal form, which must show the termination –ए:

बिना/बग़ैर हिन्दी पढ़े (हुए) 'without studying Hindi'

but seldom[1] हिन्दी पढ़ने के बिना/बग़ैर

Moreover, when the बिना or बग़ैर element of these postpositions is transposed before nouns, the के element may be deleted. Thus it is possible to use any of पैसे के बिना/बग़ैर, बिना/बग़ैर पैसे के or बिना/बग़ैर पैसे in order to express the notion 'without money'.

25.4. THE SUFFIXES -भर. -भरा. and -पूर्वक

The common suffixes -भर and -भरा are related to the verbal form भरना v.t. 'to fill' and v.i. 'to be/get filled'. The first of these suffixes is indeclinable and the juxtaposition of it and a preceding form (X) has the sense 'an entire X/full X':

पेट-भर	'a full stomach'
क्षण-भर	'for a moment' [literally 'a full moment/instant']

1. Even though either के or की can occur in conjunction with बजाय if the बजाय form is not transposed, only के can occur if the transposition does occur.

जीवन-भर '[one's] entire life'
देश-भर 'the whole nation'

The related suffix -भरा is used in conjunction with a previous word (X) to form eclinable adjective with the sense 'full of X':

दुःख भरी कहानी 'a story full of grief'
आँसू भरी आंखें 'eyes full of tears'

In Sanskritic Hindi, the suffix पूर्वक also is used with a previous form (X) in the sense 'replete with X, filled with X'. Constructions containing the suffix tend to be ısed adverbially:

विद्यार्थी अध्यापक की ओर ध्यानपूर्वक देख रहे थे।
'The students were attentively staring at the teacher'.
उनकी इच्छा मृत्यु के पश्चात् स्वर्ग में आनन्दपूर्वक रहने की थी।
'He wished to live blissfully in heaven after his death'.
[cf. मृत्यु n.f. 'death'; X के पश्चात् post 'after X']

25.5. The Particle –सा

The declinable particle –सा is found in Hindi appended to words of several different parts of speech. This form serves different linguistic functions depending on the type of word to which it is attached.

When affixed to adjectives, –सा generally indicates either a reduced or an approximate degree of the quality indicated by the adjective:

हरे-से कपड़े 'greenish clothes'
अच्छी-सी पुस्तक 'a rather good book'
सस्ता-सा खाना 'rather cheap food'
थोड़ी-सी हिन्दी 'just a little bit of Hindi'

In a few cases, –सा following an adjective can indicate an augmented degree of the quality of the adjective:

बहुत-सा पैसा 'very much money'
बहुत-से लोग 'very many people'

सा can also follow nouns or pronouns, in which case it is semantically similar to की तरह or के जैसे 'like, similar to'. The entire combination of noun or pronoun plus –सा, however, functions adjectivally, modifying either an explicit or tacitly understood noun form:

उषा-सी लड़की 'a girl like Usha'
मुझ-सा आदमी 'a man like me'
तुझ-सी लड़की को 'to a girl like you'

Frequently –सा is attached to a possessive construction.[2]

कल्लू का गीदड़ का-सा दिमाग़ है। 'Kallu is as clever as a jackal'
(literally 'Kallu has a brain like that of a jackal'.)

2. सा does not, however, cause an immediately preceding का to be converted to के.

माया की सुन्दरता किसी राजकुमारी की-सी है ।
'Maya's beauty is like that of a princess'.

The particle –सा is also encountered interspersed within verbal constructions. The -सा imparts a sense of likeness or similarity in these usages too:

भीम चला-सा गया ।
'It seems as if Bhim had left'.

उसको कुछ पुराने गाने याद आने-से लगे ।
'It was as if he/she began to remember some old songs'.

शकुन्तला की दीदी मरती[3]-सी लगती है ।
'Shakuntala's older sister looks as if she is dying'.

There are some common idioms in Hindi in which -सा is a component. The most important of these are the following :

कौन-सा 'which one ?,[4] which among a number of possibilities ?'
कौन-से गुप्ता साहब वहाँ थे ?
'Which Mr. Gupta was there ?'
आज हम कौन-सी कहानी पढ़ें ?
'Which story should we read today ?'
इतना-सा 'just so much, just a little bit'
आज मैं इतना-सा चावल खा सकता हूँ ।
'I can only eat so much rice (i.e., just a little) today'.
एक-सा 'the same, alike'
'प्रतीक्षा करना' और 'इन्तज़ार करना' के मतलब एक-से हैं ।
'[The expressions] प्रतीक्षा करना and इन्तज़ार करना have the same meaning'.

25.6. "ECHO" CONSTRUCTIONS

There exist in Hindi means for forming linguistic compounds having the sense 'X and other of its kind'. To a linguistic form is appended a nonsense word, generally a rhyme of the first linguistic item. The nonsense word is commonly made to begin with the sound व-, although such "echo" words beginning with other sounds are not unusual :

कुछ पानी-वानी पिया जाए ?
'Would you like to have some water or something else to drink ?

कमरे के फ़र्श पर काग़ज़-वाग़ज़ बिखरे थे ।
'Papers and such things were scattered on the floor of the room'.

बैठक में बच्चे पकोड़े-वकौड़े खा रहे थे ।
'The children were eating pakoras and other snacks in the sitting room'.

3. Cf. मरती imper, part. f.s. 'dying'. For discussion of the formation and use of imperfective participles v. 27.1.

4. Note that the कौन element of कौन-सा generally does not appear in the oblique form when followed by a postposition, even though the -से element is converted to -स$_{f}$. Thus कौन-से दफ़्तर में 'in which office?' appears instead of *किस-से दफ़्तर में.

In a related type of "echo" construction, a word is followed by a phonetically similar, although not necessarily rhyming, form. Unlike the "echo" constructions just discussed, however, the entire compound so formed often does not differ in meaning from the meaningful first component of the compound :

ठीक-ठाक adj. 'fine, well'
भीड़-भाड़, n.f.' crowd'
हल्ला-गुल्ला n.m. 'ruckus, tumult' [cf. हल्ला n.m. 'ruckus, tumult']

In a small number of forms, the nonsense word may actually precede the meaningful element of the compound :

आस-पास (or आसपास) adv. 'nearby, surrounding'
आमने-सामने adv. 'in front, directly opposite'.

25.7. VOCABULARY

अक़्ल	n.f. intelligence, intellect
आँसू	n.f. tear
आनंद	n.m. bliss, contentment, pleasure
इंतज़ार	n.m. waiting, expectation
क्षण	n.m. moment, instant
गधा	n.m. ass, donkey
ग़रीबी	n.f. poverty
गीदड़	n.m. jackal
जोश	n.m. enthusiasm
दिमाग़	n.m. brain, intelligence
दीदी	n.f. older sister
दृष्टि	n.f. view, vision, sight, perspective
देहांत	n.m. death
नाव	n.f. boat, ferry
नाश्ता	n.m. breakfast, snack
पाव	n.m. unit of weight equal to one-fourth of a सेर ; one-fourth, quarter
प्रार्थना	n.f. request, prayer
फ़र्श	n.m. floor, ground
बालक	n.m. (male) child, youth
बैठक	n.f. meeting; sitting room, parlor
मतलब	n.m. meaning, intent, significance
मृत्यु	n.f. death
राजकुमार	n.m. prince
वेतन	n.m. wages, salary
शक्ल	n.f. appearance, form, countenance
सेर	n.m. a unit of weight slightly greater than 2 pounds [1सेर = 4 पाव]
इतना-सा	adj. just so much, just a little bit
एक-सा	adj. the same, identical
बहुत-सा	adj. very many, a lot
X का इंतज़ार करना/होना	v.t./i. to wait for X/ for X to be expected, waited for
तैरना	v.i. to swim
पढ़ाना	v.t. to teach, instruct
बिकना	v.i. to be/get sold
बिखरना	v.i. to be scattered
मिलाना	v.t. to cause to meet, to bring together
सुनाना	v.t. to tell, relate
सुलाना	v.t. to put to sleep
अनेक	adv. several
आसपास (=आस-पास)	adv. nearby, surrounding
कुल मिला कर	adv. all in all, all together
चेहरे से	adv. in appearance
शक्ल से	adv. in appearance
सब मिलकर	adv. all together, at once
X के आसपास	post. near to X
X के पश्चात्	post. after X
X के बग़ैर	post. without X
X के बजाय	post. in place of X
X के बिना	post. without X
X के मारे	post. on account of X, by dint of X
X के सिवा (य)	post. except for X
काश	interj. would that...!
कौन-सा	inter. which (of a number of possibilities) ?

25.8. EXERCISES

25.8.1. *Translate into English*

1. उनके मित्रों के बिना, बिजली के बग़ैर, अमीर होने के मारे, मदन के अलावा; 2. सिवा मेरी चप्पलों के, बजाय उनके माता-पिता के, मारे ख़ुशी के, सिवा राम की बीवी जी के; 3. बिना काम किए (हुए), बग़ैर फ़ायदा उठाए (हुए), बिना जागे बच्चों के साथ घर में रहे (हुए), बिना उनकी सेवा किए (हुए); 4. दिन-भर काम करना, जीवन-भर का सुख, देश-भर के बालक, पेट-भर

खाना; 5. जोश-भरी आवाज; सुख-भरा जीवन, प्रेम-भरी दृष्टि, आश्चर्यपूर्वक देखना; 6. लाल-सी किताब, छोटा-सा कमरा, हल्का-सा सामान, बहुत-से बच्चे; 7. राम का-सा चेहरा, तुम-सी लड़की, गधे की-सी अक़्ल, पंकज का-सा दिमाग़, 8. कौन-सी पुस्तक, कौन-से समाचारपत्रों में, कौन-से पड़ोसियों के बारे में; 9. इतना-सा पानी, इतनी-सी मिठाइयाँ, एक-सी आवाजें, एक-से चेहरे.

25.8.2. *Translate into Hindi*

1. (use non-inverted postpositions) on account of their age, except for their children, without the policeman, in place of friendship; 2. (use inverted postpositions) without the Prime Minister, except for my three brothers, in addition to those songs, instead of these shopkeepers; 3. without staying (ठहरना) in that hotel, without eating her (own) food, without looking in our direction, without giving you (fam.) any money; 4. (use -भर) the entire week's salary, the entire night's sleep, books from the entire province, the women of the entire village; 5. (use -भरा or -पूर्वक), a life full of joy (सुख), attentively (i.e., replete with attention [ध्यान]), sinful actions (कर्म n.m.); 6. rather expensive saris, rather wet clothes, rather long poems, about the rather beautiful woman; 7. (use -सा) in a river like the Ganges, near a school like that, a brain like her's, ears like a dog's; 8. (use कौन-सा) which pea-field ? in which book ? which poems of Sūrdās ? concerning which country's independence ?; 9. the same clothes, the same opinions, with (के साथ) the same voices, identical girls.

25.8.3. *Translate into English*

1. कितना अच्छा होता कि पिताजी की मृत्यु के बाद माताजी हमारे साथ रहना चाहतीं। 2. दादीजी दिन-भर बच्चों की देखभाल करतीं, घर साफ़ करतीं, और अनेक प्रकार के दूसरे काम भी करतीं। 3. काश कि भगवान मेरी प्रार्थना सुनता। 4. ठाकुर साहब के दोनों बच्चे उनसे मिलते-जुलते हैं। 5. बैठक में पहुंचते ही श्रीमती गोपाल ने अपने बेटे जगदीश को श्रीमती शर्मा से मिला दिया। 6. कुल मिलाकर उनको सुनने पंद्रह लोग गांव से आए। 7. बिना प्रश्न पूछे हुए कुछ भी नहीं सीखा जा सकता है। 8. बग़ैर कोशिश किए जीवन में कुछ नहीं मिलेगा। 9. हमें लगा कि सारा दिन आपस में झगड़ने पर भी किरण और बलदेव के दिल मिलते-जुलते हैं। 10. राम सिंह का दिल शेर-सा नहीं समझा जा सकता है। 11. मिसेज मेनन को थोड़ी-सी पंजाबी आती है और इससे कम हिन्दी। 12. बड़े भाई साहब पढ़ने-वढ़ने के बहाने बाजार चले गये। 13. उस तरह की किताबें उस दुकान में कभी नहीं बिकतीं। 14. बिना मसाले वाला खाना बिना कपड़ों-वाले आदमी की तरह है। 15. उसके विचार में एक दोस्त के साथ तैरना अकेले तैरने से अच्छा होता है।

25.8.4. *Translate into Hindi*

1. Oh how bad it would have been if he couldn't have brought his children with him ! 2. He would sleep all day and work during the night. 3. Oh how I wish that Grandfather (paternal) wouldn't get so angry with me ! 4. It is very difficult to learn Hindi without going to India. 5. The government's hope is that all people will be able to live (बिताना) their lives without poverty. 6. Except for his two sons, there is no one to help him in the fields. 7. I want to introduce you to the pandit of that temple. 8. As soon as he entered the store he shook hands with Mr. Gupta. 9. It is very surprising that you don't resemble your mother. 10. (use –सा) It seemed as if big brother was about to leave. 11. My friend has the brain(s) of a small child. 12. Bear in mind that everyone will want to help a friend like you (fam.). 13. If I had a sister like you (int.) I wouldn't be so unhappy (i.e., I wouldn't have so much misery/woe). 14. All in all 34 students wanted to go to Madhya Pradesh with Maya (माया prop. f.). 15. Would you like to drink tea or something of that sort ?

CHAPTER 26

26.1. Causative Verbs

In other chapters of this book, pairs of verbs have been introduced that seem to function as intransitive and transitive counterparts to one another. The two members of each such pair have been similar in phonetic form, usually sharing a majority of their component sounds. The intransitive member of the pairs so far dealt with generally has signified an action conceptualized as occurring of its own accord. The transitive member of the set, by contrast, has been conceptualized as occurring through the agency of some 'doer'. This dual division of verbs into intransitive and transitive, sufficient for forms already examined, needs now be expanded into a three-way classification, with the new category being that of 'causative' verbs. The central characteristic of a causative verb is that its subject is not viewed as carrying out a verbal activity by himself, but rather is seen as bringing about the activity through an intermediary.

In a large portion of cases, the stems of causative verbs show the termination -वा. In some instances the causative in -वा alternates with a synonymous form in -आ. Causative verbs are treated as syntactically transitive, with their subjects marked with ने when the verb is in the perfective aspect. Normally the noun indicating the party who actually carries out the verbal action (as opposed to the party who causes the action to be carried out) is followed by the postposition से. A sample of causative verbs related to verb forms already introduced, as well as illustrations of the use of these causative forms, is given below :

जगवाना v.t. 'to cause to wake up/arise' [cf. जागना v.i. and जगाना v.t.]

ठीक आठ बजे प्रमोद को जगवा दो।

'Have [someone] wake up Pramod at exactly eight o'clock'.

बनवाना v.t. 'to cause to be built' [cf. बनना v.i. and बनाना v.t.]

बादशाह शाहजहाँ ने अपनी बीवी मुम्ताज़ महल की याद में ताज महल बनवाया।

'The Emperor Shah Jahan had the Taj Mahal built in memory of his wife Mumtaz Mahal'.

कटवाना v.t. 'to cause to be cut' [cf. कटना v.i. and काटना v.t.]

किसान अपने खेत का एक पेड़ कटवाना चाहता है।

'The farmer wants to have one of the trees in his field cut down'.

करवाना/कराना v.t. 'to cause to do' [cf. करना v.t.]

मैं कमलेश से आपकी मदद करवा/करा दूंगी।

'I'll have Kamlesh help you'.

26.2. Sets of Related Verbs

The vast majority of Hindi verbs belong to one or another set of related forms. The members of each such set share a common semantic core (e.g., a process of cutting is involved in each of कटना/काटना/कटवाना) as well as a set of shared phonetic features (i.e., the consonants क and ट in the illustrative trio). Moreover, the semantic and syntactic differences among the members of some one set (e.g., बनना/बनाना/बनवाना) are analogous to the differences among many other sets (e.g., पकना/पकाना/पकवाना; उठना/उठाना/उठवाना).

Unfortunately, there are complications in this seemingly orderly pattern of related verb forms. The phonetic relations among the members of a verb set need not be of the simple sort shown above. Sets exist whose members have phonetic shapes that are related to each other by complicated rules of derivation. Moreover, the semantic relations among the members of a set need not be of the simple intransitive/transitive/causative pattern outlined above. Some sets may have no intransitive member at all; others may have two semantically differentiated transitive members. In other instances, a set may have two or more members different in form, but alike in meaning. Sets differ in the number of members they contain, ranging from as many as five to as few as one. It is necessary, therefore, to divide these sets into common types, and to list other sets that do not conform to the most productive patterns.

One exceedingly common type of verb set is of the type illustrated by the forms cited above. This pattern consists of an intransitive form whose root contains one of the vowels –अ– or –इ–, (less commonly –ऐ– or –ओ–) and transitive and causative verbs formed by the addition of –आ and –वा respectively to the root of the intransitive :

हटना	'to pull back, retreat'	हटाना	'to drive back, push back'	हटवाना	'to cause to pull back'
गिरना	'to fall'	गिराना	'to fell'	गिरवाना	'to have something felled'
तैरना	'to swim'	तैराना	'to make one swim'	तैरवाना'	'to cause one to swim'
ओटना	'to boil (i)	ओटाना	'to boil (f)	ओटवाना	'to have someone boil'

Yet another phonetic alternation can be observed in many other sets. Where the transitive member of a set shows –आ–, the intransitive and causative exhibit –अ–. The sounds –ई– and –ए– in the transitive are paralleled by –इ– in the intransitive and causative. Lastly, –ऊ– and –ओ– in the transitive correspond to –उ– in the intransitive and causative:

निकलना	'to emerge'	निकालना	'to take out, remove'	निकलवाना	'to have someone remove'
पिसना	'to be ground'	पीसना	'to grind'	पिसवाना	'to have someone grind'
घिरना	'to be surrounded'	घेरना	'to surround'	घिरवाना	'to cause to be surrounded'

लुटना	'to be robbed'	लूटना	'to rob'	लुटवाना	'to have someone rob'
खुलना	'to be/get opened'	खोलना	'to open'	खुलवाना	'to have someone open'

In some sets, the pattern of vowels is seemingly the opposite of that displayed in the last cited sets of verbs. Here the intransitive member of the trio shows the root vowels –आ/ –ई–/–ए–/–ऐ–, or –ऊ–/–ओ–/–औ–, while the transitive and causative display –अ–, –इ–, and –उ– respectively:

जागना	'to wake'	जगाना	'to awaken someone'	जगवाना	'to cause to awaken'
लेटना	'to lie down'	लिटाना	'to lay down'	लिटवाना	'to have someone lie down'
बैठना	'to sit down'	बिठाना	'to seat (someone)'	बिठवाना	'to have someone seated'
भीगना	'to get drenched'	भिगाना	'to soak (something)'	भिगवाना	'to cause to soak'
घूमना	'to wander, meander'	घुमाना	'to turn (something) around	घुमवाना	'to have someone turn'

Some sets do not have an intransitive member, but show instead a distinction between two semantically distinct transitive forms:

पढ़ना	'to read, study'	पढ़ाना	'to instruct, read to'	पढ़वाना	'to cause to teach'
सीखना	'to learn'	सिखाना	'to teach'	सिखवाना	'to cause to learn'
सुनना	'to hear'	सुनाना	'to tell'	सुनवाना	'to cause to tell'
बोलना	'to speak'	बुलाना	'to call'	बुलवाना	'to have someone call'

In those cases where the root of the first member of a set ends in a long vowel, an –ल– is inserted before the –आ and –वा of the second and third members of the set respectively :

सोना	'to sleep'	सुलाना	'to put to sleep'	सुलवाना	'to cause to put to sleep'
पीना	'to drink, smoke'	पिलाना	'to give to drink, smoke'	पिलवाना	'to cause to drink or smoke'
खाना	'to eat'	खिलाना	'to feed'	खिलवाना	'to have someone feed'[1]

In some instances, transitives in –आ and corresponding causative forms in –वा are synonymous :

देना	'to give'	दिलाना/दिलवाना	'to cause to be given'

1. The -आ-/-ई-/-इ- vowel alternation in this set is irregular.

करना	'to do'	कराना/करवाना	'to cause to do'
सीना	'to sew'	सिलाना/सिलवाना	'to cause to sew'

Consonantal alternations are not unusual among the members of related verb sets. Often such consonantal variation occurs in conjunction with vowel alternations of the various kinds described above. The alternation of ट with ड़ is particularly common:

बिकना	'to be sold'	बेचना	'to sell'	बिकवाना	'to cause to be sold'
टूटना	'to break (i.)'	तोड़ना	'to break (t.)'	तुड़ाना/तुड़वाना	'to cause to break'
छूटना	'to be free, escape'	छोड़ना	'to set free'	छुड़ाना/छुड़वाना	'to cause to set free'
फूटना	'to break, split open (i)'	फोड़ना	'to break, split open (t)'	फुड़वाना	'to cause to break, split open'

In many cases, alternate forms can be found for one or the other members of a verb set. From बैठना 'to sit' may be formed either बैठाना or बिठाना 'to seat someone' and बैठवाना or बिठवाना 'to have someone seated'. Likewise, from the intransitive form भीगना 'to be wet, drenched' can be formed either of the alternate transitive forms भिगाना or the irregular भिगोना 'to drench'.

Some sets of related verbs differ from the archetypical three-member sets described above. आना 'to come' and जाना 'to go', for instance, are unique members of their sets. In contrast to these one-member sets is a group containing four members: either दिखना/दीखना (i) 'to seem, appear'; देखना (t) 'to see,'; दिखाना (t); 'to show' (alternating with the synonymous दिखलाना'); and दिखवाना 'to cause to show'. From लेना 'to take', no form is possible with the transitive suffix –आ, although a causative form लिवाना 'to cause to take' does exist. The meaning of a particular member of a verb set is often idiosyncratic. For example, from कहना 'to say' can be formed कहलाना, having the meaning 'to be called, to be named', not as one might guess 'to cause to say'. Likewise, the intransitive form मरना has the sense 'to die', whereas its transitive counterpart मारना means 'to hit, strike', not 'to make die'.[2]

It is, regretably, not possible to formulate precise rules that will always allow the prediction of what the meaning and form of each of the members of a set of related verb forms will be. The principles stated above are merely guidelines that provide the student with some understanding of a sample of the more common and productive types of sets of related verbs. Space prohibits a detailed discussion of the many exceptions to the rules stated above. Ultimately, the student needs be alert to the considerable variation in the ways that sets of related verb forms are constituted. He must bear in mind that the idiosyncratic properties of irregular verb sets ultimately have to be mastered on an individual basis.

2. The semantic element of dying in मरना is preserved in the compound मार डालना 'to kill'.

26.3. Uses of तो

The form तो is used, either by itself or in conjunction with other words, in a number of distinct ways. These various locutions function as several different parts of speech (i.e., as particles, conjunctions, and exclamations) and correspond to diverse grammatical devices in other languages.

तो is used as a conjunction in several ways. It is employed to introduce the consequent in 'if...then' sentences (cf. 24.1, 25.1):

यदि/अगर मैं मर जाऊँ तो वह दूसरी शादी करेगी ।
'She'll marry again if I die'.

It alternates with तब as the correlative to जब (cf. 22.1.2):

जब वह आई तो/तब मैं घर पर नहीं थी ।
'I wasn't at home when she came'.

Often the conjunctive use of तो has contrastive force, allowing the second clause to overturn some supposition derived from the first:

वह भूखा है तो खाता क्यों नहीं ?
'He's hungry, so why doesn't he eat?' (overturning the supposition that if he's hungry, he'll eat)..

तो is also used to introduce a conclusion reached after or as a result of the preceding discourse:

तो आप इंडिया में काफ़ी हिन्दी जान गए हैं ।
'So you have learned quiet a bit of Hindi in India'.

Lastly, conjunctive तो serves to continue a conversation, leading it to a conclusion, turning it in a new direction, or introducing a question based on the preceding discourse:

तो आपको बहुत ख़ुशी हुई होगी ।
'So you must have been quite happy'.

तो फिर तुमने क्या किया ?
'So what did you do then?'

In addition to occurring at the beginning of a clause, linking that clause to a previous clause or bit of extended discourse, तो is often used quasi-postpositionally. Here the तो is placed after some linguistic entity, be it a noun, pronoun, verb or other part of speech, a phrase, or an entire clause, but does not cause that entity to be in its oblique case, even if the entity is subject to such changes. Most commonly, this use of तो serves to link the clause in which it appears to the previous discourse, often contrasting the entity immediately preceding the तो with some parallel entity in the previous discourse or understood through context :

समय छह बजे तो है ।
'It's six o'clock (in answer to an inquiry about the time).

मैं सब तरह के जंगली जानवरों से डरता हूं । इन्द्र तो उनसे नहीं डरता ।
'I'm afraid of all kinds of wild animals, but Indra isn't afraid of them'.

वह मेरा दोस्त तो है, पर कभी-कभी मुझसे झूठ बोलता है।

'He's my friend, but sometimes he lies to me'.

उसकी सब सहेलियों को निमंत्रण भेजे गए पर सुल्ताना आई तो नहीं।

'All of her friends were sent invitations, but Sultana didn't come'.

Non-initial तो is also employed in the enumeration of a list of particulars:

एक तो मैं उसकी मदद नहीं कर सकता। दूसरे, हम दोनों में दोस्ती कुछ भी नहीं है।

'First of all, I can't help him and, secondly, there is no friendship between us'.

The combination of तो plus an immediately following सही (literally 'correct, right, true') is used at the end of the prior clause of a type of compound sentence. This usage concedes the truth of the first clause, while still asserting the second:

वह अमीर तो सही, पर ख़ुश नहीं है।

'Its true he/she is rich, but he/she isn't happy'.

वह हिन्दी बोलती तो सही पर दूसरों ने उसे मौक़ा नहीं दिया।

'She would have spoken Hindi to be sure, but others didn't give her a chance'.

The sequence नहीं तो appears in either of two functions. As a conjunction, it has the sense 'otherwise':

अपने पौधों पर पानी डालो, नहीं तो प्यासे मर जाएंगे।

'Water your plants, otherwise they'll die from lack of water'.

It can also be used as an exclamatory negative reply to questions:

क्या तुम उसकी मिठाई खा गए?

नहीं तो!

'Did you eat his/her sweets?'

'Of course not!'

The phrase तो भी is used as a conjunction synonymous with फिर भी 'nevertheless, still':

पूरे बीस समोसे खा चुका है, तो भी और मांगता है।

'He has already eaten all of twenty samosas, and still he demands more!'

26.4. VOCABULARY

कोठी	n.f. cottage, bungalow, detached house	भूखा	adj. hungry
ख़बर	n.f. news, information	सरकारी	adj. governmental, official
छत	n.f. roof, ceiling	ऊबना	v.i. to be or become bored
छुट्टी	n.f. often in pl. form छुट्टियां leave, vacation, break	कहलाना	v.i. to be called, to be referred to
ज़मीनदार	n.m. landlord, landholder	X को Y की ख़बर देना	v.t. to inform X of Y
त्योहार	n.m. festival, holiday	X को Y की ख़बर मिलना	v.i. for X to receive news of Y
दावत	n.f. party, feast	घिरना	v.i. to be surrounded
दिलचस्पी	n.f. interest, curiosity	घेरना	v.t. to surround
धूप	n.f. sun light, hot sun	छूटना	v.i. to be get free, to be left behind, to be released
निमंत्रण	n.m. invitation		
बरसात	n.f. rainy season, monsoon	टूटना	v.i. to break, shatter
		X को दिलचस्पी होना	v.i. for X to be interested in something
बीवी	n.f. wife		
मास्टर (जी/साहब)	n.m. teacher, instructor	पहुँचाना	v.t. to carry, transmit [literally 'to make arrive']
मेहरी	n.f. kitchen maid		
लाला (जी)	n.m. term of address used for shopkeepers; also respectful term of address for members of Bania and Kayasth castes	फूटना	v.i. to crack, shatter, split, burst
		फोड़ना	v.t. to crack, shatter, split, burst
		अकेले	adv. alone
लोहा	n.m. iron	अक्सर	adv. frequently, often
सच	n.m. truth; adj. true	अब की बार	adv. now, this time
हवा	n.f. wind, air	आम तौर पर	adv. generally, usually
हाल	n.m. condition, state of being	कहीं	adv somewhere or other
		ख़ास तौर पर	adv. especially
अकेला	adj. single, solitary	X की वजह से	post. because of X, on account of X
आम	adj. ordinary, everyday		
खाली	adj. empty, free (time)	मगर	conj. but
प्यासा	adj. thirsty	यहाँ तक कि	conj. to the extent that

26.5. EXERCISES

26.5.1. Select the appropriate verb from among the alternatives provided in each of the following sentences. In some cases more than one alternative may be grammatically acceptable:

1. चूल्हे पर चावल (पक/पका/पकवा) गया।
2. बढ़ई ने हमारे लिए कितनी कुर्सियां (बन/बना/बनवा) दीं।
3. क्लास में आने के बाद मास्टर साहब ने गोपाल को खिड़की के पास (बैठ/बिठा) दिया।
4. पिछले हफ़्ते हमारी दुकान तीसरी बार (लुट/लूट/लुटवा) गई।

5. सरकार का इरादा भूखों को (खाने/खिलाने/खिलवाने) का है।
6. तुम यह नया बरतन क्यों (टूट/तोड़) बैठे हो ?
7. जानवरों की हालत देखकर राजा ने उनको (छूट/छोड़/छुड़ा) दिया।
8. आनेवालों को कुछ (खा/खिला/खिलवा) कर उन्हें सोने दो।
9. किसी ने फ़र्श पर काग़ज़ (गिर/गिरा) दिया।
10. माँ ने आया से बच्चों को (सो/सुला/सुलवा) दिया।
11. नाव से अपना सामान (निकलिए/निकालिए)।
12. गाड़ी स्टेशन पर कितने बजे (पहुँच/पहुँचा) गई।
13. मैं मोची से नए जूते (बन/बना/बनवा) देता हूँ।
14. सुन्दरलाल प्रतिदिन साढ़े पांच बजे (उठता/उठाता/उठवाता) है। ठीक छह बजे वह घर के दूसरे लोगों को (जागता/जगाता) है। कभी-कभी वह किसी नौकर से अपनी छोटी बहन को (जगा/जगवा) देता है।

26.5.2. Transform the following sentences using intransitive verbs into sentences with corresponding transitives. Subjects for the sentences to be constructed are provided in parentheses:

e.g. खाना पक गया (सिद्धेश्वरी)→सिद्धेश्वरी ने खाना पका दिया (or लिया)।
1. तुम्हारा कुर्ता जल्दी धुल जाएगा (धोबी)→
2. लड़का बैठ गया (मास्टर जी)→
3. सैनिक हट गए (शत्रुओं का आक्रमण)→
4. साड़ियां बिकती हैं (दुकानदार)→
5. गिलास टूट जाएगा (उषा)→
6. उसकी कमीज़ भीग गई (बारिश)→

26.5.3. Transform the following sentences using transitive verbs into sentences with corresponding causatives. Subjects for the new sentences to be constructed are provided in parentheses:

मदन अमर को जगा देता है (रानी) →रानी मदन से अमर को जगवा देती है।
1. डाकू ग़रीब लोगों को लूट रहा था (भोला prop. m.)→
2. विष्णु भूखों को खाना खिला देगा (जमींदार)→
3. रामलाल पेड़ काटेगा (किसान)→
4. मेहरी ने पानी ओटा होगा (दादीजी)→
5. नर्स ने मरीज़ (n.m. patient, sick person) को यहाँ लिटा दिया (डाक्टर साहब)→
6. हमने उनके ठहरने का प्रबन्ध कर दिया (पिताजी)→

26.5.4. *Translate into Hindi*

1. It's true (use तो सही) her condition is poor, but she will get well quickly. 2. What is this kind of small red fruit called ? 3. Father wanted to have a cottage built for his son. 4. It is the beginning (शुरू n.f.) of August, but still the rainy season hasn't begun. 5. Generally, she has little interest in going to parties. 6. He received the news of Jamal's (जमाल prop. m.) arrival in Lucknow. 7. This kind of container isn't usually made of iron. 8. Suddenly the wind began to blow (चलना) from the north. 9. Who knows how to drive a car ? 10. One ought not to remain out in the sun for so long (इतनी देर तक). 11. The children especially liked the wild animals at (i.e., 'of') the zoo. 12. Have Panditji teach the prince to read Sanskrit. 13. All the plants will turn

green as soon as the rainy season starts. 14. I don't like to stay home by myself. 15. Have the tailor sew three or four blouses for Kiran.

SUPPLEMENTARY READING PASSAGES

A. शालीमार और निशात

भारत में अनेक दर्शनीय स्थान हैं। इनमें कुछ तो ऐसे हैं, जिनको मनुष्य ने अपने हाथों से बनाया है और कुछ ऐसे हैं जिन्हें प्रकृति ने अपने हाथों से सजाया है। इनके अतिरिक्त कुछ ऐसे भी स्थान हैं जिन्हें मनुष्य और प्रकृति दोनों ने मिलकर सजाया है। कश्मीर के शालीमार और निशात बाग़ ऐसे ही दर्शनीय स्थान हैं। शालीमार बाग़ों का राजा है तो निशात को बाग़ों की रानी कह सकते हैं।

कश्मीर की घाटी संसार की सुन्दर घाटियों में से एक है। कहीं पहाड़ों से झरने गिर रहे हैं तो कहीं मीठे पानी की बड़ी-बड़ी झीलें हैं। कहीं केसर की क्यारियां हैं तो कहीं धान के हरे-भरे खेत हैं। कहीं चिनार के विशाल वृक्ष हैं तो कहीं लंबे देवदार के। सारी घाटी फल-फूलों के बग़ीचों से भरी पड़ी है। ऐसा जान पड़ता है मानो सारा कश्मीर ही एक बहुत बड़ा बाग़ हो।

(from *APS*, p. 7)

VOCABULARY

शालीमार	prop. Shalimar (Gardens)	केसर	n.f. saffron
निशात	prop. Nishat (Gardens)	क्यारी	n.f. bed (of a garden)
दर्शनीय	adj. worth seeing	धान	n.m. rice paddy
मनुष्य	n.m. man, mankind	हरा-भरा	adj. verdant, abundant, flourishing
प्रकृति	n.f. nature		
X के अतिरिक्त	post. in addition to X	चिनार	= चनार n.m. a large tree that grows primarily on hills
बाग़	n.m. garden		
घाटी	n.f. valley, vale	विशाल	adj. large
कहीं...कहीं तो	in some places...while in other places	वृक्ष	n.m. tree
		देवदार	n.m. evergreen tree, particularly pine, cedar, and fir
झरना	n.m. spring, cascade		
मीठा पानी	n.m. fresh/clear water	X से भरी पड़ी है	lies full of X
झील	n.f. lake		

B. तीन पहेलियाँ

1.

आस-पास घास-फूस,
बीच में तबेला।
दिन-भर तो भीड़-भाड़,
रात में अकेला (उत्तर : कुआँ)

2.

बेज़बान फिर भी मैं बोलूं,
सारी दुनिया दिल पर ढो लूं।
मैं लोगों का दिल बहलाता,
अब बोलो, मैं क्या कहलाता। (उत्तर : रेडियो)

3.

पानी से निकला दरख़्त एक,
पात नहीं पर डाल अनेक।

इस दरख़्त की ठंडी छाया,
नीचे एक बैठ न पाया। (उत्तर : फ़व्वारा)

VOCABULARY

पहेली	n.f. riddle
फूस	n.m. straw, hay
तबेला	n.m. stable
बेज़बान	adj. voiceless, mute [=बे- 'without'+ज़बान n.f. 'tongue, language']
X Y पर ढो लेना	v.t. to carry the weight of X on Y [cf. ढोना v.t. to carry, cart, transport]
X का दिल बहलाना	v.t. to divert, amuse X [cf. बहलाना v.t. to make, cause to flow]
दरख़्त	n.m. tree
पात	n.m. leaf
डाल	n.f. branch
छाया	n.f. shade
फ़व्वारा	n.m. fountain

C. कंडक्टर शिकायत की पुस्तक बाप को भी नहीं देता (letter to the editor)

मैं १९ जनवरी को शाम छह बजे मौरिस नगर के स्टैंड पर बस का इन्तज़ार कर रहा था। मुझे गांव खेड़ा खुर्द जाना था। ६ बजकर ४० मिनट पर करनाल डिपो की रूट नम्बर १३७ की बस आई। डी० एच० पी० २६२७ उसका नम्बर था।

मैं ने गाड़ी रोकने के लिए हाथ दिया लेकिन ड्राइवर ने गाड़ी नहीं रोकी। मैंने फ़ौरन दूसरी गाड़ी पकड़ी। आजादपुर की लाल बत्ती पर वही १३७ नम्बर बस खड़ी थी।

मैं दूसरी बस से उतरकर झट उस पर चढ़ गया। मैंने बड़े नम्र भाव से ड्राइवर से कहा "मौरिस नगर स्टैंड पर बस क्यों नहीं रोकी ?"

ड्राइवर बड़े ग़ुस्से से बोला : "मैं क्या तेरे बाप का नौकर हूँ ?"

मैंने कंडक्टर से शिकायत की पुस्तक मांगी तो वह बोला : "कौन-सी पुस्तक ? शिकायत की पुस्तक तो मैं बाप को भी नहीं देता, तू किस खेत की मूली है ?"

मैं डी० टी० सी० के अफ़सरों से पूछना चाहता हूँ कि क्या कंडक्टर को शिकायत की पुस्तक सजा कर रखने के लिए दी गई है।

VOCABULARY

शिकायत	n.f. complaint
मौरिस नगर	prop. name of a residential colony
खेड़ा खुर्द	prop.
हाथ देना	v.t. to signal
फ़ौरन	adv. immediately
बत्ती	n.f. light
झट	adv. instantly, at once
भाव	n.m. expression, mood, tone of voice
मैं...नौकर हूँ	this is quite rude and has the sense 'who do you thing you are ?'
मूली	n.f. radish
तू...मूली है	who the hell are you ?
डी० टी० सी०	abbreviation for Delhi Transport Corporation
अफ़सर	n.m. officer

D गोस्वामी तुलसीदास

हिंदी भाषा के महाकवि संत तुलसीदास का जन्म बांदा जिले के राजापुर नामक गांव में हुआ था। इनके पिता का नाम आत्माराम और माता का नाम हुलसी था। बचपन में ही इनके माता-पिता का देहांत हो गया। यह अनाथ की भांति द्वार-द्वार भटकने लगे। साधु-संन्यासियों को इन पर दया आई। उन्होंने ही इनका पालन-पोषण किया और पढ़ाया-लिखाया। इनकी बुद्धि बड़ी तीव्र थी।

लगभग बीस वर्ष की उम्र में इनका विवाह हो गया। इनको अपनी पत्नी से बड़ा प्रेम था। वह एक बार अपने भाई के साथ पीहर चली गई। तुलसीदास अकेले नहीं रह सके और वह अपनी ससुराल जा पहुँचे। इनकी पत्नी ने इन्हें उलाहना दिया और कहा, "जितनी प्रीति आपको मुझ पर है, उसकी आधी भी यदि भगवान में होती तो आपका उद्धार हो जाता!" तुलसीदास को ये शब्द चुभ गए। यह एक क्षण भी वहाँ नहीं ठहरे, घर छोड़ कर चल दिए और साधु हो गए।

विंध्याचल का एक भाग चित्रकूट है। यह प्रदेश पहाड़ों, झरनों तथा प्राकृतिक दृश्यों के कारण बड़ा सुन्दर है। तुलसीदास यहीं रहने लगे। यह राम के बड़े भक्त थे। इन्होंने दूर-दूर तक की तीर्थ-यात्राएँ कीं।

चित्रकूट को छोड़ने के बाद तुलसीदास प्रयाग, अयोध्या और काशी में रहे। यहीं इन्होंने अपने प्रसिद्ध ग्रंथ रामचरितमानस की रचना की। इसी को रामायण भी कहते हैं। यह ग्रंथ इन्होंने संस्कृत में न लिखकर जनता की भाषा में लिखा। तुलसीदास ने दूसरे ग्रंथ भी लिखे पर रामचरितमानस ही उनकी सबसे अच्छी रचना है।

रामचरितमानस की गणना संसार के प्रसिद्ध ग्रंथों में की जाती है। भारत के सभी विद्वान इसका आदर करते हैं। उत्तर भारत में यह घर-घर पढ़ा और सुना जाता है। सचमुच इस ग्रंथ को रचकर गोस्वामी तुलसीदास ने भारतीय जनता का बड़ा उपकार किया है।

(adapted from *NPM* 4, pp. 108-12)

VOCABULARY

गोस्वामी	n.m. ascetic, spiritual leader
तुलसीदास	prop. m.
महाकवि	n.m. great poet
संत	n.m. saint
जन्म	n.m. birth
ज़िला	n.m. district
X नामक	named X
अनाथ	n.m. orphan
X की भांति	post. like X, in the manner of X
द्वार	n.m. door, gate
भटकना	v.i. to wander
द्वार-द्वार भटकना	v.i. to wander from door to door
साधु	n.m. hermit, religious mendicant
संन्यासी	n.m. ascetic, one who has renounced the world
दया	n.f. pity, compassion
X को Y पर दया आना	v.i. for X to feel pity for Y
X का पालन-पोषण करना	v.t. to raise, nourish, bring up X
पढ़ाना-लिखाना	v.t. to teach to read and write, to educate
बुद्धि	n.f. intellect
तीव्र	adj. sharp, keen
विवाह	n.m. marriage
पीहर	n.m. a wife's premarital house and family
ससुराल	n.f. the home of one's father-in-law
उलाहना	n.m. complaint
प्रीति	n.f. love, affection
उद्धार	n.m. deliverance, salvation
शब्द	n.m. word
X को Y चुभना	v.i. for Y to sting, prick X
विंध्याचल	n.m. the region of the Vindhya mountains
प्राकृतिक	adj. natural
दृश्य	n.m. scene, sight
तीर्थ-यात्रा	n.f. religious pilgrimage
प्रयाग	prop. m. the old name of Allahabad
अयोध्या	prop. f. the capital of the ancient kingdom of Kosala
काशी	prop. f. the old name for Varanasi
ग्रंथ	n.m. (sacred) book, text
रामचरितमानस	prop. m. literally 'the lake of the acts of Ram'
रचना	n.f. creation, work of art
X की रचना करना	v.t. to create, compose X
गणना	n.f. counting, reckoning, evaluation, estimation
X का आदर करना	v.t. to revere, honor X
रचना	v.t. to create, compose
X का उपकार करना	v.t. to do something of great benefit to/for X

CHAPTER 27

27.1. Imperfective Participles

Participles are forms that at one and the same time share properties of verbs and those of some other part of speech. In Hindi, participles are forms that while largely verbal in nature, function as either adjectives or adverbs. Hindi participles are one of two types, imperfective or perfective. Perfective participles (28.1.) designate completed verbal activities whereas imperfective participles represent incomplete or unfinished activities.

Imperfective participles are formed by the addition of the suffix–त– and one of the vowels -आ, –ए, or -ई directly to the verbal stem. When the participle is used adjectivally, it agrees with the noun modified in number, gender, and case. Adjectival imperfective participles frequently are expanded with one of the simple perfective forms of होना, namely हुआ, हुए, etc. :

लौटता (हुआ) आदमी	'a/the returning man'
चलती (हुई) गाड़ी	'a/the moving train'
दौड़ते (हुए) लोगों को	'to the running people'

पानी पीता (हुआ) लड़का मेरा भाई है।
'The boy (who is) drinking water is my brother'.

गाने गाता (हुआ) लड़का गांव में पहुँचा।
'The boy (who was) singing songs reached the village'.

When used adverbially, imperfective participles show the invariable suffix -ते, which is frequently expanded by हुए :

वह घर लौटते (हुए) अपने एक दोस्त से मिला।[1]
'He met one of his friends while returning home'.

प्रीति गाने गाते (हुए) गांव पहुँच गई।
'Priti reached the village singing songs (along the way)'

हमने तुमको जाते (हुए) देखा।
'We saw you going'.

---

1. Among some Hindi speakers, the termination -ती (हुई) can be used as an adverbial imperfective participle marker if the subject of the activity of the participle is female. For such individuals, this example sentence would be वह घर लौटती (हुई) अपने एक दोस्त से मिली if the subject is female.

Adverbial imperfective participles are often repeated (i.e. "reduplicated'). It is not, however, normal to amplify the participle with हुआ, हुए, etc. when such a repetition has occurred:

गुरुजी का भाषण सुनते-सुनते लड़की ऊब गई ।
'The girl got bored listening to the guru's speech'.

टी वी देखते-देखते मैं थक जाती हूँ ।
'I get tired watching television'.

Adjectival imperfective participles may be used as substantives, standing in place of understood modified nouns :

सोतों को मत जगाओ ।
'Don't wake up the sleeping'.

मरती की बुराई नहीं की जानी चाहिए ।
'A dying (woman) shouldn't be slandered'.

The repetition of an adverbial imperfective participle can be used in Hindi in a number of other important ways. It can signify that some activity or condition is going on while another event transpires :

होटल के सामने इंतज़ार करते-करते मुझे सिर दर्द होने लगा ।
'I started to get a headache while waiting in front of the hotel'.

It can indicate that some activity or state of affairs is the cause of the action designated by the primary verb of the sentence :

सारा दिन पढ़ते-पढ़ते दमयंती की आंखें कमज़ोर होने लगीं ।
'Damayanti's eyes started to get weak from reading all day'.

It can be used for gradual processes leading to some result :

पास में रहते-रहते उनमें गहरी दोस्ती हो गई ।
'A deep bond of friendship gradually developed between them from living near one another'.

And, when followed by the verbs बचना or बच जाना 'to be saved/rescued, to be left over', it can be used in the sense of English 'almost' :

वह मरते-मरते बच गया ।
'He almost died'.

गिलास टूटते-टूटते बच गया ।
'The glass almost broke'.

Adverbial imperfective participles are used in a number of different Hindi time expressions. Together with समय or वक़्त they can have the sense 'at the time of...':

जाते समय/वक़्त उसने पहचान लिया कि कोई दूसरा तैयार नहीं है ।
'When it was time to go he realized that no one else was ready'.

In the construction type X को imperfective participle होना, they denote the elapsing of time since the beginning of an activity that is still in progress:

रामलाल को सितार बजाते हुए एक महीना हुआ है ।
'Ram Lal has been playing the sitar for a month'.

Expressions containing a measure of time together with the imperfective participle of रहना have the sense 'as long as...':

मेरी जान रहते उनके घर में पैर न रखूंगा ।
'I won't even set foot in their house as long as I live'.

अँधेरा रहते बच्चे नहीं जागेंगे ।
'The children won't wake up as long as its dark'.

Some other adverbial expressions formed from the imperfective participle have idiomatic senses:

मेरे जीते जी	'as long as I'm alive'
होते-होते	'gradually, little by little'

27.2. Kinship Terms

The Hindi kinship system is vastly more complicated than that of English and most European languages. Single lexical items are found in Hindi for a larger number of familial relations than are differentiated by the lexicons of European languages. The Hindi kinship terminology system, founded as it is in the Indian joint family, reflects a family structure considerably different from that common in western culture. The translation of western kinship terms or phrases into Hindi by the mechanical substitution of seemingly corresponding elements leads to Hindi that is awkward, misleading, or completely incomprehensible to native speakers of the language. The system is complicated by the fact that a considerable gulf exists between its referential and appellative functions (i.e., between using the system to refer to individuals or to address them). Individuals who may be referred to by a particular term, often may not be addressed by the same term.

The basic set of Hindi referential kinship terms can be divided for purposes of exposition into a number of subsets, being those for basic family members paternal relations, maternal relations, relations of subsequent generations, and terms pertaining to marriage and marital status. Often several variants exist for a given familial relation, with different options reserved for distinct registers of the language. In some cases, Hindi speakers differ on the use of kinship terms. One speaker may, for example, use separate terms for father's older and younger brothers, while another may use a single term for both types of father's brother. Often kinship terms are used for ironic effect in other than their referential meanings.

The most commonly used terms for basic family members are as listed below:[2]

Father (F) : पिता, बाप
Mother (M) : माता, माँ, अम्माँ (Children's term)
Son (S) : बेटा, पुत्र
Daughter (D) : बेटी, पुत्री, कन्या
Brother (B) : भाई, भया (भैया), भ्राता

2. The following abbreviations are employed in this discussion of kinship terms: F (father), M (mother), B (brother), S (son), D (daughter), Z (sister), H (husband) W (wife), O (older), and Y (younger). For instance, the abbreviation BW is to be read as 'brother's wife'.

Sister (Z) : बहन (बहिन), भगिनी
Brother's Wife (BW) : भाभी
Sister's Husband (ZH) : बहनोई[3]

In addition to the terms listed above, the words दीदी or जीजी are often employed as terms of address in the sense 'older sister'. No comparable term exists for younger sister.

A highly developed set of terms exists in Hindi for referring to paternal relations, the most important of which are as follows:

FF: दादा	FM: दादी
FOB: ताऊ	FOBW: ताई
FYB: चाचा/काका	FYBW: चाची/काकी
FZH: फूफा	FZ: फूफी, बुआ
FBS: चचेरा भाई	FBD: चचेरी बहन
FZS: फुफेरा भाई	FZD: फुफेरी बहन

Among some speakers, the term चाचा and चाची are used as generic terms in the sense FB and FBW, with no distinction being made as to older or younger. No differentiation is made between father's older and younger sisters.

A set of maternal terms parallel to the paternal terms above is also present in Hindi:

MF: नाना	MM: नानी
MB: मामा	MBW: मामी
MZH: मौसा	MZ: मौसी
MBS: ममेरा भाई	MBD: ममेरी बहन
MZS: मौसेरा भाई	MSD: मौसेरी बहन

The kinship terms for relatives of younger generation are relatively straightforward, once the already introduced terms have been mastered:

BS: भतीजा	BD: भतीजी
ZS: भांजा	ZD: भांजी
SS: पोता	SD: पोती
DS: नाती, दोहता	DD: नातिन, दोहती

The prefix पर- is used in deriving terms for great-grandchildren from terms for grandchildren, and in deriving terms for great-grandparents from those for grandparents:

SSS: परपोता	SSD: परपोती
DSS: परनाती	DSD: परनातिन
FFF: परदादा	FFFW: परदादी
MFF: परनाना	MFFW: परनानी

3. For some Hindi speakers the term जीजा is used for an older (but not younger) sister's husband. Normally this term is used only as a term of address, with the more general बहनोई used when a purely referential form is required. A younger sister's husband is normally not addressed by a kinship term, but rather by his given name.

Hindi terms relating to marriage are particularly confusing from a western point of view. A woman upon marriage leaves the family in which she is raised (मायका or पीहर) and enters the home of her new in-laws (ससुराल).[4] Different terms are used in specifying various relations between a son-in-law and the members of his wife's family from those used in describing the relationship between a daughter-in-law and her husband's family. More terms exist for referring to a wife's in-laws than for designating the husband's, no doubt because of the fact that a husband's brothers are normally specified as being older or younger than the husband, while no such specification is made in the case of the wife's brothers. Some of the most important terms for relations by or through marriage are as follows:

Husband (H): पति, ख़ाविन्द, शौहर	Wife (W): पत्नी, बीवी (बीबी), घरवाली
Father-in-law (HF or WF): ससुर	Mother-in-law (HM or WM): सास
Son-in-law (DH) : दामाद	Daughter-in-law (SW): बहू
Brother-in-law (HOB) : जेठ	Sister-in-law (HOBW): जेठानी
(HYB): देवर	(HYBW): देवरानी
(HZH): ननदोई	(HZ): ननद
(WZH): साढ़ू	(WZ): साली
(WB) : साला	(WBW): सलहज

The use of kinship terms in addressing (as opposed to referring to) individuals is exceedingly complex, and a full discussion of this matter is beyond the scope of this introductory primer. The student should, however, be aware of the following principles. In many traditional households throughout north India, rules exist that govern the ways in which individual family members may be addressed in given situations. Thus, for example, even though a wife's husband's parents are her ससुर and सास, they are addressed with terms for father and mother. A brother's wife, whether older or younger, is referred to as भाभी. But whereas the brother's older sister is normally addressed as भाभीजी, the younger sister need be addressed by her given name. Many Hindi referential kinship terms, are, indeed, never used appellatively. The precise term to be used in addressing family members depends on the relation between the addressor and addressee, the social context, factors of age difference between various pertinent family members, and the intent of the speaker (i.e., whether being deferential, sarcastic, affectionate, etc.).

The use of Hindi kinship terms is further complicated by the fact that many terms are used in addressing individuals whose biological relationship to the speaker is other than that signified by the term. माताजी and पिताजी, for instance, are often used in addressing the parent of ones friends and acquaintances, and also in addressing respectually olders of various sorts. Several other kinship terms, originally with specific referential meanings, have come to have non-kinship applications. बाबा, originally 'grandfather' is now used to address any elderly man. बेटा (son) and बेटी (daughter) are likewise used in addressing any small children, whether biologically related to the speaker or not.

4. The terms मायका and पीहर can only be used to refer to the premarital home of a woman, whereas ससुराल can refer to the home of either a husband's or a wife's in-laws. Notice that the term ससुराल literally refers to the home of one's father-in-law (ससुर).

A number of kinship terms have pejorative connotations when used non-referentially. The terms साला (WB), ससुर (HF or WF), and साली (WZ) are particularly abusive when used appellatively (the first two corresponding to 'bastard/son of a bitch' and the second to 'bitch'), and should be avoided unless deliberate insult is intended.

A peculiarity in the Hindi system for referring to and addressing family members concerns the ways in which married women speak of or to their husbands. In many traditional homes it has been customary for a wife to avoid directly stating the name of her husband or, in fact, even referring to him explictly as husband. Rather, any of a number of types of periphrastic devices are employed. She may designate her husband as the father of one of her children "e.g., लल्लू के पिता 'Lallu's father'". She may choose locutions that avoid requiring that a name be specified (e.g., passives and other subject-less constructions). Or she may simply refer to him with a third person pronoun such as वह or वे, leaving it to the listener to deduce that the pronoun refers to the woman's husband. Often this system of 'no-naming' is extended to all elder males in a woman's family. Although still maintained in rural and traditional families, this system has fallen out of fashion in many westernized families.

In recent years the use of English kinship terms, often in conjunction with the honorific marker जी, has become quite common in westernized contexts. In families of this type it is not unexpected to hear words such as मम्मी, डेडी, वाईफ़, आंटी, and अंकल along side of native Hindi words for various familial relations.

27.3. VOCABULARY

आदर	n.m. respect, honor	बरबाद	adj ruined
इंतज़ाम	n.m. arrangement, preparation	X को आदर देना	v.t. to show/give respect to X
कृष्ण	prop. m. the god Krishna, also known as श्रीकृष्ण	X का इंतज़ाम करना/होना	v.t./i. to arrange for X/ for X to be arranged
घर वाले	n.m. pl. family members	उतारना	v.t. to bring/take down
जान	n.f. life	खिलना	v.i. to bloom
तारीफ़	n.f. praise	चिल्लाना	v.i. to scream, yell out
तैयारी	n.f. preparation	जमना	v.i. to congeal, freeze, take root
दहेज	n.m. dowry		
देवता	n.m god	जमा करना/होना	v.t./i. to gather, collect/to be gathered, to come together
देवी	n.f. goddess		
पीहर	n.m. wife's family, wife's family home		
		जीना	v.i. to live, exist
बनियान	n.f. undershirt, vest	ढूँढ़ना	v.t. to look for, search for
बाबा	n.m. term of address for an old man; grandfather	X की तैयारी करना/होना	v.t./i. to prepare for X/for preparations for X to take place
बाल-बच्चे	n.m. pl. children, progeny		
बुराई	n.f. slander, malice	X में पैर रखना	v.t. to set foot in X
बैल	n.m. ox	बजाना	v.t. to play (a musical instrument), to make sound
भाषण	n.m. speech, lecture		
भैंस	n.f. (she-) buffalo	बरबाद करना/होना	v.t./i. to ruin, destroy X/to be ruined, destroyed
मायका	n.m. wife's family, wife's family home		
		X की बुराई करना/होना	v t./i. to slander X/for X to be slandered
विवाह	n.m. wedding, marriage		
सदस्य	n.m. member	मनाना	v.t. to celebrate (a holiday), to persuade
ससुराल	n.f. father-in-law's house		
सितार	n.m. sitar (a stringed musical instrument)	हराना	v.t. to defeat
		आहिस्ता	adv. slowly, gently
सिरदर्द	n.m. headache	होते-होते	adv. gradually
कमज़ोर	adj. weak		
जमा	adj. indecl. collect, assembled		

27.4. EXERCISES

27.4.1. *Translate into English*

1. चलती कार, हंसता बच्चा, पैदल चलते लड़कों को, नाचती लड़कियों के बारे में; 2. गाते-गाते काम करना, दौड़ते-दौड़ते घर लौट आना, रोते-रोते सो जाना, खेलते-खेलते समय बिताना; 3. लौटते समय, पौधे लगाते वक़्त, खेलते समय, उठते समय; 4. मरतों की सेवा करना, खेलते-कूदतों के मुसकराते चेहरे; 5. दादाजी की जान रहते, तुम्हारे जीते जी, तेरी जान रहते, उन बच्चों के जीते जी ।

27.4.2. *Complete the following sentences:*

1. माताजी के पिताजी मेरे————————हैं। 2. माताजी की बहन मेरी——————हैं जिनके पति मेरे————हैं। 3. पिताजी के छोटे भाई मेरे————हैं जिनकी बेटियां मेरी——————हैं।4. मेरे भाई का पुत्र मेरा——————है जिसकी बहन मेरी——————है। 5. रोहिनी के भाई की बीवी उसकी————है। 6. दादाजी के पिताजी मेरे————हैं। 7. किसीकी पत्नी के पिता उसके—————हैं। 8. किसी की पत्नी की बहन उसकी——————है। 9. मेरी पुत्री का पति मेरा——————है। 10. किसी के बेटे की पत्नी उसकी————है।

27.4.3. Translate the following phrases into Hindi. In numbers 1-4 use imperfective participles wherever possible. In the remaining numbers, use single kinship terms in place of longer paraphrases where appropriate.

1. sleeping dogs, men washing clothes, women singing songs, a farmer sowing seeds; 2. to the laughing girl, towards the man climbing that tree, concerning the falling rocks, near the man [who is] studying; 3. to fall asleep while talking, to sing songs while bathing, to do puja by offering flowers, to become rich by saving money (पैसा बचाना v.t.); 4. at the time to go to the mosque, at the time of giving birth, at the time of arrival; 5. your (pol.) sister's husband, my brother's wife's sari, his sister's daughter's toys. 6. Prem's father's older brother, the teacher's grand-daughter (DD)'s name, Mr. Rahman (रहमान)'s cousin (FZS)'s home, in Vishnu (विष्णु)'s sister-in-law (WBW)'s dowry.

27.4.4. *Translate into English*

1. परसों दोपहर को हमने श्रीकांत को बाज़ार में घूमते-फिरते देखा। 2. चलती गाड़ी से नहीं उतरना चाहिए। 3. खिलते फूलों को मत तोड़ो। 4. सारा दिन दफ़्तर में काम करते-करते वे शाम तक थक जाते थे। 5. अपने घरों से भागते-भागते लोग डर से चिल्ला रहे थे। 6. कुएं में गिरकर वह डूबते-डूबते बच गया। 7. जीते जी हमें हमेशा आपकी सहायता की याद रहेगी। 8. हम अचानक समझ गए कि बालकों के साथ खेतों में खेलता हुआ वह भगवान श्रीकृष्ण होगा। 9. पहले पुत्र को पैदा करने के लिए हिन्दुस्तानी औरतें अक्सर मायके जाती हैं। 10. तुमको उस बस्ती में रहते कितने वर्ष हो गए हैं ? 11. विवाहित होने के बाद दीदीजी ससुराल में पति के परिवार को अपना ही परिवार समझने लगेंगी। 12. चाचाजी, क्या लल्लू दीदी के साथ सिनेमा जा सकता है ? 13. कहा जाता है कि सास-बहू में दोस्ती नहीं हो सकती, पर मैं इसे सच नहीं समझता। 14. क्या कपूर साहब अपने घरवालों को साथ (=अपने साथ) ले आए ? 15. तुम्हारे घर में कुल कितने रिश्तेदार रहते हैं ?

27.4.5. *Translate into Hindi*

1. We saw the children playing in a street near the mosque. 2. The man putting on a kurta is my wife's brother. 3. The rice almost got burned (use बचना) on the stove. 4. How long has your nephew (BS) been playing the sitar? 5. When it was time to go, big sister decided to stay home. 6. She grew bored working in that office every day. 7. What did your brother-in-law (WB) get by way of (i.e., in) a dowry ? 8. We were all very surprised seeing your cousin (MBS) swimming in the river. 9. Big sister, when is Usha going to get married ? 10. Gradually, all of the flowers began to bloom. 11. The woman coming down from the ox-cart (बैलगाड़ी n f.) is my aunt (FOBW). 12. This is a picture of Sri Krishna at play (i.e., of a playing Sri Krishna). 13. You will never learn anything (by) sleeping all day. 14. Living in the same village, they became good friends. 15. Seeing the children helping Mother, he started to smile.

CHAPTER 28

28.1. Perfective Participles

Perfective participles are constituted in Hindi by the addition of the adjectival suffixes –आ, –ए, and –ई directly after the verbal stem. In a small number of cases, the perfective stem to which these endings is added is irregular (cf. 10.1. and 11.1.), In contrast to the imperfective participle, which signifies a verbal activity viewed as incomplete, the perfective verbal participle represents a verbal activity as carried through to fruition or completion.

Like imperfective participles, perfective participles may be employed either adjectivally or adverbially. When adjectival, they modify some noun either explicitly stated or understood from context. The adjectival participle is often expanded with one of the forms हुआ, हुए, or हुई, with both the participle itself and the हुआ/हुए/हुई element agreeing with the modified noun in gender, number, and person:

बैठा (हुआ) आदमी	'a/the sitting (i.e., seated) man'
बैठे (हुए) आदमी	'the sitting men'
बैठे (हुए) आदमी के पास	'near the sitting man'
बैठी (हुई) औरत	'the sitting woman'
बैठी (हुई) औरतें	'the sitting women'
बैठी (हुई) औरतों के पास	'near the sitting women'

Adjectival perfective participles may be used either predicatively or attributively:

सैनिक मरे (हुए) हैं	'the soldiers are dead' [predicative use]
मरे (हुए) सैनिक	'the dead soldiers' [attributative use]

Quite often, perfective participles are used to form adjectives specifying the condition that results from the completion of a verbal activity:

चाचाजी की किताब मेज पर रखी (हुई) है ।
'Uncle's book is placed on the table'.

मेज पर रखी (हुई) किताब चाचाजी की है ।
'The book on the table is Uncle's'.

कमरे का दरवाजा खुला (हुआ) है ।
'The door to the room is open'.

कमरे के खुले (हुए) दरवाजे पर
'on the open door to the room'.

यह मेरी ख़रीदी हुई साड़ी है ।
'This is the sari I bought'.

मेरी ख़रीदी हुई साड़ी पर
'on the sari I bought'.

Adjectival perfective participles may be used as nouns, standing in place of the understood noun modified by the participle. When this occurs, the participle is conjugated a noun:

मरों (or मरे हुओं) को देखकर किसको दुःख नहीं होगा ?
'Who does not feel grief after seeing the dead?'

जीतों की प्रशंसा सब जगहों पर की जा रही थी ।
'The victors were being praised everywhere'.

Two types of formations are employed for perfective participles with adverbial force. In one, the invariable suffix–ए appears:

अपना सामान लिए (हुए) जफ़र गाड़ी से उतर गया ।
'Zafar descended from the train with his luggage'.

ज़मीन पर बैठे हुए वह औरत सब्जियाँ बेच रही है ।
'That woman (who is) sitting on the ground is selling vegetables'.

बिना गांव में रुके (हुए) आपसे दिल्ली नहीं आया जाएगा ।
'You won't be able to come to Delhi without stopping in the village' (cf.25.3).

Adverbial perfective participles constructions are also found in which the participle itself shows not the invariable ending–ए, but the –आ/ –ए/–ई of adjectival participles:

अपनी नई बनारसी साड़ी पहनी हुई शीला बाहर जाने को तैयार थी ।
'Wearing her new Benaras sari, Shila was ready to go out'.

Adverbial perfective participles frequently are reduplicated, forsaking amplification with हुए:

सारा दिन दफ़्तर में बैठे-बैठे कौन नहीं ऊबेगा ?
'Who wouldn't get bored sitting in an office all day'.

Like the imperfective participle, the perfective participle is used in sentences indicating the elapsing of time. But whereas the use of the imperfective participles denotes the elapsing of time since the inception of an activity that is still ongoing, the perfective participle in such constructions indicates the elapsing of time since the end of an already concluded activity:

राम को हिंदी सीखते हुए दो साल हो चुके हैं ।
'Ram has been learning Hindi for two years'. [action ongoing]

राम को गाय ख़रीदे हुए दो साल हो चुके हैं ।
'It's been two years since Ram bought the cow'. [action completed]

महेश को आए हुए तीन हफ़्ते हो गए हैं ।
'It's three weeks since Mahesh came'.

28.2. Reduplicative Expressions

Reduplicative expressions are those in which all or part of a linguistic form is repeated. Reduplicative expressions are quite common in Hindi, serving a number of distinct functions, and taking place vis-à-vis several different parts of speech in the language.

One of the most common senses of the repetition of linguistic forms is that of iteration, or the providing of a list of specifics. Reduplication in this sense is particularly prevalent for interrogative forms:

> वहाँ आपने क्या-क्या देखा ?
> 'What (i.e., provide specifics) did you see there?'
>
> गुरुजी का दर्शन पाने कौन-कौन आए ?
> 'Who all came to behold the Guruji?'
>
> वहाँ मैं किस-किस से मिलूँ ?
> 'With whom should I meet there?'

Another extremely common sense of reduplicated forms is that of distribution, either among a group of individuals or across space or time:

> समुद्र के किनारे-किनारे मछुओं के गांव फैले हुए हैं।
> 'Villages of fishermen are spread along the sea coast'.
>
> बच्चों को दो-दो रुपये दीजिए।
> 'Please give two rupees to each child'.
>
> लालाजी की दुकान पर तरह-तरह की चीजें बिकती हैं।
> 'You can get all kinds of things at the Lalaji's shop'.
> [cf. तरह-तरह 'all kinds of'].
>
> कारख़ाने के कार्यकर्ता अपने-अपने कार्यों में लगे हुए थे।
> 'The factory workers were all involved in their [individual] jobs'.

It is quite normal in Hindi to reduplicate various kinds of adverbs. This process often does not bring about any semantic change in the lexical meaning of the adverb;

> धीरे-धीरे बोलिए 'Please speak slowly'.

The repetition of adverbial imperfective and perfective participles discussed earlier (27.1 and 28.1.) further illustrates this tendency in Hindi to reduplicate adverbs.

In other contexts, reduplication is used in Hindi to intensify or amplify the meaning of the item being repeated:

> पहाड़ों पर गरम-गरम चाय पियो।
> 'Drink really hot tea while up in the mountains'.
>
> ठंडा-ठंडा पानी पिलाओ।
> 'Serve very cold water'.

कर constructions are to be found in which the verbal stem appears reduplicated. These constructions frequently have adverbial force:

रह-रहकर	'periodically, intermittently'
रुक-रुक कर	'haltingly'
देख-देखकर	'looking repeatedly'

28.3. Combinations of Postpositions

Sequences of simple postpositions are often employed to express complex relations holding between elements of a sentence. Some common examples of these usages are में से 'from among, out of', पर से 'from on top of', and पर का/के/की 'from on top of':

शायद उनमें से एक सफल होगा ।
'Perhaps one of them will be successful'.

वह पहाड़ पर से गिर कर मरा ।
'He fell from the top of the mountain and died'.

पहाड़ी पर की झोंपड़ी जयशंकर की है ।
'The hut at the top of the hill is Jay Shankar's.'

28.4. Onomatopoetic Expressions

Onomatopoetic words or expressions are those whose phonetic shapes are held by the speakers of a language to be iconic replicas of the meanings of the words or expressions themselves. In English, for example, the words *buzz* and *humm* are believed by many to physically resemble the sounds they signify.

Onomatopoetic expressions in Hindi are almost always reduplicative in nature, with the second form either identical to the first or derived from it by the substitution of one or a small number of sounds:

घर-घर	'rumbling, snorting noise'
टप-टप	'sound made by water dripping or falling'
खर-खर	'sound made while snoring or clearing throat'

Onomatopoetic terms of this sort are used in either direct quotation of the sound being replicated, or as adjectives modifying some noun:

झम-झम पानी 'glistening rain' [cf. झम-झम glistening]
तारे चमक रहे थे चम-चम
'The stars were glittering *cam-cam*'. [cf. चम-चम sparking, flickering, crackling].

Unlike many other languages, onomatopoetic terms in Hindi are not restricted to words indicating physical sounds (i.e., those evinced through the formation of sound waves). Moods, emotions, and even bodily motions are all treated in Hindi as though they were sounds:

झम-झम	'glistening of rain'
चम-चम	'glittering, twinkling'
सर-सर	'gliding, creeping (of a snake)'.

Onomatopoetic terms often appear in derived forms. They may become intransitive verbs through the addition of the suffix -आना. Thus from घुर-घुर can be formed the verb घुरघुराना 'to make the noise घुरघुर, to snort, rumble'. Abstract feminine nouns can be formed for onomatopoetic terms by the addition of -आहट, literally 'sound, trace, indication'. From टप-टप is formed the term टपटपाहट 'sound of water falling':

पानी की टपटपाहट की आवाज़ सुनाई दे रही थी ।
'The sound of water falling could be heard'.

28.5. A Further Use of बनना

The intransitive verb बनना, literally 'to be made', often occurs in the sense 'to become, to be constituted'. In such cases, it is closely synonymous with हो जाना:

इस तरह काम करते-करते तुमको अमीर बनना चाहिए ।
'You ought to get rich working in this way'.

Together with थोड़े 'hardly', बनना exists in the idiom X Y से Zथोड़े बनना 'X hardly will become Z from doing Y, doing Y doesn't make X a Z':

टाई लगाने से प्रोफ़ेसर थोड़े बनते हैं ।
'Wearing a tie doesn't make you a professor'.

28 6. Interrogatives Used as Exclamations

In many languages, words that ordinarily function as interrogatives can also serve as exclamations. The English clause 'Oh how lovely is the morning' is not, indeed, a query about the degree of loveliness exhibited by a particular morning, but rather an exclamation of delight. In Hindi, too, interrogative forms often have exclamatory force:

वह कितनी अच्छी लड़की है ।
'What a good girl she is!'

कैसी अद्‌भुत है यह धरती हमारी ।
'How marvelous is this world of ours!'

वे तो कितनी ही बार जीत गए ।
'Oh how many times he was victorious!'

28.7. Clause-Final न and क्या

In colloquial Hindi, the negative marker न and the question word क्या often appeal after a verb at the end of a clause. These usages are alternates for other more formal devices in Hindi for asking questions requiring a yes or no answer:

हमारे साथ खाएँगे न ?
'Won't you eat with us?'

साफ़ कपड़े साथ ले आया क्या ?
'Did he bring the clean clothes with him?'

उसने जो कहा, ठीक है न/क्या ?
'Is what he said correct?'

न also appears at the end of a sentence in a sense equivalent to German *nicht wahr*, French *n'est ce-pas*, or English *is that so, right*:

तुम उसके दोस्त हो न ?
'You're his friend, aren't you?'

This use of न also appears together with verbs in the negative:

वह घर में मदद नहीं करता न ?
'He doesn't help in the house, does he?'

28.8. VOCABULARY

कला	n.f. art
क्षेत्र	n.m. field
गेहूँ	n.m. wheat
घास	n.f. grass
चश्मा	n.m. (pair of) eyeglasses
जाल	n.m. net
जिम्मेदारी	n.f. responsibility
तरस	n.m. compassion, pity
ताँबा	n.m. copper
तुलना	n.f. comparison
दर्शन	n.m. sight, presence; philosophy
पहाड़ी	n.f. hill
पीतल	n.m. brass
बादल	n.m. cloud
मछली	n.f. fish
मछुआ	n.m. fisherman
रूप	n.m. form, shape, beauty
रूपरेखा	n.f. outline
लकड़ी	n.f. wood
व्याकरण	n.m. grammar
शब्द	n.m. word
शब्दकोश	n.m. dictionary
शेर	n.m. lion
संगीत	n.m. music
सहारा	n.m. support
हिम्मत	n.f. courage
अद्‌भुत	adj. extraordinary
टेढ़ा	adj. crooked, bent
बनारसी	adj. from Benaras
भारी	adj. heavy, weighty
व्यस्त	adj. busy, occupied
साफ़	adj. clear, clean; adv. clearly
होशियार	adj. clever
चमकना	v.i. to glitter, sparkle
जुड़ना	v.i. to be linked, connected, joined
जोड़ना	v.t. to unite, link, connect
X को (Y पर) तरस आना	v.i. for X to feel compassion/pity for Y
X का दर्शन पाना	v.t. to behold X, to catch a glimpse of X, to meet X
पिघलना	v.i. to melt
फंसाना	v.t. to cause to become entrapped
फटना	v.i. to burst, tear, rip, split
फाड़ना	v.t. to tear, rip, split
फैलाना	v.t. to spread out
X को Y की हिम्मत होना	v.i. for X to have the courage to do Y
परे	adv. away, afar
भीतर	adv. inside
X की तुलना में	post. in comparison to X
X से परे	post. beyond X
X के बावजूद	post. in spite of X
X के भीतर	post. inside X
X के रूप में	post. in the form/guise of X
X के सहारे	post. with the support of X

28.9. EXERCISES

28.9.1. *Translate into English*

1. पिघली बर्फ़, जुड़े पैसे, जाल में फ़ंसी चिड़ियाँ, फटा काग़ज़, जली हुई लकड़ी; 2. बादलों के पीछे निकला हुआ सूरज, ताँबे और पीतल के बने बर्तन, अपने मित्रों से लिया हुआ सहारा, अशोक की लिखी हुई किताब; 3. आहिस्ता-आहिस्ता बोलना, ठंडे-ठंडे पानी का एक गिलास, रुक-रुक कर गुरुजी के प्रश्नों का उत्तर देना, तरह-तरह की मछलियों को नदी में तैरते देखना; 4. जयशंकर के दोस्तों में से दो, मेज़ पर से गिरना, कार के पीछे से सामान निकालना; 5. कितने अच्छे समोसे! ; कितनी होशियार बच्ची !, कैसा सुन्दर रूप !, कितनी भारी ज़िम्मेदारी !, 6. श्याम (prop. m) को हम पर तरस न आने के बावजूद, बनारसी साड़ियों की तुलना में, अच्छे व्याकरण और शब्दकोश के सहारे !

28.9.2. *Translate into Hindi*

1. broken toys, plucked flowers, glittering stars, torn clothes; 2. with the boy (who had) climbed up the hill, to harvest (काटना) the wheat planted in the fields, to ask the man standing in front of the store, to grasp the fish (that had) become trapped in the net; 3. in spite of being our enemies, in the form of an outline of Hindi grammar, beyond the Himalaya (हिमालय) mountains, in spite of their living in Madhya Pradesh, inside the wooden house; 4. how many beautiful children!, what a beautiful garden!, what busy people!, what a crooked nose!; 5. to behold the Prime Minister, to feel pity for the dead of the city, to have the courage to leave one's home, to leave one's home, to rescue the six birds (who were) trapped in the nets.

28.9.3. *Translate into English*

1. मेज़ पर से आंटी का दिया हुआ चश्मा उठा लाओ। 2. युद्ध में मरे हुओं की बुराई कभी नहीं की जानी चाहिए नहीं तो हमारे मरने पर लोग हमारी भी बुराई करेंगे। 3. हरी-हरी घास पर लेटे-लेटे, चलते बादलों को देखते-देखते, प्रकृति का मज़ा (n.m. enjoyment) किसको नहीं आता। 4. द्विवेदी जी का दर्शन पाए हुए मुझे चार-पांच साल हो चुके हैं। 5. बिजली चमक रही है चम-चम, लगा बरसने पानी झम-झम। (adapted from a childern's poem) 6. सारा दिन काफ़ी हाउस में बैठे-बैठे इंजीनियर बनोगे कैसे? 7. इस अद्भुत विवाह से दोनों परिवारों को जोड़ दिया गया। 8. साहित्य, संगीत, दर्शन तथा कला के क्षेत्रों में रवीन्द्रनाथ टैगोर का बहुत ऊंचा स्थान था। 9. मेज़ पर गंदे पैर फैलाए अपने ससुर को देखकर मालती अपने अन्दर जलती थी, पर वह क्या करती। 10. मुझमें भूखे शेर के पास जाने की हिम्मत होती तो मैं उसका नाश्ता बन जाता। 11. दूर-दूर के गांवों से लोग गांधीजी का दर्शन पाने इकट्ठे हुए। 12. आजकल अपने बच्चों को खिलाने-पिलाने की भारी ज़िम्मेदारी आसानी से नहीं सही जाती। 13. नदी के किनारे-किनारे अपने जाल फैलाए हुए मछुए मछलियाँ फंसाने का काम कर रहे थे। 14. तुम्हारी नई कहानी की रूपरेखा इतनी लम्बी नहीं होती तो शायद साफ़-साफ़ समझी जाती। 15. अपने दोस्तों और परिवारवालों के सहारे किसी भी तरह की मुसीबत सही जा सकती।

28.9.4. *Translate into Hindi*

1. Give the boy (who is) drenched by the rain some dry (सूखा) clothes. 2. The days that have gone by (use बीतना) will never return again. 3. Please pick up the toys that are scattered on the ground. 4. It's been three weeks since Father set off for Pakistan. 5. Show the tailor (दरज़ी) your kurta so that he can see where it is torn. 6. Tulsīdās and Sūrdās are among the most famous poets of the Hindi language. 7. Mrs. Gopal gave each of the children two rupees. 8. I certainly don't have the courage to confront Mr. Sharma in front of his friends. 9. One shouldn't buy cut fruit in the market 10. It is forbidden to enter (i.e. ascend) into a moving bus (बस n.f.). 11. Nothing is ever accomplished without trying. 12. All the people standing there were surprised upon seeing the queen's beauty. 13. In spite of being located (i.e. situated) on a hill, that village's weather is very hot. 14. All that the fishermen caught in their nets were heavy rocks.

CHAPTER 29

29.1. Participles + रहना

Persistence, either in carrying out an activity or in the state resulting from the completion of that activity, is expressed in Hindi by either the imperfective or perfective participle followed immediately by the verb रहना. Constructions so formed conventionally are expressed in English by the words *keep(s) on*, *continue(s) to*, *persist(s) in*, and the like, although other phrases may be more appropriate in specific contexts.

The imperfective participle followed by रहना indicates the sustained continuity of or presistence in activities that are conceptualized as incomplete, whether habitual or progressive:

थके होने पर भी चाचाजी रात तक लिखते रहे ।

'Even though he was tired, Uncle kept on writing into the night'.

जीते रहो ।

'Be well!' [literally, 'keep on living'. This a popular salutation, used at the end of conversations.]

उसे संस्कृत सीखने में कम दिलचस्पी है, फिर भी पढ़ती रहेगी ।

'She has little interest in learning Sanskrit, but still she will keep on studying it'.

आशा है कि भविष्य में इस तरह का उत्सव होता रहेगा ।

'It is hoped that this kind of celebrating may continue in the future'.

रहना following a perfective participle indicates persistence or continuation of the state or condition resulting from the completion of the activity of the verb represented by the participle:

मोती चार दिन अपनी चारपाई पर बेहोश लेटा रहा ।

'Moti lay unconscious on his charpai for four days'.

उठने की कोई जरूरत नहीं जनाब, बैठे रहिए ।

'There's no need to get up, Sir. Please stay seated'.

शराब की बोतल अलमारी में छिपी रही ।

'The bottle of liquor remained hidden in the almirah'.

Normally, the participles employed in these constructions of persistence are not amplified with हुआ, हुए, etc.

29.2. Indirect Commands

An indirect command is one that is not given directly to the party who is desired to perform something, but rather is conveyed to the ultimate performer through an intermediary. It thus generally has the sense 'tell X to do Y', 'have X do Y', etc.

The normal format for an indirect command in Hindi is X से/को oblique infinitive = Y] को कहना 'to tell X to do Y':

राम को/से घर जाने को कहो।
'Tell Ram to go home'.
दीदी को/से सब्जियाँ ख़रीदने को कहिए।
'Please tell big sister to buy some vegetables'.

The clause stating the desired activity occasionally is transposed to a position after the verb, which then normally is placed in the subjunctive:

राम को/से कहो कि वह घर जाए।
दीदी से/को कहिए कि वह सब्जियाँ ख़रीदे।

The use of को in the above examples is somewhat less polite than the use of से. The former implies that the act of telling is unidirectional, i.e., that it does not invite a response. The latter, by contrast, leaves open the possibility of a response to the bearer of the command.

29.3 Stylistic Shifts of Word Order

In conversational Hindi, the order of the constituent parts of a sentence often differs markedly from that seen in formal styles of the language. Deviations in word order can be quite substantial, involving all or some of the major components of a sentence.

It is beyond the scope of this primer to discuss all of the types of permutations of word order that can occur in the spoken language. Some shifts, however, are of such general occurrence that even the beginning student should be aware of their existence.

In one important syntactic permutation, a word or phrase is placed after the verb in sentence final position:

बहुत काम किया उसने।
'He did a lot of work'.
मुझे अच्छा शब्दकोश चाहिए हिन्दी का।
'I need a good Hindi dictionary'.
रसीले आम मिलेंगे वहाँ पर।
'You'll get juicy mangoes there'.
पानी जरूर बरसेगा शाम तक।
'It will certainly rain by evening'.

In another shift, an attributive adjective, often a possessive phrase, is moved after the noun it modifies:

भाभीजी उसकी अशोक होटल में ठहरेंगी।
'His sister-in-law (BW) will stay in the Ashoka Hotel'.
यह बैल हमारा कुछ काम का नहीं है।
'This ox of ours is good for nothing'.

Forms of the copula होना frequently are found moved to the beginning of colloquial sentences:

है तो महंगा, लेकिन ख़रीद लो ।
'It's expensive, but buy it anyway'.

हूँ तो अमरीकन, पर हिन्दुस्तानी गाने मुझे अच्छे लगते हैं ।
'I am American, but I like Indian songs'.

Words or phrases can also be displaced to the beginning of a sentence or clause:

उसकी बीवी को मैं जानता हूँ ।
'I know his wife'.

इस तरह का खाना यहाँ खाया नहीं जाता ।
'This kind of food isn't eaten around here'.

It is quite possible for more than one syntactic permutation to occur within the same sentence:

हूँ तो मैं दिल्ली का, पर पैदा हुआ बंबई में ।
'I am from Delhi, but I was born in Bombay'.

बातें बुरी-बुरी कहीं तुमने ।
'You have said very bad things'.

In general, the displacement of a word or phrase to the beginning of a sentence serves to bring that word or phrase into greater prominence than is normal. Displacement to the end of a sentence is more complex, and can occur either to emphasize or de-emphasize a form. When the subject of the sentence has been moved to the end of the sentence, however, it is almost always for purposes of de-emphasis:

मामाजी के यहाँ रहते हो तुम ?
'Do you live with your (maternal) uncle?'

In this last example, the word तुम is included as almost an afterthought, and is said at the conclusion of the main portion of the sentence with a minimal amount of stress.

29.4. POLITENESS FORMULAE

As should be apparent, the means for the expression of politeness are quite different in Hindi from their counterparts in English. It has already been shown (7.5) how the use of honorific pronouns with plural verbal agreement, markers such as जी and साहब, and plural pronominal forms can be used to convey respect or deference towards an individual addressed or spoken about. But this by no means exhausts grammatical devices for employing polite or respectful speech. Although it is not obligatory or even common in Hindi to use separate words corresponding to the English 'please', such words do exist and are encountered in the formal style of the language. The most common of these are कृपा करके, कृपया, and मेहरबानी करके :

कृपा करके बच्चों की देख-रेख कीजिए ।
'Please look after the children'.

मेहरबानी करके काग़ज़ दिल्ली से साथ ले आइए ।
'Kindly bring the papers with you from Delhi'.

The words कृपा and मेहरबानी may be combined with करना to form conjunct verbs that are linked with की to an oblique infinitive:

ठीक समय पर आने की कृपा/मेहरबानी कीजिए ।

'Please be so kind as to come right on time'. [literally, 'please do the kindness of coming right on time'.]

पढ़ने के बाद पुस्तक वापिस करने की कृपा कीजिए ।

'Would you please be so kind as to return the book when you've finished reading it'.

A special genre of respect-bestowing vocabulary items may be employed during polite speech. This genre includes several substitutes for ordinary verbs (e.g., पधारना for आना, तशरीफ़ आना for अंदर जाना, तशरीफ़ रखना for बैठना, and फ़रमाना for कहना, बोलना, or करना. These substitute usages are particularly characteristic of refined speech in Urdu, although they are employed to some degree throughout the Hindi-Urdu speaking world:

पधारिए, रह्‌मान साहब । तशरीफ़ रखिए यहाँ पर ।

'Please come in Mr. Rahman. Won't you sit down over here'.

बादशाह सलामत ने दरबार में इकट्ठे हुए वज़ीरों से फ़रमाया कि

'The Emperor said to his ministers (who were) assembled in his court...'

It is also possible to convey politeness through the adoption of a level of diction in which one speaks disparagingly of oneself and one's own, but in glowing terms of all that concerns the person addressed. Thus one's own home becomes a ग़रीबीखाना, literally 'poverty house', but the addressed's home is a दौलतख़ाना 'home of wealth/riches'. The addressed may be referred to as आक़ा 'leader, master' or जनाब 'sir', while the speaker refers to himself as नाचीज़ 'nothing, servant' or ग़ुलाम 'slave'. These usages, too, are most characteristic of elevated Urdu.

29.5. ज़रा AND क्यों न

The word ज़रा may be used as an indeclinable adjective in the sense 'a little, a bit'. It is occasionally followed by the declinable suffix -सा:

ज़रा (-सा) पानी 'a little bit of water'

ज़रा-सी देर 'a little while'

As an adverb, ज़रा has the sense 'a little, a bit, just':

ज़रा ठहरो 'just wait a bit'

Often, adverbial ज़रा at the beginning of a sentence has the effect of softening a command or request. This usage roughly corresponds to the English phrase 'why don't you':

ज़रा मेरे साथ सिनेमा चलो ।

'Why don't you come to the movies with me'.

ज़रा बाहर निकल कर देखो ।

'Why don't you come outside and look'.

क्यों न may be used very much in the manner of ज़रा to soften requests and commands:

क्यों न मेरे साथ सिनेमा चलो ।

क्यों न चांदनी चौक की सैर करें ।

'Why don't we take a stroll in Chandni Chowk'.

29.6. EXPRESSIONS OF COMPULSION

The adjectives बाध्य and मजबूर 'compelled, obligated' are used, together with other elements, to express the compulsion or obligation to carry out some activity. Normally, an infinitival phrase is employed to indicate that which needs to be carried out. This phrase is linked to the adjective बाध्य or मजबूर by the postposition पर. The बाध्य or मजबूर element is combined with either होना or करना, depending on whether one wishes to refer to the state of being compelled or to the activity of compelling someone else respectively. A summary of important expressions for compulsion is given below:

X oblique infinitive [=Y] पर बाध्य/मजबूर होना
'for X to be compelled to do Y'.[1]
X Y को oblique infinitive [=Z] पर बाध्य/मजबूर करना
'for X to compel Y to do Z'

मैं यहाँ ठहरने पर बाध्य/मजबूर हूँ ।
'I am compelled to stay here'.
विजय ने मुझे यहाँ ठहरने पर बाध्य/मजबूर किया ।
'Vijay compelled me to stay here'.

In expressing prevention from doing something (as opposed to compulsion to carry it out) से (and occasionally को) is substituted for पर and either of the verbs मना करना (v.t. 'to forbid') or रोकना substituted for बाध्य/मजबूर करना :

माताजी ने कमेली को शादी करने से मना कर दिया ।
'Mother forbade/stopped Kameli from getting married'.

29.7. वैसे तो

वैसे तो at the beginning of a clause serves as an extremely loose conjunction, linking a clause to some previous discourse. Often the construction has contrastive sense, distinguishing that which is to follow from that which might be supposed or presupposed from earlier discourse:

विद्वान-सा लगता है । वैसे तो बेपढ़ा किसान है ।
'He seems like a wise man, but actually he's an illiterate farmer'.
वैसे तो यहाँ लोग ऐसे कपड़े नहीं पहनते । लेकिन आज होली का त्यौहार है, इसलिए रंग-बिरंगे कपड़े पहने आए हैं ।
'Ordinarily people don't wear clothes like these. But today is Holi and that's why people are wearing (such) colorful clothes'.

1. It is, of course, also possible to use infinitives + होना or पड़ना, as well as indirect verb constructions with ज़रूरत or आवश्यकता, to express the obligation or necessity to carry out some action (cf. 17.2-17.4.).

29.8. Vocabulary

अलमारी	n.f. almirah
उत्सव	n.m. festival, celebration
चांदनी चौक	n.m. Chandni Chowk [a famous market in Old Delhi]
चारपाई	n.f. charpai [a kind of bed made of wood and rope]
चौक	n.m. market, marketplace
तार	n.m. wire, telegram
देख-रेख	n.f. supervision, care
पूछताछ	n.f. inquiry
बादशाह	n.m. emperor, king
भविष्य	n.m. future
वज़ीर	n.m. minister, adviser
शराब	n.f. liquor
होली	n.f. Holi [a Hindu festival]
काम का	adj. useful
गोल	adj. round
ख़ूबसूरत	adj. beautiful
बराबर	adj. equal; adv. regularly
बाध्य	adj. compelled
बेकार	adj. vain, useless, good for nothing
बेपढ़ा	adj. illiterate
बेहोश	adj. unconscious
मजबूर	adj. compelled
रंग-बिरंगा	adj. colorful, multi-colored
रसीला	adj. juicy
X की कृपा करना	v.t. to be so kind as to do X
ख़ुशी मनाना	v.t. to celebrate, rejoice
छिपना	v.i. to hide, to be hidden
टंगना	v.i. to hang
टांगना	v.t. to hang, suspend
तशरीफ़ रखना	v.t. to sit
तशरीफ़ लाना	v.t. to come
तार देना	v.t. to wire, to send a telegram
X की देख-रेख करना/होना	v.t./i. to supervise, care for X/ for X to be supervised, cared for
धकेलना	v.t. to push
पधारना	v.i. hon. to go, come, arrive
पूछताछ करना	v.t. to inquire
फ़रमाना	v.t. hon. to speak, say, talk
बाध्य करना/होना	v.t./i. to compel/to be compelled
मजबूर करना/होना	v.t./i. to compel/to be compelled
X से/को मना करना	v.t. to forbid to do X
X की मेहरबानी करना	v.t. to be so kind as to do X
कृपया	adv. please, kindly
कृपा करके	adv. please, kindly
क्यों न	adv. cf. 29.5.
ज़रा	adv. cf. 29.5.; adj. indec. a little, a bit
मेहरबानी करके	adv. please, kindly
X के बराबर	post. equal to X, the same as X
वैसे तो	conj. actually, ordinarily
जनाब	interj. Sir!

CHAPTER 30

30.1. -आ करना

It has already been shown (8.2.) that Hindi possesses a verbal aspect, the habitual, one of whose main functions is to describe actions or sets of circumstances that are repetitive, regular, or recurring in some manner. The language has, however, another construction that can be invoked to indicate the repetitiveness of verbal activities. In this construction, the main verb shows what appears to be its perfective participle with the invariable suffix -आ. This participle is immediately followed by करना, which may be freely conjugated. The repetitiveness indicated by this construction is of a specific kind, to wit, that arising through force of habit or a recurrent pattern of behavior:

राम अपनी बहनों से मिलने आया करता था ।
'Ram made a habit of coming to see his sisters'.

अपने पाठ ध्यान से पढ़ा करो ।
'Study your lessons carefully' (i.e., make a habit of studying your lessons carefully).

उन दिनों राम से हमारी बातें अक्सर हुआ करती थीं ।
'We used to talk to Ram frequently those days'.

When जाना is the main verb of such constructions, जाया appears as the first element in place of the expected गया :

माधुरी रोज़ बाज़ार जाया करती थी ।
'Madhuri made a habit of going to the market every day'.

30.2. Indirect Quotation

Indirect quotation is the process whereby one relates to another that which was said by a third party. Such reportage can be direct, in which case a verbatim account is provided, or indirect, in which a paraphrase is offered. In written English, the distinction between direct and indirect quotation is quite clear, with the use of quotation marks required for the former. In spoken English, by contrast, the difference between the two is often blurred, with given sentences ambiguous between senses embodying the two types of quotation.[1]

Indirect quotation in Hindi is carried out by the use of one or another verb of speaking (e.g., कहना 'to say', पूछना 'to ask', पेश करना 'to request', बोलना 'to speak', फ़रमाना

1. Thus, for example, the two written sentences ***John said I'm coming tomorrow*** and ***John said, "I'm coming tomorrow"*** are realized identically in the spoken language.

'to say'), the conjunction कि and a following clause giving the actual reportage. The reportage clause in Hindi differs in an important way from the corresponding clause in English sentences of indirect quotation. In an English sentence such as '*John said that he was coming*' the words *he was coming* constitute the speakers paraphrase of which John actually said. In his actual speech John would not have used the third person pronoun *he*, but rather the first person *I*. Nor would John actually have said *was coming*, but most likely would have expressed his intent with some expression such as *am coming*. In Hindi, indirect quotations of the type *John said that he was coming* can be formed in one of two ways. In the more common, and also more traditional, way the reportage clause has the appearance of a direct quotation, regardless of whether or not it is a paraphrase:

राम ने कहा कि मैं आ रहा हूँ।
'Ram said that he was coming' or
'Ram said, "I am coming." '
गप्पू ने पूछा कि मैं यहाँ बैठ जाऊँ।
'Gappu asked if he might sit down here' or
'Gappu asked, "May I sit down here ?" '

The कि element is often deleted in sentences of indirect reportage:

राम ने पूछा (कि) मैं आऊँ।
'Ram asked if he might come in'.

The other pattern, no doubt under the influence of European languages, follows the English system for indirect quotation:

राम ने कहा कि वह आ रहा है।
'Ram said that he (either Ram or another party) was coming'.

Of the two patterns, the first is by far the more common, particularly in ordinary speech and non-westernized writing. The second pattern is, however, becoming more widely seen in written Hindi, and may well become even more common as a result of increased use of quotation marks and other English punctuation devices.

30.3. Unexpressed General Nouns

It is not uncommon to find in Hindi constructions in which the possessive post-position की is seemingly unconnected to any noun with which it stands in grammatical agreement. In such cases, the की can often be assumed to be connected to some feminine noun with very general sense such as बात 'matter, thing', 'time, occasion' or the like, which has been deleted :

वह वहाँ जाया करती थी। अब की नहीं गई।
'She used to make a habit of going there, but she didn't go this time'.
[with deletion of बार]
पहले स्कूल और कालेज में पढ़ाई पूरी कर लो, फिर अमरीका जाने की सोचना।
'First finish school and college, and then think of going to America'.
[with deletion of बात]

30.4. FURTHER PROPERTIES OF ही

The quasi-postpositional[2] particle ही appears in a wide variety of syntactic contexts in Hindi. Its meaning, and consequently its translation, varies greatly depending on the specific syntactic context in which it appears.

ही is extensively used as an emphatic marker, generally with a sense of exclusion (cf. 8.5.). It combines with many preceding pronouns and adverbs to form single word contractions. Some of the most common of these are the following:

यह+ही→यही	हम+ही→हमी
वह+ही→वही	अब+ही→अभी
इस+ही→इसी	तब+ही→तभी
उस+ही→उसी	जब+ही→जभी
इन+ही→इन्हीं	सब+ही→सभी
उन+ही→उन्हीं	यहाँ+ही→यहीं
तुम+ही→तुम्हीं	वहाँ+ही→वहीं
	कहाँ+ही→कहीं

The contractions कभी (=कब+ही) and कहीं (=कहां+ही) have meanings not predictable from the meanings of their constituents. The former has the sense 'sometime (or other)' and the latter 'some place (or other)'.

The placement of ही when following phrases that include postpositions is most idiosyncratic, and considerable variation is to be observed. In general, however, certain tendencies can be pointed out. Sequences of a noun and following postposition are, at least in the formal written language, often broken up by ही :

राम ही के लिए	'only for Ram'
दिल्ली ही में	'only in Delhi'

Sequences in which the order of postposition and ही is switched are, however, also encountered:

दिल्ली में ही	'only in Delhi'
मैं तुमसे ही प्रेम करता हूँ।	'I love only you'.

There exist syntactic constructions in which the placement of हीं before the postposition is mandated and others in which the order of these elements is reversed. In some cases, both options may be permissible, but with a slight difference of meaning between the two alternatives. In other cases, no difference of meaning may be discernible. The complexity of the placement of ही relative to preceding forms that include a postposition is particularly noticeable where pronouns are involved. Thus, for example, ही is incorporated into a contraction with a pronoun in such phrases as इसी का 'of this very one', उसी का 'of that very one', इन्हीं का 'of these very ones', and उन्हीं का 'of those very ones', but serves as an independent element following possessive pronouns in मेरा ही 'mine (and no one else's)', तेरा ही 'yours (int.)', हमारा ही 'our', तुम्हारा ही 'yours (fam.)' and आपका ही 'yours (pol.)'.

---

2. i.e., it occurs after the words with which it is associated, but does not cause them to appear in oblique case forms.

When interspersed in or appended to verbal constructions, ही effects diverse semantic changes depending on the nature of the verbal construction involved. Where the verb expresses futurity, an appended ही can specify the certainty of the action:

झा साहब हमसे मिलेंगे ही।

'Mr. Jha will certainly meet with us'.

With verbs specifying the completion of an action or describing a state or condition resulting from the carrying out of some activity, ही indicates priorness:

चाचाजी ने वह किताब ख़रीदी ही थी कि उनको याद आया कि ऐसी किताब उनके पास है।

'Uncle had already bought that book when he realized that he already had one like it'.

ही is also found in compound sentences in which the ही is interspersed in the verbal component of the prior clause and the second clause is introduced with the conjunction कि. The specific sense of the ही...कि construction varies according to the nature of the verbal elements in the two clauses being conjoined. Samples of these construction types include the following:

अमित जाने ही वाला था कि कोई उसका नाम पुकारने लगा।

'Amit was just about to go when someone started to call his name'

राष्ट्रपति दिल्ली पहुंचे ही थे कि बाढ़ का समाचार प्राप्त हुआ।

'The President had just arrived in Delhi when the news of the flood was received'.

मनिंद्र सो ही रहा था कि चोर उसके कमरे में घुस आया।

'The thief crept into Manindra's room even while he was sleeping'.

30.5. Compound Subjects

There is no single method in Hindi by which verbs are made to agree with compound noun phrases. In general, there are two methods by which such agreement takes place.

In the first pattern, a verb form agrees in number and gender with the closer of two coordinate nominal entitles, or the closest if there are three or more:

एक थाली और कुछ बर्तन मेज़ पर रखे थे।

कुछ बर्तन और एक थाली मेज़ पर रखी थी।

'A platter and some utensils were on the table'.

In the other pattern, a kind of "summing up" is carried out in which the compound subject is viewed as an aggregate whole. Normally a verb agreeing with such a subject is marked as masculine and plural, unless each of the components of the subject is itself feminine, in which case the verb is marked as feminine plural :

राम और उसकी बहन हमारे यहाँ आए।

'Ram and his sister came to our place'.

सीता और उसकी बहन हमारे यहाँ आईं।

'Sita and her sister came to our place'.

एक कुरता/और तीन कमीजें फ़र्श पर पड़े थे (or पड़ी थीं)।

'A kurta and three shirts were lying on the floor'.

Often words such as सब, दोनों, तीनों, etc. are used in forming aggregate subjects by the summing up method:

सीता और राम दोनों आपके यहाँ आएंगे।

'Both Sita and Ram will come to your place'.

एक कुरता और तीन कमीजें सब फर्श पर पड़े थे।

30.6. INTENSIVE COMPOUND VERB CONSTRUCTIONS

A type of compound verb construction exists in Hindi in which, unlike the majority of compound verb constructions discussed earlier (cf. 19.1.ff.), the prior member is not uninflected, but rather either shows one of the adjectival inflections –आ, –ए, or –ई, with the choice among these alternates determined by the number and gender of the grammatical subject, or the invariable adverbial suffix –ए. There is a wide range of semantic effects brought about by the use of such constructions, generally referred to as 'intensive', with the specific effect in any given instance being related to the nature of the V_1 and V_2 elements constituting the compound.

Intensive showing the adjectival suffix -आ/-ए/ -ई attached to the V_1 are primarily limited to compounds having intransitive V_1 elements. In general, these compounds indicate that the primary verbal activity is in progress, impending, or in a state requiring immediate resolution. In some cases, however, any semantic difference between an intensive compound and a corresponding compound without an intensive suffix is either extremely subtle or totally imperceptible:

सुमित्रा दुःख से मरी जा रही थी।

'Sumitra was (gradually) dying from grief'.

घनघोर बादल आकाश में फैले जा रहे थे।

'Dense clouds were spreading in the sky'.

Intensives showing the invariable adverbial suffix -ए are by and large restricted to compounds with transitive V_1 members. Often these transitive intensives are used rhetorically to add greater authority, certainty, or emphasis to what is being said:

मैं सचमुच यह सब खाना खाए जाऊँगा।

'I will certainly eat up all of this food'.

मैं तुमको कहे देता हूँ कि....

'Truly I say unto you that...'.

Intensives are also to be found in Hindi that violate the above stated generalizations about the transitivity or intransitivity of V_1 elements. For example, intransitive V_1 elements are to be found that may co-occur with either –आ/ –ए / –ई or with the invariable -ए:

पानी उबला/उबले जा रहा था।

'The water was about to boil'.

It may be noted that a small number of verbal constructions already discussed involving motion (i.e., चला जाना, चला आना, भागा जाना, etc. [16.6.]) can properly be considered intensives of the type treated here.

30.7. Vocabulary

आग	n.f. fire	उबलना	v.i. to boil
जाड़ा	n.m. cold	उबालना	v.t. to boil
थाली	n.f. plate, platter	छूना	v.t. to touch
पढ़ाई	n.f. education	दबना	v.i. to be pressed down, to be subdued
पुरुष	n.m. person, man	दबाना	v.t. to depress, subdue, press down
प्यार	n.m. love	पुकारना	v.t. to call, cry out
बाढ़	n.f. flood	पेश करना	v.t. to present, offer
मनुष्य	n.m. man, human being	प्राप्त करना/होना	v.t./i. to receive/to be received
मर्द	n.m. man	प्यार करना	v.t. to love
मेम (साहब)	n f. madam (usually a western woman)	बंधना	v.i. to be tied, fastened
राज्य	n.m. state, reign, rule	बांधना	v.t. to tie, fasten
राष्ट्रपति	n.m. president (of a nation)	मुड़ना	v.i. to turn (back), bend, be folded
वसंत	n.m. spring (season)	मोड़ना	v.t. to turn (back), bend, fold
समाचार	n.m. news	लदना	v.i. to be laden
समाज	n.m. society	लादना	v.t. to load, carry
हृदय	n.m. heart	सताना	v.t. to torment
अनिवार्य	adj. compulsory	अनजाने	adv. unknowingly, unwittingly
अन्य	adj. other	आख़िर	adv. finally, at last
घनघोर	adj. thick, dense	नज़दीक	adv. nearby
ख़ामोश	adj. silent	लगातार	adv. continuously
नंगा	adj. naked	X के अनुकूल	post. in accordance with X
नन्हा	adj. tiny, small	X के नज़दीक	post. near to X
फीका	adj. tasteless, vapid		
बेचारा	adj. helpless, unfortunate		
भला	adj. good		
मैला	adj. dirty, filthy		
आग लगाना	v.t. to ignite		

CHAPTER 31

31.1. Imperfective Participle+जाना

In order to describe a verbal action that is conceptualized as a gradual progression from one state or condition to another, the imperfective participle (i.e., the stem+ता/ते/ती) followed by some form of जाना is used. The imperfective participle and the जाना show agreement in gender and number with the subject of the clause

ज्यों-ज्यों रातें लंबी होती जाती हैं त्यों-त्यों दिन छोटे होते जाते हैं।
'The days grow shorter as the nights grow longer'.

भारतीय साहित्यकारों के संसार में रेणु की प्रशंसा बढ़ती जा रही है।
'Renu is being increasingly praised in the world of Indian literary figures' [रेणु prop. m. Phanishvarnath "Renu," a contemporary Hindi writer, best known for his novels, short stories, and plays.]

31.2. A Construction with बनना

The intransitive verb बनना, literally 'to get/be made', is employed in a special construction with capabilitive sense. The schema of this construction is noun+से+imperfective participle+बनना. The participle shows the invariable adverbial ending -ते. The entire locution almost always is in the negative and has the sense that X cannot manage to carry out the activity expressed by the imperfective participle:

सुधीर से हिन्दी में एक भी शब्द बोलते नहीं बनता।
'Sudhir can't manage to speak even a single word of Hindi'.

इतनी लंबी बीमारी के बाद रमेश से बैठते नहीं बनेगा।
'Ramesh won't even be able to sit down after such a long illness'.

तुमसे इतनी चौड़ी नदी पार करते नहीं बनेगा।
'You won't be able to cross such a wide river'.

31.3. Some Arithmetic Formulae

There is considerable variation in Hindi in the means for describing simple arithmetic computations. The four basic arithmetic functions, i.e., addition, subtraction, multiplication, and division, are each verbalized by a somewhat lengthy formula, which may be reduced in several different ways for purposes of recitation.

Addition: X को Y में जोड़ना 'to add X to Y'
आठ और/धन/जमा आठ सोलह (होते हैं) 'eight and eight are sixteen'

Subtraction: X में से Y को घटाना 'to substract Y from X'
दस ऋण/नफ़ी पांच पांच (होते हैं) 'ten minus five is five'

Multiplication: X को Y से गुणा करना — 'to multiply X by Y'
दो गुणित/ज़रब चार आठ (होते हैं) — 'two times four is eight'
Division: X को Y से भाग देना — 'to divide X by Y'
बीस भाजित/विभाजित/तक़सीम पांच चार (होते हैं) — 'twenty divided by five is four'.

A special set of Hindi numbers often is employed in recited multiplication tables. These words have the particular sense 'times one', 'times two', etc.:

एकम	'times one'; e.g.,	चार एकम चार	'four times one is four'
दूनी	'times two'; e.g.,	तीन दूनी छः	'three times two is six'
तिया	'times three'; e.g.	दो तिया छः	'two times three is six'
चौका	'times four'; e.g.,	तीन चौका बारह	'three times four is twelve'
पंचे	'times five'; e.g.,	दो पंचे दस	'two times five is ten'
छठा	'times six'; e.g.,	चार छठा चौबीस	'four times six is twenty-four'
सत्ता	'times seven'; e.g.,	दो सत्ता चौदह	'two times seven is fourteen'
अट्ठा	'times eight'; e.g.,	एक अट्ठा आठ	'one times eight is eight'
नवां	'times nine'; e.g.,	पांच नवां पैंतालीस	'five times nine is forty-five'
दहाम	'times ten'; e.g.,	तीन दहाम तीस	'three times ten is thirty'

31.4. Relative-Correlative Compounds

Several expressions occur in Hindi in which a relative form is joined in a compound with its corresponding correlative. These compounds are used in Hindi with adverbial force:

ज्यों-त्यों (कर के)
जैसे-तैसे
जैसा-तैसा } 'somehow or other'

ख़ैर जैसे-तैसे/ज्यों-त्यों खरे साहब को यहाँ ले आना ।
'Bring Mr. Khare here any way you can'.
जैसा-तैसा काम चल रहा है ।
'Somehow or other the work is getting done'.

जैसे-का-तैसा
ज्यों-का-त्यों } 'exactly as it was'

सौ रुपये का नोट जैसे-का-तैसा/ज्यों-का-त्यों पड़ा था, किसी ने नहीं लिया ।
'The hundred rupee note was lying exactly as it was; no one had taken it'.

जहाँ-का-तहाँ — 'in the same place as before'
पुस्तक पढ़ने के बाद प्रसादजी ने उसे जहाँ-का-तहाँ रख दिया ।
'After he finished reading it, Mr. Prasad put the book back in the same place'.

जहाँ-तहाँ — 'here and there, everywhere'
कमरे में सारा सामान जहाँ-तहाँ बिखरा पड़ा था ।
'All of the luggage was lying scattered all over the room'.

A related compound जैसे-को-तैसा is used as a masculine noun with the sense 'tit for tat, retaliation':

जब श्यामू चोर के यहाँ भी चोरी हो गई तब लोगों ने यही कहा कि जैसे-को-तैसा मिला ।
'When a robbery occurred at the home of Shyamu the thief, people said that he had gotten what he deserved (i.e., that he had received tit for tat)'.

31.5. The Use of English in Hindi

English words and phrases are employed by Hindi speakers of all backgrounds. Many words of English origin are so ubiquitous in Hindi that, by any stretch of the imagination, they have become Hindi words. Forms such as फ़ोन, स्कूल, कार, फ़्लैट, रेडियो, प्रोग्राम, रेलवे, प्लेटफ़ार्म, and टाइम-टेबल are now reckoned as Hindi vocabulary items and are so listed in many Hindi dictionaries. Often these words coexist alongside तत्सम neologisms, with the use of the latter restricted to the most formal styles of Hindi (e.g., लाइब्रेरी alternating with पुस्तकालय n.m.).

The use of English words and phrases is far more widespread in colloquial Hindi than it is in the written forms of the language. Indeed, among many urban speakers of Hindi, English words, phrases, and even sentences are scattered freely within Hindi discourse. Speakers switch back and forth among Hindi, English, and other languages, using one or another of these languages for rhetorical, stylistic, or emotional effect. Written Hindi is far less tolerant of such mixing than is the spoken language. In general, the written language does not look with favour on the use of English words that have not been incorporated into the Hindi lexicon (i.e., that have not been natived as Hindi vocabulary). But there are exceptions to this. In fiction, one often encounters a considerable quantity of English in reported dialogue:

"हाऊ मीन," अंजू ने तेजी से कहा।
"क्या खयाल है अंजू डार्लिंग ?" लड़के ने उसे भींचते हुए कहा।
"चलो, होस्टल लौट चलें।"
"इतनी जल्दी ?"
"हां।"
"क्यों ?"
"पागल न बनो। ऐसा बढ़िया मौका जिंदगी में बार-बार हाथ नहीं आता।"
"नहीं रोमियो, नहीं। अभी नहीं।"[1]

The incorporation of English forms and sentences in Hindi is not devoid of linguistic regularity. The borrowing of linguistic forms from one language to another entails the modification of the borrowed entities so as to meet the phonological and syntactic requirements of the borrower language. English words brought into Hindi are seldomed pronounced in the same was as they would be in English (whether the British or the American variety). Rather, they are pronounced using Hindi sounds, as well as Hindi stress and intonation rules. The loan word होटल 'hotel' is not spoken, as in English, with stress on the second syllable, but rather on the first. By contrast, अस्पताल 'hospital' is stressed on the final syllable, not on the initial syllable as in English. English alveolar stops (i.e., *t* and *d*) normally appear in Hindi as retroflexes, the English alveolar series of consonants not being represented in Hindi and lying midway between Hindi's retroflex and dental series (e.g., टेस्ट test', डिग्री 'degee', डिस्ट्रिक्ट 'district')[2]. The *th* in English words such as *third* and *theatre* (phonetically an interdental voiceless fricative) is expressed in Hindi as an aspirated, voiceless, dental stop (थर्ड, थियेटर).

1. Gulshan Nanda, भंवर ['whirlpool']. New Delhi (Hindi Book Center, 1972), p. 12.
2. Note that the word अस्पताल is an exception to this rule.

There is substantial modification of the English vowels in words borrowed by Hindi. The short *e* sound in words such as *entrance* and *engine* is generally represented as an इ in Hindi (इंट्रेंस, इंजन.)

Many English diphthongs in Hindi are broken up into two independent vowels. In writing, these elements are separated by a य element (e.g., एयर इंडिया 'Air India', डायरी 'diary'). The *o* in English words like *order* and *coffee* generally is realized as आ, which in writing occasionally is spelled with a superscript diacritic (ऑडर, कॉफ़ी [cf. 2.4.]).

It is beyond the scope of this primer to discuss all of the conventions by which English loan words are pronounced in Hindi and written in *devanāgarī*. Suffice it to say that these borrowings involve a process of adaptation whereby English forms are modified so as to bring them into accord with the structural demands of Hindi and its writing system.

31.6. Derivational Suffixes Denoting Gender

Several suffixes are used in Hindi to derive feminine nouns from corresponding masculine ones. There are three major functions that can by served by these suffixes. They can form diminutives, they can specify the wife of some party, or they can indicate the female member of a pair. Often the addition of one of these suffixes also entails a modification of the stem to which it is affixed. The most common suffixes used in forming feminines are as follows:

–ई : लड़का 'boy' ~ लड़की 'girl'; बंदर 'monkey' ~ बंदरी 'she-monkey', रस्सा 'rope' ~ रस्सी 'string, twine'

-इया: कुत्ता 'dog' ~ कुतिया 'bitch'; बूढ़ा 'old man' ~ बुढ़िया 'old woman'; डिब्बा 'compartment, box' ~ डिबिया 'small compartment, box'

–इन: सुनार 'goldsmith' ~ सुनारिन 'goldsmith's wife'; धोबी 'washerman' धोबिन 'washerwoman, washerman's wife'

–आइन: ठाकुर 'member of ठाकुर caste' ~ ठकुराइन 'wife of ठाकुर, female member of ठाकुर caste'; चौबे 'member of चौबे caste' ~ चौबाइन 'wife of चौबे, female member of चौबे caste'

–आनी : नौकर 'servant' ~ नौकरानी 'servant's wife, female servant'; देवर 'husband's younger brother' ~ देवरानी 'husband's younger brother's wife'

–नी : ऊंट 'camel' ~ ऊंटनी 'female camel'; हाथी 'elephant' ~ हथिनी 'female elephant'; मोर 'peacock' ~ मोरनी 'peahen'

Occasionally feminines may be derived from masculines by the addition of either of two different suffixes. Thus one finds both पंडिताइन and पंडितानी in referring to the wife of a पंडित.

In some cases a word for specifying masculine gender is derived from a corresponding feminine rather than vice versa: भैंस 'she-buffalo' ~ भैंसा 'he-buffalo'; रांड़ 'widow' ~ रंड़ुआ 'widower'.

31.7. Vocabulary

कर्त्तव्य	n.m. duty	ओढ़ना	v.t. to cover (the body), to wrap
चोरी	n.f. theft	खोदना	v.t. to dig
ज़िंदगी	n.f. life	गुणा करना	v.t. to multiply
तेज़ी	n.f. swiftness, sharpness	छाना	v.i. (for darkness, clouds, etc.) to spread
दिक़्क़त	n.f. difficulty, trouble	नक़ल करना	v.t. to copy
निश्चय	n.m. decision	पार करना	v.t. to cross
नियम	n.m. rule, principle	पीटना	v.t. to beat
नेता	n.m. II. leader	बढ़ना	v.i. to advance, increase
परिवर्तन	n.m. change, development	बिखेरना	v.t. to scatter
पोशाक	n.f. clothes, attire	बिगड़ना	v.i. to spoil, to deteriorate
प्रभाव	n.m. influence	बिगाड़ना	v.t. to spoil, ruin
प्रेमिका	n.f. lover	भटकना	v.i. to wander stray
प्रेमी	n.m. lover	भाग देना	v.t. to divide
फ़ैसला	n.m. decision	भींचना	v.t. to embrace, squeeze
बीमारी	n.f. disease	हाथ आना	v.i. (for an opportunity) to be at hand
मूल्य	n.m. value, price	एकाएक	adv. all of a sudden, suddenly
विषय	n.m. topic, subject	तेज़ी से	adv. quickly
व्यापार	n.m. business, trade	शीघ्र	adv. quickly
समस्या	n.f. problem	X के मुताबिक़	post. in accordance with X
साहित्यकार	n.m. writer, literary figure	X के विषय में	post. on the topic of X, concerning X
सिलसिला	n.m. respect, context	X के सिलसिले में	post. in respect to X, concerning X
अंतिम	adj. final	ख़ैर	interj. all right, well
अपरिचित	adj. unknown, unfamiliar		
आधुनिक	adj. modern		
नक़ली	adj. imitation		
परिचित	adj. familiar		
प्रस्तुत	adj. submitted, presented		
भोला-भाला	adj. guileless, innocent		

SUPPLEMENTARY READING PASSAGES

A. महात्मा गांधी

राष्ट्रपिता महात्मा गांधी एक महान युग निर्माता थे। भारत को स्वतंत्र कराने के लिए उन्होंने अपना सारा जीवन बलिदान कर दिया। यदि महात्मा गांधी राष्ट्रीय आन्दोलन की बागडोर न संभालते तो यह निश्चित था कि भारत को १९४७ ई० में स्वतंत्रता प्राप्त न होती। वे सर्वदा मानव मात्र की सेवा में लगे रहते थे। अंग्रेज़ों की सब चालें उनके आगे फीकी पड़ जाती थीं।

महात्मा गांधी ने हरिजनों के उद्धार के लिए भारी प्रयत्न किया। छुआ-छूत को समाप्त करने के लिए उन्होंने हरिजन नामक समाचारपत्र भी निकाला। महात्मा गांधी भारत में एक योगी महापुरुष थे। उन्होंने सत्य, अहिंसा तथा प्रेम का आश्रय लेकर अंग्रेजों को पराजित किया। ३० जनवरी १९४८ ई० को एक नासमझ युवक ने उनकी हत्या कर दी। आज हमारे प्रिय बापू हमारे बीच नहीं हैं, किन्तु उनके महान आदर्श हमारे पथ-प्रदर्शक हैं। इनके आदर्शों से प्रेरित होकर एक विदेशी निर्माता ने भारतीय सरकार के सहयोग से इनके जीवन पर १९८१ में एक फ़िल्म का निर्माण किया।

(from *DBSSE*, p. 10)

Vocabulary

राष्ट्रपिता	n.m. father of the nation
महान	adj. great
युग	n.m. era, epoch
निर्माता	n.m. builder, producer
बलिदान करना	v.t. to sacrifice
राष्ट्रीय	adj. national
आन्दोलन	n.m. movement, agitation
X की बागडोर संभालना	v.t. to hold the reins of X
निश्चित	adj. definite, certain
सर्वदा	adv. always
मानव	n.m. man, mankind
मात्र	partl. =ही
चाल	n.f. trick
X की चालें फीकी पड़ना	v.i. for X's tricks to have no effect
हरिजन	n.m. a term (literally 'people of God') coined by Gandhi for referring to untouchables
उद्धार	n.m. uplift, improvement
प्रयत्न	n.m. effort, attempt
छुआछूत	n.f. untouchability
समाप्त करना	v.t. to eradicate, complete
X नामक	named X
योगी	n.m. here used as adj. having yogic powers, ascetic
महापुरुष	n.m. great man
सत्य	n.m. truth
X का आश्रय लेना	v.t. to make use of X, to take shelter in X
पराजित करना	v.t. to defeat
नासमझ	adj. ignorant, unwise
युवक	n.m. youth
X की हत्या करना	v.t. to murder/kill X
बापू	n.m. father; an affectionate term for referring to Gandhi
आदर्श	n.m. ideal, model
पथ-प्रदर्शक	n.m. guide, leader
X से प्रेरित होना	v.i. to be inspired by X
सहयोग	n.m. cooperation, collaboration
X का निर्माण करना	v.t. to construct/make X

B. एक बूंद

ज्यों निकलकर बादलों की गोद से,
थी अभी एक बूंद कुछ आगे बढ़ी ।
सोचने फिर-फिर यही जी में लगी,
आह ! क्यों घर छोड़ कर मैं यों कढ़ी ।।१।।
देव ! मेरे भाग्य में है क्या बदा,
मैं बचूंगी या मिलूंगी धूल में ।
या जलूंगी गिर अंगारे पर किसी,
चू पड़ूंगी या कमल के फूल में ।।२।।
बह गयी उस काल एक ऐसी हवा,
वह समुन्दर ओर आई अनमनी ।
एक सुन्दर सीप का मुँह था खुला,
वह उसी में जा पड़ी मोती बनी ।।३।।
लोग यों ही हैं झिझकते, सोचते,
जब कि उनको छोड़ना पड़ता है घर ।
किन्तु घर को छोड़ना अक्सर उन्हें,
बूंद लौं कुछ और ही देता है कर ।।४।।

अयोध्या सिंह उपाध्याय 'हरिऔध'

Vocabulary

बूंद	n.f. drop	गिर	= गिर कर
गोद	n.f. womb, lap	अंगारा	n.m. ember, live coal
थी . . .बढ़ी ।	= बढ़ी थी	चूना	v.i. to drop, leak, ooze
आगे बढ़ना	v.i. to come forward, advance	कमल	n.m. lotus
		बहना	v.i. to flow
सोचने . . . लगी	= जी में यही फिर-फिर सोचने लगी	काल	n.m. time
फिर-फिर	= बार-बार	समुन्दर	= समुद्र
यों	= ऐसे	ओर	= की ओर
कढ़ना	v.i. to come out, fly away	अनमना	adj. dispirited, disconsolate
दैव	n.m. fate, fortune	सीप	n.f. oyster
भाग्य	n.m. fate, fortune	झिझकना	v.i. to hesitate
बदा	adj. fated	X लौं	like/resembling X
धूल	n.f. dirt, dust	कुछ और ही	something different

C. जबान का रस

रामू से उसकी बीवी, मां और बाप सभी तंग थे। वह कोई काम नहीं करता था और निठल्ला बैठा रहता। दोस्तों के साथ गप्पें हांकता और दिन काटता।

बीवी रोज़ ताने देती—निखट्टू काम के न काज के, दुश्मन अनाज के।

बीवी के तानों से तंग आकर वह रोज़गार के लिए गांव से चल पड़ा। धोती के छोर में कुछ चावल बांध लिए।

चलते-चलते दोपहर हो गई। एक पेड़ के नीचे उसने आराम किया और फिर चल पड़ा।

सांझ के समय रामू एक गांव में पहुंचा। इधर- उधर रात बिताने के लिए ठौर ठिकाना देखा। सामने एक बुढ़िया का घर दिखाई पड़ा।

—माई ! जय रामजी की !

—जय रामजी की, बेटा !

—माई ! रात रहने को जगह मिल जाएगी ?

—बेटा ! कहाँ से आ रहे हो ?

—मलका से।

—यहां दरवाज़े के पास पड़े रहना।

—माई ! यह चावल है, ज़रा उबाल देना, मैं खा लूंगा।

रामू ने धोती के छोर से चावल खोल कर दे दिए।

बुढ़िया ने चावल राँधने के लिए जलती हुई अंगीठी पर चढ़ा दिए। रामू बेकार बैठा इधर-उधर झांकने लगा। ड्योढ़ी में भैंस बंधी हुई थी।

—माई, यह भैंस अपनी है ?

—हां !

—कितना दूध देती है ?

—दस सेर।

—माई, अपनी इस ड्योढ़ी का दरवाज़ा तो बहुत छोटा रखा है।

—हां, बेटा।

—अगर आपकी भैंस मर जाए, तो यह दरवाज़े में से कैसे निकाली जा सकेगी ?

बुढ़िया लाल-पीली हो उठी, क्रोध से बोली—ले अपने चावल सम्हाल और यहाँ से चलता बन। मेरी भैंस क्यों मरे, तू ही न मर जाए।

बुढ़िया ने उबल रहे चावलों का पतीला रामू की धोती में उलट दिया।

रामू धोती में चावल डाले गांव में घूम रहा था और ठौर ठिकाने की तलाश कर रहा था। चावलों से पानी बह रहा था।

रास्ते में किसी ने पूछा—अबे ! यह क्या चू रहा है?
रामू ने तुरन्त जवाब दिया—ज़बान का रस।
सो मित्रो, ज़बान पर क़ाबू रखना चाहिए और सोच समझ कर बात करनी चाहिए।

(adapted from *PKK*, pp. 6-7)

VOCABULARY

ज़बान	n.f. speech, tongue, language
X से तंग होना आना	v.i. to be fed up with X
निठल्ला	adj. idle, unemployed
गप्पें हांकना	v.t. to gossip loudly and obnoxiously
ताना	n.m. taunt
निखट्टू	n.m. indolent person, good-for-nothing
कामकाज	n.m. work, business
दुश्मन	n.m. enemy
अनाज	n.m. corn, grain
काम के न काज के, दुश्मन अनाज के	You don't do any kind of work; what a parasite (lit. 'enemy of grain') you are!
रोज़गार	n.m. employment
छोर	n.m. end, extremity
आराम करना	v.t. to rest
सांझ	n.f. dusk, evening
ठौर-ठिकाना	n.m. place, location
माई	n.f. mother, old woman
राँधना	v.t. to cook
अंगीठी	n.f. a small coal-burning stove
बेकार	adj. idle, useless
झांकना	v.i. to peep, peer
ड्योढ़ी	n.f. vestibule, porch
अपनी	here = आपकी
लाल पीला होना	v.i. to boil over in anger
क्रोध	n.m. anger
सम्हालना	v.t. to take in one's charge
मेरी भैंस...मर जाए	Why should my buffalo die ? You're the one who ought to die.
उबले रहे चावल =	उबलते चावल
पतीला	n.m. kettle
अबे	interj. hey !
सो	conj. thus, so
X पर काबू रखना	v.t. to have/keep control over X

GUIDE TO FURTHER STUDY

The student who after completing this primer wishes to continue the study of Hindi faces no shortage of materials to use, although he will have to exercise care in selecting appropriate tools for specific purposes. In the remarks that follow I offer some recommendations as to pedagogical tools that I have found helpful for developing skills in each of several different areas of Hindi.

Without doubt, the major reference grammar of Hindi is still that of Kellogg, particularly as concerns the structures of Hindi regional dialects. Although the Hindi described in his work is in many regards archaic, Kellogg's grammar is an indispensable source of information for any serious student of Hindi. In addition to the Kellogg work, there are many other reference grammars and language courses available for Hindi, some of which are of utility. Among these reference grammars, I have found those by the Central Hindi Directorate, Lal, McGregor, S.N. Sharma, and Srivastava to have the best overall coverage of grammatical points. The Hindi course by Porizka, although not designed as a reference tool, contains a sufficiently large amount of information to enable it to be used as a reference grammar of the language. Hook's *Hindi Structures: Intermediate Level* provides excellent treatment of many grammatical constructions not normally covered in elementary language courses.

Several sets of materials are available for the student who wishes to develop conversational skills in Hindi. In the United States, the standard manual of colloquial Hindi is that by Gumperz and Rumery, although it has become somewhat outdated. Other materials by Fairbanks and Pandit, Fairbanks and Misra, Jagannathan and Bahri, Pattanayak, Sharma and Stone, and Smith and Weightman also are useful. The manual by Gambhir, *Spoken Hindi-Urdu*, is especially helpful in developing oral skills at the second or subsequent year level. Tape recorded oral exercises are available in conjunction with many published language courses.

Unfortunately, an inadequate number of readers is available for the study of Hindi. Most of those that do exist either have fallen out of print or are difficult to obtain. In my own teaching, I have found it helpful to have students read various graded children's readers in use in Hindi-medium grade schools in India. In the past, I have used those published by the राष्ट्रीय शैक्षिक अनुसंधान और प्रशिक्षण परिषद् for the kindergarten through fifth grade to be suitable for use in the first year of instruction at the university level. The राष्ट्र भारती readers, intended for the sixth through eighth grades in India, are suitable for our intermediate (i.e., second year) classes at the university level. Those students who have completed this primer should be able to tackle the राष्ट्र भारती readers without undue difficulty. The Sohomer and Jain reader is also recommended to such students. In the bibliography at the end of this section I have also listed several other readers that can be examined with profit by the interested student.

The situation with regard to Hindi language dictionaries has improved considerably in the past few years, and there are many dictionaries that can be recommended to students. Among Hindi-English dictionaries, those by Bahri, Chaturvedi and Tiwari, and Mohan and Kapur are particularly useful. Pathak's Hindi-English dictionary, although widely available, is somewhat less acceptable for students than the works already named. Among English-Hindi dictionaries, that by Bulcke is probably still the best, although *The Oxford Progressive English-Hindi Dictionary* has many strengths. The advanced student of Hindi is well advised to obtain a Hindi-Hindi dictionary, with the बृहत् हिन्दी कोश (Kalika Prasad, et. al., eds.) particularly recommended. For those requiring an unabridged dictionary of Hindi giving extensive citations of the use of forms throughout the history of Hindi, the हिन्दी शब्दसागर (Shyamsundar Das, ed.) is indispensable. Often the student will, in the course of his study of Hindi, encounter idioms that are not glossed in standard dictionaries. The हिन्दी मुहावरा कोश, edited by Bholanath Tiwari, is a most helpful tool in tracking down the meanings of such idioms.

The student who wishes to acquire a mastery of the Hindi language cannot, of course, do so merely by reading pedagogical or reference works. Such works, while necessary, only provide a framework for beginning the systematic study of the language. Real mastery is an ongoing process, something that is attained through emersion in the language in its social context. For this it is necessary to speak, read, and write Hindi as much as possible. One can read edited materials or do programmed exercises for only so long. Conversational fluency is attained by speaking Hindi with native speakers of the language. The way to learn how to write Hindi is to write it as much as possible and to have one's own efforts corrected by someone fully literate in the language. And the way to improve one's reading ability in a language is to read. There is no shortage of things to read in Hindi. The sooner the student abandons edited materials and moves on to "real" Hindi the better. Magazines, newspapers, academic, literary, and popular books of all kinds, advertisements, pamphlets, encyclopedias, telephone directories, food wrappers, inserts in pharmaceutical packages, street signs, public notices, and countless other things are printed in Hindi throughout much of north India. My best advice to the student is to read widely in the various styles of the language and to read often. Only by so doing can any real fluency be attained and reading be changed from an act of tedium to one that gives pleasure.

A Selected List of Hindi Reference Materials

Grammars and Language Courses

Central Hindi Directorate, Ministry of Education and Social Welfare, Government of India. *A Basic Grammar of Modern Hindi* (*Spoken and Written*), 3rd edition. New Delhi. 1975.

Fairbanks, Gordon H. and Bal Govind Misra. *Spoken and Written Hindi*. Ithaca. Cornell University Press. 1966.

———and P.B. Pandit. *Hindi: A Spoken Approach*. Poona. Deccan College, 1965.

Gambhir, Surendra K. *Spoken Hindi-Urdu*. Madison. University of Wisconsin, Center for South Asian Studies. 1978.

Gumperz, John J. and June Rumery. *Conversational Hindi-Urdu.* Devanagari edition by Ripley Moore and S.M. Jaiswal. Delhi. Radhakrishna Prakashan. 1967. 2 volumes.

Hook, Peter Edwin. *Hindi Structures: Intermediate Level.* Michigan Papers on South and Southeast Asia. The University of Michigan. 1979.

Jagannathan, V.R. and Ujjal Singh Bahri. *Introductory Course in Spoken Hindi: A Microwave Approach to Language Teaching* (SIIL series in Indian languages and linguistics, no. 2). Chandigarh. Bahri Publications. 1973.

Kachru, Yamuna and Rajeshwari Pandharipande. *Intermediate Hindi.* Delhi. Motilal Banarsidass. 1983.

Kellogg, Samuel H. *A Grammar of the Hindī Language: in which are treated the High Hindī, Braj, and the Eastern Hindī of the Rāmāyaṇ of Tulsī Dās, also the colloquial dialects of Rājputānā, Kumāon, Avadh, Rīwā, Bhojpūr, Magadha, Maithila, etc., with copious philological notes.* With notes on pronunciation by T. Grahame Bailey. 1st Indian edition. New Delhi. Oriental Books Reprint Corp. 1972. (reprint of 1938 edition; original edition 1875).

Lal, Hazari. *Lal's New Exhaustive Hindi Grammar: comprehensive and clearly explained with meaningful examples.* Ajmer. Vijay Pustak Bhandar. 1963.

McGregor, Ronald Stuart. *Outline of Hindi Grammar (with Exercises).* Oxford. Oxford University Press. 1972. Revised edition 1975.

Pořízka, Vincenc. *Hindī Language Course.* Prague. Státní pedagogické nakladatelstvi. 1963. Revised edition 1972.

Scholberg, Henry C. *Concise Grammar of the Hindi Language.* 3rd edition. London. Oxford University Press, 1968. (reprint of 1955 edition).

Sharma, Deoki N. and James W. Stone. *Hindi, An Active Introduction.* Washington, D.C., Foreign Service Institute, Department of State. 1970.

Sharma, S.N. *Hindi Grammar and Translation.* 3rd edition. Lakhani Book Depot. Bombay. 1960.

Smith, R. Caldwell and S.C.R. Weightman. *Introductory Hindi Course.* Revised edition. Landour Language School, Mussoorie. 1979.

Southworth, Franklin C. *The Student's Hindi-Urdu Reference Manual.* Tucson. University of Arizona Press. 1971.

Srivastava, Murlidhar. *The Elements of Hindi Grammar.* Delhi. Motilal Banarsidass. 1969.

Van Olphen, H.H. *First-year Hindi Course.* Austin. University of Texas, Dept. of Oriental and African Languages and Literatures. 1985.

Readers

Chandola, Anoop. *A Systematic Translation of Hindi Urdu into English.* Tucson. University of Arizona Press. 1970.

Harris, Richard M. and Rama Nath Sharma. *A Basic Hindi Reader.* Ithaca. Cornell University Press. 1969.

Nilsson, Usha, tr. *Hindi Stories : A Dual Language Anthology (for Area and Advanced*

Language Students). Madison. University of Wisconsin, South Asia Language and Area Center. 1975.

———. *Intermediate Hindi*. Madison. University of Wisconsin, Indian Language and Area Center, 1967.

———. *Readings in Hindi Literature*. Madison. University of Wisconsin, Indian Language and Area Center. 1967. 2 volumes.

राष्ट्र भारती (Parts 1, 2, and 3). New Delhi· राष्ट्रीय शैक्षिक अनुसंधान प्रशिक्षण परिषद्. New Delhi. 1968.

Schomer, Karine and Usha Jain. *Second Year Hindi Reader*. Berkeley. University of California, Center for South and Southeast Asia Studies. 1983.

Vatuk, Ved Prakash and Norman Zide. *An Advanced Reader in Modern Hindi Poetry* (*for Foreign Students*). Delhi. Alankar Prakashan. 1976.

Zide, Norman, et. al. *A Premchand Reader*. Honolulu. East-West Center Press. 1965.

Dictionaries

Bahri, Hardev. *Learners' Hindi-English Dictionary* (शिक्षार्थी हिन्दी-अंग्रेजी शब्दकोश). Delhi Rajpal and Sons. 1981.

Bulcke, C., S. J. अंग्रेजी-हिन्दी कोश (*An English-Hindi Dictionary*). New Delhi. S. Chand. 1982.

Chaturvedi, Mahendra and Bholanath Tiwari. *A Practical Hindi-English Dictionary* (व्यावहारिक हिन्दी-अंग्रेजी कोश). 2nd edition. Delhi. National Publishing House. 1975.

Das, Shyamsundar (ed.) हिन्दी शब्दसागर. Varanasi. Nagari Pracarini Sabha. 1965-75. 11 volumes.

Mohan, Brij and Badrinath Kapoor (eds.). *Meenakshi Hindi-English Dictionary* (मीनाक्षी हिन्दी-अंग्रेजी कोश). Meerut and Delhi. Meenakshi Prakashan. 1980.

Pathak, R. C. (comp. and ed.). *Bhargava's Standard Illustrated Dictionary of the Hindi Language* (*Hindi-English Edition*). 5th revised and enlarged edition. Varanasi. Bhargava Book Depot. 1968.

———. *Bhargava's Standard Illustrated Dictionary of the Hindi Language* (*Anglo-Hindi Edition*). 12th revised and enlarged edition. Varanasi. Bhargava Book Depot. 1970.

Platts, John T. *A Dictionary of Urdū, Classical Hindī, and English*. Oxford. Oxford University Press. 1884.

Prasad, Kalika et. al. (eds.). बृहत् हिन्दी कोश. 3rd edition. Varanasi. Jñānamaṇḍal Limited 1965.

Tiwari, Bholanath (ed.). हिन्दी मुहावरा कोश. 3rd edition. Allahabad. Kitab Mahal. 1977.

Vira, Raghu. *A Comprehensive English-Hindi Dictionary of Govermnental and Educational Words and Phrases*. New Delhi. International Academy of Indian Culture. 1976.

Verma, S. K. and R. N. Sahai. *The Oxford Progressive English-Hindi Dictionary*. Delhi. Oxford University Press. 1977.

HINDI-ENGLISH GLOSSARY

The Hindi-English glossary given below contains, with certain exceptions, all lexical items introduced in the vocabulary sections of this primer. Not included are most proper nouns indicating persons and places, obvious English loan words, numbers over ten (11.2. and 11.3.), names of days of the week and months (19.7., 20.11., 21 5.), kinship terms other than those for immediate family members (27.2.), non-nominative forms of pronouns (8.4., 10.2., 11.1.), onomatopoetic expressions (28.4.), echo forms (25.6.), and special locutions in the honorific register of Hindi (29.4.).

Entries in the glossary for idioms and other multi-word constructions are listed according to the semantically most prominent component. Thus इसलिए 'therefore' is to be found in the entry for लिए and X पर / के ऊपर क्रोध करना 'to get angry with X' in that for क्रोध 'anger'.

अंग्रेज़ी	prop. f. English language; adj. English
अंडा	n.m. egg
अंत	n.m. end; अंत में adv. finally, in the end
अंतिम	adj. final
अंदर	adv. inside; X के अंदर post. inside X
अंधेरा	n.m. darkness
अकेला	adj. single, solitary
अकेले	adv. alone
अक़्ल	n.f. intelligence, intellect
अक्सर	adv. frequently
अगर	conj. if
अगरचे	conj. even though
अगला	adj. next, coming
अचानक	adv. suddenly, all of a sudden, unexpectedly
अच्छा	adj. good; interj. good, well
अजनबी	n.m. stranger
अत्यंत	adv. extremely, excessively
अथवा	conj. or
अद्भुत	adj. extraordinary

अधिक	adj. more, much, many; adv. much
अधिकतर	adv. mostly, generally
अधिकारी	n.m. authority, official
अध्यापक	n.m. teacher
अनजाने	adv. unknowingly, unwittingly
अनिवार्य	adj. compulsory
X के अनुकूल	post. in accordance with X
अनुगृहीत	adj. obliged, grateful
अनुचित	adj. improper
X का अनुभव करना/ होना	v.t./i. to experience X/ for X to be experienced
X के अनुसार	post. according to X
अनेक	adj. several
अन्य	adj. other
अपना	refl. poss. pron. one's own
अपने आप	adv. by oneself, of one's own accord
अपरिचित	adj. unknown, unfamiliar
X की अपेक्षा	post. in comparison with X
अफ़सोस	n.m. sorrow, grief, regret; X को अफ़सोस होना v.i. for X to regret
अब	adv. now; अब की बार adv. now, this time
अभी	adv. right away, immediately
अमरीकन	n.m. American
अमीर	adj. rich
अर्थात्	conj. that is to say
अलग	adj. separate, distinct
अलमारी	n.f. almirah
X के अलावा	post. besides X, in addition to X
अवश्य	adv. certainly
अवसर	n.m. opportunity, occasion
असल में	adv. in fact
अस्पताल	n.m. hospital
आँख	n.f. eye
आँगन	n.m. courtyard
आँसू	n.f. tear
आकाश	n.m. sky
X पर आक्रमण करना	v.t. to attack X

आख़िर	adv. finally, at last
आग	n.f. fire
आग लगाना	v.t. to ignite
आगे	adv. straight ahead, forward; X के आगे post. ahead of X
आज	adv. today
आजकल	adv. nowadays
आज़ाद	adj. independent, free
आज़ादी	n.f. independence, freedom
आटा	n.n. whole wheat flour
X की आदत डालना	v.t. to form the habit of X
आदमी	n.m. man, person
आदर	n.m. respect, honor; X को आदर देना v.t. to show/give respect to X
आदि	partl. et cetera
आधा	adj. half
आधी रात	n.f. midnight
आधुनिक	adj. modern
आनंद	n.m. bliss, contentment, pleasure
आना	v.i. to come
आप	2.pl.hon. personal pron.; आप (ही) adv. alone, by oneself; आप की आप adv. by oneself, to oneself; आप से आप adv. by oneself, of one's own accord
आपस में	adv. among themselves
आपसी	adj. mutual, reciprocal
आपा	n.f. self
आबादी	n.m. population, populace
आभारी	adj. grateful, obliged
आम	n.m. mango
आम	adj. ordinary; आम तौर पर adv. generally, usually
आमने-सामने	adv. in front, directly opposite
आया	n.f. nursemaid
आरंभ करना/होना	v.t./i. to begin, start
आराम से	adv. comfortably
आलू	n.m. potato
आवश्यकता	n.f. necessity; X को Y की आवश्यकता होना v.i. for X to need or require Y
आवाज़	n.f. voice, sound, noise
आशा	n.f. hope; आशा करना v.t. to hope; X को आशा होना v.i. for X to hope

आश्चर्य n.m. surprise, astonishment; X को आश्चर्य होना v.i. for X to be surprised
आसपास adv. nearby; X के आसपास post. surrounding X
आसानी से adv. easily
आह interj. used in expressing surprise
आहिस्ता adv. slowly, gently

इंतज़ाम n.m. arrangement, preparation; X का इंतज़ाम करना/होना v.t./i. to arrange for X/for X to be arranged
इंतज़ार n.m. waiting, expectation; X का इंतज़ार करना/होना v.t./i. to wait for X/for X to be waited for
इकट्ठा adj. frequently indecl. gathered, collected; इकट्ठा करना/होना v.t./i. to gather together/to be gathered together
इच्छा n.f. wish, desire; X की इच्छा करना v.t. to desire, wish for X
इतना adj. this much/ many; इतना-सा adj. just so much, just a little bit
इतिहास n.m. history
इधर adv. in this direction, hither; इधर-उधर adv. here and there, everywhere
इमारत n.f. building
इरादा n.m. intention
X का इस्तेमाल करना/होना v.t./i. to use X/for X to be used

ईद prop. f. Id (a Muslim festival)
ईदगाह n.m. a place of assembly for offering Id prayers
ईसाई n.m. Christian

उँगली n.f. finger
उगना v.i. to grow
उगाना v.t. to grow
उचित adj. proper, correct
उठना v.i. to rise, get up, wake up
उठवाना v.t. to cause to rise, get up, wake up
उठाना v t. to lift up
उड़ना v.i. to fly
उतना adj. that much, that many
उतरना v.i. to descend, come down

उतारना	v.t. to bring down, take down
उत्तर	n.m. answer, reply; X को उत्तर देना v.t. to reply to X
उत्तर	n.m. north; X के उत्तर post. to the north of X
उत्सव	n.m. festival, celebration
उदास	adj. sad
उद्देश्य	n.m. purpose, aim, intention
उधर	adv. in that direction, thither
उपन्यास	n.m. novel
उपयोगी	adj. useful
उबलना	v.i. to boil
उबालना	v.t. to boil
उम्र	n.f. age
उर्दू	prop. f. Urdu language
उलटना	v.t./i. to overturn/to be overturned
ऊँचा	adj. high, tall
ऊन	n.f. wool
ऊपर	adj. above; X के ऊपर post. on top of X, above X
ऊबना	v.i. to be bored
एक-एक करके	adv. one by one
एक-सा	adj. the same, identical
एकता	n.f. unity, solidarity
एकाएक	adv. at once, suddenly, totally
एकदम	adv. all of a sudden, suddenly
ऐसा	adj. this kind of, of this sort
ऐसे	adv. in this manner, thus
ओढ़ना	v.t. to cover (the body), to wrap
ओर	n.f. direction; X की ओर post. in the direction of X, towards X; X की ओर से post. from X, from the direction of X
ओह	interj. used in addressing or invoking someone
ओहो	interj. used in expressing surprise
औटना	v.i. to boil
औटवाना	v.t. to have someone boil
औटाना	v.t. to boil

ग्रौर	conj. and adj. additional; ग्रौर भी adj. in addition, additional, even more
ग्रौरत	n.f. woman
कई	pron. and adj. several
कक्षा	n.f. grade, class
कच्चा	adj. unripe, shoddy, unsubstantial, made of clay or mud, raw
कटना	v.i. to be cut, for time to elapse or be spent
कटवाना	v.t. to cause to cut, to have cut
कठिन	adj. difficult
कनिष्ठ	adj. youngest
कन्या	n.f. daughter
कपड़ा	n.m. cloth, material; कपड़े n.m.pl. clothes
कब	inter. when?
कभी	adv. at some time (or other)
कम	adj. few, little; adv. on few occasions, seldom; कम करना/होना v.t./i. to make less/to diminish, become less; कम-से-कम adv. at least
कमज़ोर	adj weak
कमरा	n.m. room
कमाना	v.t. to earn
कमीज़	n.f. shirt
कर	n.m. tax, taxes; कर लगना/लगाना v.i./t. for taxes to be levied/to levy taxes
करना	v.t. to do
करवाना	v.t. to cause to do
कराना	v.t. to cause to do
क़रीब	adj. approximately
कर्त्तव्य	n.m. duty
कल	adv. yesterday; tomorrow
क़लम	n.f. pen
कला	n.f. art
कवि	n.m. poet
कविता	n.f. poem
कष्ट	n.m. inconvenience, bother; X को कष्ट देना v.t. to bother X, to inconvenience X
कहना	v.t. to say
कहलाना	v.i. to be called, to be referred to as

कहाँ inter. where; कहां से inter. from where?, whence?
कहानी n.f. story, tale
कहीं adv somewhere (or other); कहीं...न conj. lest
कांपना v.i. to tremble, shake
का poss. post. (7.3.)
काग़ज़ n.m. paper
काटना v.t. to cut, to spend time
कान n.m. ear
काफ़ी adj. enough, sufficient, adequate; adv. quite
कॉफ़ी n.f. coffee
काम n.m. work, task; काम करना v.t. to work; काम का adj. useful; X को काम होना v.i. for X to have work to do
कार n.f. car, automobile
कारख़ाना n.m. factory
कारण n.m. reason; इस कारण conj. therefore; X के कारण post. because of X, on account of X
कार्य n.m. work, deed, action
कार्यकर्ता n.m. worker
काला adj. black
कालेज n.m. college
काश कि... conj. would that...
किंतु conj. but
कि conj. that, when, or, if
कितना inter. how much?, how many?; कितनी बार inter. how often?, how many times?; कितने में inter. for how much?; कितने बजे inter. when?, at what time?
किताब n.f. book
किधर inter. in which direction?, whither?; किधर से inter. from which direction?
किनारा n.m. edge, border, bank; X के किनारे (पर) post. on the banks of X by the side of X
किसान n.m. farmer
कुआँ n.m. well
कुछ pron. and adj. some, a few, an amount of; adv. somewhat, a little, a bit; कुछ-न-कुछ pron. and adj. something or other
कुत्ता n.m. dog
कुमारी n.f. Miss

कुरता n.m. kurta (a kind of loose fitting upper garment)
कुरसी n.f. chair
कुल adv. all in all, in sum, in toto; कुल मिलाकर adv. all in all, in sum, in toto
कूदना v.i. to jump
कृपया adv. please, kindly
कृपा n.f. favor, kindness; कृपा करके adv. please, kindly; X की कृपा करना v.t. to be so kind as to do X
केला n.m. banana
केवल adv. only, just
कैसा inter. what kind of
कैसे inter. how?, in what manner?
को post. see 8.3.
कोई pron. and adj. someone, something; कोई-न-कोई someone (or other), something (or other)
कोठी n.f. cottage, bungalow, detached house
कौआ n.m. crow
कौन inter. who?; कौन-सा inter. which (of a number of alternatives)?
क्या inter. what?; marker of yes/no question; interj. used in expressing surprise; क्या X. . .क्या Y conj. whether X or Y
क्यों inter. why?; क्यों न see 29.5.
क्योंकि conj. because
क्रोध n.m. anger; X को Y पर/के ऊपर क्रोध आना v.i. for X to be angry with Y; X पर/के ऊपर क्रोध करना v.t. to get angry with X
क्षण n.m. moment, instant
क्षेत्र n.m. field

खड़ा adj. standing
ख़त्म adj. completed, finished; ख़त्म करना/होना v.t./i. to complete/to be completed
ख़बर n.f. news, information; X को Y की ख़बर मिलना v.i. for X to be informed of Y
ख़याल n.m. opinion, meaning
ख़राब adj. bad, spoiled
ख़रीदना v.t. to buy
ख़र्च n.m. expenditure; X का ख़र्च करना/होना v.t./i. to spend X/for X to be spent
खाँसना v.i. to cough

खादी	n.f. home-spun cloth
खाना	n.m. food; v.t. to eat
ख़ामोश	adj. silent
ख़ाली	adj. empty, free (time)
ख़ास	adj. special; ख़ास कर adv. especially; ख़ास तौर पर adv. especially
खिड़की	n.f. window
खिलना	v.i. to bloom
खिलवाना	v.t. to cause to feed
खिलाना	v.t. to feed, to give to eat, to cause to bloom
खिलौना	n.m. toy
ख़ुद (ही)	adv. by oneself, of one's own accord
ख़ुदा	n.m. God; ख़ुदा जाने ... God knows (who/where/what/why etc...)
खुलना	v.i. to open
खुलवाना	v.t. to have someone open
खुला	adj. open
ख़ुश	adj. happy, pleased
ख़ुशी	n.f. happiness, pleasure; ख़ुशी मनाना v.t. to celebrate, rejoice; X को ख़ुशी होना v.i. for X to be glad, happy
ख़ूबसूरत	adj. beautiful
खेत	n.m. field
खेलना	v.i. to play
ख़ैर	interj. all right, well
खोदना	v.t. to dig
खोलना	v.t. to open
गंगा	prop. f. the river Ganges
गंदा	adj. dirty
गधा	n.m. ass, donkey
गरम	adj. hot, warm
गरमी	n.f. heat, warmth; गरमियां n.f.pl. summer, hot season; X को गरमी लगना v.i. to X to feel hot, warm
ग़रीब	adj. poor
ग़रीबी	n.f. poverty
ग़लत	adj. wrong, incorrect
ग़लती	n.f. mistake, error
गला	n.m. throat
गली	n.f. narrow street, lane

गले मिलना	v.i. to embrace, hug
गहरा	adj. deep, dark, profound
गाँव	n.m. village
गाड़ी	n.f. cart, train, vehicle
गाना	n.m. song; v.t. to sing
गाय	n.f. cow
गाली	n.f. curse, abuse; X को गाली (गालियां) देना v.t. to curse, abuse X
गाहक	n.m. customer
गिरना	v.i. to fall
गिरवाना	v.i. to have something felled
गिराना	v.t. to fell
गिलास	n.m. glass (for drinking)
गीदड़	n.m. jackal
गीला	adj. wet, moist
गुजराती	prop. f. the Gujarati language
गुणा करना	v.t. to multiply
गुरु	n.m. guru, spiritual master, teacher
ग़ुलाबी	adj. rose colored, pink
ग़ुलाम	n.m. slave
ग़ुस्सा	n.m. anger, rage
गेहूँ	n.m. wheat
गोल	adj. round
घंटा	n.m. hour
X से घटकर	post. inferior to X, less than X
घटना	n.f. incident, event
घड़ी	n.f. watch, clock
घनघोर	adj. thick, dense
घबराना	v.i. to be bothered, to be vexed
घर	n.m. house, home
घास	n.f. grass
घिरना	v.i. to be surrounded
घिरवाना	v.t. to cause to surround
घी	n.m. clarified butter
घुमवाना	v.t. to cause to turn, rotate, revolve
घमाना	v.t. to turn, rotate
घुसना	v.i. to enter

घूमना v.i. to wander, meander, stroll; v.i. घूमना-फिरना to wander, meander, stroll

घेरना v.t. to surround

चक्कर n.m. dizziness; X को चक्कर आना v.i. for X to become dizzy

चटनी n.f. chutney

चढ़ना v.i. to rise, ascend, climb up

चढ़ाना v.t. to raise, elevate, to give as an offering, to place on a fire for cooking

चपरासी n.m. peon

चपाती n.f. chapati (a kind of thin fried bread made from whole wheat flour)

चप्पल n.f. sandal

चमकना v.i. glitter, sparkle

चलना v.i. to go, move, progress; चल बसना v.i. to die; चला आना v.i. to depart, set off (toward speaker); चला जाना v.i. to go, depart, set off (away from speaker)

चलाना v.t. to drive, cause to move, set in motion

चश्मा n.m. (pair of) eye glasses

चाँद n.m. moon

चाँदी n.f. silver

चाक़ू n.m. penknife

चाय n.f. tea

चारपाई n.f. charpai (a kind of bed made of rope and having a wooden frame)

चावल n.m. (often pl.) rice

चाह n.f. wish

चाहना v.t. to want, wish

चाहे conj. regardless of the fact that...; चाहे X ... चाहे Y conj. whether X or Y

चिड़िया n.f. bird

चिड़ियाघर n.m. zoo

चिल्लाना v.i. scream, yell

चीज़ n.f. thing

चीनी n.f. sugar

चुप adj. silent; चुप करना/होना v.t./i. to make quiet, to silence/to become silent

चुपचाप adv. silently, stealthily
चूँकि conj. because
चूड़ी n.f. bangle
चूना v.i. to leak, ooze
चूल्हा n.m. stove, hearth
चेहरा n.m. face, countenance, appearance; चेहरे से adv. in appearance
चोट n.f. injury, blow; X को चोट लगना v.i. for X to get injured
चोर n.m. thief
चोरी n.f. theft
चौक n.m. market, marketplace; crossing
चौड़ा adj. wide

छत n.f. roof; ceiling
छात्र n.m. student
छात्रा n.f. student (female)
छात्रवृत्ति n.f. scholarship
छाना v.i. to spread
छिपना v.i. to hide, to be hidden
छि: interj. used in expressing disgust
छींकना v.t. to sneeze
छुट्टी (छुटटियाँ) n.f. leave, vacation, break, holiday
छुड़वाना v.t. to cause to set free
छुड़ाना v.t. to cause to set free
छुपना v.i. to hide, to be hidden
छूटना v.i. to be free, to leave, to be left behind
छूना v.t. to touch
छोटा adj. small, young, younger
छोड़ना v.t. to give up, renounce, abandon, forsake; X को छोड़ कर post. except for X

जंगल n.m. woods, forest, jungle
जंगली adj. wild
जगवाना v.t. to cause to wake up
जगह n.f. place
जगाना v.t. to wake someone up
जनता n.f. populace, the people
जब rel. adv. when

जमना	v.i. to congeal; freeze; take root
जमा	adj. indecl. collected, assembled; जमा करना/होना v.t./i. to gather, collect/to come together, to be gathered, collected.
ज़मीन	n.f. ground, land
ज़मीनदार	n.m. landlord, landholder
जय	n.f. victory; X की जय हो! victory to X!
ज़रा	adj. indecl. a little, a bit. Also see 29.5.
ज़रूर	adv. certainly
ज़रूरत	n.f. necessity; X को Y की ज़रूरत होना v.i. for X to need or require Y
ज़रूरी	adj. important, necessary
जलना	v.i. to burn, be ignited, be jealous
जलाना	v.t. to burn, ignite
जल्दी	adv. early, quickly, swiftly; जल्दी करना v.t. to hurry; X को जल्दी होना v.i. for X to be in a hurry
जवाब	n.m. answer, reply
जहाँ	rel. adv. where
जागना	v.i. to wake up, arise
जाड़ा	n.m. cold, winter
जान	n.f. life, animation
जानना	v.t. to know
जानवर	n.m. animal
जाना	v.i. to go
जाल	n.m. net
ज़िंदगी	n.f. life
ज़िंदा	adj. indecl. alive
जितना	rel. adj. as much, as many
जिधर	rel. adv. in which direction, whither
ज़िम्मेदारी	n.f. responsibility
जिससे (कि)	conj. so that
जी	honorific marker; n.m. heart, mind, soul, will; X में Y का जी लगना v.i. for X to be happy, contented in X
जीतना	v.i. to be victorious, to win
जीना	v.i. to live, exist
जीवन	n.m. life, existence
ज़ुकाम	n.m. cold
जुड़ना	v.i. to be linked, connected, conjoined
जूता	n.m. shoe

जैसा rel. adj. of which kind
जैसे rel. adv. in which manner, as; conj. as if; X के जैसे post. like X, in the manner of; जैसे ही ... वैसे ही as soon as...then
जो rel. pron. who, that, which
जोड़ना v.t. to unite, connect
जोश n.m. enthusiasm
ज़्यादा adj. much, more, many, too much, too many; adv. excessively
ज़्यादातर adv. mostly, generally
ज्येष्ठ adj. eldest
ज्यों ही...त्यों ही as soon as...then

झगड़ना v.i. to quarrel, fight
झूठ n.m. lie, falsehood
झोंपड़ी n.f. hut, small cottage

टंगना v.i. to hang
टांग n.f. leg
टांगना v.t. to hang
टिकट n.m. postage stamp, ticket
टूटना v.i. to break
टेढ़ा adj. crooked, bent

ठंड n.f. cold; X को ठंड लगना v.i. for X to feel cold
ठंडा adj. cold
ठहरना v.i. to wait, stay
ठीक adj. correct, right; ठीक-ठाक adj. fine, well

डर n.m. fear; X को डर लगना v.i. for X to be/feel afraid
डरना v.i. to fear, be afraid
डालना v.t. to put in, place, insert, pour
डूबना v.i. to sink, drown
डेढ़ adj. one and a half

ढाई adj. two and a half
ढूँढ़ना v.t. to look for, search for

तम्बाकू n.m. tobacco
तक post. until, as far as

तथा	conj. and
तब	adv. then, at that time
तबीयत	n.f. disposition, condition, state of health
तभी	adv. just then
तमाशा	n.m. spectacle, big event
तरफ़	n.f. direction; किस तरफ़ inter. in which direction?; X की तरफ़ post. towards X; X के चारों तरफ़ post. all around X, surrounding X
तरस	n.m. compassion, pity; X को Y पर तरस आना v.i. for X to feel compassion for Y
तरह	n.f. manner, way, kind, sort; किस तरह inter. in what manner?, how?; किस तरह का inter. of what kind?; किसी तरह adv. somehow (or other); X की तरह post. like X, in the manner of X
X की तलाश करना/होना	v.t./i. to look for, search for X/ for X to be looked for
तशरीफ़ रखना	v.t. to sit down
तशरीफ़ लाना	v.i. come in, enter
तस्वीर	n.f. picture; तस्वीर खींचना v.t. to take/draw a picture
ताँबा	n.m. copper
ताकि	conj. so that
ताज़ा	adj. fresh
ताज महल	prop. m. the Taj Mahal
तार	n.m. wire, telegram; तार देना v.t. to wire, to send a telegram
तारा	n.m. star
तारीख़	n.m. date
तारीफ़	n.f. praise
तालाब	n.m. tank, pond
तीसरा	adj. third
तुड़वाना	v.t. to cause to break
तुड़ाना	v.t. to cause to break
तुम	2.pl.fam. personal pron.
तुरंत	adv. immediately
तुलना	n.f. comparison; X की तुलना में post. in comparison to X
तू	2.s.int. personal pron.
तेज़	adj. quick, swift, sharp; adv. quickly, swiftly
तेज़ी	n.f. swiftness, sharpness; तेज़ी से adv. quickly
तैयार	adj. ready, prepared

तैयारी — n.f. preparation; X की तैयारी करना/होना v.t./i. to prepare X, to prepare for X/ preparation for X to take place
तरना — v.i. to float, swim
तैरवाना — v.t. to cause to swim
तैराना — v.t. to make swim
तो भी — conj. still, nevertheless
तोड़ना — v.t. to break
त्योहार — n.m. holiday, festival

थकना — v.i. to become tired
थप्पड़ — n.m. slap; थप्पड़ देना v.t. to slap
थाली — n.f. plate, platter
थू — interj. used in expressing disgust
थैला — n.m. bag, sack
थोड़ा — adj. a little, some; थोड़ा-बहुत adj. some, a little; adv. somewhat
थोड़े — adv. seldom, hardly

दक्षिण — n.m. south; X के दक्षिण post. to the south of X
दफ़्तर — n.m. office
दबना — v.i. to be pressed down; to be subdued
दबाना — v.t. to depress, to press down; to subdue
दरवाज़ा — n.m. door
दर्द — n.m. pain
दर्शन — n.m. sight; presence; philosophy; X का दर्शन पाना v.t. to behold X, to catch a glimpse of X
दही — n.m. curds, yoghurt
दहेज — n.m. dowry
दाम — n.m. price, cost
दाल — n.f. lentils
दावत — n.f. party, feast
दाहिना — adj. right; X की दाहिनी तरफ़/ओर post. to the right side of X
दाहिने — adv. to the right; X के दाहिने हाथ पर post. to the right side of X
दिक़्क़त — n.f. difficulty, trouble
दिखना — v.i. to seem, appear
दिखाई देना — v.i. to be seen, appear
दिखाई पड़ना — v.i. to be seen, appear
दिखलाना — v.t. to show, exhibit, display

दिखवाना v.t. to cause to show
दिखाना v.t. to show
दिन n.m. day; दिन-भर adv. all day
दिनांक n.m. date, day
दिमाग़ n.m. brain; intelligence
दिल n.m. heart; X और Y के दिल मिलना v.i. for X and Y to be in agreement, for X and Y to be sympathetic to each other; X में Y का दिल लगना v.i. for Y to be happy/contented in X; दिल लगाकर adv. intently, diligently, from the depths of one's heart
दिलचस्प adj. interesting
दिलचस्पी n.f. interest, curiosity; X को दिलचस्पी होना v.i. for X to be interested in something
दिलवाना v.t. to cause to give
दिलाना v.t. to cause to give
दीखना (=दिखना) v.i. to seem, appear
दीप n.m. earthen lamp
दीवाली prop. f. Hindu festival of Diwali (= Dipavali)
दुकान n.f. store, shop
दुकानदार n.m. shopkeeper
दुगुना adj. twice as much
दुबला-पतला adj. thin, skinny
दुहराना v.t. to repeat
दुःख n.m. grief, sadness; X को दुःख होना v.i. for X to be sad, unhappy
दूध n.m. milk
दूर adj. distant, far; adv. far away; X से दूर post. far from X
दूसरा adj. second, another
दृष्टि n.f. view, vision, sight, perspective
देखना v.t. to see, look; देख लेना v.t. to take a look
देखभाल n.f. care, custody, supervision; X की देखभाल करना v.t. to look after, supervise X
देख-रेख n.f. supervision, care; X की देख-रेख करना/होना v.t./i. to supervise, care for X/ for X to be supervised, cared for
देना v.t. to give
देर n.f. delay, interval of time; देर से adv. late; X को देर होना v.i. for X to be late, for X to be delayed
देवता n.m. II god
देश n.m. country, nation

देशी adj. native, indigenous, local
देहांत n.m. death
देहात n.m. countryside
दोनों pron. adj. both
दोपहर n.f. noon, afternoon; दोपहर को adv. at noon, in the afternoon
दोस्त n.m. friend
दोस्ती n.f. friendship
दौड़ना v.i. to run
X के दौरान post. during X
X के द्वारा post. by, through, through the agency of X

धकेलना v.t. to push
धन्यवाद expression of gratitude
धरती n.f. earth, land
धर्म n.m. dharma, righteousness, religion
धीरे adv. slowly
धूप n.f. sunlight, heat of sun
धोती n.f. dhoti (a cloth garment worn wrapped around the waist and covering the bottom half of the body)
धोना v.t. to wash, clean
धोबी n.m. washerman
ध्यान n.m. concentration, attention, care; ध्यान से adv. carefully, attentively

नंगा adj. naked
न adv. negative marker; न ... न conj. neither ... nor; न जाने ... who knows (what, why, where, etc.)...
नक़ल करना v.t. to copy
नक़ली adj. imitation, fake
नगर n.m. city
नज़दीक adj. nearby; X के नजदीक post. near to X
X को Y नज़र आना v.i. for Y to come into X's sight, for X to see Y
नदी n.f. river
नन्हा adj. tiny, small
नमक n.m. salt
नमकीन n.f. salty snack
नमस्कार expression of greeting
नमस्ते expression of greeting

नमाज़ n.f. prayer (of Muslims); नमाज़ पढ़ना v.t. (for Muslims) to pray
नया adj. new
नहलाना v.t. to bathe (someone else)
नहाना v.i. to bathe (oneself)
नही adv. negative marker; नहीं तो conj otherwise
नाई n.m. barber
नाक n.f. nose
नाचना v.i. to dance
नाम n.m. name
नापसंद adj. displeasing, disliked
नाव n.f. boat, ferry
नाश्ता n.m. snack, breakfast
निकलना v.i. to come out (of something), to emerge
निकलवाना v.t. to have someone remove
निकालना v.t. to remove, take out, to bring out
नित्य adv. always, eternally
निमंत्रण n.m. invitation
नियम n.m. rule, principle, law
निरंतर adv. continuously
निवासी n.m. resident
निश्चय n.m. decision; X का निश्चय करना/होना v.t./i. to decide X/ for X to be decided
निश्चित adj. definite
नींद n.f. sleep, sleepiness; X को नींद आना v.i. for X to feel sleepy
नीचा adj. low
नीचे adv. below; X के नीचे post. below X
नीला adj. blue
नेता n.m. II leader
नौकर n.m. servant
नौकरानी n.f. female servant
नौजवान n.m. young man, youth

पंजाबी prop. f. the Panjabi language; adj. Panjabi
पंडित n.m. pandit
पकड़ना v.t. to grasp, catch, seize
पकना v.i. to be cooked, to cook
पकवाना v.t. to cause to cook

पका adj. ripe
पकाना v.t. to cook
पकौड़ा n.m. pakora (a kind of vegetable fritter)
पक्का adj. substantial; built of brick (as opposed to mud); solid
पक्ष n.m. side, flank; faction
पड़ना v.i. to fall, lie
पड़ा adj. lying
पड़ोस n.m. neighborhood
पड़ोसी n.m. neighbor
पढ़ना v.t. to study, read
पढ़वाना v.t. to cause to be read
पढ़ाई n.f. education
पढ़ाना v.t. to teach, instruct
पतला adj. thin, lean
पता n.m. information; address; knowledge; X को पता चलना कि ... v.i. for X to find out, learn that...; X को Y पता होना v.i. for X to know Y (where Y is information of some kind)
पति n.m. husband, lord
पत्थर n.m. rock, stone
पत्नी n.f. wife
पत्र n.m. letter
पधारना v.i. to come, arrive, enter, go
पपीता n.m. papaya
पर post. on, at, by
पर conj. but
परंतु conj. but
परसों adv. the day after tomorrow; the day before yesterday
परस्पर adj. mutual, reciprocal
परिचय n.m. familiarity, acquaintance; X को Y का परिचय देना v.t. to introduce Y to X
परिचित adj. familiar
परिवर्तन n.m. change, transformation, development
परिवार n.m. family
परिश्रम n.m. hard work, labor
परिश्रमी adj. hard working, industrious
परीक्षा n.f. examination, test
पुरुष n.m. person, man

परे	adv. away; X से परे post. beyond X
पवित्र	adj. holy, sacred
X के पश्चात्	post. after X
पश्चिम	n.m. west; X के पश्चिम post. to the west of X
X को Y पसंद आना/होना	v.i. for X to like Y
पहचानना	v.t. to recognize
पहनना	v.t. to put on, wear
पहर	n.f. an interval of three hours
पहला	adj. first
पहले	adv. before, earlier, previously; X के/से पहले post. before X
पहाड़	n.m. mountain, mountain range
पहाड़ी	n.f. hill
पहुँचना	v.i. to reach, arrive
पहुँचाना	v.t. convey, transmit, carry
पागल	adj. crazy, mad
पागलपन	n.m. madness
पाठ	n.m. chapter, lesson
पाठशाला	n.f. elementary school, grade school
पाना	v.t. to find
पानी	n.m. water
पाप	n.m. sin
X के पार	post. on the other side of X, across X
पार करना	v.t. to cross (over)
पालना	v.t. to protect, keep, raise
पाव	n.m. one fourth, quarter; unit of weight equal to one fourth of a ser
X के पास	post. near X, in X's possession
पिघलना	v.i. to melt
पिछला	adj. last, previous
पिता	n.m. II. father
पिलवाना	v.t. to cause to drink or smoke
पिलाना	v.t. to give to drink
पिसना	v.i. to be ground
पिसवाना	v.t. to have someone grind
पीछे	adv. behind; X के पीछे behind X
पीटना	v.t. to beat

पीठ n.f. back
पीतल n.m. brass
पीना v.t. to drink, smoke
पीपल n.m. pipal tree
पीला adj. yellow
पीसना v.t. to grind
पीहर n.m. wife's family, wife's family home
पुकारना v.t. to call, cry out
पुत्र n.m. son
पुत्री n.f. daughter
पुराना adj. old (of things)
पुलिस n.f. police
पुस्तक n.f. book
पूछताछ n.f. inquiry; पूछताछ करना v.t. to inquire
पूछना v.t. to ask
पूजा n.f. prayer (of Hindus); पूजा करना v.t. to pray (of Hindus)
पूजाघर n.m. place for doing puja, place of worship
पूरा adj. complete; पूरा करना/होना v.t./i. to complete/to be completed
पूरी n.f. puri (a kind of bread made of whole wheat flour and fried in hot oil)
पूर्णिमा n.f. day of the full moon
पूर्व n.m. east; X के पूर्व post. to the east of X;
पूर्व adv. previously
X-पूर्वक suffix. replete with X, filled with X
पेट n.m. stomach
पेड़ n.m. tree
पेन्सिल n.f. pencil
पेश करना v.t. to request, present, offer
पैदल adv. on foot
पैदा adj. indecl. born, produced, grown; पैदा करना/होना v.t./i. to give birth, produce/to be born, to be produced, to be grown
पैर n.m. foot; X में पैर रखना v.t. to set foot in X
पैसा n.m. money, paisa (= 1/100 of a rupee); पैसे n.m.pl. money
पोशाक n.f. clothes, attire
पौधा n.m. a small plant, seedling
पौन/पौना adj. three quarters
प्याज़ n.m. onion

प्यार	n.m. love; X को प्यार करना v.t. to love X
प्यास	n.f. thirst; X को प्यास लगना v.i. for X to be thirsty
प्यासा	adj. thirsty
प्रकार	n.m. kind, sort, variety, manner; किस प्रकार का inter. of what kind?
प्रकाशित	adj. published; प्रकाशित करना/होना v.t./i. to publish/to be published
X के प्रति	post. towards X, with regard to X, as concerns X
प्रति दिन	adv. every day
X की प्रतीक्षा करना/होना	v.t./i. to wait for X/ for X to be waited for
X को प्रतीत होना	v.i. to seem, appear to X
प्रदेश	n.m. state, province
प्रधान मंत्री	n.m. Prime Minister
प्रबंध	n.m. arrangement; X का प्रबन्ध करना / होना v.t./i. to arrange for X/ for X to be arranged
प्रभाव	n.m. influence
प्रयोग	n.m. use, employment; X का प्रयोग करना/ होना v.t./i. to use, employ X/ for X to be used, employed
प्रशंसा	n.f. praise; X की प्रशंसा करना/होना v.t./i. to praise X/ for X to be praised
प्रश्न	n.m. question; X से प्रश्न पूछना v.t. to ask a question of X, to inquire of X
प्रसन्न	adj. happy
प्रसन्नता	n.f. happiness, pleasure; X को प्रसन्नता होना v.i. for X to be happy, for X to be pleased
प्रसिद्ध	adj. famous
प्रस्तुत	adj. submitted, presented
प्रातःकाल	n.m. and adv. early morning
प्राप्त करना/होना	v.t./i. to receive/to be received
प्रायः	adv. usually, generally
प्रिय	adj. dear, beloved
प्रेम	n.m. love
प्रेमिका	n.f. lover
प्रेमी	n.m. lover
फंसाना	v.t. to cause to become entrapped
फटना	v.i. to burst, tear, rip, split
फ़रमाना	v.t. to speak, say, talk

फ़र्श	n.m. floor, ground
फल	n.m. fruit
फलवाला	n.m. fruit seller
फाड़ना	v.t. to tear, rip, split
फ़ायदा	n.m. benefit; X का फ़ायदा उठाना v.t. to take advantage of X
फिर	adv. again, then; फिर भी conj. nevertheless, still
फिरना	v.i. to turn, revolve, wander
फीका	adj. tasteless, vapid
फड़वाना	v.t. to cause to break, split open
फूटना	v.i. to crack, shatter, split, burst
फूल	n.m. flower; फूल चढ़ाना v.t. to make an offering of flowers (usually as part of a religious rite)
फेंकना	v.t. to throw, throw away, hurl
फैलना	v.i. to spread
फैलाना	v.t. to spread out
फ़ैसला	n.m. decision
फोड़ना	v.t. to break, split open, burst
बंगाली	prop. f. the Bengali language; adj. Bengali
बंद	adj. closed; बंद करना/होना v.t./i. to close/to be closed
बंधना	v.i. to be tied, to be fastened
बग़ीचा	n.m. garden
X के बिना	post. without X
बचना	v.i. to escape; be left over; survive; accumulate
बचपन	n.m. childhood
बचाना	v.t. to save, protect; collect; rescue
बच्चा	n.m. child
बच्ची	n.f. child (female)
बजना	v.i. to sound, (for the hour) to strike, to emit a sound
बजाना	v.t. to play (a musical instrument), to make sound
X के बजाय	post. instead of X
बटा	over, divided by
बड़ा	adj. large, great, older; adv. very
बढ़ई	n.m. carpenter
बढ़ना	v.i. to advance, increase; X से बढ़कर post. better than X, superior to X

बढ़िया	adj. indecl. good, fine, nice
बताना	v.t. to tell
बत्ती	n.f. lamp
बदन	n.m. body
बदमाश	n.m. hooligan
बदमाशी	n.f. hooliganism
बदलना	v.t./i. to change (something)/to change
X के बदले	post. in place of X, in exchange for X
बधाई	n.f. greetings
बनना	v.i. to be or get made
बनवाना	v.t. to cause to make
बनाना	v.t. to make
बनारसी	adj. from Benaras (= Varanasi)
बनियान	n.f. undershirt, vest
बरतन	n.m. cooking utensil
बरबाद	adj. ruined, destroyed; बरबाद करना/होना v.t./i. to ruin, destroy/to be ruined, destroyed
बरसना	v.i. to rain, shower
बरसात	n.f. rainy season
बराबर	adj. equal; adv. regularly; X के बराबर post. equal to X, the same as X
बर्फ़	n.f. snow, ice; बर्फ़ गिरना v.i. to snow
बलवान	adj. strong
बसना	v.i. to be located, settled, situated
बस्ती	n.f. colony, residential community
बहन (बहिन)	n.f. sister
बहाना	n.m. excuse, pretext; X के बहाने post. on the pretext of X
बहुत	adv. very; बहुत-सा adj. many, quite a few, much, a lot of
बहू	n.f. daughter-in-law
बांधना	v.t. to tie, fasten
बांसुरी	n.f. flute
बांह	n.f. arm
बाक़ी	adj. remaining
बाज़ार	n.m. marketplace, bazaar
बाज़ी	n.f. wager, bet; बाज़ी लगना v.i. for a bet to be wagered; बाज़ी लगाना v.t. to wager a bet

बाढ़	n.f. flood
बात	n.f. matter, discussion; X से बात करना v.t. to converse with X; X की Y से बात (बातें) होना v.i. for X to converse with Y
X के बाद	post. after X
बाद में	adv. afterwards
बादल	n.m. cloud
बादशाह	n.m. emperor, king
बाध्य	adj. compelled, obligated; बाध्य करना/होना v.t./i. to compel/ to be compelled
बाप	n.m. father
बाप रे बाप	interj. used in expressing grief or distress
बायाँ	adj. left; X की बाईं तरफ़/ओर post. to the left side of X; बाएँ adv. to the left; X के बाएँ हाथ पर post. to the left side of X
बार	n.f. time, occasion; बार-बार adv. time and again, over and over
बारिश	n.f. rain; बारिश होना v.i. to rain
X के बारे में	post. concerning X
बाल-बच्चे	n.m. pl. children, progeny
बालक	n.m. male child, youth
X के बावजूद	post. in spite of X
बाहर	adv. outside; X के बाहर post. outside X
बिकना	v.i. to be sold
बिकवाना	v.t. to cause to sell
बिखरना	v.i. to be scattered
बिखेरना	v.t. to scatter
बिगड़ना	v.i. to spoil, deteriorate
बिगाड़ना	v.t. to spoil, ruin
बिजली	n.f. electricity, lightening
बिठवाना	v.t. to have someone seated
बिठाना	v.t. to seat (someone)
बिताना	v.t. to spend time
X के बिना	post. without X
बिलकुल	adv. completely, entirely, absolutely
बिल्ली	n.f. cat
X के बीच	post. in the middle of X
बीज	n.m. seed
बीतना	v.i. for time to elapse or be spent

बीमार	adj. sick, ill; बीमार पड़ जाना v.i. to fall sick
बीमारी	n.f. disease, illness
बीवी (बीबी)	n.f. wife
बुख़ार	n.m. fever; X को बुख़ार आना v.i. for X to develop a fever
बुढ़िया	n.f. old woman
बुरा	adj. bad
बुराई	n.f. slander, malice; X की बुराई करना/होना v.t /i. to slander X/ for X to be slandered
बुलवाना	v.t. to have someone call
बुलाना	v.t. to call
बूढ़ा	n.m. old man; adj. old, ancient
बेकार	adj. vain, useless, good-for-nothing
बेचना	v.t. to sell
बेचारा	adj. helpless, unfortunate
बेटा	n.m. son
बेटी	n.f. daughter
बेपढ़ा	adj. illiterate
बेहोश	adj. unconscious
बैठक	n.f. meeting; sitting room, parlor
बैठना	v.i. to sit down
बैठा	adj. seated, sitting
बैल	n.m. ox, bullock
बोना	v.t. to sow
बोलचाल	n.f. speech, manner of speaking, conversation
बोलना	v.t. to speak
भक्त	n.m. devotee. follower
भगवान	n.m. God; भगवान जाने...God knows (who, what, why, etc.)...
भजन	n.m. devotional song, hymn
भटकना	v.i. to wander, stray, meander
X-भर	suffix. a full X, an entire X
भरना	v.t. to fill; v.i. to become full
X-भरा	adj. suffix. full of X
भला	adj. good
भवन	n.m. residence, house, building
भविष्य	n.m. future
भाई	n.m brother

भाग n.m. part, share, portion; भाग देना v.t. to divide

भागना v.i. to flee, escape; भागा आना v.i. to flee, escape, set off in flight (motion towards the speaker); भागा जाना v.i. to flee, escape, set off in flight (motion away from speaker)

भारत prop. m. India

भारतीय adj. Indian

भारी adj. heavy, weighty, serious

भाषण n.m. speech, lecture

भाषा n.f. language

भिगवाना v.t. to cause to soak

भिगाना v.t. to soak

भींचना v.t. to embrace, squeeze

भी partl. indicating inclusion (see 8.5 and 23.4.); X भी...Y भी conj. both X and Y

भीगना v.i. to get drenched

भीड़ n.f. crowd, multitude, throng; भीड़-भाड़ n.f. crowd

भीतर adv. inside; X के भीतर post. inside X

भूख n.f. hunger; X को भूख लगना v.i. for X to be hungry

भूखा adj. hungry

भूल n.f. error, mistake

भूलना v.t./v.i. to forget; भूल जाना v.i. to forget

भेजना v.t. to send

भेड़ n.f. sheep

भैंस n.f. (she-) buffalo

भोजन n.m. food

भोला-भाला adj. guileless, innocent

मंज़िल n.f. storey, floor (of building)

मंत्री n.m. minister (of à government), secretary (of a government or organization)

मंदिर n.m. temple

मगर conj. but

मछली n.f. fish

मछुवा (मछुआ) n.m. fisherman

मज़दूर n.m. worker, laborer
मजबूर adj. compelled; मजबूर करना/होना v.t./i. to compel/to be compelled
X का मज़ाक़ उड़ाना v.t. to ridicule X, to make fun of X
मटर n.f. pea
मत n.m. opinion; adv. negative marker
मतलब n.m. meaning, intent, significance
मदद n.f. help, assistance; X की मदद करना/होना v.t./i. to help X/ for X to be helped
मधुर adv. sweet, melliflous
मन n.m. mind, inclination, intention, wish; मन लगाकर adv. intently, diligently, conscientiously; मन ही मन adv. inwardly, to oneself
मना adj. indecl. forbidden; मना करना v.t. to forbid
मनाना v.t. to persuade
मनुष्य n.m. man, human being
मरना v.i. to die
मराठी prop. f. the Marathi language
मर्द n.m. man
मशहूर adj. famous
मसाला n.m. spice, spices
महंगा adj. expensive
महरी n.k. kitchen maid
महीना n.m. month
माँ n.f. mother
मांगना v.t. to demand
मांस n.m. meat
माता n.f. mother
मानना v.t. to accept, believe
मानों (मानो) conj. as if
माफ़ करना v.t. to excuse, pardon
X को Y माफ़िक़ आना v.i. for Y to suit X
मामला n.m. affair, matter
मामूली adj. ordinary, routine
मायका n.m. wife's family, wife's family home or village
मारना v.t. to strike, hit; मार खाना v.t. to get beaten, to suffer a beating; मार डालना v.t. to kill

X के मारे	post. on account of X, by dint of X
मालिक	n.m. boss, employer, superior
X को Y मालूम होना	v.i. for X to know Y; X को मालूम होना (in hab.) v.i. to see, appear to X
मास्टर (जी/साहब)	n.m. teacher, instructor
मिट्टी	n.f. clay, earth, soil
मिठाई	n.f. sweet, sweetmeat
मित्र	n.m. friend
मित्रता	n.f. friendship
मिनट	n.m. minute
मिर्च	n.f. pepper
मिलना	v.i. to be available, to be obtained, to be found, to meet, to resemble (see 16.2.)
मिलाना	v.t. to cause to meet, bring together (see 16.2.)
मीठा	adj. sweet
मुँह	n.m. mouth; X की तरफ़/ओर मुँह करना v.t. to turn one's face towards X; X की तरफ़/ओर मुँह होना v.i. for one's face to be turned towards X
मुड़ना	v.i. to turn back; bend; fold
X के मुताबिक़	post. in accordance with X
मुश्किल	n.f. difficulty; adj. difficult
मुसलमान	n.m. Muslim
मुसीबत	n.f. calamity, hardship
मुस्कराना	v.i. to smile
मुस्कराहट	n.f. smile
मूर्ति	n.f. statue, idol
मूल्य	n.m. value, price
मृत्यु	n.f. death
में	post. in, among
मेज़	n.f. table
मेम साहब	n.f. madam (usually a western woman)
मेला	n.m. fair, festival
मेहनत	n.f. hard work; मेहनत करना v.t. to do hard work
मेहरबानी	n.f. favor, kindness; मेहरबानी करके adv. please, kindly; X की मेहरबानी करना v.t. to be so kind as to do X
मैं	l.s. personal pron.
मैदा	n.m. white (bleached) flour
मैदान	n.m. field
मैला	adj. dirty, filthy

मोची n.m. cobbler
मोज़ा n.m. sock
मोटा adj. fat
मोती n.m. pearl
मोर n.m. peacock
मौक़ा n.m. opportunity, occasion, chance; X को मौक़ा मिलना v.i. for X to get an opportunity
मौसम n.m. weather; season

यदि...(तो) conj. if...(then)
यद्यपि...तथापि conj. even though...still
यमुना prop. f. the river Yamuna
यह 3.s. prox. personal and demonstrative pron.
यहाँ adv. here; X के यहाँ post. at X's place; यहाँ तक कि conj. to the extent that
यहीं adv. right here
या conj. or; या X...या Y conj. either X... or Y
याद n.f. memory, remembrance; X को Y (की) याद आना v.i. for Y to come to mind, to be recalled, for X to remember Y; याद करना v.t. to memorize; याद रखना v.t. to bear in mind, remember; X को Y की याद रहना v.i. for X to continue to remember Y
यानी conj. that is to say
युद्ध n.m. war
ये 3. pl. prox. personal and demonstrative pron.
यों ही (यूँ ही) adv. casually, by chance, in this manner, thus

रंग n.m. color; रंग-बिरंगा adj. colorful
रखना v.t. to place, put, keep, store
रस n.m. juice
रसीला adj. juicy
रसोई n.f. kitchen
रहना v.i. to live, dwell, remain; रह-रहकर v.i. adv. periodically, intermittently
राजकुमार n.m. prince
राजकुमारी n.f. princess
राजधानी n.f. capital city
राजा n.m.II. king

राज्य	n.m. state, reign, rule
रात	n.f. night; रात को adv. at night
रानी	n.f. queen
राय	n.f. opinion
राष्ट्रपति	n.m. President
रास्ता	n.m. path, road, way
रिवाज़	n.m. custom
रिश्तेदार	n.m. relative
रुकना	v.i. to stop; रुक-रुककर adv. haltingly
रुपया	n.m. rupee; money
रूप	n.m. form, shape; beauty; X के रूप में post. in the form, guise of X
रूपरेखा	n.f. outline
रेशम	n.m. silk
रोकना	v.t. to stop
रोज़	n.m. day; adv. daily, every day
रोटी	n.f. bread
रोना	v.i. to cry, weep
लंबा	adj. long, tall
लकड़ी	n.f. wood
लगना	See 15.5., 16.3., 22.5., and 24.5.
लगभग	adv. approximately
लगातार	adv. continuously
लगाना	v.t. to install, place, plant (see 24.5.)
लड़का	n.m. boy
लड़की	n.f. girl
लड़ना	v.i. to fight
लदना	v.i. to be laden
लहसुन	n.m. garlic
लादना	v.t. to load, carry
लाना	v.t. to bring
लाभ	n.m. benefit; X से लाभ उठाना v.t. to derive benefit from X
लाल	adj. red
लाल क़िला	prop. m. the Red Fort (in Delhi)
इस लिए	conj. therefore; इस लिए कि conj. because; किस लिए inter. why?; X के लिए post. for X, for the benefit of X
लिखना	v.t. to write

लिटवाना	v.t. to have someone lie down
लिटाना	v.t. to lay down
लिफ़ाफ़ा	n.m. envelope
लुटना	v.i. to be robbed
लुटवाना	v.t. to have someone rob
लूटना	v.t. to rob
लेकिन	conj. but
लेख	n.m. article
लेखक	n.m. writer, author
लेटना	v.i. to lie down
लेना	v.t. to take; ले आना v.t. to bring someone or something somewhere; ले जाना v.t. to take someone or something somewhere
लोग	n.m.pl. people
लोहा	n.m. iron
लौटना	v.i. to return
वक़्त	n.m. time, occasion
वग़ैरह	partl. et cetera
वजह	n.f. reason, explanation; इस वजह से conj. therefore; X की वजह से post. because of X, on account of X
वज़ीर	n.m. minister, adviser
वर्ष	n.m. year
वर्षगाँठ	n.f. birthday celebration
वसंत	n.m. Spring
वस्तु	n.f. thing
वह	3.s. non-prox. personal and demonstrative pron.
वहाँ	adv. there
वहीं	adv. right there
वापस	adv. back; वापस आना v.i. to come back; वापस जाना v.i. to go back
वाराणसी	prop. f. Varanasi (= Benaras)
वास्तव में	adv. in fact
वाह	interj. used in expressing appreciation
विचार	n.m. opinion, judgement
विद्यार्थी	n.m. student
विद्वान	n.m. scholar
विवाह	n.m. wedding, marriage
विवाहित	adj. married

विशेष	adj. special; विशेषकर adv. especially
विश्वविद्यालय	n.m. university
X में/पर विश्वास करना/होना	v.t./i. to place trust in X, to trust X/ for X to be trusted
विषय	n.m. topic, subject; X के विषय में, post. on the topic of X, concerning X, about X
वे	3.pl. non-prox. personal and demonstrative pron.
वेतन	n.m. wages, salary
वैर	n.m. hatred, hostility
वैसा	adj. that kind of
वैसे	adv. in that manner, thus; वैसे तो conj. actually, ordinarily
व्यस्त	adj. busy, occupied
व्याकरण	n.m. grammar
व्यापार	n.m. business, trade
शक्ति	n.f. power
शक्ल	n.f. form, appearance; शक्ल से adv. in appearance
शत्रु	n.m. enemy
शब्द	n.m. word
शब्दकोश	n.m. dictionary
शराब	n.f. liquor, wine
शरीर	n.m. body
शहर	n.m. city
शादी	n.f. wedding, marriage; X की शादी करना v.t. to marry (with) X, to get X married; X से Y की शादी करना v.t. to marry Y to X; X की शादी होना v.i. for X to get married
शाबाश	interj. used in expressing appreciation
शाम	n.f. evening; शाम को adv. in the evening
शास्त्र	n. sacred text, scripture
शिकायत	n.f. complaint; X की शिकायत करना v.t. to complain, to issue a complaint
शीघ्र	adv. quickly
शुक्रिया	thank you
शुद्ध	adj. pure; refined; Sanskritized
शुरू करना/होना	v.t./i. to begin
शेर	n.m. lion
शेष	n.m. remainder; adj. remaining

श्री	Mr.
श्रीमती	Mrs.
श्रीमान	Mr.
श्रेष्ठ	adj. best
संकरा	adj. narrow
X के संग	post. together with X
संगीत	n.m. music
संतरा	n.m. orange
संतोष	n.m. satisfaction; X को संतोष होना v.i. for X to get pleasure, satisfaction
संध्या	n.f. evening
संबंध	n.m. relationship, connection; X के संबंध म post. concerning X, on the matter of X
संभव	adj. possible
संसार	n.m. world
संस्कृत	prop. f. the Sanskrit language
सख़्त	adj. hard, arduous, harsh; adv. completely
सच	n.m. truth; adj. true
सचमुच	adv. truly
सच्चा	adj. true
सच्चाई	n.f. truth
सजना	v.i. to be decorated, adorned
सजाना	v.t. to decorate, adorn
सड़क	n.f. street
सताना	v.t. to torment
सदस्य	n.m. member
सदा	adv. always
सन्	n.m. year (in dates)
सप्ताह	n.m. week
सफ़र	n.m. trip; X का सफ़र करना v.t. to travel to X
सफल	adj. successful
सफलता	n.f. success
सफ़ेद	adj white
सब	pron. pl. all
सब्ज़ी	n.f. vegetable
समझना	v.i./t. to understand; X Y को Z समझना v.t. for X to consider Y to be Z

समय n.m. time, occasion; इस समय adv. now, at this time; उस समय adv. then, at that time; किस समय inter. when?
समस्या n.f. problem
समाचार n.m. news
समाचारपत्र n.m. newspaper
समाज n.m. society
X के समान post. like X, the same as X, equal to X
समुद्र n.m. ocean, sea
समोसा n.m. samosa (a triangular shaped pastry filled with vegetables or meat)
सरकार n.f. government
सरकारी adj. governmental, official
सरदी n.f. cold; सरदियाँ n.f.pl. winter, the cold season
सलाम expression of greeting among Muslims
सवा adj. one and a quarter
सवाल n.m. question
सवेरा n.m. the morning
सवेरे adv. in the morning
सस्ता adj. cheap, inexpensive
सहना v.t. to endure, tolerate
सहायता n.f. help, support, assistance, aid; X की सहायता करना v.t. to help, assist X
सहारा n.m. support; X के सहारे post. with the support of X
सही adj. correct, right, true
सहेली n.f. (female) friend (of a female)
सांस n.f. breath; सांस लेना v.t. to breathe
साड़ी n.f. sari
साढ़े adj. plus half (used with numbers greater than two)
साथ adv. together, side by side; X के साथ post. together with X; X के साथ हो लेना v.i. to accompany X; साथ-साथ adv. all together
साफ़ adj. clean, clear, pure; साफ़ करना v.t. to clean; साफ़-सुथरा adj. neat and clean
X का सामना करना v.t. to challenge X, to confront X
सामने adv. in front, opposite; X के सामने post. opposite X, in front of X
सामान n.m. luggage, materials, paraphernalia
सारा adj. all, entire
साल n.m. year

साहब n.m. master, boss; Mr.
साहित्य n.m. literature
साहित्यकार n.m. writer, literary figure
सिखवाना v.t. to cause to learn
सिखाना v.t. to teach
सितार n.m. sitar
सिर n.m. head
सिरदर्द n.m. headache
सिर्फ़ adv. only, just
सिलवाना v.t. to cause to sew
सिलसिला n.m. respect, context; X के सिलसिले में post. with respect to X, concerning X
सिलाना v.t. to cause to sew
X के सिवा (सिवाय) post. except for X
सीखना v.t. to learn
सीधा adj. straight
सीधे adv. straight, straight ahead
सीना v.i. to sew
सुंदर adj. beautiful
सुंदरता n.f. beauty
सुख n.m. happiness; X को सुख होना v.i. for X to be happy, for X to get satisfaction, contentment
सुनना v.t. to hear
सुनाई देना v.i. to be audible, to be heard
सुनाई पड़ना v.i. to be audible, to be heard
सुनाना v.t. to tell, relate
सुबह n.m. morning; adv. in the morning
सुरक्षित adj. protected, safe
सुलवाना v.t. to cause to put to sleep
सुलाना v.t. to put to sleep
सूती adj. cotton
सूरज n.m. the sun
से post. from, by, since
सेब n.m. apple
सेर n.m. a unit of weight slightly greater than two pounds
सेवा n.f. service, aid; X की सेवा करना/ होना v.t./i. to serve, assist X/ for X to be served, assisted

सैनिक n.m. soldier

सैर n.f. stroll, stip, excursion, walk; X की सैर करना v.t. to wander around X, to make a trip to X

सोचना v.t. to think

सोना n.m. gold

सोना v.i. to sleep, to go to sleep

स्त्री n.f. woman

स्थान n.m. place; X के स्थान पर/में post. in place of X

स्थिति n.f. situation, circumstance, condition

स्वतंत्र adj. independent, free

स्वतंत्रता n.f. independence, freedom

स्वयं adv. personally, by oneself

स्वर्ग n.m. heaven

स्वागत n.m. welcome; X का स्वागत करना/होना v.t./i. to welcome X/ for X to be welcomed

स्वास्थ्य n.m. health

स्वीकार करना/होना v.t./i. to accept/to be accepted

हंसी n.f. laughter; X को हंसी आना v.i. for X to laugh, smile

हंसना v.i. to laugh, smile

हटना v.i. to pull back, retreat, desist

हटवाना v.t. to cause to pull back

हटाना v.t. to drive back, push back

हफ़्ता n.m. week

हम 1.pl. personal and demonstrative pron.

हमेशा adv. always

हर adj. each, every

हरा adj. green

हराना v.t. to defeat

हल n.m. plough; हल जोतना v.t. to plough

हलका adj. light (color or weight)

हलवाई n.m. sweet seller

हल्ला n.m. ruckus, tumult; हल्ला-गुल्ला n.m. ruckus, tumult

हवा n.f. air, wind

हाँ adv. yes

हाथ n.m. hand; हाथ आना v.i. (for an opportunity) to be at hand; X के हाथ/हाथों post. by X, through the agency of X

हाय	interj. used in expressing grief or distress
हारना	v.i. to be defeated
हाल	n.m. condition, state of being
हालत	n.f. state, condition
हालांकि	conj. even though
हिंदुस्तान	prop. m. India
हिंदुस्तानी	adj. Indian
हिंदी	prop. the Hindi language
हिंदू	n.m. Hindu
हिम्मत	n.f. courage, audacity; X को Y की हिम्मत होना v.i. for X to have the courage to do Y
हिलना	v.i. to stir, move, wag
हिलाना	v.t. to stir, move, wag
हिस्सा	n.m. part, share, portion
ही	partl. see 8.5., 9.4., 21.3., and 30.4.
हृदय	n.m. heart
हे	interj. used in addressing or invoking
होना	v.i. to be; X (से) होकर adv. via X; हो जाना v.i. to become, happen, occur, be completed; हो लेना v.i. (for work) to be completed; हो सकता है कि ... it is possible that...; होते-होते adv. gradually, little by little
होली	prop. f. Holi (a Hindu festival)
होशियार	adv. clever